# TABLE OF CONTENTS

REGIONS OF RECENT URBANIZATION AND MODERNIZATION

PROSPECT AND RETROSPECT: METHODOLOGICAL AND SYNTHETIC
PERSPECTIVES

# LIST OF ILLUSTRATIONS

# LIST OF TABLES

# PREFACE

Chauncy Dennison Harris has studied and taught geography at the University of Chicago for more than forty-five years, during which he earned a worldwide reputation for his contributions to urban geography, Soviet studies, and geographical bibliography. It is fitting, in addition to all the honors he has received elsewhere, that he be honored by his immediate colleagues. We have chosen to celebrate the close of his departmental responsibilities with a volume that in its subject, structure, and style reflects the breadth and diversity of the scholarly community he helped shape. It serves as the Department's tribute to Chauncy Harris' professional accomplishments, and in its devotion to an urban theme the volume has aimed not only to focus interest upon a sphere in which he has done seminal work, but also to call on the respect and contributions of a very wide, international circle of urban geographical scholars that reflects particularly well his extensive global involvement within the profession.

It was apparent from the outset that essays covering each inhabited region of the earth could not be accommodated within one volume. The solution adopted was to invite contributors who collectively could cover many of the critical urban realms of the world, most as residents of the regions they are writing about, and who in addition all have personal associations with Chauncy Harris, some reaching back decades. Contributors were asked to write about urban change in the modern period, with attention to processes of urbanization and internal structural change they felt to be important. They were also asked to consider aspects of urban modernization, whatever that would connote in their respective regional contexts. Above all, they were given latitude to write about what seemed to them significant and appropriate in the circumstances. Some have chosen to stress broad regional patterns of urbanization more than internal city conditions, others to concentrate attention on specific intraurban problems; some focus on changes in the last few years, others on the path of change since the Second World War, and still others offer a long historical perspective within which to assess contemporary change. These variations stem partly from the dictates of regional experience, partly from individual preference and judgement. The diversity of approach serves to avoid a mechanical survey of the subject, we hope, and augments the thematic richness of the collection.

The editor makes no claim that these essays represent a tightly coherent phalanx of thought on a compact geographical problem. Modern urban change is too complex for such narrowness, and the multiplicity of geographical viewpoints on this general topic too interesting and fruitful to be forced into a rigid formula for presentation. What the contributors do offer in these essays is an impressive range of analytical approaches, empirical organization, and interpretative perspective on--as well as a surprising array of concurring and dissenting conclusions about--the manifold nature of contemporary urbanism. This collection of international geographical statements on urban change, then, provides a window on the discipline's intellectual and practical approach to a pressing concern in global human settlement studies.

We are especially grateful to these colleagues for their keen interest and "labor of love" in contributing these essays. A vote of special thanks is due one contributor for joining the project under unexpected circumstances: following a protracted effort to secure an essay on contemporary Soviet urban change--a topic close to Harris' personal research interests--by a Soviet geographer, which unfortunately came to nothing, Theodore Shabad assumed responsibility, at very short notice, for that chapter. Invited essays on urban change in the Arab realm and in Australia and New Zealand in the end did not materialize.

In Chicago, several people who have given valuable help toward planning this enterprise deserve special mention. Marvin W. Mikesell gave unstinting support and encouragement at all stages, and his good council is particularly appreciated. Kathleen Zar, formerly Geography Bibliographer at Regenstein Library and now Head of Reference Services at the University's Crerar Science Library, assisted in many bibliographic ways with the preliminary business of establishing eligible contributors. Edith Harris delved into her storehouse of personal recollections to help ensure the selection of contributors whose close associations with Chauncy were beyond doubt. Bill and Cheng Borchert stepped in at a critical point, and at very short notice, to undertake the careful translation of the essay on Beijing, and their efforts to ensure a faithful rendition then included a hand-carried draft to the author in China for review! Kathleen N. Conzen lent the editor valuable help in translating the Argentine essay from its original German. We particularly appreciate the willingness of several of the authors to submit their essays in English, though it is not their native language. The staff of the Regenstein Library Reference Department rendered extensive service in checking cited material in various languages, and in particular Eizaburo Okuizumi, Japanese specialist in the Library's Far Eastern Collection, gave valuable assistance in deciphering Japanese reference sources. Bernard Lalor, Managing Editor of the *Research Papers Series*, labored long to bring the various parts of this publication together for the printer, and Francine Atwell and Katie Walsh used their special skills to coax intelligible text from the computer. Betsy Brooks and Kathy Sellers worked hard to harmonize the various idiosyncracies in the cartographic material for the volume, and redrafted several maps and graphs.

It is a pleasure to acknowledge the support of the Social Sciences Division of the University of Chicago, granted under Dean William H. Kruskal, which has materially aided the production of this book.

November 24th, 1985                                                                                    M.P.C.

# THE FRAMEWORK

# Chapter I

# INTRODUCTION: GEOGRAPHICAL APPROACHES TO MODERN URBAN CHANGE

Michael P. Conzen

Urban change, continuous and complex, is endemic to the maturation of the modern world economy. There is a seeming imperative behind the global integration of regional market systems that produces accelerated and practically ubiquitous urban change of almost bewildering variety and consequence. So broad a phenomenon interests scholars in numerous disciplines, and for many the key changes are summed up conceptually in the process of urbanization. This fundamental notion is so inclusive that numerous definitions of it and related concepts have gained currency, and their specific usage in the present context needs clarifying.[1]

Urbanization from a geographical perspective is a regionally varied social process of settlement intensification shaped according to environmental endowments and principles of spatial order producing a network of built environments created by and interacting with changing human needs. The process is a deeply historical one that has by now affected most if not all cultures, in a chronological pattern suggesting strong diffusionary influences working with differential speed to transform regional societies. Its modern outcome is a global pattern or network of "urban" settlements of great internal functional and morphological diversity with highly variable relations to the larger society and economy from region to region.[2]

---

1. A useful interdisciplinary introduction to various interpretations of the process of urbanization is Philip M. Hauser and Leo F. Schnore, eds., *The Study of Urbanization* (New York: Wiley, 1965). For a useful discussion of the distinctions between urbanization and urbanism, see Paul Wheatley, "The Concept of Urbanism," in *Man, Settlement and Urbanism,* ed. Peter J. Ucko, Ruth Tringham, and G.W. Dimbleby (Cambridge, MA: Schenkman Publishing Co., 1972), pp. 601-637. See also Eric E. Lampard, "The Nature of Urbanization," in *Visions of the Modern City: Essays in History, Art, and Literature,* ed. W. Sharpe and L. Wallock (New York: Columbia University Heyman Center for the Humanities, 1982), pp. 47-96.

2. Geographical discussions of urbanization include Brian J.L. Berry, *Comparative Urbanization: Divergent Paths in the Twentieth Century* (New York: St. Martin's Press, 1981); Arthur E. Smailes, "The Definition and Measurement of Urbanization," in *Essays on World Urbanization,* ed. Ronald Jones (London: George Philip and Son, 1975), pp. 1-18; *Harold Carter, The Study of Urban Geography* (London: Edward Arnold, 3rd ed., 1981), pp. 16-36; and Larry S. Bourne and Robert Sinclair, "Introduction," in *Urbanization and Settlement Systems: International Perspectives,* ed. Larry S. Bourne, Robert Sinclair, and Kazimierz Dziewoński

In common with other geographical phenomena, urbanization can be approached along four systematic dimensions: topical, regional, historical, and comparative. The very complexity of intertwined urban processes is usually a barrier to understanding unless it can be separated into its component parts. Hence, topical studies contribute by sorting out and linking elements with direct and immediate causal connections, with emphasis on the laws that regulate order in geographical space, regardless of localized setting. Regional analysis adds to this by considering the vital modifications in what would otherwise be taken as universal urban processes introduced by the particular confluence of forces acting in, and the unique circumstances of, a given regional setting. The historical study of urban processes in geography establishes the directions and amounts of change in spatial organization over time, with special attention to continuities and discontinuities, and exposes the incremental and intertial as well as the radical changes they produce in the evolved, cumulative character of urban structures on the earth's surface. The comparative method takes the results of regional and temporal study and gauges how like or unalike the evolved regional expressions of urbanization actually are from place to place, and from culture to culture.

With this broad geographical view of urbanization, it follows that such notions as urban growth and urban development are but descriptive components of the general process. The traditional distinction made in economic analysis that growth and development represent different types and degrees of structural change in the system is generally accepted. And urbanism, then, as a characteristic state or level of social organization definable with reference to time and place, represents a benchmark of settlement evolution long attained in all the regional cases addressed here.

It is possible to consider the interplay of critical components in urban organization in a timeless fashion, as if suspended in a perpetual functional equilibrium, but history and common sense compel an evolutionary perspective. Some writers, viewing human settlement development from the most detached standpoint, see it falling into three fundamental ages--pre-urban, urban, and post-urban--and predict that advanced societies are now shifting rapidly from the middle to the latter stage.[3] Whether or

---

(Oxford: Oxford University Press, 1984), pp. 1-19.

3. See Pedro Armillas,"Urban Revolution: The Concept of Civilization," *The International Encyclopedia of the Social Sciences,* vol. 16 (New York and Glencoe, IL: Macmillan Co. and The Free Press, 1968), pp. 218-221; Ivan Light, *Cities in World Perspective* (New York: Macmillan Publishing Co., 1983), pp. 3-25. For anxieties about the end of urban civilization, see Kenneth E. Boulding, "The Death

not this is a useful chronology, there is little doubt that massive
urban transformations are taking place across all continents in
concert with the economic realignments of the maturing world-system,
and the geographical pattern of urbanization apparent at any given
point in time merely captures a cross-section of a dynamic global
process having operated long in some regions and more briefly in
others.

### The World's Urban Settlement Matrix

The great differences in historical urbanization, particularly
the advancement and penetration of urbanism in the life of regions
and nations, together with the diversity of present levels and rates
of change in the various dimensions of urbanism, make it difficult
to establish a common base against which to measure the trends
observable in individual localities. The only reasonable means of
establishing a context for the specific findings of the essays that
follow is to sketch with summary statistics the broad spatial
patterns of urban development, and allow the qualitative differences
to emerge in later discussion.

The most widely followed measure of urbanization is the
proportion that the urban population comprises of the total
population of a particular region at any moment in time. At the
global scale, considerable variations exist between major regions
(table 1.1) and individual countries (figure 1.1). Since the
distribution of general population in relation to land and resources
varies so widely from region to region around the world and
statistics are gathered for political units of widely variable size,
high rates of urbanization (as just defined) can result in
contrasting environments. Northwest European countries contain
numerous cities of all sizes as well as quite dense rural
populations, whereas Canada, for example, ranks high on the
urbanization scale because vast areas contain almost no rural
population at all, as does Australia. Conversely, some African
countries, particularly in the Sahelian realm, contain miniscule
proportions of their populations in urban places--and have very few
cities of any size--while China and India maintain low urbanization
rates in spite of numerous large cities because of their vast and
often densely distributed rural populations. Though such
differences are masked by the simple statistical ratio, it does
reveal a surprisingly coherent global pattern of gradients from high

---

of the City: A Frightened Look at Postcivilization," in *The Historian and the
City*, ed. Oscar Handlin and John Burchard (Cambridge, MA: M.I.T. Press and Harvard
University Press, 1963), pp. 133-145, and Paul-Henry Chombart de Lauwe, *La Fin des
villes: Mythe ou réalité* (Paris: Calmann-Levy, 1982).

to low values. The Western Hemisphere comprises generally high
ratios, as does Europe and northern Asia, the Mediterranean rim, and
the southern Pacific (figure 1.1). Eastern and southern Asia and
most of Africa exhibit low ratios. The correspondence between this
pattern and one of general economic development is not overwhelming,
but certain obvious parallellisms exist.

When the geography of urbanization thus defined is considered
in the light of the distribution of very large cities, the
relationship is again not entirely simple (figures 1.1 and 1.2).
The pattern of cities (or more properly urban agglomerations) with
over one million inhabitants in 1980 shows dense concentrations in
Europe, the United States, the eastern and central parts of the
Soviet Union, and northern China. Other "million" cities are more
scattered, sometimes one to a country--hinting at the urban
"primacy" often symptomatic of developing regions.[4] This reflection
of primacy is more dramatic in the distribution of agglomerations
with over five million people, with places such as Jakarta, Manila,
Shanghai, and Cairo standing out in areas of low general
urbanization. Most striking is the prospect that 16 of 28
additional metropolises projected to surpass five million

TABLE 1.1.
PROPORTION OF POPULATION LIVING IN CITIES (IN PERCENTAGES),
BY MAJOR WORLD REGION

| Region | 1950 | 1970 | 1980 | 2000 |
|--------|------|------|------|------|
| WORLD | 29.0 | 37.5 | 41.3 | 51.3 |
| Australia & Oceania | 61.2 | 70.8 | 75.9 | 83.0 |
| North America | 63.8 | 70.5 | 73.7 | 80.8 |
| Europe | 53.7 | 63.9 | 68.8 | 77.1 |
| Soviet Union | 39.3 | 56.7 | 64.8 | 76.1 |
| Latin America | 41.2 | 57.4 | 64.7 | 75.2 |
| East Asia | 16.7 | 28.6 | 33.1 | 45.4 |
| Africa | 14.5 | 22.9 | 28.9 | 42.5 |
| South Asia | 15.7 | 20.5 | 24.0 | 36.1 |

Source: *Patterns of Urban and Rural Population Growth* (United Nations Population
Study no. 68, 1980), Table 8, p. 16.

---

4. Brian J.L. Berry, "City Size Distribution and Economic Development,"
*Economic Development and Cultural Change* 9 (1961): 573-587.

BRIESEMEISTER'S ELLIPTICAL
EQUAL AREA PROJECTION

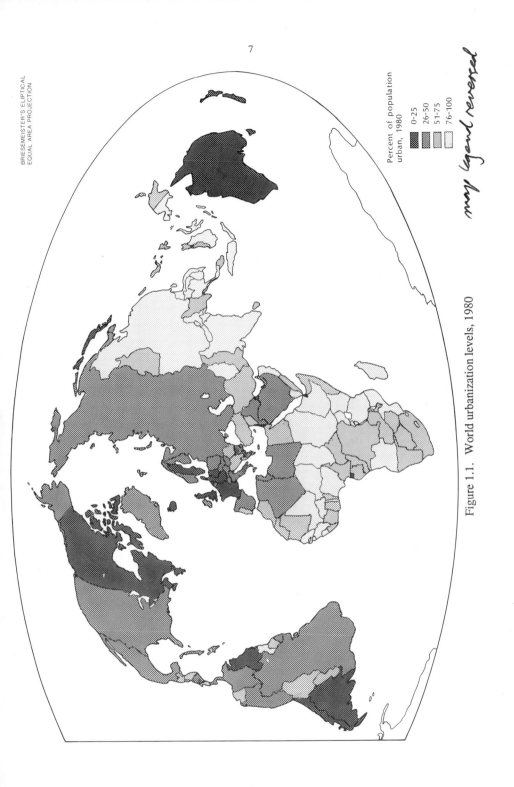

Percent of population
urban, 1980

0-25
26-50
51-75
76-100

*map legend reversed*

Figure 1.1.  World urbanization levels, 1980

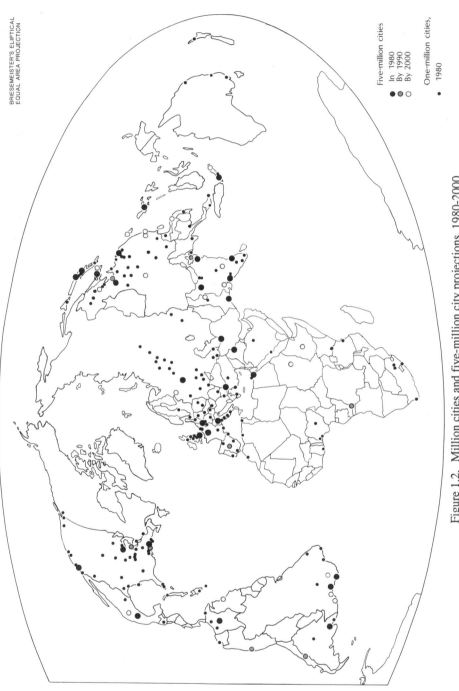

BRIESEMEISTER'S ELIPTICAL
EQUAL AREA PROJECTION

Five-million cities
In 1980
By 1990
By 2000

One-million cities,
1980

Figure 1.2. Million cities and five-million city projections, 1980–2000

inhabitants by the year 2000 are located in countries with very low urbanized levels (five in China alone).[5] It is evident that such focussed urban growth will nudge many developing countries towards the urbanized levels of the more developed nations, but not necessarily with the solid ranks of secondary cities characteristic of the latter group.[6]

If overall rates of increase in national urban population are viewed against the backdrop of general comparative population size, the theme of demographic convergence is given further support (figure 1.3). Projections of aggregate percentage urban growth between 1980 and 2000 reveal that the greatest expansions of urban population are likely to occur in the currently least urbanized countries and that in strictly numerical terms the impact is probably going to be felt most keenly in India, Bangladesh, and Nigeria. Weaker shifts are anticipated for the United States and the Soviet Union, and the smallest changes in already heavily-urbanized Europe and Japan.

Such patterns as these fail to do more than hint at the multitude of particular trends in and responses to urbanization that individual regions experience. It is axiomatic that demographic convergence of the statistical measures of urbanization between countries over the relatively short period of two decades or even half a century certainly masks fundamental differences in the way cultures respond to pressures for and shape the character of urban transformation. Advanced technology may allow cities to "skip" some developmental phases of urban development that older urbanized societies have experienced, but this in no way implies that they will acquire the same nature or functional organization, and urban values might well differ strongly. Much of this flux and variability is associated with the concept of "modernization."

### "Modernization" as a Stage of Urbanization

Modernization as an historical construct is a slippery term.[7] Long-established European nation-states have been "modernizing" for a significant period of time, in some cases from the breakup of

---

5. The evidence used in the preparation of the table and maps is drawn from *Patterns of Urban and Rural Population Growth* (New York: United Nations Department of International Economic and Social Affairs, Population Studies, no. 68, 1980). This source has an advantage over others in that the compilers attempted to standardize as much as possible the statistical definitions of urban places employed by the reporting countries, and they prepared an elaborate model with which to make prognostications about future urban population levels.

6. Dennis Rondinelli, *Secondary Cities in Developing Countries: Policies and Diffusing Urbanization* (Beverly Hills, CA: Sage Publications, 1983).

7. See discussions in Gino Germani, ed., *Modernization, Urbanization, and the Urban Crisis* (Boston: Little, Brown and Co., 1973).

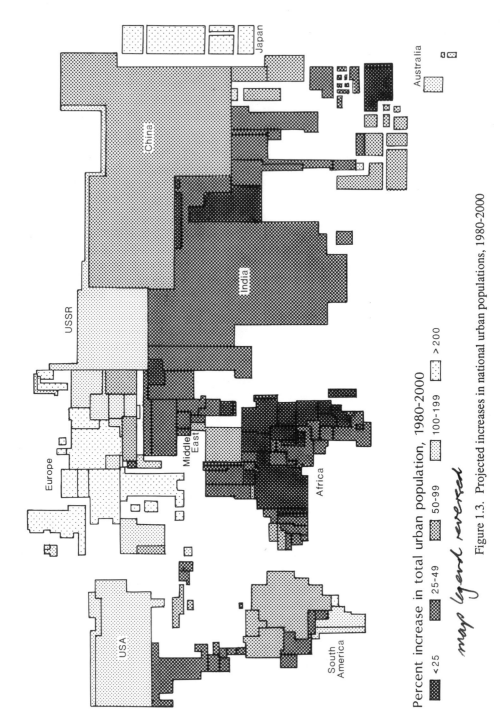

Percent increase in total urban population, 1980-2000

<25    25-49    50-99    100-199    >200

*map legend reversed*

Figure 1.3.   Projected increases in national urban populations, 1980-2000

their feudal order in the fifteenth and sixteenth centuries.
"Modern" history is frequently defined as beginning, indeed, with
the emergence of capitalism and the rise of the nation-state. And
yet modernization in economically advanced countries is often
invoked in a shorter-term sense to mean any transition, consciously
planned or not, from one distinct organizational state to another.
With respect to less-developed regions in the world, "modernization"
carries a wide array of meanings, from accelerated growth and
development in order to eliminate the development gap, to a form of
cultural hegemony for the economic powers where "modernization" is
seen as a Westernism with distinct global-political overtones.[8]

In its benign form, modernization, it is argued, consists of
mechanisms by which economic growth and development are introduced
or enhanced, economic and social infrastructure  provided, and
governmental stability and efficiency promoted--all with a desirable
rise in general "quality of life" as a crowning achievement. Given
the geographical inequality in the distribution of advanced
socio-economic development, this conception of modernization has
motivated Western and Third World countries to work towards a
contemplated convergence of development levels through the provision
and investment of foreign aid and international development
programs.[9]

A more critical stance is taken by those who argue that
modernization is essentially a Western strategy to maintain economic
world hegemony by favoring developments that tie Third World
countries ever more tightly to the needs of the advanced nations.[10]
This view carries both an economic critique based on the inability
of lesser developed regions either to catch up or to gain economic
flexibility in their external relations, and also a cultural
critique based on the perceived imposition of Western cultural
values about what is modern and socially desirable.[11]

---

8 . Terry G. McGee, *The Urbanization Process in the Third World:
Explorations in Search of a Theory* (London:  Bell, 1971).  See also M. Francis
Abraham, *Perspectives on Modernization:  Towards a General Theory of Third World
Development* (Washington, D.C.: University Press of America, 1980).

9 . Part of this body of thought regards urbanization as a beneficial agent
of development in Third World countries.  Exemplary of such thinking is the search
for a demonstrable causal link between the two: see Arthur S. Banks and David L.
Carr, "Urbanization and Modernization:  A Longitudinal Analysis," *Studies in
Comparative International Development* 9 (Summer, 1974): 26-45, and M. A. Qadeer,
"Do Cities 'Modernize' the Developing Countries?  An Examination of the South
Asian Experience," *Comparative Studies in Society and History* 16 (June, 1974):
266-83.  In this present volume, however, concern is not so much with cities as
sources of modernization in development regions, but rather with the impact on and
consequences for cities of current forces of modernization.

10 . David Harvey, *The Urbanization of Capital:  Studies in the History and
Theory of Capitalist Urbanization* (Baltimore:  Johns Hopkins University Press,
1985), p. 216.

11 . Leonard Berry and Robert W. Kates, eds., *Making the Most of the Least*

In recent years, a less ethnocentric consensus has been emerging over the terms of the development debate. Particularly with the lessons of overindustrialization and overly large-scale agricultural projects in full view and the implications of selective deindustrialization in advanced nations sinking in, there is more attention now to possible indigenous forms of development within the changing world-system. But the long-term consequences for urban growth and change of decades of traditional development policies, both in the developed and less developed realms, have yet to be measured, let alone suitably coped with.[12] Cities have long been viewed as centers of cultural innovation and change and as loci of advanced living standards relative to those of their rural surroundings. But in both realms there are signs of a possible collapse in this principle, for different reasons. It is more difficult to sustain a belief in the inevitability of progress and the centrality of cities in that progress, for example, when further economic restructuring of "modernized" regions devalues the giant infrastructure of whole cities and regions through severe industrial withdrawal, abandonment, and mass unemployment.[13] Similarly, in other settings, the fruits of modernization are more complicated to assess when the rate of improvement in urban facilities and services is dwarfed by uncontrolled rural in-migration. The shift towards more appropriate normative notions of urban modernization in different regions, however, does not in any way affect or deter the increasingly powerful interregional economic integration of cities and regions the world over—an integration not endowed with any particular a priori geographical equality of resources or benefits.

### The Regional Impact of Modernization

This volume seeks to examine the geographical conditions of urban change in a wide variety of localities around the globe. In doing this, there is no avoiding the historical diversity of regional urban experience, and it seems fitting to consider even modern urban change in terms of countries and regions grouped within the framework of broad cultural realms possessing at the large scale something of a common historical urban heritage.[14] The scheme

---

(New York: Holmes and Meier Publishers, 1979); Ignacy Sachs, *The Discovery of the Third World* (Cambridge, MA: M.I.T. Press, 1976).

12 . Michael Pacione, ed., *Problems and Planning in Third World Cities* (New York: St. Martins Press, 1981); Harry W. Richardson, "National Urban Development Strategies in Developing Countries," *Urban Studies* 18 (October 1981): 267-284.

13 . See the essays in F. Blackaby, ed., *De-Industrialisation* (London: Heineman, National Institute of Economic and Social Research Economic Policy Papers 2, 1979).

14 . There is no accepted worldwide cultural-genetic typology of cities to

favored here recognizes different local traditions of urbanism but, concerned as it is primarily with the impact of *modern* urban change, does not necessarily separate them unless modern change acts upon them in vastly different ways.[15]

It seems reasonable to argue that European countries share a history of long and continuous urban change from classical times to the industrialized present, representing a clear heterogenetic tradition in which the role of cities in regional and interregional relations has been constantly evolving and in which the modern, industrialized phase represents a comparatively minor, evolutionary discontinuity with the region's past development.[16] By contrast, there are regions with ancient urban traditions--the Middle and Far Easts--much older than Europe's, but where those traditions became settled in orthogenetic fashion for long periods of time until disrupted by modern European colonialism and the mercantile-industrial pressures it brought.[17] A third category comprises regions of relatively recent, European-inspired urbanization associated with overseas settlement and commercial domination by European national groups, generally among indigenous peoples without long-sustained urban traditions of their own.[18] This brings the exploration full circle since North American urbanism, though little over three hundred years old, now ranks with that of Europe as highly advanced, technically innovative, and globally

---

lend precise structure to this idea. Generally, studies differentiating towns into groups based on common cultural heritage have confined themselves to relatively small regions, and the few discussions at the global scale have not offered any satisfactory cartographic regionalizations. The most resilient, but still geographically impressionistic, conception is that of Robert Redfield and Milton B. Singer, "The Cultural Role of Cities," *Economic Development and Cultural Change* 3 (October 1954): 53-73, which introduced the distinction between orthogenetic and heterogenetic urban evolution, a paper that drew approving comments at the time from Chauncy Harris: see his "Orthogenetic and Heterogenetic Cities in the Modern World," *Economic Development and Cultural Change* 3 (October 1954): 76-77. A useful recent overview of this problem of global typology is Burkhard Hofmeister, "Die Stadtstruktur im interkulturellen Vergleich," *Geographische Rundschau* 34 (1982): 482-488. Also interesting is the collection of essays in John Agnew, John Mercer, and David Sopher, eds., *The City in Cultural Context* (Boston: Allen and Unwin, 1984), although these essays do not address the problem of defining a cultural-genetic regional system for viewing the world's urban realms.

15. Thus, the continuities and discontinuities in urban change broadly conceived over long periods of time are considered culturally more important than such criteria as present population density and the distinction between "new" and "old" lands as such, or the contrast in styles of modern government. Cf. Bourne et al., *Urbanization and Settlement Systems* (footnote 2).

16. Elizabeth Lichtenberger, "The Nature of European Urbanism," *Geoforum* 4 (1970): 45-62, and "The Changing Nature of European Urbanization," in *Urbanization and Counterurbanization,* ed. Brian J.L. Berry (Beverly Hills, CA: Sage Publications, 1976), pp. 81-107.

17. The classic study of oriental urban origins is Paul Wheatley, *The Pivot of the Four Quarters: A Preliminary Enquiry into the Origins of the Ancient Chinese City* (Chicago: Aldine Publishing Co., 1971).

18. This three-fold classification is clearly open to challenge on many grounds, and there are obvious internal variations and contradictions in each category, but it serves well to structure the contributions that make up this book.

influential. Insofar as world urbanism is, for better or worse, strongly affected by the urban dynamics of countries circling the North Atlantic Ocean, the collection closes with essays devoted to questions of advanced urbanism, viewed in a strong socio-cultural light.

### Recurrent Themes

Most of the essays in this collection deal with issues concerning national or large regional systems of cities.[19] Several extend this concern to cover problems of urban growth as it affects cities as places to live. Several common themes run through these chapters, notwithstanding the diverse cultural, economic, and political backgrounds of the urban traditions considered. Their variable relevance spans the spectrum of economic development from "advanced" to "developing;" some are universal, others geographically more limited.

Perhaps the most striking theme is the stage of almost "total" urbanization that North America and Western Europe may be approaching as the twenty-first century draws near. This is evident not so much in the crude urbanized population ratio per se (although Britain is far advanced in this respect) as by the "reach" of urbanization as a physical and functional reality--commuting is the prime integrator--extending well beyond the urban fringe deep into rural zones and diminishing the differences between regions. Implicit throughout Michael Wise's autobiographical assessment of British urban and regional planning, it is documented in Harold Mayer's review of American and Canadian cities and forms the starting point for Brian Berry's essay on advanced urbanism. In his view, we are moving beyond an orientation to the "economics of location" in favor of preoccupation with the political and cultural terms of social change. Allied with this is the theme of shifting emphasis from production to services that many advanced economies are now experiencing. In addition to America and Britain, France and West Germany also show signs of this change in their urban

---

[19]. There have been several previous attempts at international surveys of regional systems of cities, mostly by geographers. The two most extensive collections are Jones, *Essays on World Urbanization* (footnote 2) and Bourne et al., *Urbanization and Settlement Systems* (footnote 2), both products of symposia organized by working groups of the International Geographical Union; neither one covers all countries or world regions, though Bourne's collection is both more recent and more comprehensive. A recent text covers similar ground in a less formalistic and more coherent way: Stanley D. Brunn and Jack F. Williams, eds., *Cities of the World: World Regional Urban Development* (New York: Harper and Row, 1983). Other substantial writing on urban patterns and trends at the global scale by social scientists has tended to focus on less developed regions: see especially Janet Abu-Lughod and Richard Hay, eds., *Third World Urbanization* (New York: Methuen, 1979); Alan Gilbert and Josef Gugler, *Cities, Poverty, and Development: Urbanization in the Third World* (Oxford: Oxford University Press, 1983); Pradip K. Ghosh, ed., *Urban Development in the Third World* (Westport, CT: Greenwood Press, 1984).

employment structure, as noted in the essays by Jacqueline Beaujeu-Garnier and Peter Schöller respectively. By contrast, East Bloc countries such as East Germany, Poland, and the Soviet Union are still firmly committed to industrial expansion through, if anything, a proportionate *increase* in workforce devoted to manufacturing, as the chapters by Schöller, Kazimierz Dziewoński, and Theodore Shabad make clear.

Related to these themes is the problem of regional obsolescence, when industries are no longer competitive through loss of comparative advantage. The consequences of job losses and social stress highlight the dilemma faced in many such cases: bring jobs to where the people are, or move people to where the jobs are? This is especially acute in Britain, as Wise discusses, considering the historical investments in the industrial cities of Britain, but it is also not unknown even in command economies such as the Soviet Union, as Shabad notes in connection with the metallurgical district south of Moscow. Regional eclipse is often associated with economic and demographic concentration around favored places, such as capital cities, and this theme, with its policy implications and its counterpoint in deconcentration and decentralization, informs all the essays concerned with Europe (particularly France) and emerges also in David Amiran and Avie Schachar's chapter on Israel and Shinzo Kiuchi's essay on Tokyo.

Deconcentration within great cities, whether by government planning or market mechanism, directly affects the upkeep of urban infrastructure and the changing social relations in residential and employment terms. Here, the contrasts between the automobile-based urban cultures of Western Europe, North America, and Japan on one hand, in which residence and social patterning are strongly regulated by the housing market and lifestyle preferences, and Eastern Bloc countries on the other, in which work places as employment opportunities largely define the geography of housing and occupational patterns, is striking. Evidence of contrasts like these can be found particularly in the chapters by Schöller, Jörg Güssefeldt and Walter Manshard, Mayer, Kiuchi, Shabad, and Dziewoński.

If we consider common themes in the setting of less developed regions, several *leitmotive* stand out. Perhaps one of the most fundamental is what Akin Mabogunje refers to as "backwash" urbanization, a process particularly rife in Africa in which flawed policies such as import-substituting industrialization depress investments in the agricultural sector to the point where rural-to-urban migration is irresistible and inevitable. Such a situation produces among other things sharp differences between rural and urban standards of living, urban primacy within the regional system of cities, "dual circuits" in the economy (and often significant "informal" sectors), and tremendous problems of squatter settlements within and on the edge of cities. This theme forms the main concern of Mabogunje's essay, and it receives strong indirect support in Speridião Faissol's chapter on Brazil. Faissol, however, views the process as having a distinct geographical morphology to it: industrial-urban development impulses emanating from large cities in favored "core" areas over time diffusing, however slowly, to more peripheral areas. Both writers agree that industrial urbanism in these circumstances is the driving force behind so-called development. The resulting squatter settlements figure prominently in Africa and Latin America, as noted in the essays by Mabogunje, Herbert Wilhelmy on Argentina, and Faissol on Brazil.

Primacy stands as one of the most dominant characteristics of urbanism in developing countries, and no consensus exists on its policy significance. Even in advanced countries an early history of primate development has resulted in "relict primacy" (London and Paris are the obvious cases) that to this day stimulates policies of urban containment of capital city growth in various ways (see the essays by Wise and Beaujeu-Garnier). Prolonged industrial development has somewhat blunted the primacy evident in the urban hierarchy of such countries, but the pattern is starker in such settings as Mexico, Latin America, and several countries of Southeast Asia, as the chapters by Maria Gutiérrez de MacGregor, Wilhelmy, Faissol, and Norton Ginsburg attest. Some argue that primacy is inherently bad in that it confines development to too few favored places and thus hinders broad diffusion, while others, Ginsburg and Güssefeldt and Manshard among them, seem to suggest that development should be introduced where it is most efficient and diffuse as widely as enterprise deems it appropriate. Policies of subsidizing uneconomic places in the periphery may thus be costly and misguided. Evidence on this point is offered at a small scale in Israel where Amiran and Shachar note that Development Towns have not proven particularly viable after tariff supports were relaxed.

A corollary theme in all this is the pressure of Westernization felt throughout the developing world. Allied to what has been termed "the technological imperative," this theme runs through the essays of Mabogunje, Ginsburg, and R.L. Singh and R.P.B. Singh on India, implicitly suggesting that Western ideas, meaning mainly American and West European ideas (and advice), are not necessarily the most appropriate stock from which to forge solutions for local developing regions. A consistent outcome in such settings is the sharpening of differentials between the living standard of rural and urban areas, and this is commented upon by several writers here, including Faissol on Brazil, and even Shabad on the Soviet Union, who stresses the contrast there with the virtual lack of such differentials in North America.

In many cases, governments have little leverage in forming effective policies to cope with the symptoms of urban pathology, such as the explosion in squatter settlements, because the causes lie largely outside their direct contol. They can do little beyond legitimizing them and try catching up in the provision of amenities. In other cases, governments have considerable scope in determining the character of urban change. This is particularly true where political ideology is close to the surface. Examples of this theme abound in this collection: the large ceremonial central squares in such cities as East Berlin, Tian-an Men Square in Beijing, the Development Towns in Israel (in part to help settle immigrants), for example. It is noted by both Shabad and Dziewoński that state policies aimed at heavy industrialization and export investments are often accompanied by severe underinvestment in urban infrastructure--a situation that George Hoffmann, referring specifically to Greece and Yugoslavia, calls "underurbanization."

Where urbanization seems to be under a plausible degree of control, government policies can concern themselves with such issues as urban containment, such as limiting the accommodation of new residents and passing land use measures such as greenbelts and satelite cities, as well as more subtle concerns, such as preservation of historical fabric for general social aims (see Hou Ren-Zhi's essay on central Beijing). When the whole basis of urban change is dependent on largely external factors of economic development in an international entrepreneurial context, more intractable questions assert themselves. The most dramatic one followed by several of the authors in this book is: Are cities really changing whole populations to an urban way of life, and is this becoming more homogeneous with time? Jean Gottmann's closing essay on "orbits" draws out the patterns of cultural interchange that have invigorated urbanism on both sides of the North Atlantic, but concludes that urbanization is not in itself an arbitrarily convergent force. Human diversity will still evolve highly varied forms of urbanism worldwide. This holds some meaning for less developed regions where urbanization has a flimsier historical hold on regional experience. Rapid migration of rural populations to cities may well result, as several authors suggest, in the "peasantization" of cities--a point made here not only in the African context, but also with reference to Southeastern Europe--and offer the prospect for major new forms of cultural assimilation and nonassimilation between city and country.

In general, then, the theme binding these essays together revolves around the modernization of cities and urban life and what this means, viewed particularly from the perspective of city systems and internal urban spatial organization. Thus, modern urban change is approached as either gradual or rapid, evolutionary or revolutionary, based on indigenous traditions or strongly affected by outside influences. These dimensions clearly vary from continent to continent, but in all there are both creative as well as disruptive tensions that exist in each region between its historical legacy, its developmental goals, and the homogenizing forces of the modern world economic system. Such relationships are reflected in the urbanization rates, urban spatial structure, and urban culture--including local approaches to the "management" of urbanization--of each region. In this light, the following essays offer a substantial agenda of worldwide urban geographical issues for reflection and debate.

REGIONS OF LONG AND CONTINUOUS MODERNIZATION

# Chapter II

# URBAN AND REGIONAL CHANGE IN BRITAIN FROM A PERSONAL PERSPECTIVE

## Michael J. Wise

Memories of Chauncy Harris are for me inseparable from international gatherings. The international community of geographers is greatly in his debt for the wise leadership which he gave as Vice-President and then as Secretary-General of the International Geographical Union. It was his aim to build on the work of his predecessors, to recruit more nations to the Union, to enhance the range and depth of international communication. Chauncy Harris was always at the center of discussions, patient and considerate in negotiation, clear and far-seeing in advice and decision. Partly from his knowledge of many languages but more from the confidence engendered by his true friendships with geographers all over the world, he symbolised the international unity of geographers in the search for scholarship. It is Chauncy's own eminence as a scholar that has been the decisive factor in his influence. His work in urban geography is known the world over. His studies of the Soviet Union, of Japan, and of their cities have been carried out with a skill and care that inspired respect from the geographers of those countries. His work in documenting periodicals and publications has given him an unsurpassed knowledge of geographers and their work the world over. Chauncy Harris has stood consistently for the unity of science: the international geographical community has immense cause to be grateful to him.

### Early Experiences of Urban Environments

When some of us return home from international meetings we become absorbed, at least for part of our time, in problems of national concern. This essay reflects my interest in issues of urban change and regional planning in Britain.

W.H. Auden once wrote:

Clearer  than Scafell Pike, my heart has stamped on
The view from Birmingham to Wolverhampton,

and the urban landscapes of the Birmingham-Black Country conurbation
are deeply engraven in my early memories. Travelling by train
between my parents' home in Handsworth, a northern suburb of
Birmingham, and Stafford where my grand-parents lived, I recall the
night sky lit up by the flames from the blast furnaces which had
survived the decline of the Black Country iron industry. Mackinder
had written of the district at the turn of the century as "one great
workshop, both above ground and below. At night it is lurid with
the flames of the iron furnaces: by day it appears one vast
loosely-knit town of humble homes amid cinder heaps and fields
stripped of vegetation by smoke and fumes."[1] The trams which linked
the industrial towns, separated one from another by slag heaps, coal
spoil, and water filled clay pits, clanked their way through
terraces of cottages and workers' houses. The smoke had cleared:
no longer was employment found mainly in coal mining and the iron
and steel industries; the secondary metal trades had taken over and
engineering had become a major employer. Birmingham was different:
no trace of coal and iron here. Handsworth was the home of many
small masters and craftsmen who worked in the gun and jewelry
quarters, a short tram ride away, in what would now be called the
"inner city." On the other side of the city were metal, especially
nonferrous metal, industries. Great factories were growing on the
edge of the city producing motorcars, motorcycles, tires and
accessories, as well as providing consumer goods, food and drink for
the growing urban population.

As we travelled by train around the country on holidays or on
school expeditions, I became aware of the great differences between
my home district and other great urban districts. The rectangular
cotton mills of Lancashire dominating the terrace houses; the pit
heads of South Wales with the small, coal grimed miners walking home
down the valleys; the bare expanses of derelict land of the lower
Swansea Valley--such scenes left seeds which some inspired teaching
by the geography master at my secondary school helped to germinate.
London was different again: journeys to my aunt's home in Plumstead,
later to be demolished in the London blitz, were a source of special
excitement. There was the speed of the the two-hour express, the
arrival at Euston, the descent into the underground railway system
to London Bridge Station and then another railway journey to
Woolwich. Birmingham was a big city but in London there was urban
growth on a new scale, a whole system of cities in itself. The

---

1. Halford J. Mackinder, *Britain and the British Seas,* 2nd ed. (Oxford:
Clarendon Press, 1907), p. 265.

history of Britain was displayed in its buildings, marvels to the
boy brought up in a Victorian industrial city. And there was the
sense of being in the place where the really important decisions
were made. I had never heard the word "hierarchy" but a feeling for
relative scale and for functional differences emerged. Later, I was
to find Mackinder's chapter on London and "the urban community of
South-East England" touching a deep chord.[2]

Bicycling around the West Midlands, I watched the changes
taking place in the urban landscape. The Birmingham-Wolverhampton
new road appeared, cutting through the derelict land, rather than
through the towns, a product of the public investment program of the
depression years. Birmingham had what one of its early historians,
William Hutton, had termed "the itch for building" and vast
municipal housing estates sprang up with tree-lined curving roads,
houses with gardens, open spaces for recreation, designed (as I
later perceived) with some regard to garden city ideas. Matching
them for number and speed of building were the semi-detached houses
of the speculative builder selling for £450 or a little more
depending on size, garage, and prestige of the area.
Suburbanization was in full swing: the local palaces of the cinema
chains and the brewery-financed public houses commanded street
junctions and gave their names to focal points and tram termini. As
the suburbs spread, the more flexible motorbus supplemented the wire
or trackbound trolley buses and trams. New industrial estates
appeared away from railways or canals: I did not then know the term
"footloose" industries. About 1930 we acquired our first radio,
electric light was installed, and the gas mantle disappeared.
Birmingham's civic motto was "Forward," and among all cities it was
a leader in municipal enterprise with gas, electricity undertakings,
a water department which piped supplies from the Elan valley, far
away in the Welsh hills--even its own savings bank. To display the
growing city, the city transport provided cheap fares for week-end
rides around its outer circle bus route. Nor was recreation
forgotten, for in addition to the municipal parks there were the
lovely Lickey Hills, the local equivalent of London's Hampstead
Heath.

By 1930 my family had moved to the eastern side of the city to
a semi-detached house on a small experimental model village known as
the Ideal Village.[3] My father had secured the headship of a school

---

2. Mackinder, chap. 14, pp. 231-259, especially pp. 257-8.

3. Michael J. Wise, "An Early Experiment in Suburban Development: The Ideal
Village, Birmingham", in *Landscape and Industry*, ed. E. Grant and P. Newby
(London: Middlesex Polytechnic, 1982), pp. 151-156.

in the slums in the lowlying land of Garrison Lane wedged between smoky factory chimneys and railway embankments. There I would go, when I could, to help him by teaching a group of backward readers. He introduced me to the environment from which the school population was drawn. We would go through arches into the courtyards of back-to-back houses, with their central privies and taps, into which the sunlight seemed never to come. Yes, he would explain, slum clearance was going on but it would take time to clear away so many unfit houses and to provide decent environments.[4]

Later, one memorable day, in 1938, I was summoned, as an undergraduate, to the office of the head of the Department of Geography in which I was a student to be confronted with a set of 1:2,500 maps of the city of Birmingham. He said that a royal commission had been appointed to enquire into the geographical distribution of the industrial population of Great Britain and to consider the social, economic, and other disadvantages arising from the concentration of industries and the industrial population in large towns and to report on the remedial measures that were necessary. The commission had, he said, little evidence on the location of industries, their relation to housing, and the residence of the workforce. Would I please, therefore, mount my bicycle and survey the location of industry in Birmingham? Little, he said, had been done by geographers to study industry in towns since G.G. Chisholm's work on Edinburgh[5] (I later found some, though not many, exceptions to this statement),[6] and the time was ripe to show that geogrpahy possessed ideas and techniques which could be applied to the betterment of the environment. So geomorphology had, henceforth, to take second place, and I found myself in a new world peopled, on the one hand, by theorists—notably Alfred Weber—and, on the other, by the men and women who organized the factories, large and small, in a great industrial city.

The maps revealed three "rings" of urban housing: an inner area of mixed development containing small scale industrial quarters and factories side by side with slum housing, a middle ring of monotonous terraces of architecturally deplorable but for the most part structurally sound houses built before 1914, and an outer ring of suburban housing built either by the city under the duties

---

4. See Bournville Village Trust, *When We Build Again* (London: Allen and Unwin, 1941).

5. George G. Chisholm, "The Development of the Industries of Edinburgh and the Edinburgh District," *Scottish Geographical Magazine* 26 (1914): 312-21.

6. For example Douglas H. Smith, *The Industries of Greater London* (London: P.S. King and Son, 1933).

imposed by the housing act 1919 to provide adequate housing for rent or by the speculative builders for sale. There were exceptions, like the large, expensive houses of Edgbaston.

Radiating from the city along the main canal, railway, and road routes were the manufacturing sectors, with their public utilities, railway carriage workshops, and tire, automobile, and electrical engineering factories. I have often compared the maps since with the models of Burgess, Hoyt, and Harris and Ullman![7]

The maps were duly exhibited to the royal commission and there was in the air much thought and discussion about more effective town and regional planning, of halting the growth of greater London, especially in view of its strategic danger in the face of the expected air raids, of stopping cities from sprawling outwards and ribboning along main roads, and of alleviating the plight of many industrial areas such as South Wales, the Tyne, and the Clyde, where heavy structural unemployment was persistent. The expected war came, so did the air raids. Then for some years I was far away from Britain and out of touch. But my thoughts turned frequently to family and friends living at either end of the road from Birmingham to Wolverhampton and to what was being done in Britain to plan for the better environment which would arise in the post-war years. How well could industrial districts adapt to new circumstances? In what ways could assistance from government be most usefully given? How could plans for industrial re-generation be linked to plans for better cities and for the countryside?

### Post-War Policies and Plans

Lewis Mumford remarked in 1948 that "the foreign observer has ceased to be astonished at the quality of the thought that has gone into the surveys and plans for the redevelopment of urban England."[8] He was referring especially to the remarkable flowering of thought stimulated by the crisis of the war about the nature of the future society and environment. Of the needs for physical re-development there was no doubt. Conventry lay in ruins and in many other cities vast bombed-out or badly damaged areas lay in wait for reconstruction. There had been no addition to the stock of civilian housing, the slums remained uncleared. Arrears of maintenance to the urban infrastructure had accumulated: transport systems, in particular, were badly run down and in need of new investment.

---

7. See summary map in Michael J. Wise, *Birmingham and Its Regional Setting* (Birmingham: British Association Scientific Survey, 1950), fig. 44.

8. Lewis Mumford, "Foreword" to West Midland Group on Post-War Planning and Reconstruction, *Conurbation* (London: Architectural Press, 1948).

Basic industries had to be adjusted from the needs of war to those
of peace. It was not only physical reconstruction that was in mind:
society had to be refashioned and the Beveridge Plan with its theme
of social security formed a keystone. Three reports, the Barlow,
Scott, and Uthwatt Reports, had focused discussion on post-war urban
and regional planning issues. The Barlow report of 1940 is the most
relevant to our theme.[9] It examined the advantages and disadvantages
of the growth of great connurbations, pointing especially to the
problems of overcrowding, congestion, and pollution. Greater London
had become an "immense liability" and the continued drift of
population to south-east England constituted a "social and economic
problem which demands immediate attention." The outward sprawl of
London had to be arrested. Equally important was the need to
stimulate the industries and environments of those industrial
districts of South Wales, the north-east and north-west of England
and Scotland whose basic industries, largely heavy industries, had
been in decline. Diversification of their industrial bases was
overdue. Meanwhile the Scott Report[10] had emphasized the
conservation of agricultural land, especially the best land, which
in the pre-war years had been lost to urban growth at what had
seemed an alarming rate. The hand of L. Dudley Stamp, whose land
utilization survey of Britain[11] had clearly revealed the land-use
changes that were in progress, was evident in that report.

Many groups had been formed during the war years to think out
in urban and regional terms the practical implications of such
policy trends. I was fortunate enough to be able in 1946 to join in
the preparation by one of the most influential of them, the West
Midland Group on Post-War Reconstruction and Planning, of a planning
survey of the Birmingham-Black Country conurbation.[12] The
illustrations of the scarred landscapes that lay between Birmingham
and Wolverhampton gave added force to the analyses of land uses and
the call for "the radical physical re-planning of the whole area of
the conurbation and of the surrounding countryside." New improved
towns and cities were to be created in a green setting created from
reclaimed derelict land linked to what Elihu Burritt, the American
Consul, had once termed the "green borderland."[13] Social, as well as

9. Royal Commission on the Geographical Distribution of the Industrial
Population, *Report* (London: H.M.S.O., *Cmd.* 6153, 1940). (The "Barlow" Report).

10. Ministry of Works and Planning, *Report of the Committee on Land
Utilisation in Rural Areas* (London: H.M.S.O., 1945). (The "Scott" Report).

11. L. Dudley Stamp, *The Land of Britain: Its Use and Mis-Use* (London:
Longman, 1948).

12. West Midland Group, *Conurbation.*

economic needs were to be regarded in creating the new urban
environments. Coordination in regional planning between the
different interests, sectors, and professions was essential.

Much more influential nationally was the greater London plan
which the architect-planner Sir Patrick Abercrombie had prepared
between 1942 and 1944 and which was accepted in basic principle by
the governemnt in 1946. It was more influential, not only because
it offered a plan for the greatest city and its region, but also
because it provided principles which were to be adopted widely,
albeit with some delay, in other regions of Britain.[14] The plan
assumed that it would be possible to hold the population of greater
London stable at a little over 10 million and that new industrial
growth would be restrained. London could then be remodelled by
reducing the population of inner London by some 1.25 million so
relieving overcrowding and enabling slum clearance to proceed.
There would be a massive redistribution of population and employment
to new and expanded towns lying beyond a green belt. Within the
green belt, new development would be rigidly controlled, thus
preventing further urban sprawl. It was a grand conception.

In other cities of Britain the rubble was cleared. The plans
for Coventry and the rebuilding of Coventry Cathedral symbolized the
general, national desire for a new urban Britain. The Distribution
of Industry Act of 1946 and the Town and Country Planning Act of
1947 provided the powers.

There were great achievements and we can point only to some of
them. Eight new towns around London were built: Hemel Hempstead,
Harlow, Hatfield, Welwyn Garden City, Stevenage, Basildon, Crawley,
Bracknell, and successfully offered new medium-scale environments
for industry and housing. "Neighbourhood areas" were centered on
local schools, shops, and health centers to foster community living.
Pedestrian precincts, segregation of industry from housing,
separation of traffic from houses, new designs, all brought admiring
architect-planners from far afield.[15] In the long term they have
proved a very profitable investment. Between 1952 and 1958, 120,000
people were to move to the London new towns, together with 45,000 to
housing estates beyond the edge of the connurbation and 10,000 to
existing towns with which the then London County Council had agreed

---

13 . Elihu Burritt, *Walks in the Black Country and Its Green Borderland*,
(London: Sampson Low, 1868).

14 . Sir Patrick Abercrombie, *Greater London Plan 1948* (London: H.M.S.O.,
1945)

15 . Town and Country Planning Association, *New Towns Come of Age,* reprint
of *Town and Country Planning* 36 (Jan-Feb. 1968).

expansion schemes. Planned decentralization was going well.

A second achievement was in the clearance of the slums of the inner cities. Birmingham was especially quick to designate areas for compulsory redevelopment, to demolish slums, and to replace them with comprehensive development areas embodying current ideas of traffic segregation, community provision, ample open space. Leeds, Manchester and, a city of smaller size, Wolverhampton were other leaders in housing reconstruction efforts.[16]

Progress was also made in stimulating industrial growth in what came to be called the development areas. The establishment of new factories and the expansion of older ones in Greater London and the West Midlands, the more prosperous industrial areas, was rigidly controlled.[17] Programs of financial assistance to enterprises establishing themselves in, or moving to, the Development Areas were introduced. Industrial estates were provided in these areas, providing factory buildings in advance and with common services. In an age of full employment the Development Areas offered available labor supplies, an important attraction. Some, in Scotland especially, were successful in attracting investment from overseas, notably from the United States. Plans for reclaiming derelict land were framed: the Lower Swansea Valley Project, for example, began work in 1961.[18]

It was a daring experiment in national reconstruction: except on the fringe of the major cities where Green Belt controls held firm and where, with some exceptions, the urban edge has been fossilized to this day, the urban landscape was on the move. Demolition of slums was matched by the building of new towns in the countryside. Control of further industrial growth in London contrasted with the new factories springing up in South Wales, Tyneside, and Clydeside. Nationalization of the coal mining industry brought new plans for the modernization of mines and the sinking of new ones. Physical planning had national purposes and social aims.

### Second Thoughts

But by the early 1960s inadequacies in the post-war policies were being appreciated and new problems were emerging, some of them as products of the earlier policies. The assumption that, following

---

16. Maurice B. Stedman and Peter A. Wood, "Urban Renewal in Birmingham," *Geography* 50 (1965): 1-17.

17. John W. House, ed., *The UK Space: Resources, Environment and the Future,* 2nd ed. (London: Weidenfeld and Nicolson, 1977), pp. 22-23.

18. K.J. Hilton, "The Lower Swansea Valley Project," *Geography* 48 (1963): 296-299.

a post-war bulge in population growth, population trends would
revert to the pre-war pattern of low growth had been falsified. To
natural increase of population had been added, after 1956, an influx
of immigrants mainly from the Commonwealth. Whereas official
projections had forecast an increase of population for England and
Wales of 2 million for 1951-71, there was a growth of no less than
2.6 million by 1961. It had not proven so easy to arrest the growth
of population and employment in South-east England as had been
expected. In the new towns, with their youthful population
structures, large numbers of school-leavers were entering the labor
market: the desired range of jobs in new towns of limited size was
not available and commuting to London was on the increase. The
population of the main built-up area of the London conurbation had
indeed fallen, but the rate of household formation and the demand
for separate dwellings had increased more rapidly than had been
expected. Voluntary decentralization had gathered pace, assisted by
the personal mobility given by rising car ownership and by
electrification and dieselization of the railways. A great wave of
population increase surrounded the London conurbation, and the
villages and small towns were losing their original character as
private housing intruded and as commuters to central London took up
the dwellings of the former rural population. The city was indeed
coming to the countryside.[19] The strength and scale of
decentralization called for regional planning on a new scale. A
leading regional planner, A.G. Powell, wrote "in and beyond the
Green Belt movements of population and industrial expansion have,
with the aid of the motor car, created an embryonic conurbation a
hundred miles wide."[20] A new positive regional planning framework
was required.

There was dissatisfaction too with the pace of economic and
urban transformation in the Development Areas. Between 1952 and
1958 the London region with 27 percent of the population of England
and Wales had received over 40 percent of the additional employment,
a much greater share than the Barlow Report envisaged. The gains
from introducing new industries into the Development Areas were
being substantially offset by declines in employment in basic
industries, notably in coal mining. As as increasing importation of
relatively cheap oil turned the post-war coal shortage into a coal
surplus, such declines were to continue. Unemployment in the

---

19. Raymond E. Pahl, *Urbs in Rure,* London School of Economics Geographical
Papers, 1965.

20. A.G. Powell, "The Recent Development of Greater London," *Advancement of
Science* 22 (1966): 571-588.

Development Areas remained higher than the national average and rose in the recession of 1958-59. Powell was quite forthright: "the economic background of the Barlow Report is a thing of the past and planning based on it is equally out-dated." Barlow had viewed the control of the location of manufacturing industry as the key to the location of population, but manufacturing was now employing a declining proportion of the population and it was the service industries that were growing, and growing especially fast in London. Could, or should, planning break the trends? Was it not more realistic to accept the trends and plan for them?

Now based in London, I was drawn into the discussion of these questions and, in 1960, wrote that there seems "a prima facie case for considering present planning policies ineffective to deal with modern conditions."[21] Too little regard had been given, I suggested, to changing economic conditions and particularly to the ways in which the geographical values of different industrial regions had changed. Town and regional planning had to accept at least some responsibility for the economic welfare of the country. In this light, locational policies had been based too heavily on short term welfare considerations and too sparsely on the longer term need for economic efficiency. It was desirable also to coordinate more closely the policies of government departments and nationalized industries in their regional and locational aspects. Such arguments led to the view that planning should take fresh aims and purposes with the positive objective of adjusting old urban and industrial patterns to new needs. If the Development Areas were to be modernized, a more far-reaching program of investment would be required, involving an accelerated reorganization of present patterns of settlement and population. Were there not ways of improving basic conditions and services in the older industrial regions to provide attractive conditions for the location and growth of secondary and tertiary industry? But a realistic view had also to be taken of the forces making for growth in the South-east of England where the "city-region" of London[22] had a radius of some fifty miles outwards from Westminster. A new planning appreciation was required.

There was a further reason for reviewing earlier policies. While in the London region planned decentalization had proceeded satisfactorily, this was not the case in all regions. The West

---

21. Michael J. Wise, "Some Economic Trends Influencing Planning Policies," *Journal of the Town Planning Institute* 46 (1960): 30-39.

22. Michael J. Wise, "The City Region," *Advancement of Science* 22 (1966): 571-588.

Midlands was one such case.[23] A regional plan had been prepared by
Sir Patrick Abercrombie and Herbert Jackson in 1948. An overspill
problem from the central Birmingham-Black Country conurbation was
identified and recommendations were made for dispersal to towns
capable of expansion which lay towards the fringe of the region.
The conurbation was itself divided between a number of local
government authorities and one of the recommendations of the plan
was that the conurbation should be treated as a single planning unit
with an overall planning authority. By far the largest authority in
the connurbation, Birmingham, remained largely unconvinced of the
need for dispersal of employment and industry, quite unlike the
London County Council which had fostered decentralization. While
Birmingham had undertaken negotiations for overspill agreements with
other local authorities ih the early 1950s, these had had only
strictly limited results. It saw the best solution to its problems
of lack of available space for its very large scale and well
organized housing program in a large extension of the city to the
south into an area of land which lay within the jurisdiction of a
neighboring county council.

There developed in 1959 a now celebrated planning "battle"
over the proposals to develop at Wythall. The principles at issue
between the central urban and the more rurally oriented county
authorities were the extent to which the conurbation should be
extended further and the intrusion into the Green Belt which this
would precipitate. Objections were made on the part of those living
in the smaller towns and villages within the commuter zone of
Birmingham, but outside the city itself, to the supposed damage
which such a major urban intrusion would represent. Birmingham's
requirements were real and solutions were eventually found. Schemes
for new town development, at Redditch to the south, and at Dawley
(now called Telford) in Shropshire, where the development could be
combined with the reclamation of the landscape of the old Shropshire
coalfield, were devised and put into effect. There was also
agreement to the extension of Birmingham to the east in the large
Chelmsley Wood Estate for about 50,000 people and, later, to some
smaller extensions to the south.

## Policy Responses in the 1960s

The reinforcement of policies for industrial location was an
immediate response to such trends with the tightening of controls on
approvals for industrial development in southern England and an

---

23. Michael J. Wise, "The Birmingham-Black Country Conurbation in Its
Regional Setting," *Geography* 57 (1972): 89-104.

expansion of factory building in the Development Areas.  Previous legislation for the distribution of industry was replaced in 1960 by a new Local Employment Act under which any locality in which unemployment existed above a certain level became eligible for help as a Development District.  When employment improved, assistance was withdrawn.  The apparent flexibility of this measure was soon seen as a disadvantage for the prospect of consistent help became uncertain.  The criticism was also made that the assistance would go, by definition, to places that were unfavorable for modern industrial development rather than to those, perhaps even only a few miles away, which had much greater potential.  The scheme was abandoned in 1966 when a new Industrial Development Act was passed defining development areas widely.  A further step in 1967 was the designation of Special Development Areas, with higher rates of assistance, to certain districts of the coalfields where mine closures resulted in high rates of localized unemployment.

Evidence provided by Howard is also relevant.[24] He showed that the total volume of industrial movement involved about 53,000 jobs per year in 1945-51, 35,000 per year in 1952-59, and 46,000 per year in 1960-65.  In the first period the less prosperous regions received about two-thirds of all manufacturing movement as measured by jobs.  In the second period the main flow of jobs was from Greater London to the rest of South-east England.  But in the early 1960s the less prosperous areas were again the principal recipients.

New ground was broken in studies of two regions, North-east England and central Scotland, and the government published White Papers in 1963.  These formally introduced into British planning the concept of the "growth zone," a modification and adaptation of Perroux's growth pole idea.  The White Papers included maps of the proposed growth zones.  That for the North-east was too wide an area, no doubt for local political reasons, to be a very effective instrument.  Those for central Scotland were more precisely defined to coincide with locations for new towns and overspill centers or with access points on the improving transport infrastructure: the Forth Bridge, for example, was opened in 1964.  D.R. Diamond, writing in 1965,[25] viewed these proposals as "the latest and very valuable step in the creation for Scotland of an effective regional planning system."  There, in a region with its own partly separate

24. R.S. Howard, *The Movement of Manufacturing Industry in the U.K. 1945-65* (London: H.M.S.O., 1968) and see discussion by Manners in Gerald Manners, David E. Keeble, Brian Rodgers, and Kenneth Warren, *Regional Development in Britain* (London: John Wiley, 1972), chap. 1.

25. Derek R. Diamond in "Regional Planning Problems in Great Britain," ed. A.A.L. Caesar and David E. Keeble, *Advancement of Science* 22 (1965): 177-185.

governmental system, it had been possible to achieve a considerable degree of co-ordination in planning for urban development, housing, industrial development, the social services, transport, and the infrastructure.

In 1964 came, with a change of government, a major review of regional planning strategy and organization. A new Department of Economic Affairs took responsibility for the coordination of regional development action while administration of industrial location policy remained in the hands of the Board of Trade and physical planning policy with the Ministry of Housing and Local Government. Britain was divided into ten planning regions. For each region an Economic Planning Council was created with members from local governemnt, industry and other representative interests. Each council was assisted by an Economic Planning Board composed of representatives of the regional offices of the government departments involved in making decisions affecting the regional economy and environment. The new system was intended to provide, at the national level, a way of reconciling competition between regions and, at the regional level, a mechanism for the coordination of interests which had previously been lacking.

There had already been an attempt to inititate a new set of regional surveys and plans directed by central government planners in Whitehall. The *South East Study* in 1964 was the first.[26] The inadequacy of the Abercrombie decentralization strategy, in the light of the new wave of population growth, led the authors to conclude that one million people would need to be transferred from London by 1981 and that homes would also need to be provided outside London for a further 2.5 million people. The strategy devised embodied a growth zone concept in proposing large counter-magnet towns which would act as major centers in the South-east and a new wave of larger New Towns. Not all the proposals were accepted in the form offered but many important urban developments have their origins in this scheme, for example the expansion of Swindon, Peterborough, and Northampton New Towns and the idea which emerged as Milton Keynes New Town with a target population of a quarter of a million located over 45 miles from London.

The Economic Planning Councils were required to produce their own regional designs for the future, in effect visions of the future regional economic geography of the country. Assembled together they provide an impressive picture of the national prospect viewed at a

---

26. Ministry of Housing and Local Government, *The South East Study 1961-81* (London: H.M.S.O., 1964).

time when growth was very much in the air.  Space precludes
individual discussion but a little must be said about the *Strategy
for the South-East* which appeared in 1967.[27] While a number of the
elements in the 1964 study were incorporated the strategy had a
growth-sector base to it with tongues of development aligned along
the main radial communication lines emanating from London.  Its
population targets were somewhat lower than those accepted in 1964
but nevertheless substantial.  The strategy also made provision for
some major development in infrastructure, notably a third London
airport (which was to become the subject, as it still is, of further
detailed inquiry).

To complete the story, reference must be made to a third
study, produced by a planning team drawn from national and local
government departments and from the Economic Planning Council, which
was intended to examine the practicability of the alternative
proposals, to establish their feasibility, and to consider the
longer term implications for the period up to 2001.  Two models were
advanced for testing, one based on the sectoral approach and a
second which placed greater emphasis on existing trends in
population growth and gave more importance to growth in areas
relatively close to London.  The *Strategic Plan for the South-East*
which emerged was a relatively flexible scheme which anticipated a
London reduced to 7 millions, provided for some growth in
counter-magnets, but placed much more growth in and around existing
nuclei near to London.  It has been described as a "flexible and
appropriate framework within which to shape the future human
geography of the region."[28]

Perhaps enough has been said to indicate the flavor of this
exciting phase of regional planning, in which many geographers and
geographically trained planners played influential parts.  Not all
the regional surveys and plans were as optimistic in tone as those
for the south east.  Papers coming from the West Midlands, for
example, a region which had been regarded as, next to greater London
region, a major growth area and where growth, indeed, had been
restricted in favor of transferring enterprises to development
areas, carried ominous undertones.[29] The region was too dependent on
manufacturing industry and relatively poorly endowed with service

27. South East Economic Planning Council, *A Strategy for the South-East*
(London: H.M.S.O., 1967).

28. South East Joint Planning Team, *Strategic Plan for the South-East*
(London: H.M.S.O., 1970).

29. West Midlands Economic Planning Council, *The West Midlands: An Economic
Appraisal* (London, H.M.S.O., 1971).

industries. Manufacturing itself was too dependent on the automobile and its linked industries. Labor productivity was low. Diversification was desirable.

A new wave of New Town construction was in progress, often, though not invariably, focused on existing towns farther away from the main city and with larger population targets than those of the first wave around London. Particular use was made of the New Towns concept in plans for the Development Areas: five were designated in Scotland.[30]

The 1960s were also years of thought about the internal structure of cities. Green Belts, on the whole, held well; decentralization on a regional basis was the rule. But how to adapt cities to the motor vehicle which was accounting year by year for a greater proportion of the passenger and freight movements? In 1951 there was one car for every 21 people, in 1974 one for every four. Britain was slow to develop its motorway network but the program which was instituted in 1955 began to show major results in the 1960s. A first major product, the M1 linking London with the West and East Midland regions, has shown an impressive economic rate of return. Built quickly to deal with the heavy volumes of traffic on this major axis, insufficient attention was given to the environmental aspects of its design. The lesson was learned and, aided by the work of the Advisory Committee on the Landscape Treatment of Trunk Roads,[31] subsequent motorway and major inter-city road development has been environmentally more sensitive. The Buchanan Report of 1963 exercised a considerable influence on road and traffic planning within cities.[32] Its concepts of "distributor" roads carrying traffic into and around towns have been easier to apply in New Towns than in old though many examples exist of the adaptation of older road networks to the new ideas. Traffic restriction schemes and the creation of "environmental areas" freed from through-traffic have greatly improved conditions in residential areas and in shopping precincts. Less fruitful have been a number of schemes for urban motorway development. Birmingham, it is true, successfully completed its inner ring road but that concept had been born in the 1920s. The scheme for three major new ring roads within the London conurbation advanced in the Greater London Plan of 1968 aroused intense opposition on environmental grounds, and only some

---

30. Richard Lawton, *The UK Space,* ed. J.W. House, chap. 2.

31. Bruno de Hamel, *Roads and the Environment* (London: H.M.S.O. for Department of the Environment, 1976).

32. Colin D. Buchanan, *Traffic in Towns* (London: H.M.S.O., 1963).

limited parts of it have been built as intended.  Priority was given
instead to the construction of a motorway (M25) circling the
conurbation within the Green Belt and designed to carry
through-traffic around the urban area.  But this was a task for the
1970s and early 1980s.  A new departure was made in the Transport
Act of 1968 with the introduction of government grants for public
transport and the establishment of Passenger Transport Authorities
for the main conurbations serving about 37 percent of the
population.  The principle of support for public transport has
subsequently been maintained though not without controversy over
scale and method.

It was a decade, then, of regional planning involving
modification of the earlier post-war planning policies and
objectives to meet the circumstances of population increase, greater
mobility of individuals and industry, the desire for growth, and
also the increased rate of decline in the larger conurbations and
cities and the stronger tendencies for decentralization from cities
of smaller size.

### "Emptying" Cities: The Need for New Policies

Before considering the main trends in urban and regional
change of the 1970s, I must refer to the remarkable study carried
out by Hall, Gracey, and Drewett published in 1973 as *The
Containment of Urban England*.[33] The study was in two parts: the
first concentrated on the processes of urban and metropolitan growth
in the post-war period and the second examined the planning system
and gave a verdict on its results.  A period of unprecendentedly
rapid urban growth was brilliantly depicted.  The larger
metropolitan areas had reached stagnation, even decline, especially
in their inner areas.  In the faster growing regions this had been
accompanied by the rapid expansion of smaller, peripheral
metropolitan areas, a trend especially noticeable around London.
Peripheral growth had been less in evidence in the regions of weaker
economic growth where the overall result was one of stagnation.
Decentralization from urban core areas to the metropolitan rings had
not yet been fully matched in the distribution of employment, though
that situation appeared to be changing.  Decentralization had been
earliest and fastest in the larger metropolitan areas and some of
the biggest had been recording absolute losses from their core areas
in the 1960s, for example, London, Manchester, Newcastle, and

---

33. Peter G. Hall, Harry Gracey, Roy Drewett, and Ray Thomas, *The
Containment of Urban England,* 2 vols. (London: Allen and Unwin, 1973); see also
Peter G. Hall, "The Containment of Urban England," *Geographical Journal* 140
(1974): 386-417.

Liverpool. But relative decentralization was taking place also in the smaller metropolitan areas. Hall advanced a model of decentralizing urban change which has been much tested subsequently. Urban change was not simply a matter of growth from metropolitan area to megalopolis. While an English megalopolis could be recognized, stretching from the English Channel to Lancashire, it consisted of 63 metropolitan areas within each of which decentralization processes had been variably at work. In the largest the earlier rates of growth had slowed and, in some, reversed.

Turning to the success of planning policies, Hall found that the policy of urban containment, with the Green Belt as a main instrument, had indeed worked. The amount of land converted from rural to urban use had been minimized and kept compact. A second, probably less intended feature had been the growing separation of residential areas from employment locations, leading to the further suburbanization of the population. Hall drew attention, thirdly, to the escalation in land and property values which, if not wholly the product of planning policies, had been facilitated by them. He drew the sobering conclusion that the system had not achieved one, at least, of the major objectives of the founding fathers of British planning in providing for the "lower income groups, whether in high-rise municipal housing in the cities, or in adequate privately-rented housing in these same cities, or in small and poorly equipped new housing at the urban periphery," nearly as much as for the home-owning middle classes. While, perhaps, this conclusion under-estimates the extent to which change for the better had been brought to urban slum environments and is a criticism as much of economic and social, as of planning, systems, it was a lesson which was to have much point in the later 1970s.

Towards the end of the 1960s the natural increase of population had declined and, by contrast with the 5 percent increases of 1951-61 and 1971-81, the population increase 1971-81 was of the order only of 0.5 percent. Decline in the crude birth rate was an important factor. The North West and North of England and Scotland all declined in population; the South West, East Anglia, and the East Midlands grew. The South East declined slightly. There appeared to be a continued shift of population from north to south but a key element in change was the presence or absence within a given region of a major conurbation, for it was there that the most dramatic changes took place.[34] The population of

---

34. W. Randolph and S. Robert, "Population Re-distribution in Great Britain

Greater London fell during the decade by three quarters of a million
to 6.7 millions; its inner areas declined by 17.7 percent. Glasgow
city declined by 22.3 percent. Greater Manchester by 17.4 percent,
Liverpool by 16.4 percent. Liverpool had fallen in 20 years from
three-quarters of a million to only just over half a million. In
the 1961-71 decade, declines had been most obvious in the inner
areas of the major cities: these continued, but decline in 1971-81
spread also to the outer areas of the main cities and conurbations.
Population loss spread also to many smaller cities.

By contrast, high relative increases were found, especially in
areas in the outer metropolitan fringes. An arc of increase
extended from the Solent to the Wash. Many rural areas showed
increases and, in some remoter rural areas, a reversal of previous
trends to decline. On the whole, the Development Areas showed
decline but the effects of North Sea oil development showed up
clearly in North-east Scotland. Generally the shifts have been
regarded as showing a deepening and an extension of the
decentralization trends of the 1960s. Clearly the implications for
the inner areas of the great cities are ominous, but before
discussing these a little must be said about another trend--the rise
of unemployment.

There had been, since the mid-1960s, a major decentralization
of jobs from most of the large industrial areas to their surrounding
districts. This had been evident notably in Greater London, the
West Midlands, Manchester, and on Clydeside; matched by job decline
in the inner areas. The national rate of unemployment had risen a
little during 1970-72, fell in 1973-74, and then rose to 6.7 percent
by 1980. For a brief period in 1975-76 there was a tendency for a
decline in the differences in unemployment rates between Greater
London and, say, Glasgow and Tyneside. Thereafter the differences
widened again and by 1980 Liverpool had a rate of 13.6 percent,
Glasgow 11.4 percent, and Tyneside 10.8 percent compared with 4.1
percent for Greater London. The areas of traditionally high
unemployment have suffered worst in this new age of mass
unemployment.

These trends must be viewed against major changes in
employment structure which have been in progress. Over the fifteen
years 1965-1980 manufacturing industry shed about 1,730,000 workers,
a decline of 21 percent while the service industries grew by some

---

1971-81," *Town and Country Planning* 50 (1981): 227-230; and "Beyond
Decentralization: The Evolution of Population Distribution in England and Wales,
1961-81," *Geoforum* 14 (1983): 75-102.

1,950,000, an increase of 18 percent.[35] There was much discussion of
the so-called "de-industrialization process," though it remains to
be seen whether the term is fully apt or whether the process has
been a complex one of industrial adaptation within which the seeds
of regeneration have been sown.

Nevertheless it is understandable, at a time when high rates
of unemployment had spread even to the West Midlands and to the
inner districts of Greater London, that enthusiasm for regional
policy in its existing form greatly waned.  It was, said its
critics, too widespread in its application, too expensive in
relation to the number of jobs created, too inclined to create
capital-intensive rather than labor-intensive development.  Should
not the emphasis be placed on energizing economic growth and on
encouraging new opportunities for employment wherever these might
arise?  Should not more advantage be taken of the opportunities for
growth in southern England, especially in relation to the greatly
increased share which Western Europe now held in patterns of trade
and the markets that awaited British exports?  While the Industry
Acts of 1972 and 1975 increased the assistance given to firms to
move to or develop within the assisted areas, by 1976 the Greater
London Council had reversed its long standing policy of encouraging
firms to decentralize from the conurbation and was considering how
best to foster industrial redevelopment in its inner areas of high
unemployment.

A new government elected in 1978 undertook a review of
regional industrial location policy as a whole, limiting
expenditure, reducing the size of the assisted areas, and putting
new emphasis on development through the creation of enterprise
zones.  In these small, carefully selected areas, situated in all
regions of the country, advantages to location are offered,
including the removal of certain town and country planning
constraints.  The most recent statement of policy in 1983 puts more
faith in "the natural adjustment of labor markets" to be brought
about by improving the comparative advantages of the assisted areas
through lower wages and unit costs and increased productivity.
Reflecting the change in the country's industrial structure it
places more emphasis on guiding the service industries to the areas
of need.  The criteria for making grants to firms will be tightened
to favor job-creating projects.[36]

---

35. John E. Martin,"La Desindustrialisation de la Grande Bretagne," *Revue
d'Économie Régionale et Urbaine* 4 (1981): 283-289.

36. *Regional Industrial Development* (London, H.M.S.O. *Cmnd.* 9111, 1983);
see also discussion of regional policy in Regional Studies Association, *Report of*

Meanwhile the problems, in the age of decentralization, of the "Unequal City" exemplified by the localized unemployment, high death rates of industrial firms, and run-down infrastructure of the inner cities have also attracted specific and urgent attention. In 1977 a program for the inner cities became a central element in government planning policy and the Inner Urban Areas Act of 1978 established a program of assistance organized through partnership schemes between central and local government authorities and other measures for certain defined areas. Frameworks for inner area strategies were advanced in a series of studies of areas in London, Liverpool, and Birmingham.[37] As has been shown, the problems are complex and involve issues of poverty and social disadvantage as well as lack of locally available job opportunities. They involve tasks of environmental reconstruction which must be carried out with sensitivity to local needs as well as to regional requirements. The situation contains a number of enigmas, not least the continuance of high land values that appear out of proportion to current demands. While there are some specifically local elements, the situation as a whole reflects an over-investment in the facilities on the fringe of the decentralizing city and the belated recognition of the deepening problems, at a time of economic recession, of the inner areas. There are signs of progress: more local community involvement, with a change in attitudes and priorities. Cities are resourceful and new approaches to the improvement of their "livability" are emerging. But the problems will not disappear quickly.

### Continuing Tasks

I turn again to Lewis Mumford. When he came to Britain shortly after the end of the Second World War, he quoted the remark made by Emerson during his visit at the time of the great depression of 1847: "England is no country for faint-hearted people." Mumford extended Emerson's observations to suggest that here lay the "political intelligence, administrative skill and the civic probity and courage that will transform the old handicaps into fresh opportunities."[38] Mumford was thinking ahead to the new problems that faced the transformation of the industrial city, blighted by war, through a period of immense economic, technical, and social change. There have been great successes but many failures. One of

---

*an Inquiry into Regional Problems in the U.K.* (Norwich: Geo Books, 1983).

37. See, for example, Llewelyn-Davies, Weeks, Forestier-Walker, and Bor, *Unequal City: Final Report of the Birmingham Inner Area Study* (London: H.M.S.O., for the Department of the Environment, 1977).

38. Mumford, see footnote 8.

the basic difficulties is that of relating two very different time scales of action.  Action to regenerate old industrial regions must be carried through consistently over a quarter of a century or more; the reconstruction of the urban environment may be achieved somewhat more quickly, yet not without a degree of planning, whether by government or private agencies, over the long term.  Economic circumstances can change overnight, however, as happened in the early 1970s, and, at the best of times, the vision of the economic planner is short or medium term in real substance.  A satisfactory relationship between economic and environmental planning is difficult to establish.

Then there is the age-old question of the causes of things. How far do the problems of the assisted or "development" areas reflect problems of locational disadvantage or of industrial structure?  Are they indeed regional problems in a geographical sense or local manifestations of economic changes taking place at the national level?  Why had progress been made in adapting industry and environment in some areas, coastal South Wales, for example, more rapidly than in others, the North East, Merseyside, or Glasgow?

Similar questions may be asked of the inner city problems. Are these the effects of decentralization and of new investments which have made locations away from the large urban centers more attractive?  Or do they reflect broader changes in the organization of industrial production which have increased the strength of large corporations and reduced the attraction of the city to smaller firms by lessening the importance of intra-urban linkages.  By extension, it is argued that the changes in industrial organization and production are on such a scale as to affect adversely the traditional role of the large city in the urban system as a whole. "The urban hierarchy", it has been said, "consists of a number of large centers lacking a contemporary functional role in the organization of private production."  The role of the conurbation, in this view, remains only in employment for the public sector and in local population serving activities.  The policy problems, in these circumstances, may then be to find roles for the conurbations that will justify their fixed investment in urban infrastructure and provide greater opportunities for jobs for the people who live there.[39]

---

39 . Martin E. Frost and Nigel A. Spence, "Policy Responses to Urban and Regional Economic Change in Britain," *Geographical Journal* 147 (1981): 321-349; see also Nigel A. Spence et al., *British Cities:  An Analysis of Urban Change* (Oxford: Pergamon, 1982).

Such a task raises the question of where major
responsibilities for change in the large cities are to lie. Little
has been said in this essay about the changes that have been made in
the local government organization for cities or about changes in the
balance between central and local government responsibility. The
large metropolitan authorities which were set up in 1974 for the
major conurbations, in order to achieve the strategic planning that
seemed then to be necessary, have been, in the view of the present
government, both ineffective and expensive, and plans for their
abolition are in hand. This situation, and other government
actions, suggest a move to more centralized authority. But
solutions may come eventually from cooperation between central and
local government to promote action that will generate the growth of
new employment opportunities and will re-create, in the problem
areas, attractive environments for individual and community life
(figure 2.1).

Urban and regional planning has contributed greatly to the
transformation of post-war Britain. The achievements would have
been still greater had it been possible to adapt policies and
practice to the pace of change and to the appearance of new
problems. But, perhaps, time lags of this kind are inevitable in
democratic society and are a necessary part of the price that is
paid for the time spent, not merely in identifying new trends, but
in resolving argument about new policies. Perhaps, again, as
Michael Chisholm suggests.[40] There has been too much emphasis on
responding to the needs of areas and not enough on securing that
economic efficiency and growth which is an enabling factor in the
process of regional economic improvement.

### The Scene Transformed

The Birmingham to Wolverhampton road is still busy but its
role has changed. Through-traffic now moves rapidly along Motorways
5 and 6 which join in the heart of the conurbation. Junctions to
the motorways, most famous among them the controversial "spaghetti
junction" at Aston, in Birmingham, carry traffic out of the
conurbation on to the national motorway net. By nipping in and out
of the junctions, local and interregional movements may be made
swiftly. Distances have shortened. While the Birmingham-Black
Country conurbation remains an identifiable physical unit, it is now
the core of a much larger, more widespread "city region." The

---

40. Michael Chisholm, "City, Region and - What Kind Of Problem", chap. 2 in
*The Expanding City, Essays in Honour of Jean Gottmann,* ed. John Patten. (London:
Academic Press, 1983).

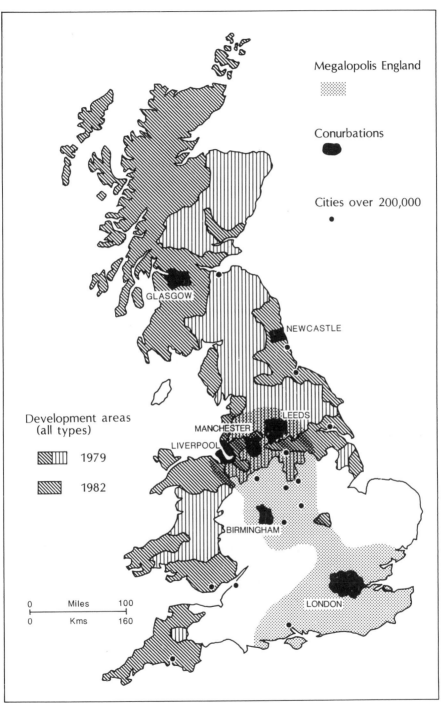

Figure 2.1. British metropolitan areas

decentralization of people and jobs to places beyond the surrounding Green Belt has brought into being a "central urban complex" for the West Midlands. It may be likened to a constellation of towns extending to a radius of 30 miles or so from central Birmingham, with the fastest growth on the fringe. Industry has changed its character: no longer are the local industrial linkages, which provided the economic base for the concentration of people, houses and factories, any longer a significant element. Many of the smaller factories and work-places have gone. The industrial villages of the Victorian Age, so brilliantly described by Francis Brett Young,[41] have changed their appearance and lost their localness.

In many ways it is a landscape for the better: the derelict land of the age of coal, clay, and iron has been reclaimed and put to new uses, though the demand for roadstone has led to further scarring by the immense quarries into the Rowley Hills that dominate the road. The canal tunnels under the limestone hills, north of Dudley, carry barges only for visitors and tourists, and industrial museums brilliantly reveal the origins of the industrial region. It is easier to write history than to find from history the best paths into the future.

Today industrial life is depressed: in particular, the sad history in the 1970s of the automobile industry has left its mark. But at the same time there are signs of innovation and growth. The automobile industry has survived; it is efficient again and not short of new models and ideas. Very close to the Birmingham-Wolverhampton road is a new enterprise zone. The motorway junction had improved accessibility and had confirmed the region's centrality in the transport map of southern Britain. The service industries are growing in an area that was short of them. True, at either end of the road, in inner Birmingham and in Wolverhampton, as well as in nearby old industrial towns, there are "inner city" problems to be solved. Housing needs modernization and renewal; there are local community tensions, some of them ethnic in origin, to be eased; skills to be changed and new jobs found.

What I have been trying to express is the view that the geographer interested in the study of urban and regional change cannot stand aside from the discussion of the causes and processes of change. Nor can he isolate himself from the discussion of policy, for it will be better informed for the contribution that

---

41. Leslie J. Jay, "The Black Country of Francis Brett Young," *Transactions of the Institute of British Geographers* 66 (1975): 57-72.

geographical approaches to regional study can make. Nor, finally, should we draw the wrong conclusions from disappointments and "failures" of planning policies. Through the rigorous examination of trends and the identification of forces, through the development of new ideas about the use and organization of space, better paths to progress can be offered for discussion and choice. The post-war geography of the West Midlands, indeed of Britain, is "intimately bound up with the post-war history of planning: each has changed the other."[42] Happily a new generation of geographers has taken up the challenge in Britain, much better equipped methodologically than their predecessors, and the issues of urban and regional change and of planning policies are being pursued with new vigor.[43]

---

42. Gordon Cherry, "Post-War Development Strategies for the West Midland Conurbation," address to Institute of British Geographers, 1973, (mimeo).

43. See, for example, John B. Goddard and Anthony G. Champion, eds., *The Urban and Regional Transformation of Britain* (London: Methuen, 1983) and references cited therein; also David Keeble, *Industrial Location and Planning in the United Kingdom* (London: Methuen, 1976).

# Chapter III

# URBANIZATION IN FRANCE SINCE WORLD WAR II

Jacqueline Beaujeu-Garnier

The French urban landscape has changed extraordinarily in the last forty years. Even the most casual observer cannot help but notice and marvel at the change. To the old low-profile towns with their local materials and picturesque architecture, differing with each region, have been added, or have been substituted, new vertical constructions, in concrete, whose geometric design stands out in the middle of traditional neighborhoods, or juxtapose one another in blocks rising above the low town. Surrounding the cities are the suburbs, more and more extended, supported and favored by the axes of modern transportation. Recent building lots continue their regular alignment into cultivated fields or glades in the middle of forests. There are even entirely new cities which have appeared in rural areas. Construction sites appear everywhere and a short trip to the countryside makes it evident that, in the country as well, the customs and attitudes of the inhabitants have greatly evolved as a result of the contact with city life.

France has not been immune to this powerful movement of *urbanization* which is one of the major events of the last half century in every country in the world. Roughly 28.2 percent of the world's population lived in cities with more than 5,000 inhabitants in 1950, 41 percent in 1975, and the movement has not yet ended. Even if we must be somewhat wary of statistics established with criteria differing from one state to another, the phenomenon is no less surprising for its intensity and its rapidity. Beyond more or less arbitrary statistical definitions the notion of urbanization is much more complex, including at the same time a localization, a life style, and a psychological attitude. It embodies not only spatial manifestations, but sociological interpretations as well. It is this double aspect which we shall treat in this essay on urbanization in France.[1]

---

1 . Recent general works on French urban geography and urbanism include Jacqueline Beaujeu-Garnier, *Géographie urbaine* (Paris: Edition Masson, 1980), and idem, ed., *La France des villes,* 6 Vols. (Paris: La Documentation Française,

## The Notion of Urbanization

The quantitative measure of the notion of urbanization has never been, and doubtless never will be, incontestably defined. The lower limit of the population considered to be urban varies from one state to another. In France, since 1846, all those living in groups of more than 2,000 persons are officially considered part of the urban population. If this criterion was acceptable at the time, it is now quite outdated. According to this definition, the urban population reached 22 million inhabitants in 1936, 52 percent of the total population, and 73 percent in 1975 with 38 million.

Challenging this definition, various authors have proposed setting the lower limit at 3,000 inhabitants.[2] Others have deliberately sacrificed the small towns and taken as a starting point 10,000 or even 20,000 inhabitants.[3] This elimination of the lower categories has the disadvantage of concealing a very important phenomenon, namely, the change in the role of small towns in the national urban frame.

Aside from this quantitative approach, desirable but always more or less debatable, one must acknowledge the importance of qualitative change. At the present time, in most of France, there are phenomena of "urban contamination" of the country. A large number of villages have a rural non-farm population, and the behavior of this population tends more and more to resemble that of the city dwellers. In other words, a homogenization of the population, more sensitive in life style or reactions than in spatial localization. These caveats aside, what do the statistics say?

### Growth of the Urban Population

The last five censuses (1954, 1962, 1968, 1975, 1982) permit us to measure the volume of growth and to observe its general orientation, even if the changes in the definition of one or another point during this period render the exact measurement difficult. Between 1946 and 1975, the urban population increased 190 percent for the whole of France, while the global urban population progressed only 130 percent. While 56 percent of the French lived in an urban township in 1954, this grew to 78 percent in 1982.

1978-1980); Jean Borde, Pierre Barrère, and Micheline Cassou-Mounat, *Les Villes françaises* (Paris: Edition Masson, 1980); Denise Pumain, *La Dynamique des villes,* (Paris: Economica, 1982); Thérèse Saint-Julien, *Croissance industrielle et système urbain,* (Paris: Economica, 1982).

2. Georges Dupeux, *Atlas historique de l'urbanisation de la France* (Paris: CNRS, 1911-1975).

3. Philippe Pinchemel et al., *La France,* 2 Vols. (Paris: A. Colin, 1981).

During this same period, the number of towns with more than 50,000 inhabitants went from 63 to 107. Not only did the number of urban townships increase, but the population of these urban townships increased as well (table 3.1).

Two immediate comments are in order. First, all the figures for population are on the increase, except for towns of from 10,000 to 20,000 inhabitants. Record growth is shown by towns which can be considered large by French standards: for the base of 100 in 1946, we have progressed to a growth index of 277 for towns of more than 100,000 inhabitants and to 426 for those with more 250,000. The Paris metropolitan area, until 1946 distinguished by its growth rate, reached only 188 by 1982. There are some obvious irregularities to explain.

The second remark concerns the number of "urban units." To take into account the new forms of this explosion "whose rhythm was like that of the nineteenth century, at the time of the Industrial Revolution," statisticians have had to present the census results in a different manner. To the concept of the traditionally defined "isolated town" was added that of the agglomeration, whose definition, established by the *Institut National de la Statistique et des Études Economique* (INSEE) in 1952, was modified for each later census (1967-1974) to take into consideration the general expansion of population, which greatly overflowed the borders of the townships included in the large agglomerations. Despite these successive modifications, the fundamental principles underlying the definition include continuity of building, strong growth of a population with many young people and a certain density, and regular migration of workers converging on the center. This combination of town and agglomerations is called an *urban unit*. Thus, the agglomeration of Lyon contains 73 townships, 55 in Lille's agglomeration, and 22 in that of Marseille. The number of townships so classified depends more on their areal size than their population. The two agglomerations of Lyon and Marseille, for example, have approximately the same population--just over a million. With the great wave of urbanization taking place, the number of isolated urban communities decreased from 1,085 in 1962 to 872 in 1975, while that of the agglomerations has almost tripled (282 to 769), and the number of urban communities included has jumped from 1,454 to 3,587 places.

Another important consequence of urbanization is found in the definition of "zones of industrial and urban population" *(zones de peuplement industriel et urbain or ZPIU),* which the statisticians

TABLE 3.1

EVOLUTION OF THE URBAN POPULATION
BY CATEGORY OF URBAN UNITS

|  | 1946 | | 1975 | |
|---|---|---|---|---|
|  | N | Population | N | Population |
| 3,000 - 5,000 | 325 | 1,257,452 | 426 | 1,629,699 |
| 5,000 - 7,500 | 175 | 1,052,270 | 211 | 1,305,817 |
| 7,500 - 10,000 | 88 | 761,727 | 106 | 920,211 |
| 10,000 - 20,000 | 155 | 2,092,622 | 143 | 1,994,857 |
| 20,000 - 50,000 | 90 | 2,716,742 | 113 | 3,589,379 |
| 50,000 - 100,000 | 22 | 1,638,461 | 47 | 3,354,002 |
| 100,000 - 200,000 | 10 | 1,359,993 | 26 | 3,768,153 |
| 200,000 - 250,000 | 4 | 869,480 | 7 | 1,543,367 |
| 250,000 - 500,000 | 2 | 698,340 | 12 | 4,225,662 |
| 500,000 and + | 2 | 1,149,139 | 4 | 3,636,883 |
| Aggl. by | 1 | 4,433,336 | 1 | 8,374,024 |
| TOTAL | 874 | 18,029,562 | 1,096 | 34,342,054 |

TABLE 3.2

GROWTH OF AND BALANCE AMONG URBAN SIZE CLASSES
1946-1975

| Category of urban units | Population in 1975, on base 100 in 1946 | Evolution of the relative importance, on base 100 in 1946 |
|---|---|---|
| 3,000 - 5,000 | 130 | 67 |
| 5,000 - 7,000 | 124 | 66 |
| 7,500 - 10,000 | 121 | 64 |
| 10,000 - 20,000 | 95 | 50 |
| 20,000 - 50,000 | 132 | 70 |
| 50,000 - 100,000 | 205 | 107 |
| 100,000 - 200,000 | 277 | 146 |
| 200,000 - 250,000 | 178 | 94 |
| 250,000 and + | 426 | 223 |
| Aggl. by | 188 | 99 |
| Total urban population | 190 | / |
| Total French population | 130 | / |

have established to take into account the rural areas where industry is located. The *ZPIU* are even more spread out than the agglomerations since they can include several urban units and of course rural townships. In France in 1975, there were 881 *ZPIU* including 1,641 urban units, the majority of which were formed by both an urbanized area and a rural one. There are 150 *ZPIU* which spread out over several departments, and 12 even extend beyond the borders. A total of 83 percent of the French population is included in these *ZPIU* zones.

## A Differentiated Growth

The cities have had a different evolution not only with respect to their size. If we study what change occurred from one census to another, rather than for the period as a whole, we notice that the overall growth was rapid from 1954 to 1968 and slowed down after 1970.[4] The only exception to this rule is the category of urban units with fewer than 5,000 inhabitants. The Parisian agglomeration has been the most strongly affected. Natural increase remains positive and more or less stable for all the urban units, but it is the migratory balance that weakens and becomes negative in the capital region (table 3.2). The most favorable situation remains that of towns with more than 250,000 inhabitants, both in terms of natural growth as well as the migratory balance. This has great relevance for land planning policy.

Another differentiation in growth is linked to the regional position of the cities (figures 3.1 and 3.2). Three domains seem particularly favored for the period. First, there is the periphery of the Paris metropolitan area and its extensions, particularly the Loire valley (Orléans, Tours). A second favored domain is the Lyon metropolitan area and the alpine region (Grenoble). Thirdly, there is the edge of the Mediterranean region and, during the first period, especially the cities of the Languedoc-Roussillon (Montpeiller, Perpignan, Nîmes), and then, between 1968 and 1975, the towns of the Bas-Rhône, of lower Provence (Nice, Ajaccio). Completing the picture are several isolated cities in the west of France (Caen, Rennes, Nantes, Bordeau, and Pau), as well as the group of towns on the threshold of the Saône-Rhin and its surroundings (Dijon, Besançon, Montbéliard, Mulhouse, Colmar) and isolated centers of the Massif Central (Clermont-Ferrand, Limoges, Brive) and the center of the Bassin d'Aquitaine (Toulouse). Among

---

4. Denise Pumain and Thérèse Saint-Julien, "Les Dimensions du changement urbaine," Mémoire CNRS, Paris, 1978.

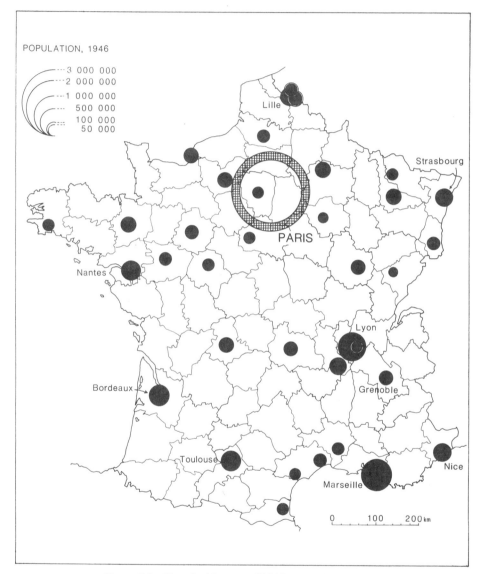

Figure 3.1.  French cities over 50,000 population in 1946

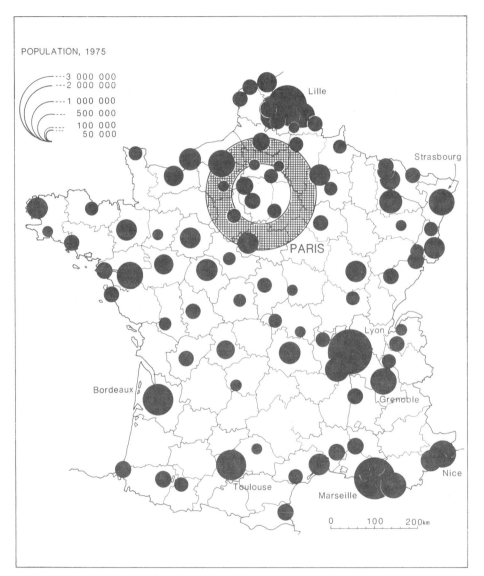

Figure 3.2.  French cities over 50,000 population in 1975

cities of more than 50,000 inhabitants, there have been some
negative growth trends in the northern coal-mining region and its
surroundings (Bruay, Lens, Douai) and in the mining and industrial
towns of northern Lorraine (Longwy, Forbach, Hagondange).
Elsewhere, growth occurred recently in urban units which had a
negative growth rate during the first period (such as Annecy,
Cannes-Grasse).

Do these disparities in the growth rate and in their regional
distribution result solely from a spontaneous movement?  In fact,
the French urban network as it exists today owes a great deal to
historical heritage and, more recently, to new attempts at land
planning.

### The Historical Legacy

The historical record shows that the French urban network as
we know it today was essentially set as early as the end of the
Middle Ages, starting with an important Gallo-Roman inheritance and
numerous foundations of cities that were fortified to defend the
neighboring flat country over the centuries.  This explains the
localization of most of our cities: they are almost always
established so as to profit from either a route for trade or a
support for the defense of this same route in the event of conflict.
Thus we find them above valleys, near main routes, along river
banks, at all the major crossroads.  Some were especially
constructed to serve as military bases in case of military emergency
(bastides in the Southwest, new cities) and more specifically for
the defense of a border (Vauban's fortifications to protect the
northeastern border).  From these beginnings the cities clung to
their nuclear sites which sometimes developed secondary components
to facilitate access to them (Laon, for example, built initially on
its isolated hill, has descended onto the plain).

Such towns also retain a distinct physical character: main
communication axes in the present street systems, circular rings
marking urban growth, including the peripheral boulevards of Paris).
Embellished and expanded in the seventeenth and eighteenth
centuries, they became more majestic, more populated, opened by new
architectural perspectives, enriched by the construction of mansions
and palaces intended for enriched bourgeois as well as for the most
esteemed noble families.  These vestiges are what give most French
cities their personality and certain aspects of their power of
attraction.

During the Industrial Revolution, which began at the end of the eighteenth century, most of the West European countries experienced a great influx of new city-dwellers and an efflorescence of cities, as with Great Britain and the German and Belgian territories. France however, was only partially touched by this phenomenon, and it was delayed. This abnormality has several explanations. First, the French mobilized their energy for a political revolution and suffered the consequences. Second, major industry came from coal, and France had comparatively little of this combustible. Lastly, from the beginning of the nineteenth century, France, which had had a great demographic impulse in the last decades of the eighteenth century (28 million inhabitants in 1801, the most populated country in Europe), registered a steady decrease in the birth rate and consequently in the rate of population growth (a 50 percent increase between 1800 and 1940, as compared with a tripling in the British Isles and Germany and a quadrupling in Belgium and the Netherlands!).

Nevertheless, several industrial and mining towns appeared or increased their population: among the first were Roubaix (textiles), le Havre, Mulhouse, Tourcoing (textiles), St-Etienne. Thus, industry demonstrated its urbanizing power, but without the force it had in the neighboring countries. The urban hierarchy proved remarkable stable and the same linear relations were respected throughout the nineteenth century, Paris being, of course, the exception. On the eve of World War II, France still seemed to be a relatively under-urbanized country. The proportion of the active farm population was much higher than in the neighboring countries in northern and central Europe. The quality of the soil, the attachment to the land, the small rustic property explain the persistence of a dense rural population. However, some exceptions began to appear, especially in the north where the Paris region, which prefigured England at the time, already had 80 percent of its population urban.

### Towards an Urban Policy

The Second World War was a breaking point. Several towns were destroyed and others seriously damaged (Saint-Nazaire, Lorient, Dunkerque). To rebuild and transform the national economy, planning was resorted to and, for the first time, the French were absorbed with an urban policy. An important recovery of the birthrate, from 1943 on, produced a new generation for whom education and employment had to be provided. Agricultural productivity required improvement and, consequently, the number of farmers had to be reduced. Until around 1973 and the beginning of the economic difficulties linked to the oil crisis, rural youth were induced to leave the farms, and they do so at the rate of 100,000 per year. These circumstances provided direct and indirect stimuli for urban growth.

But not any sort of growth. In the policy which has taken shape and will be continually amended, two notions are to be retained. First of all, following certain economists (F. Perroux, J. Boudeville) there is land planning--which emerged in France as early as 1950--based on the notion of *growth poles,* and by extension *growth centers,* in particular urban centers. In addition, the campaign against the excessive domination of Paris (the Paris agglomeration in 1946 contained 24.8 percent of the French urban population) has become the major imperative of any policy of voluntary urbanism. This double orientation is expressed by two sets of objectives: to slow down the development of the capital city and to create a certain number of vigorous poles of development elsewhere in France. The policy of *decentralization* is codified by the decrees of 1955-1957, which forbid almost all construction of new industrial enterprises in the Paris metropolitan area.[5] Decentralization of tertiary activities was left for later, but has been applied since the 1970s. In all, an estimated one million people have been kept from settling in Paris, as a result of these regulations. The second point is expressed by the policy of *capitals of equilibrium.*

There are eight of these capitals: they are located at the extremities of France, as far as possible from Paris. They are Lille, Nancy-Metz, Strasbourg, Lyon (associated with Grenoble and Saint-Etienne), Marseille, Toulouse, Bordeaux, and Nantes. Aside from their particular location, they are also characterized by a higher level of tertiary activities than less populated cities. By virtue of their selection, they were favored by the central government, which preferentially implanted certain facilities. For example, Nantes received a university, Lyon gained head offices and an international airport as well as a new business district (La Part-Dieu), Toulouse a space center, and Marseille a group of heavy industries nearby. In all, these eight capitals, classed in the category of more than 250,000 inhabitants, have had the greatest demographic growth since 1954: approximately two million inhabitants, as many as the Parisian agglomeration.

---

5. Michel Rochefort and J. Hautreux, *Le Niveau supérieur de l'armature urbaine française* (Paris: Commissariat Général du Plan, 1963).

Beside these "equilibrium" capitals we must make room for the *regional capitals*. For administrative reasons France was divided into 22 economic regions, each including several departments and having as its county seat the most important city (for example, Dijon for Bourgogne, Rennes for Bretagne, Montpellier for Languedoc-Roussillon). These cities, generally classed in the category of 100,000 to 250,000 inhabitants, were equally favored by the central government, especially for administrative services, the relocation of certain decentralized agencies, and the production of some specialty goods. They occupy the second place in the general scheme of urban growth. Somewhat later, the state chose still a third group of priviledged places: the *medium-sized* towns, whose statistical definition has never been very clear (between 20,000 and 100,000 inhabitants, or between 50,000 and 200,000?). In any case, they also had the right to certain favors and particularly to contracts allowing them to arrange certain aspects, such as improving their appearance and the environment of their citizens. To date, the last act of the official policy of the *Délégation à l'Aménagement du Territoire et à l'Action Régionale (DATAR)* which was quite eclectic and flexible, and no doubt too ambitious for the means available, was to consider the fate of the *small towns* of fewer than 10,000 inhabitants which appear as the poles in the center of a rural "country," which they furnish with facilities and services essential to modern life.

Increasing urban populations have not been the only concern of this policy; long-term forecasting and rational development of the agglomeration have received equal attention. For this purpose the *Schéma Directeur d'Aménagement et d'Urbanisme (SDAU)* and the *Plan d'Occupation du Sol (POS)* have been prepared which define land use according to precepts of urbanism designed to improve the "quality of life." The delivery of a construction permit, absolutely necessary for any construction be it public, private, residential, or functional, permits the necessary verifications. The *SDAU* can apply to an entire region, or to an agglomeration, or to a single town. It looks twenty years ahead based on what exists and what must be modified. It has suggestive rather than coercive powers. The *POS,* on the contrary, is a precise planning mechanism, based on construction permits needed for development of any kind, which controls land use down to the urban block itself: it anticipates the height of buildings and their use (residences, offices, industries) and carries the weight of law. It is with these two planning tools that, for the past thirty yers, the containment and direction of urban France has been pursued.

## Important Changes in the Cities

Expressions of growth are found not only in the rise of demographic curves. Towns are more populated and more numerous, and they have also changed aspect. Tall buildings constructed in groups in the suburbs, neighborhoods with geometric allotment, concentration of certain activities (industrial zones, shopping centers, supermarkets, and hypermarkets) diversify and transform the urban landscape.

To cope with this increase in the number of city dwellers, we have considered building "new towns," planned entirely in advance. Their localization is designed to correct certain faults of existing urbanization. In the north of France, Villeneuve d'Ascq is destined to be the super-center of the "conurbation" of Lille-Roubaix-Tourcoing.[6] Similarly, Le Mirail is intended as a second city to Toulouse; Le Vaudreuil extends the urban complex of le Havre-Rouen; Isle d'Abeau, located in the country to the east of the Lyon agglomeration, was intended for new inhabitants descending from the northern Alps towards the region of Lyon; and lastly, in the Paris region, five "new towns" are under construction. These towns grow rapidly, they have young populations and an attempt is made to bring residence and employment closer together. The creation of new activities is strongly encouraged, as is cultural and university expansion and the development of amusement and leisure activities.

## Space and Urbanization

This wave of urban development has had a considerable impact on space, either directly by occupation of the ground or indirectly by the crowding beyond the limits set by statistics. The new urbanization is a large consumer of space. The "new town" of Cergy-Pontoise (to the northwest of Paris) takes up the same space for 200,000 inhabitants as does Paris for 2,130,000 (which has had almost three million inhabitants in the past). This absorption of good agricultual land drives away the farmers and diminishes harvests. The market-gardeners, in particular, producers of fresh vegetables for the neighboring towns, are pushed further and further away. We are witnessing a land speculation favoring the owners of land classified as "constructible" by planning declarations, while simultaneously penalizing those whose land is destined by virtue of location to remain agricultural. There is severe competition for land, which is characteristic of all countries having a liberal

---

6. The term "conurbation" refers here to an agglomeration formed by several neighboring towns whose suburbs coalesce.

economy and private land ownership.[7]

To explain the general evolution of the urban web, the cost of
land and several related phenomena must be considered. In the
center of the city the costs are generally highest and can be born
only by highly profitable activities (banks, commerce, services,
etc.). This is the general rule. However, in certain cases the old
historical centers are devalued by worn-out building stock, housing
an urban proletariat with low incomes. An attempt has been made
during the past few years to evacuate these disadvantaged residents
from the city centers. In this manner, entire portions of the old
town in Bordeaux and Toulouse have been destroyed and rebuilt in an
ultra-modern style. On the margins of these central sections there
are more or less comfortable residential areas, followed by more
distant suburbs which continue along the important axes of
communication. Statistics show the center becoming more unpopulated
with each census. Rings of suburbs extend progressively outward
towards the periphery. But we are witnessing a new phenomenon, the
"rurbanization" or what I have called the *redéversement urbain.*"
To have more room, to be closer to nature, to be housed more
inexpensively, many French people live further and further away from
the city centers. For some, the ecologically-minded, for example,
it is a supposed return to a more natural life. For others, it is
an attempt to house at a lower cost a young family with children.
In certain cases the family continues to live in a rural family home
while the working members go to the factory. Thus, certain firms
established in towns having a reduced labor force assemble their
personnel from dozens of kilometers around. The Peugeot factories
in Montbéliard, for example, go to pick up their workers every day
even as far as the southern part of the Vosges, the north of the
Jura, and the northeast of the Doubs plain. These displacements are
tiring and costly, but those concerned, for economic reasons or by
inclination, accept them willingly. As for the firm's officials,
they often prefer this scattered residence which renders the workers
more isolated and less pugnacious.

Lastly, the diffusion of city dwellers in space is also
accomplished by *second homes.* It is a very popular practice in
France to possess a home in the country or at the seaside or in some
pleasant location where one spends short vacations and weekends.
These homes are often old rural dwellings which have been restored
and improved, and many villages around the large cities are

---

7. This theme is well covered in Jean Bastié, *La Croissance de la banlieue
parisienne* (Paris: P.U.F. 1964).

populated only by commuters and owners of second homes. A new life style is being established and one may once again ask "Where does urbanization end?"

## The Case of Paris

The Parisian agglomeration is the giant of French urbanization and a giant which has for a long time inspired a certain suspicion. This distrust was embodied after 1950 in a genuine urban policy *against the capital* (decentralization, taxation, prohibitions affecting certain enterprises and certain offices). Conversely, certain cities or regions were subsidized to permit them to become industrialized, often receiving those industries barred from the Paris metropolitan area. But the purpose was not only to stop the demographic growth but also to reorganize the use of space. This was the object of the 1965 urban master plan for the Paris region, in 1965, altered four or five times in detail since but with the fundamental principles in tact. The schema favors the growth of a linear agglomeration from the northwest to the southeast while freezing development towards the northeast (Forest of Montmorency, Roissy-Charles de Gaulle airport) and the southwest (Forests of Rambouillet and Fontainebleau). To house the new peripheral inhabitants, the construction of five "new towns" are being built (Cergy-Pontoise, Saint-Quentin en Yvelines, Evry, Melun-Sénart, Val-de-Marne). It is also intended to systematize industrial growth and important commercial centers, and to bring life to certain towns in the suburbs, near Paris, which have lacked their own civic and cultural facilities. These places were designated *restructuring poles*. For Paris itself, a master plan was proposed in 1967, setting out the major zones for planning the capital.

The statistics of the last two censuses (1975 and 1982) show great changes in the demography of the Paris metropolitan area. The population increase, which has progressed 1.6 percent per year between 1954 and 1962, fell to 0.53 percent between 1968 and 1975 and, within the same boundaries, was twice as weak between 1975 and 1982. The evolution is highly differentiated: the city of Paris lost 124,000 people (5.6 percent), the near suburbs lost 72,000 (-2 percent), while the distant suburbs gained 390,000 inhabitants (+10.8 percent) including 170,000 for the five "new towns."

These variable trends of population distribution have multiple consequences. Paris, which has lost nearly 800,000 inhabitants since its population peak, is beginning to have oversized facilities (hospitals, schools), while such facilities are still too sparse or lacking in the furthest suburbs. The density in the capital has fallen from 26,855 inhabitants per square kilometer in 1954 to 20,400 in 1982. The workers, in particular, have left the city, as has industry. In contrast, tertiary positions have remained stable and even increased. Despite the transfer of a certain number of agencies and establishments to the suburbs, the need for a daily labor force remains high and commuting involves over a million inhabitants. These movements have become more complicated: to the morning flux towards Paris is now added the outflow of Parisians commuting to relocated activities in the suburbs. Not surprisingly, there are transportation difficulties: the necessity of improving public transport, heavily in deficit, and the slowness and cost of using private automobiles.

These facts are characteristic of the evolution of all great modern capitals. One may ask if the simple variations in the price of land, acccording to the demand, would not have had analogous results. There exist laws of supply and demand and voluntary decisions sometimes have a double effect. Developing public transportation would in the end make it easier for people to live further away and, consequently, there is the possibility of further increases in commutation. On the other hand, it would enable the users to save time and weariness. This is but one example of the complexities of planning applied to urbanization.

### Towards a Generalized Urbanization

To close this evocation of the multiple problems that urbanization has brought out in France today, we can return to the initial question. Where does urbanization end? All studies demonstrate the phenomenon which characterizes the large agglomerations: population decline in the center, the diffusion of population density further and further towards the edges. By the census of 1982, all the large cities of France have been affected. On the other hand, by means of repeated contacts, the imbrication of residences, identical information generalized by the mass-media etc., there is a certain homogenization of the population. The progress made by telecommunications will accentuate this homogenization still further. It will no longer be necessary to live in a city to live like a city-dweller. Certain parts of the French countryside such as those surrounding the Paris metropolitan area have already reached this stage more or less. Conversely, the urban cores threaten to explode with the specialization of functional localizations (industrial zones, commercial centers),

Consequently the role of cities is seriously menanced. Perhaps certain traditional classifications between urban population and rural population are in need of revision in those countries with the same type of civilization as France. But this is a suggestion, not an assertion of fact.

# Chapter IV

# COMPARATIVE URBAN CHANGE IN
# WEST AND EAST GERMANY

Peter Schöller

## The Division of Germany: Problems and Questions

For a comparative study of urban changes central Europe offers a unique field, due to the recent partitioning and differentiation of an old and highly developed national settlement system and the accelerated change of city functions, urban structures, and urban landscape caused by divergent political forces and socio-economic systems.[1] The division of Germany and her capital Berlin, resulting from Hitler's war and the defeat of the Reich, began with the establishment of four zones of Allied occupation and led to the foundation of two German republics in the West and the East in 1949.

Traditionally, the term "East Germany" refers to the former Prussian territories of Silesia, Western Prussia, Pomerania, and Eastern Prussia. These regions, mainly situated east of the Oder-Neisse boundary, were incorporated into the People's Republic of Poland and the Soviet Union after 1945, the German population being forcibly evicted. As the result of the westward shift of Poland and Russia, the German Democratic Republic (GDR), including the old core areas of Mitteldeutschland, is now internationally known as East Germany; the Federal Republic as West Germany.

The founding of two separate German states was more a reflection of global politics than of national causes.[2] In their respective constitutions of 1949, both East and West Germany proclaimed their status as provisional until such time as unity could be achieved again. The growing conflict between international

---

1. Useful general works setting regional urban geography in a comparative context are Burkhard Hofmeister, *Die Stadtstruktur: Ihre Ausprägung in den verschiedenen Kulturräumen der Erde* (Darmstadt: Wissenschaftliche Buchgesellschaft, 1980); Elizabeth Lichtenberger, "The Nature of European Urbanism," *Geoforum* 4 (1970): 45-62; and Peter Scholler, *Die deutschen Städte* (Wiesbaden: F. Steiner, 1967).

2. Synthetic works on Germany with some discussion of urban change are Thomas H. Elkins, *Germany*, rev. ed. (New York: Praeger, 1968); Pierre George, *Géographie de l'Europe central* (Paris: Presses Universitairies de France, 1964); and Karl Sinnhuber, *Germany: Its Geography and Growth* (London: J. Murray, 1970).

power-blocs, however, led to their assimilation into opposing
spheres of ideology, military power, and economic organization.
Such ties resulted in the need for separate identities: East Germany
had to change her constitution twice, abolish her federal structure
(1952), and build a highly fortified, almost impenetrable boundary
toward the West (1961) in order to stop her citizens from fleeing to
West Germany. The constitution and the politics of the Federal
Republic, on the other hand, adhere to this day to the goal of
national unity, even though it is commonly believed that
reunification will remain a problem for generations hence--above all
due to the continuously diverging forces of social and economic
development.

In dealing with existing realities of world power-blocs and
ideologies, Germans on both sides have been able to achieve some
means of co-existence: official relations, a substantial quantity of
duty-free trade, postal and telephone communication which even in
the hardest of times has never been interrupted for long periods.
Most importantly, every year millions of Germans visit their
relatives and friends in the other state, even though travel from
east to west is restricted mainly to aged and retired people.
Furthermore, western radio and television stations serve as
influential factors of information and communication, providing
common links across the border.

In order to comprehend the effects of this border and the more
recent problems of geographical change, one has to realize that the
boundary has no historical or cultural precedent. Norman Pounds and
others have tried to justify the dividing line with the argument
that the border is based on old and established geographic
differences, but such an assertion disregards the earlier
geographical judgments of these same writers. Basic historical and
structural distinctions between older settled areas and later
colonized districts do, of course, exist. Such regional
differences, however, do not represent or even remotely resemble the
present territories of the Federal Republic or the German Democratic
Republic.[3]

The regions between the Harz Mountains, the Thuringian Forest,
and the Erz Mountains (also known as Ore Mountains) were once
described by R.E. Dickinson as "the heartland of Germany;" this area
is not what is historically referred to as "East Germany."[4] The

---

3. See Norman J.G. Pounds, *Divided Germany and Berlin* (Princeton, N.J.: Van
Nostrand, 1962), and Peter Schöller, "The Division of Germany--Based on Historical
Geography? A Reply to N.J.G. Pounds' *Divided Germany and Berlin*," *Erdkunde* 19
(1965): 161-64.

regions of the former Zone of Soviet Occupation, as established in 1945, have as much or as little in common as the three territories of western occupation. The urban centers of Western Pomerania and Thuringia, of the textile belt of Saxony, and the "lake district" of Mecklenburg reflect contrasts as sharp as those to be found between the most different regions of West Germany.

In both Germanies the real problem of regional and federal planning is still that of overcoming contrasts between North and South. The movement of traffic and exchange of ideas has mainly been on a West-East basis and has therefore created obvious similarities in neighboring regions across the border; to some extent this continues even today.

### The Development of an Urban System in Germany

The evolution of an urban system, especially in neighboring areas, cannot be seperated along the present political border between East and West Germany. Since the high Middle Ages, the formation of an elaborate network of urban centers has taken place in three major phases. Apart from older Roman settlements in western and southern Germany and the ensuing rise of episcopal centers, urban growth and development was predominantly shaped by trade and market functions. During the twelfth century, central urban markets were established as permanent places of exchange. A great number of small towns with their rural umland-areas were integrated into the hinterlands of larger central cities, while regional centers of a higher order offerred specialized services and permanent, long-distance trade with world markets. A classic example for the integration of supraregional trade cities and local markets into a hierarchical order is the Hanseatic League. This economic and social federation of cities in northern Germany and around the Baltic Sea had formed a distinct, although variable and interchangeable, system of three to four city ranks: headquarter city, quarter city, principal, and sub-city. The pattern of urban centers with different ranks and economic relations determined the entire network of cities around Köln, Lübeck, Stralsund, Erfurt, and Danzig, and such systems even survived the decline of the *Hanse* during the sixteenth century.

A second phase is associated with the time of absolutism and feudal territories, when urban development was characterized by political functions. In contrast to centralized nations like Britain and France, the map of Germany remained a colorful, if

---

4. Robert E. Dickinson, *Germany* (London: Methuen, 1953).

archaic, mosaic of small and larger territories. During the
eighteenth and nineteenth centuries the number of states and free
cities declined, but the reign of political particularism survived
the Napoleonic era and continued to influence urban development.
New capitals in principalities and kingdoms emerged with political,
administrative, and cultural functions. Dresden, Stuttgart, Potsdam
and Kassel, Dessau and Karlsruhe, Schwerin and Oldenburg, Meiningen
and Arolsen are striking examples of the rise of such
*Residenzstädte,* reflecting the very different levels of size and
power. In general, the newly founded cities and their political
functions only enlarged and altered the old established urban
network, they did not destroy it.

The third phase is identified with industrialization and
centralization. The Industrial Revolution, the construction of
railroads, and political and economic unification, culminating in
the founding of the Second German Reich in 1871, caused the most
fundamental change in the structure of the urban system since the
Middle Ages.[5] Textile and iron manufacture gave rise to new cities
and towns, especially in Saxony and Rhineland-Westphalia. Coal
mining, closely linked to iron and steel industries, created a new
type of industrial agglomeration near the rivers of the Ruhr and the
Saar and in Upper Silesia. The dramatic transformation in the size
and distribution of cities was fully demonstrable by 1925 (figure
4.1).

The modern era also brought about a more concentrated,
centralized urban expansion: the main centers of the pre-industrial
urban system--capitals, higher regional centers and large port
cities--were ideal for those industries which depended more on
labor, communications, and markets than on raw materials. Hamburg,
Bremen, Stettin and Königsberg, Breslau, Dresden, Leipzig, Hannover,
Köln, Frankfurt, Stuttgart, Nürnberg and München, all large regional
centers, now accelerated their growth with additional industrial
functions.[6] The most striking example was Berlin. By 1925, the
capital of the new Reich had become both the largest industrial city
and the superior political, economic, and cultural metropolis in
Germany and thus the only German city with cosmopolitan appeal as a
"world city," at least in the years between 1910 and 1934.

---

5. Erwin Scheu, *Des Reiches wirtschaftliche Einheit* (Breslau: F. Hirt,
1924).

6. Robert S. Dickinson, *The City Region in Western Europe* (London:
Routledge and Kegan Paul, 1967).

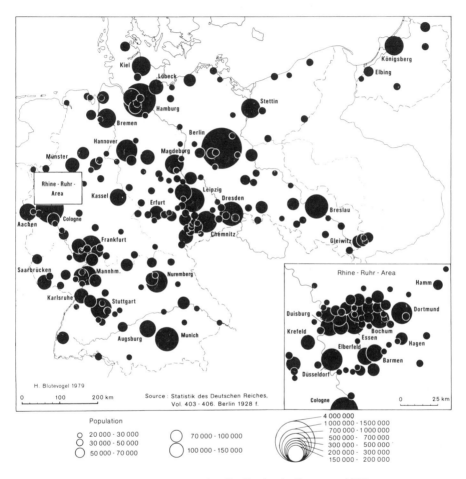

Figure 4.1.   Urban size distribution in Germany, 1925

## War Damages and Urban Reconstruction

Terrestrial combat and battles on German soil caused relatively little damage; by the time the Allies invaded the Reich the cities had been largely bombed out in air raids. The loss of housing and industrial buildings was colossal. The infrastructure and the transport networks, on the other hand, were more easily and rapidly put into functioning order than could have been expected. Thus, the degree of war destruction had little effect on the structure of the urban network as a whole, yet air raids had reduced both the size and the function of a number of cities. In the zone of Soviet occupation these effects would remain far longer than in the Western zones.

All regions and every type and size of city had been individually affected. The highest percentage of war damages was found in the cities of the northwest and in the western regions. In general, there was practically no large city which remained intact; in many, more than fifty percent of all housing facilities had been destroyed: Berlin, Hamburg, Bremen, Hannover, Dortmund, Essen, Köln, Frankfurt, Dresden, Nürnberg, and Stuttgart.[7] At the end of the war more than a dozen towns were almost completely in ruins: in the east the cities of Prenzlau, Pasewalk, Halberstadt and in the west Paderborn, Bocholt, Dülmen, Wesel, Duren (99 percent destroyed), Hanau, Pforzheim, Würzburg. Only a few non-industrial or peripheral towns had suffered little or no damage: Heidelberg, Speyer, Konstanz, Passau in western and southern Germany; Halle on the Saale, Görlitz, Greifswald, and Schwerin in the east.

During the first two years after the war, living conditions in all four zones of Allied occupation were quite similar: ruins, hunger, overcrowded living spaces, and dismantled industries made up the day-to-day existence. Nonetheless, the new spirit of freedom and hope after the liberation from Nazi terror encouraged initiative and activities on a broad scale. Even before the currency reform in 1948, the turning point of economic recovery, the three western zones took the lead in urban reconstruction. As Roy Mellor has observed, "The emphasis was on housing, so bombed-out townspeople could move back from the country-side or undamaged small towns, where the new element of the expellees had intensified pressure on an already strained infrastructure. The upsurge in economic life gave a further impetus to reconstruction, with speed rather than

---

7. See *Statistisches Jahrbuch deutscher Gemeinden* (Braunschweig: Deutsche Städtetag, 1949), and the statistical register accompanying Karl Gassdorf and Manfred Langhans-Ratzeburg, *Kriegsfolgen-Karte Westdeutschland, 1939-1950* scale 1:500,000 (Frankfurt/M.-Höchst: Verlagsbuchhandlung Gassdorf, 1950).

planning for future needs as the major consideration."[8]

In the east normality was harder to come by. In the west the Marshall Plan and the new market economy smoothed the way for an accelerated economic boom, while the new republic in the east had to pay much heavier and more long drawn out reparations in dismantled industrial machinery as well as in goods. Clearing up the debris and ruins had gone much faster than in the west, but reconstruction jolted. The state concentrated all efforts on industrial production. Large open spaces in the hearts of cities, cleared of ruins, would remain--in some cases, even until the present day. But here, too, life continued; Hitler's theatrical "vision of the destruction of a people" did not take place. Both parts of Germany have lost the bulk of their historical architecture. Entire city cores which over centuries had developed into harmonic, organic quarters--like Nürnberg's and Braunschweig's medieval centers or the magnificent Baroque-cities of Dresden and Würzburg--went up in flames. Many historic buildings, churches, cathedrals, castles, stately homes, townhalls, and townhouses were heavily damaged but could be rescued; in both German states the younger generation today can hardly appreciate from what ruins the "economic wonder" arose. To be sure, also some historic buildings were later torn down merely to be replaced by new "modern" constructions.

From early on, both reconstruction and unneccesary or even forced destruction were in sharper contrast in the east. The architecture and the gardens of the Dresden Zwinger are renowned as symbols of artful restoration, but the destruction of feudal and royal city mansions in Berlin and Potsdam, to name only a few, was mandated to make room for the new Socialist representation in the downtown areas. Such propagandistic appeal did not exist in the West. Here, in general, more was saved and more was restored. The reasons are quite obvious: there were more funds to be spent by government, churches, and towns, but there was also more civic initiative and more conservationist concern.

### The Border within Germany and Its Consequences

Following older administrative borders, which had cut across closely linked economic and social exchange, the line between the zones of occupation became one of the most consequential in Europe. Only the peculiarity of West Berlin with her air-corridors and transit routes for railroads and highways obscures the fact that regional and supra-regional networks of communication have been

---

8. Roy E.H. Mellor, *The Two Germanies* (New York: Barnes and Noble, 1978), p. 343.

severed: 34 railroad lines, 23 highways, 140 country roads, and
thousands of local passages end at the border between east and
west.[9]

The disadvantages of turning a formerly central region into a
peripheral, dead-end zone have not been overcome to this day on
either side of the border. On the western side numerous economic
subvention schemes could not prevent a decline in population in this
critical border zone, together with an unemployment rate above the
federal average. Relief measures were most successful in larger
cities and regional centers. On the eastern side a similar
development can be observed. Here, too, most cities along the
border have grown up mainly since 1970--even along the wall
surrounding West Berlin; the population in rural areas, though,
often is still below the figures from before the war. The intricate
buffer system, several miles deep, erected to prevent people from
fleeing the country, also prevents traveling, visiting, and even
moving toward the border.

But the impact of such a dividing line extends beyond the
proximity of the border itself. A number of lines of communication
between cities with central positions and functional areas have been
severed. Cities like Lübeck, Duderstadt, and Hof in the Federal
Republic have lost part of their rural catchment area; on the
eastern side centers like Salzwedel, Eisenach, and Sonneberg have
similarly been affected. Such losses of centrality can only be
compensated by new specialized urban functions.

For East Germany, however, the problems of her eastern border
are far more striking. Schwedt, Frankfurt/Oder, Forst, and Görlitz
lost their suburbs across the river or, as in the case of Guben and
Küstrin, even their historic cores. For decades the border
districts remained a problem of regional development. Therefore, it
does not come as a surprise that two reconstruction priorities were
placed on sites along the eastern border: Eisenhüttenstadt (founded
in 1952 as Stalinstadt) was the first "socialist city" with heavy
industry, followed later by Schwedt as a petrochemical and refining
center. To support the cities along the borders East Germany also
used administrative functions. When the federal structure was
abolished in 1952, Frankfurt/Oder and the small town of Suhl in
South Thuringia became the seats of district administration. In the
north, Rostock was made a super-regional center and large seaport.

---

9. The best recent survey of the intra-German boundary is Gerd Ritter and
Joseph G. Hajdu, *Die deutsch-deutsche Grenze: Analyse ihrer räumlichen
Auswirkungen und der raumwirksamen Staatstätigkeit in den Grenzgebieten* (Köln:
Selbstverlag Schneider-Wiese, 1982).

Rostock now had to accommodate some functions of the leading harbor towns Hamburg and Stettin, both outside East Germany. Thus, a new major center was developed for the underdeveloped north and the coastal district.

## Urban Growth and Decline: Changes in the Settlement System

If a system of settlements defines itself through division of labor as well as the interaction of functions, then by 1945 Germany no longer had a common system. Even though the structure and appearance of the German city network noticeably diverged only after 1954, the disintegration of functions had already been prompted by the different occupation forces. From that point onward different stages of independent formation of urban systems can be discerned. For years West Berlin had unofficially served secondary functions of supply and communication for East Berlin and surrounding areas; the construction of the wall in 1961 made it necessary to integrate this part alone of the former capital into the western city system, even though it does not lie under the jurisdiction of the Federal Republic.[10]

After the war the western cities had to accommodate waves of immigrants. People evacuated during the years of air raids returned, prisoners of war were released, expellees started to move from their rural camps, and millions of refugees and emigrants from East Germany and from the GDR poured into the cities, which were still largely in ruins. But such migration accelerated the reconstruction and supported the efforts for public and private housing facilities. After the first housing act of the Federal Republic had been passed in 1950, more than two million public housing units were built in six years. Even at that time the growth in housing units stood in excess of half a million annually, while in East Germany during this time even the moderate goal of 40,000 to 80,000 apartments per year was hardly ever reached. In 1955, only 33,000 living units were constructed while in the same year West Germany boasted 563,000 new apartments.[11]

Nearly all West German cities had regained their prewar population levels by 1960, and some surpassed them. In East Germany anomalies of city growth persist to the present day. The most striking decline was registered in the heavily destroyed cities and

---

10. Hans H. Blotevogel, Manfred Hommel, and Peter Schöller, "The Urban System of the Federal Republic of Germany," *Acta Geographica Lovaniensia* 22 (1982): 163-206.

11. For background on postwar housing activity see Dietrich Storbeck, *Die Wohnungswirtschaft in Mitteldeutschland* (Bonn and Berlin: Deutscher Bundes-Verlag, 1963).

towns. The upper echelons of the urban hierarchy were particularly truncated: Berlin, Leipzig, Dresden, and Magdeburg never reached their former size. This contrast alone contradicts the frequent argument that there is no substantial difference in the population development of cities between East and West Germany, merely a time-lag (figure 4.2).

There are, however, more profound differences, concerning the nature of urban forces.[12] "Cities were built by industry for industry," runs the Soviet motto that was transmitted into the "Guidelines for City Planning in the GDR" in 1950. Thus, in the East all efforts were focused on production sites. In contrast to the West, where processes of concentration and dispersion were varied and autonomous, in the East the government, led by the Communist Party, determined all investments for industry, housing, trade, traffic, and public services; in short, it planned and ordered the development of all sectors of the settlement structure. Early on in both German states the emphasis was on such heavy industries as mining and iron and steel production. In the west the region of the Ruhr took priority. In the east, lacking its own heavy industries, policy called for new sites for basic industries, policy called for new sites for basic industries and associated housing to be established: Eisenhüttenstadt (iron and steel production), Hoyerswerda (soft-coal), and later Schwedt and Halle-Neustadt (petrochemicals). Developments since 1955 have separated the two systems even more (figure 4.3).[13]

In West Germany, affluence, higher demands for housing, increased motorization, and a disproportionate growth in the tertiary sector led to intensified downtown concentration and sprawling suburbanization. The cores of cities decreased in population, inner urban areas stopped growing in density and merely expanded. Since 1960, the development of settlements can only be conceptualized in terms of functional city regions. The spatial effects and tendencies continue even though the birth rate is declining. Today the decrease of inhabitants in many big cities, especially in the northern and central areas, is largely concealed by migration and the high birth rate among foreign guestworkers.

---

12. Peter Schöller, "Veränderungen im Zentralitätsgefüge deutscher Städte: Ein Vergleich der Entwicklungstendenzen in West und Ost," *Deutscher Geographentag Bad Godesberg* (1967), pp. 243-50.

13. Peter Schöller, "Die neuen Städte der DDR in Zuzammenhang der Gesamtentwicklung des Städtewesens und der Zentralität," *Forschungen und Sitzungsberichte der Akademie fur Raumforschung und Landsplanung* 88 (1974): 299-324.

73

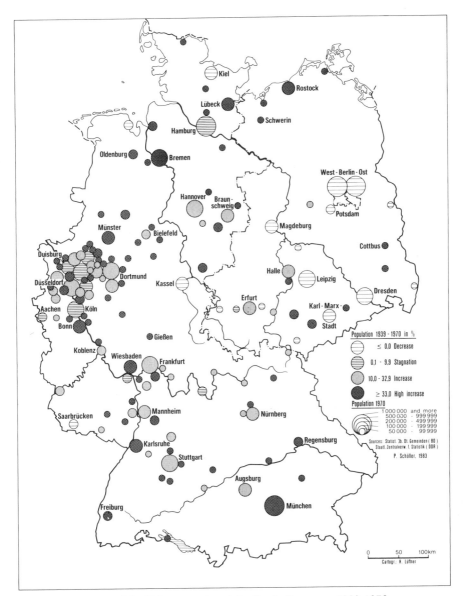

Figure 4.2. Urban growth and decline in Germany, 1939-1970

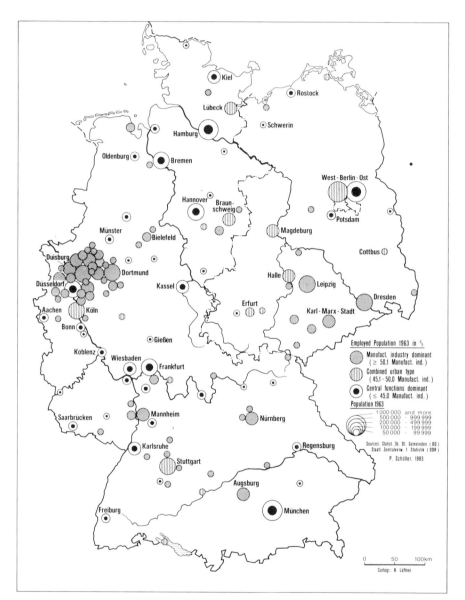

Figure 4.3. Major urban functions

In the German Democratic Republic, only a few cities achieved growth and economic boom during the decade after 1955. Increased nationalization and concentration of commerce and services denied existing centers the most basic foundation which in the past had made them central places and which had been the impetus to expansion. Numerous centers lost their functions, in particular those which had not become county or district seats or industrial sites with high priority.[14] In a planned economy even the economic apparatus of trade, services, and culture belong to the sphere of government administration. Therefore, it is not surprising that towns with country and district seat status *(Kreis-* and *Bezirksstädte)* were particularly strengthened.[15] Similarly, the population in district towns of a higher order, the Bezirks-Hauptorte, increased in population by 45.9 percent between 1950 and 1980 (figure 4.4).[16]

The centrality of places in West Germany took a different path for obvious reasons. More flexible, differentiated, and better adapted to economic conditions and spatial patterns of social conduct, free trade, and consumption, these cities experienced numerous changes in the system of central places. Mobility increased, while the orientation toward centers became variable. In general, however, the continuity of city-forming functions of the prewar and postwar periods have had a stabilizing effect on the settlement system in the Federal Republic. Distribution, density, functional orientation, and the core area character of these cities remain reinforcing factors in the spatial organization of this country.

Only the highest rank in the urban hierarchy remained severed, unfilled: the West German settlement system lacks its apex, the capital. This has led to an extreme decentralization of national leadership. Bonn, consciously chosen as provisional seat of the federal government can only fulfill capital functions as part of the city-region Düsseldorf-Köln-Bonn. There are other "semi-capitals" such as Frankfurt, headquarters for financial and economic organizations; Hamburg, the ocean gateway and press center; München, presenting itself as cultural capital; and Hannover, Karlsruhe, Nürnberg, and Stuttgart with more specialized functions. But even

---

14. Frankdieter Grimm and Ingrid Hönsch, "Zur Typisierung der Zentren in der DDR nach ihrer Umlandbedeutung," *Petermanns Geographische Mitteilungen* 118 (1974): 282-288.

15. Frankdieter Grimm, "Die Kreisstädte der DDR und ihre Rolle im Siedlungssystem," *Geographische Berichte* 19 (1974): 229-247.

16. Population statistics are given in *Statistisches Jahrbuch der DDR* (Berlin: VEB Deutscher Zentralverlag, annual).

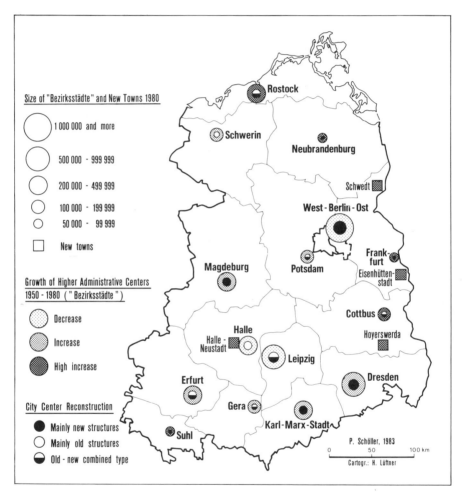

Figure 4.4. Aspects of urban change in the GDR

such distributions and divisions of functions have a structural link to German history--the tradition of an active regionalism with its strong, lively regional capitals.[17]

### Differences and Similarities in Housing and Urban Culture

There are few aspects of living which have taken such different and often contradictory courses in East and West Germany as housing. While in the West, as a substantial part of a free market economy, housing facilities expanded more quickly and more in accord with the needs and preferences of the population, the housing supply in East Germany was linked to the priorities of the government and the norms of the Soviet-ruled bloc. That meant few single-family homes and also smaller apartments than before the war, while collective services were improved. A decisive step in the history of German architecture was the 1955 program for the industrialization of housing construction, the *Industrialisierung und Typisierung des Bauens in der DDR.*[18] The new methods of production and assembly of prefabricated elements resulted in an era of extreme standardization; uniformity and monotony dominated the appearance of new cities and new settlements. Often the tracks of assembly cranes determined the layout of these housing developments.[19] Since 1969, the tendency toward a higher concentration of buildings has only added to the grim appearance of such complexes.

But even in the Federal Republic of Germany new construction projects since 1945 have rarely approached ideal solutions. To be sure, the cult of the façade and ideological statement was hardly ever applied, but the monotony of row houses exists here, too. Attempts to build cities and new neighborhoods geared to the convenience of automobile traffic have proven misguided. Unregulated urban sprawl spilled cities into open country. Even in 1960, 47 percent of all new homes were built as single houses. Such a destruction of rural hinterlands created several complications: it meant increased traffic problems in the inner cities, higher costs for utilities and services. It also diminished the recreation areas around cities and encouraged a certain detachment of the citizens

---

17 . Peter Schöller, Willi W. Puls, and Hanns J. Buchholz, eds., "Federal Republic of Germany: Spatial Development and Problems," *Bochumer Geographische Arbeiten* 38 (1980).

18 . The turning point is documented in "Die Baukonferenz der Deutschen Demokratischen Republik vom 3. bis 6. April 1955," *Die Bauwirtschaft,* vol. 2 (Berlin: Regierung der DDR; Ministerium fur Aufbau, 1955); see especially chapters by Walter Ulbricht, "Die neuen Aufgaben im nationalen Aufbau" and Gerhard Kosel, "Über Industrialisierung und Typisierung."

19 . See *Architektur und Städtebau in der DDR* (Leipzig: Deutsche Bauakademie, 1969).

from urban traditions.

Since 1970, city and regional planning in the west is concerned with a concept of settlements along development axes, with new priorities outside the inner-city region to accommodate the preference for "green" housing sites. Meanwhile, the average size of an apartment has doubled in comparison to East Germany. But there, too, new impulses have emerged. Since 1971, single-family houses have been permitted, and are even subsidized; however, the number of privately-owned properties must not exceed ten to fifteen percent of all new housing facilities. Not long after this reform, housing programs gained priority in order to overcome the enormous shortage of apartments. Such a new appreciation of the problem has to be viewed in the context of older buildings falling completely apart.

The severest shortcoming of the East German housing policy was the utter neglect of older buildings. While in the Federal Republic older houses were either renovated or replaced without fuss, in the East large sections of surviving residential areas and commercial cores simply decayed. Rents were fixed at the level of 1944; building materials and craftsmen were perpetually in short supply, making fundamental renovation quite impossible. Despite a considerable change of policy in 1979, the decades of neglect, however, can never be made good.

The divergent development of housing between West and East is quite apparent (figure 4.5), but a glimpse behind the facade of the buildings will render a different impression. Here the separation has left less searing marks--far less than the Eastern government would like to assert for ideological reasons, although far more than poorly-informed Western public opinion might acknowledge. One of the most astonishing phenomena is the continuity of several, mostly uncelebrated, common traits: not only habits, fashions, and social conduct, but also values, preferences, and modes of life in private, familial, and social spheres remain alike for Germans in the East and in the West. Despite Eastern propaganda and Western ignorance, some quite baffling correspondences in clothes, slang, recreation, and room and garden design, even the names preferred for christening infants, can be observed. To be sure, West German television has continuously influenced East German tastes, but that alone does not account for the overwhelmingly congruent patterns. Visits from relatives, conscious and subconscious continuation of older traditions, and efforts to sustain a private sphere in opposition to the

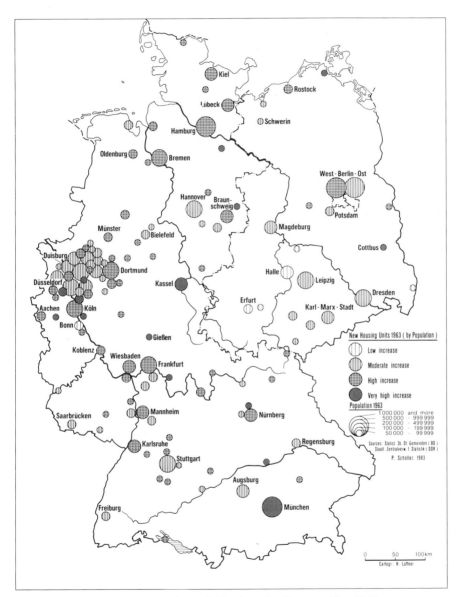

Figure 4.5.  Housing activities in major German cities, 1963

overpowering influence of the Party and the government apparatus also help account for such affinities.

## Capitalist City versus Socialist City?

Almost all East German publications concerned with urbanism make the claim that East Germany has accomplished the concept of a "socialist city," of a better, more humane environment than the Western city--characterized as a jungle of capitalism based on profit, speculation and exploitation.[20] This claim, however, rings hollow, not only in the new cities but also in the new housing complexes of older cities and in reconstructed urban cores. More and more shortcomings are acknowledged, at least regarding the past. Models once acclaimed are now criticized, though such criticism is aimed more at ideological postulates than at confronting the real needs of the people. The ideology of developing a new and better socialist society found expression in new structures of municipal life in the cores of cities and towns.[21] Enormous squares in the city centers were created for party rallies and official celebrations, broad avenues as *Hauptmagistrale* for parades and festivals, colossal "palaces of culture" and domineering party and administration buildings as "a monumental expression of the people's power." But the social life in these new centers has rarely lived up to expectations.[22] The magisterial avenues became throughways, ill-proportioned vacant spaces continue to smother the spontaneity of city life, and the nationalization and concentration of shopping in department stores and warehouse-style facilities has reduced the attractiveness of shopping streets.

Western city centers, on the other hand, reveal a colorful, diverse structure of businesses and shops, densely clustered due to real estate prices. Competition and advertising, private initiative, and the power of banks are witness to the fact that under capitalism "servicing" means not only the distribution of goods but that variety and consumer choice in shopping, clearly basic needs, are much more honored than in a socialist society.[23]

---

20. See Adolph Karger and Frank Werner, "Die Sozialistische Stadt," *Geographische Rundschau* 34 (1982): 519-28, and Hans H. Heineberg, "Service Centers in East and West Berlin," in *The Socialist City,* ed. R. Anthony French and F.E. Ian Hamilton (Chichester: Wiley, 1979), pp. 305-34.

21. Edmund Collein, "Der Aufbau der Stadtzentren in der Deutschen Demokratischen Republik," *Deutsche Architektur* 4 (1955): 532-45.

22. The problems created by such feudalistic elements of city planning and the recent changes of several German "Magistralen" are discussed in Peter Schöller, "Paradigma Berlin: Lehren aus einer Anomalie--Fragen und Thesen zur Stadtgeographie," *Geographische Rundschau* 26 (1974): 425-34.

23. H. Heineberg, "Zentren in West und Ost-Berlin," *Bochumer Geographische Arbeiten* Sonderreihe 9 (1977).

However, besides the profit-oriented world of consumption, important
cultural, educational, and civil functions, as well as sport,
health, and recreational institutions, have been conserved or
rebuilt and expanded. The tradition of civil institutions for the
general and common civic spirit have not been discontinued, either
in the west or in the east of Germany (figure 4.6).

Thus, despite tendencies to the contrary, cities in the west
and in the east cannot simply be classified as "capitalist" or
"socialist." Such dualistic classification would serve only to
describe some superficial aspects. It would also fail to take the
people into consideration, people who live and work in these cities
and towns. The majority of inhabitants in the east conform as
little to the "socialist human model" as the citizens in the west
portray a pure capitalist system.

Still, one should stress that the co-existence of different
models of society within Germany offers special insights. Real
estate offers a case in point. While the traditional forms of
property ownership have prevented a better reformulation of urban
structure in the Federal Republic, the example of East Germany
proves that even when the rights of private land ownership have been
taken away, this does not necessarily lead to a better land-use
structure. In all redesigned city centers planning and construction
were out of balance and influenced by misleading ideological
statements. Rarely have the actual needs of the population been
given priority. But since in the west only a few satisfying
architectural solutions have been achieved in the city centers, a
positive revaluation of historic urban fabric not surprisingly
followed.

### City Conservation and a Common Historical Heritage

The rediscovery of historical dimensions in German cities has
certainly been provoked by the inadequacies of modern socialist and
capitalist city planning and architecture. But of equal importance
are trends of supra-national significance: nostalgia, the quest for
ambience, and neo-historicism. The need to revalorize the urban
core areas was quite real, in order to reinforce civic life in the
face of Western "suburbia" and Eastern "socialist housing comlexes."
The re-awakening of the hearts of towns could only be achieved by
creating zones exclusively reserved for pedestrians.[24] Since the
1950s in the West and the 1960s in the East, an extensive network of
pedestrian zones in almost all historic small and medium-size towns

---

24. Rolf Monheim, "Fussgängerbereiche und Fussgängerverkehr in Stadtzentren
in der Bundesrepublik Deutschland," *Bonner Geographische Abhandlungen* 64 (1980).

Figure 4.6. Cultural activities in German cities: Theaters

has been established.

One should not overlook the surprising fact that civic life in East Germany is generally much more conservative than in West Germany: an ever constant "local awareness," a patronage for regional and local history, a thoroughly "bourgeois" restaurant life, a successful struggle against street violence, the prohibition of open sex and pornography, and the continuation and cultivation of the music and theater tradition with the high standards of central Germany (figure 4.6). The cultural life, geared toward the classical repertory and its faithful presentation, is often more substantial and less aimed at fads, fashions, and profits than in comparable western centers.

The Federal Republic is still in the lead in matters of city conservation. Even buildings from the nineteenth and twentieth centuries are being conserved and restored as much as possible. The era of replacing entire neighborhoods is definitely over.[25] In East Germany, however, such drastic measures are still in use. There, leveling entire sections of towns is not always dependent on the poor condition of the buildings. In most cases the party decides what should be viewed as "national cultural heritage." In the years between 1945 and 1960, the government in the east issued ideological pleas for Germany's unity and its common cultural heritage;[26] but this was also the era when large Stalinist constructions produced the sharpest contrast with cities in the "other" Germany. Later, when delimitation and independent socialism were proclaimed, new measures of functional construction reconciled the gap with the western cities.[27] Still, developments in the Soviet Union have a decisive influence on official predilections.

In general, however, the return to a common heritage of German city planning on both sides of the dividing line can only be encouraging: a deeper understanding of both the divergent developments and the remaining unity contribute to a more relaxed, sensible, considerate co-existence of both German states in the future.

---

25 . For a sampling of the literature on this topic, see Hans P. Bahrdt, *Humaner Städtebau,* rev. Ed. (Hamburg: Wegner, 1968); Friedrich Tamms and Wilhelm Wortmann, *Städtebau* (Darmstadt: Wissenschaftliche Buchgesellschaft, 1973); and Ule Lammert, *Zu Problemen des Städtebaus der achtziger Jahre* (Berlin: Akademie-Verlag, 1982).

26 . See *Fur einen fortschritlichen Städtebau, fur eine neue deutsche Architektur* (Leipzig: Deutsche Bauakademie, 1951), and *Programmerklärung der Deutschen Bauakademie und des Bundes Deutscher Architekten zur Verteidigung der Einheit der Deutschen Architektur* (Berlin: Deutsche Bauakademie, 1954).

27 . See *Architektur in der DDR* (Berlin: Deutsche Bauakademie, 1979).

# Chapter V

# CURRENT CHANGES IN POLISH CITIES AND URBAN LIFE

Kazimierz Dziewoński

In 1946 the urban population of Poland stood at about seven and a half million, which represented 31.8 percent of the total population.[1] By 1950 it rose to 9.6 million (39 percent), and by 1982 it had reached 21.7 million (59.5 percent). In relation to 1950, a year of change in Poland fron post-war resettlement and reconstruction to processes of peaceful development--processes of forced industrialization and urbanization--the present urban ratio marks a growth of some 125 percent. In other words, for every four persons living in statistically urban areas in 1950 there were by 1982 more than nine.

During the same period the number of dwellings in cities grew from 2.7 to 6.4 million and of occupied rooms from 6.6 to 20.1 million, showing an increase of 136.4 percent and 205.5 percent for dwellings and rooms respectively. Compared with the growth of urban population this indicates a significant, although still insufficient, improvement in housing conditions. The main problem in housing conditions at present is the disparity between the number of families and dwellings.

According to the 1978 National Census, the age structure of dwellings was as follows: 16.6 percent were built before 1918, 23.0 percent during the interwar years (1918-1944), and since 1945 37.2 percent by 1970 and 23.2 percent between 1971 and 1978. Thus by 1978 three out of every five dwellings had been constructed after 1945. Polish cities as they are today, in terms of the majority of their population and physical substance, represent an achievement of the post-war years!

---

1. Statistics employed in this essay are drawn from the following sources: *Statistical Yearbook* (Warsaw: Central Statistical Office, 1947-1950, after 1956 annually); *Statystyka miast i osiedli 1945-1965* (Warsaw: Central Statistical Office, 1967); *Rocznik Statystyczny Miast, 1980* (Warsaw: Central Statistical Office, 1981).

## Urban Growth Rates

However, the distribution and growth of population and buildings was not even in either time or space. Considering the period after 1950 in terms of five-year intervals, urban growth was strongest during 1951-1955 (6.3 percent per annum) and 1956-1960 (3.3 percent). Then it fell in the 1960s to 1.8 percent, increasing in 1971-1975 to 2.2 percent, after which it fell steadily to 1.4 percent in recent years. This growth was due both to natural increase and in-migration from rural areas. In some years the changes in administrative status and boundaries also played a significant role. They were especially important in the 1950s, accounting for about two-fifths of the total urban increase. Later they accounted for no more than about one-tenth, and after 1975 ceased to have an influence on urban growth. The natural increase was higher than that due to migration up to 1965, when a combination of generally falling birth rates and constant rates of rural-to-urban migrations resulted in larger net migration gains. After 1975, however, urbanward migration slowed and birth rates rose again. The natural increase in cities has risen from the low of 6.4 percent in 1969 to 9.4 percent in 1982, representing the new demographic high. Rural-to-urban migration fell from a high of about a quarter-million to about 120,000 in 1982.

Although urbanization was strong and rapid in Poland over the last thirty years, the degree of centralization was rather limited. The largest cities (100,000 population or more in 1960) grew by 34 percent between 1950 and 1960, and by 17 percent between 1960 and 1970. By contrast, towns with populations between 20,000 and 100,000 grew 46 and 22 percent over the two periods, while those under 20,000 showed growth rates of 36 and 23 percent respectively. It is obvious that the growth of the middle-size cities was the strongest throughout the period before 1970.

The decade of the 1970s witnessed a major differentiation in the growth behavior of different cities, however, despite aggregate growth rates similar to past performance (in which growth was rather evenly distributed between the various size-classes of cities, with the exception of new industrial towns and villages). There were several causes behind such a change.

First, a radical redistribution of administrative functions was introduced in 1975 (creation of more smaller regional units --voivodships--and liquidation of one hierarchical level in the territorial organization of local government--poviats). Second, new industrial development was strongly concentrated in a few areas, such as the copper mining districts of Lower Silesia and the sulphur mining areas of the Vistula plain, the seaports on the Bay of Gdansk, and several centers of chemical and machine industries. Third, the so-called "action for the reunification of German families," which had been agreed on by the state authorities, led to significant outflows of population in some areas, mainly in Upper Silesia. Finally, declines in rural-to-urban migration led in part to an increase in the importance and significance of movements from smaller to larger cities. As a result of this last cause certain smaller cities with limited economic bases began to lose population.

## The Geography of Differential Growth Patterns

Strong regional differences in the pace and structure of urbanization, however, have been evident for a long time. These have been described in several publications,[2] and such discussions have yielded three zones of distinct and specific character. The first is the great southern mining and industrial conurbation of Upper Silesia and Cracow, at present in an advanced phase of urban development (that is, of supraregional integration of several smaller industrial or mining regions and urban agglomerations).

The second zone comprises the central regions of Poland, characterized by urbanization. These central regions form distinct western and eastern clusters. The western group has a densely developed network of small cities, well developed and developing middle-sized cities, and some moderately growing urban agglomerations. The eastern group exhibits an urban network clearly dominated by the large urban agglomeration of the national capital, Warsaw, and the traditional center of textile industry, the city of Lodz.

The third zone consists of the remaining, less urbanized regions mainly in the north and east where at present the growth of cities is the most intense, but also the most regionally diversified. In the north-western regions the development of cities of all sizes is more or less balanced by strongly growing agglomerations around the ports at the estuaries of the main rivers, the Vistula and the Odra. In the eastern part urban growth is almost completely concentrated in the regionally largest cities. Finally, in the south-eastern and central areas urban growth is concentrated in the numerous middle-sized cities, which are remarkably close to each other in size.

---

2. E.g., Prace Geograficzne, *Rozmieszczanie i magracje ludności a system osadniczy Polski Ludowej*, ed. Kazimierz Dziewoński, Andrzej Gawryszewski et al., no. 117 (Warsaw: Polish Academy of Sciences, Institute of Geography and Spatial Organization, 1977).

Beyond such variations, there are systematic regional differences in the relationship between industrialization (as measured by percentage of the proportion of employment that is industrial) and urbanization (as measured by the proportion of the population that is urban). Three latitudinal zones can be identified: a southern one, where industrialization is stronger than urbanization, a central one in which these two basic processes are balanced, and a northern one, where urbanization seems to precede and be further advanced than industrialization. As a consequence the southern areas are characterized by extensive commuting to work while in the north, with the exception of the port agglomeration in the Bay of Gdansk, commuting is practically nonexistent.

Within these broad patterns, recent years have witnessed some changes. With regard to the main urban agglomerations and the largest cities changes have not been marked. These urban areas have all been growing at a rate below the national urban average (193.2 growth index) (except for the Gdansk and Katowice agglomerations during 1980-1982 with index values of 103.7 and 103.3 respectively--for the first time since 1946 slightly higher than the national average). Cities in the next size group, those between 100,000 and 300,000 inhabitants, have been growing much faster, although their growth in the crisis years of 1980-1982 has fallen to the rates characteristic for urban agglomerations. Their differentiation was not very large as their functions were generally similar.

Medium-sized cities (between 30,000 and 100,000 inhabitants), particularly those which in 1975 became the capitals of newly created voivodships, experienced very strong growth ranging within the eight years from 20 to 50 percent, with smaller cities growing more rapidly than the larger ones.

The smaller towns formed an extremely varied class. Some, such as the industrial new towns or villages, grew very quickly while others, at the opposite end of the spectrum, actually lost population, particularly towns with poor accesibility and without developed services for the neighboring rural population. Unexpectedly, few of the more than 200 centers which up to 1975 had been seats of the poviat administration lost population. Altogether, only seven now have smaller populations than in 1975, and even in these cases the decline was partly due to other causes such as emigration abroad (reunification of German families) and redundancies in local industries.

In consequence, the introduction of a new regional administrative structure may be described from an urban development perspective as a success. It increased signigicantly the number of regional centers from about 20 to more than 50, thus strengthening the polycentric structure of the national settlement system. It counterbalanced, or even weakened, the dominance of urban agglomerations, especially the three largest ones of Katowice, Warsaw, and Gdansk.

### Typologies of the Polish Urban Settlement System

So far in this essay Polish cities have been differentiated on the basis of their size, as follows: urban agglomerations, the largest cities, large and middle-sized cities, as well as smaller and small cities. But in the past decade several more complex classifications have been undertaken and corresponding typologies established. From the functional point of view one presented by M. Jerczynski is generally considered to be the best (figure 5.1).[3] He based his typology on functional dominance and interrelations between employment and residential functions in the cities as well as on their size, thereby incorporating three dimensions in his typology.

With respect to the relationship between work and residence he identified five categories: cities with very strong dominance of work function (major labor markets), with strong dominance of work function, with a balance between work and residence, with strong residential dominance, and with very strong dominance of residential function (the latter representing true dormitory cities). Among cities with dominant employment functions he distinguished ten classes: purely agricultural, industrial, service centers, and six mixed classes, such as agricultural and industrial, industrial and agricultural, industrial and service, service and industrial, service and agricultural, agricultural and service centers, and finally cities without any clearly dominant functions.

Jerczynski employed traditional statistical classes in analyzing relationships with city size, namely places under 5,000, 5,000 - 20,000, 20,000-50,000, and over 100,000 inhabitants. By classifying all 814 settlements which had urban status in 1973, he established that 43.5 percent of all cities showed strong employment functions, and extensive commuting, 37.4 percent balanced employment and residential functions, and only 19.1 percent were predominantly

---

3. Merek Jerczynski, "Funkcje i typt funcjonalne polskich miast (zagadnienia dominacji funkcjonalnej)," in *Statystyka Polski* 85 (Warsaw: Central Statistical Office, 1977), pp. 20-73.

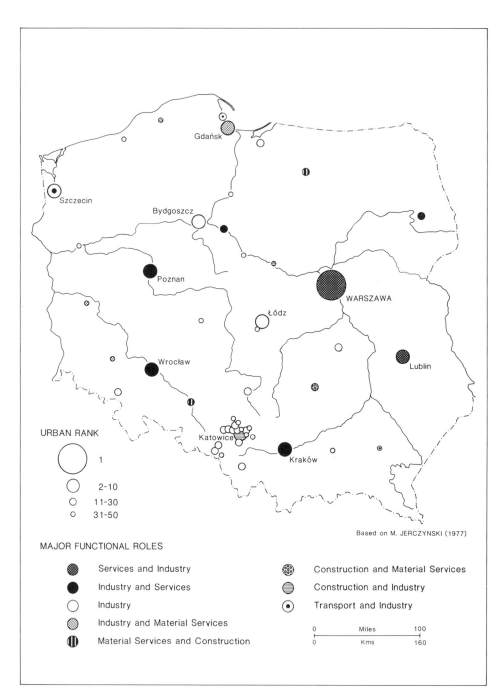

Figure 5.1. Types of Polish urban centers

residential towns. In the analysis of functional dominance only six out of ten classes were well represented: industrial (24.1 percent), service with industrial (20.1 percent), service (7.4 percent), towns without dominant functions (7.4 percent), and agricultural with service (6.2 percent). The 27 largest cities, however, belonged to only three classes: 14 industrial, 8 industrial with service, and 5 service with industrial. This well illustrates the present stage in the development of socialist cities, characterized by both overemployment in industry and underemployment in services. A similar dominance of those three classes prevails in all size categories over 5,000 population, with a mixture of industrial and service functions gaining representation over functions lower down the urban hierarchy. Only in the class below 5,000 inhabitants were all categories more or less evenly distributed.

Jercynski examined patterns of change between 1960 and 1973. The growth of cities in the 1973 class of 20-50,000 population was the strongest (38.2 percent) followed by the classes of 5-20,000 and 50-100,000 population (30.9 and 30.2 percent respectively). The growth in all other classes was under the national average mean (28.0 percent). At the same time, the cities with very strong employment dominance grew by 47.5 percent, cities with strong employment dominance by 31.9 percent, while all other classes grew at a similar, and much lower, rate of about 20.0 percent, well below the national average. Finally, among the heavy employment centers, cities with industrial and service as well as service with industrial emphasis grew the most, being the only classes with indices above the national average.

Recently, other typologies of Polish cities have been developed. One is based on demographic characteristics[4] and another addresses differences in living conditions.[5] The demographic typology prepared by Mrs. E. Pytel-Tafel is based on the division of the whole population system into three subsystems: one of demographic characteristics sensu stricto, another of professional and social structures, and the third of migratory patterns. By use of factorial analysis the latent elements are identified for each of the three subsystems and also for all of them taken together. For demographic characteristics three factors appear to be the most significant: the demographic effects and consequence of the post-war

---

4. E. Pytel-Tafel, *Struktury demograficzna jako czynnik rożnicujący zbior miast polskich,* doctoral thesis (Warsaw: Polish Academy of Sciences, Institute of Geography and Spatial Organization, 1981).

5. Alina Muzioł-Węcławowicz, *Typologia miast Polski na podstawie zróżnicowania warunków życia,* doctoral thesis (Warsaw: Polish Academy of Sciences, Institute of Geography and Spatial Organization, 1981).

resettlement, the demographic results of forced industrialization, and the differences in sex structure of the population. In the analysis of professional and social structures, professional-social status is most associated with differentiation, with age structure and level of education coming second, and professional activity together with level of services is third in importance. In the migrational subsystem direction of migratory flows (mainly rural-to-urban) is the most significant, followed by intensity of in-migration and population mobility.

The factorial analysis of all characteristics taken together shows a high interdependence of the three subsystems. Four of the factors defined earlier for the subsystems appear very important in accounting for the diversity of the whole set. These include dominant economic function and social structure, the effects of post-war migrations, age structure and level of education, and direction of migratory flows. In the analysis of the whole system they rank as the first, second, fourth, and sixth of all factors. The third represents the polarization of population in the productive age by sex, and the fifth the intensity of migration.

The conclusion that emerges from this analysis is that the post-war resettlement and migrations still represent the most important element of the present demographic diversity of Polish cities. More recent migrations, connected with processes of industrialization and urbanization--the first forced and the second delayed--are now progressively modifying this basic pattern. Also, the regional variations are still stronger than those connected with the hierarchical structure of settlement. So far, the location of a city is more important in demographic differentiation than its size.

A typology of living conditions in Polish cities has been offered by Mrs. Muzioł-Węcławowicz who faced a real difficulty in choosing suitable statistical data among those available. Again, the whole obtained set of information was split into subsystems, this time four in number: housing conditions, social services sensu stricto, technical infrastructure, and shopping and gastronomic services. Notwithstanding problems of incomplete data, the three main factors identified with the aid of factorial analysis explain only 47.3 percent of the common variance of 20 analytical characteristics. These factors are identified as service equipment, employment in health services, and, ranking only third, housing conditions. The comparatively minor role of housing conditions in the present diversity of Polish cities marks the success of economic policies in leveling the standards of technical equipment in building new dwellings and in egalitarian methods for their allocation. In the general typology the size of cities is the most imortant factor. The dominant economic functions (which in Poland, incidentally, are strongly correlated with city size) appear less important. The historical factor of past political, cultural, and economic development, both at the macroscale and at the level of regional variations, is still very important in accounting for diversity of housing conditions. Industrialization and the emergence of urban agglomerations so far rank only second in such an accounting.

Both these typologies raise a central question which at present cannot be answered: how long will it take for the impact of modern industrialization and state-directed urbanization to overtake the basic inter-city differences created by the post-war migrations and earlier historical divisions?

### The Importance of Workplaces in Defining the Internal Spatial Structure of Polish Cities

Let us now turn to changes in the internal structure and patterns of cities. It is desirable to begin by noting several phenomena recently observed or identified in Poland. They may also exist in other countries and regions but to my knowledge they have not yet received much scrutiny. Most important is the relation between residence and work-place. In Polish cities this particular linkage forms large scale patterns in the distribution of dwellings. Work places, when highly concentrated, strongly influence the distribution of all remaining elements of urban structure. Moreover, they cause characteristic deformations in traffic patterns. Consequently the decentralization of employment nodes has a greater impact on urban structure than similar decentralization of residential areas or other elements.

In a detailed study of all types of journeys-to-work in the city of Łodz (roughly 800,000 inhabitants) by Jerzy Dzieciuchowicz, it emerged clearly that for all types of workers and professionals there exists a specific zone, at a certain distance from their workplace, which contains the largest number of these workers.[6] The distance and the size may vary, but for all larger or concentrated employment nodes the phenomenon persists. In services and industries employing large numbers of women this zone is narrower, while for those employing staffs with higher professional

---

6. Jerzy Z. Dzieciuchowicz, *Rozkłady przestrzenne dojazdów do pracy ludności wielkiego miasta (na przykładzie Łodzi)*, Studies of the Committee for Space Economy and Regional Planning, 66 (Warsaw: Polish Scientific Publishers, 1979).

qualifications it is more distant and extensive. Therefore, to characterize the distribution of employed people by their residence it is necessary to state its size and structure, as well as the distance from which all in general, and the largest number in particular, come. It has usually been assumed that the number of workers coming to a particular workplace diminishes with increasing distance from it, although factors such as transport facilities, quality of housing, environmental advantages or disadvantages, both natural and social, may distort such distributions. Nevertheless, distance has always been considered as the decisive factor. However, in my opinion, the concept of maximum possible residence at any given distance requires modification of the traditional approach. The notion of a probability of finding a dwelling should be introduced. With other conditions being equal, it has to increase in square relation to the distance. The influence of increasing distance is positive here, while so far only the negative impact (increased commuting effort) has been recognized. Only when such probabilities are greater than the demand for dwellings of employees from specific workplaces, does the distance become the decisive negative factor. In cases in which employment is smaller in number than the available dwellings in the vicinity, neither the negative nor the positive impact of distance influences the distribution of dwellings. However, such smaller places of work are ususally concentrated in the core of the city or in and around some local foci of services and centers of social and economic daily life. Therefore the distribution of either positive or negative attributes of distance in relation to the distribution of dwellings comes into play again.

This relationship would suggest that around the urban core, in which a very large number of workplaces concentrate, its cumulative effect should create at some specific distance a maximum density of workers and their families, their dwellings, and therefore their residential densities. This may provide a quite different explanation for the well known Clark density curve with its crater at the city center. Nevertheless, it should be remembered that the number of inhabitants is not necessarily proportional to densities in given distance zones. The effect of the area increasing in square relation to the distance partially or completely cancels the increase in densities due to the increase in distance. One final point: for various reasons, such as the size of the city core or of very large industrial plants, the workplace has to be considered not as a point but as an area. The "insulation zone" for noxious industries, also, should be included in the area.

Workplaces influence the location of not only dwellings but also of all services, whether economic, social, or cultural. This is particularly true of the daily services, such as transport facilities, shopping areas, nurseries, and schools (especially the professional schools). Workplaces are foci where people concentrate daily. By their importance they are able to exert significant influence on the location of other urban elements, either indirectly or by conscious efforts of the industrial management. Studies both for Upper Silesia and the city of Lodz leave no doubt of their signficance.[7] Such influences are complex. Workplaces are located either in relation to the already existing housing and services or, as stated, they exert significant impact on the distribution and location of all other elements. The actual direction of influence depends on the temporal precedence. The influence may be both positive (attracting) or negative (repulsing). Whatever the case, it is obviously important to consider the internal structure of cities not only from the point of view of residential distribution, but also of workplace distribution.

### Transportation and Land Use Structure

There is also a definite polarization in Polish cities of traffic patterns in relation to the central business district and urban core. With growing distance from these areas transport becomes increasingly unidirectional, with traffic to and from these core zones predominating more and more over all other directions. Within the core traffic becomes multidirectional. The polarization of traffic orientation may be easily linked on the one hand with the theory of population potential and, on the other, with the dominance of concentric patterns in the spatial structure of central areas and sectoral patterns in the external parts of a city or urban agglomeration.

A similar polarization can also be observed in land and building utilization. In the urban core the numerous functions are mixed together, while in the external parts they are predominantly seperated. In such instances, they can be expressed through a mathematical formulation of density distribution and differential land rents, especially in their more complex forms. Such formulations are useful in the case of complex forms for simulating

---

7. Jan Rajman, *Procesy urbanizacyjne na obrzeżu Górnośląskiego Okręgu Przemysłowego po II Wojnie Światowej,* Monographs of the Higher School of Pedagogics, 7 (Cracow, 1979) and Ludwik Straszewicz, and Stanisław Liszewski, "Research Reports Pertaining to the Impact of Industrial Enterprises and Plants on Urban Structures and Land Utilization in Łódź" (Warsaw, Polish Academy of Sciences, Institute of Geography and Spatial Organization, 1981).

real urban structures and patterns.[8] The classic theory of concentric land use zones based on the differential rentability of various functions and uses needs to be at least partly reformulated. The central areas are not characterized by a specific succession of functions and uses but by their mixing.[9] It is only in the outlying areas and suburbs that polarization takes place. It is interesting to note that some sociologists came lately to the realization that the city itself may be defined by its heterogeneity, multifunctional character, and complex social structures.[10]

Returning to the concentric patterns, if all directions of traffic in each successive ring are added together, their total structure is similar, containing all directions with probably the same or similar frequency. However, in the case of land utilization this is not true. With the exception of the center or core there are specific sequences of dominance of different land uses--a probabilistic implementation of the widely recognized Thünian rings, which were deduced theoretically from the existence of differential land rent.

In dealing with all these phenomena their change over time has to be assumed implicitly. Even in individual cases, when a certain stability is observed, it is usually temporary depending much on a wider stability of the community as a whole or even more broadly on that of the whole society. However, when such changes take place they are not simultaneous. It seems clear that the answer to the question "Where do people live?" depends heavily on the question "What are they doing, and where?" In most modern societies there is a large and growing number of people who possess independent sources of income. Still, in Poland, the large majority of people have to work for a living and the question "Where do they work?" is decisive for the location of their dwellings, even in an era of modern transport which increases mobility and lengthens the distances they are able to cover on their way to work. Therefore, as noted earlier, the spatial structure of a city and changes in it really should be interpreted in relation to the location and locational changes of workplaces.

---

8 . Lionel J. March, "Urban Systems: A Generalized Distribution Function," in *London Papers in Regional Science,* ed. A.G. Wilson, 2 ed. (London: Pion Ltd., 1971), pp. 157-170.

9 . James A. Quinn, *Human Ecology* (New York: Prentice-Hall, 1950); Leo F. Schnore, "On the Spatial Structure of Cities in the Two Americas," in *The Study of Urbanization,* ed. P.M. Hauser and L.F. Schnore (New York: John Wiley and Sons, 1965), pp. 347-398.

10. Jan Węgleński, *Urbanizacja. Kontrowersja wokół pojęcča,* (Warsaw: Polish Scientific Publishers, 1983).

In recent research on the social ecology of Polish cities, Grzegorz Węcławowicz found to his surprise that the concentration of the night population in the city of Radom (about 200,000 inhabitants) was higher than the daytime one.[11] He studied solely the stable population of the city. For example, he included among the daytime population only those people who live in an area in the town and do not work outside it and the people from the outside who either worked or attended schools in the city. He did not take into account the temporary visitors such as shopppers or short-term customers of other services. Based on an analysis of census tracts, he found that the larger industries and services have moved to the outer zone in this city, a trend seemingly characteristic of most Polish cities, particularly the industrial ones. The importance of this phenomenon for understanding current and future development and urban change in Poland appears to be great. Perhaps we should interpret it in terms of urban economic bases, but with particular attention to a fine calibration both in space and through time.

### Urban Core and Urban Fringe

There are yet other, well known trends in Polish urban geography, similar to those taking place in other countries; maybe less intense but perhaps clearer to observe. Among these the transformation of the city core and the emergence of large housing estates and new towns on the outskirts of older centers should be included.

In the majority of Polish cities the central areas were heavily damaged, indeed, sometimes completely destroyed during the Second World War. During reconstruction they were modernized and their housing conditions technically equalized. Arterial streets were usually widened and reshaped in the form of circular bypass roads. The process of closing off many narrow internal streets for traffic has already begun, especially in larger cities. In the few historical cities where the ancient centers survived the war their rehabilitation, indeed their thorough reconstruction, is by now sorely needed. In some cases as with Cracow, Toun, and Zamosc, rehabilitation has been approved and actually begun.

The emergence of large housing estates with very high development densities is now typical in Polish cities of all sizes. Such construction is now widely criticized, for it has led smaller cities to some very unhappy and incongruous results. These

---

11. Grzegorz Węcławowicz, "The socio-spatial structure of Radom in 1978," paper presented at the Seventh British-Polish Geographical Seminar, Jablonna, Poland, 1983.

developments were imposed by the building industry, and in an effort to satisfy the very strong demand for new housing the industry came to depend with unnecessary severity on the technology of large precast concrete panels for use in high towers and apartment blocks. As a result we have now, almost everywhere, around older cities dispersed areas of intensively developed housing estates, often without adequate services, connected by arterial roads with city centers and industrial zones. Such a pattern of urban development is at present characteristic for cities of all sizes. In large cities it has created some heavy traffic and transport problems. In the smaller towns, however, it has led to the almost complete disintegration of their formerly coherent plan and appearance.

With the emergence of strong pressures for and efforts towards preservation of agricultural land, these forms of urban development are now being significantly checked. Some new, more integrated patterns of development will now have to be developed and applied, although it may require a radical reorganization of the building industry.

Polish cities, with their quick growth and major achievements in reconstruction and development, are nevertheless characterized by serious disfunctions and disparities. These are not so evident in social or class divisions--in this regard the egalitarian social ideals, along with government social and cultural policies, have achieved evident successes. There are, for example, no areas inhabited by the very poor in destitute conditions (slums), nor are there any significantly large, rich districts. Disfunctions and disparities are the consequence of forced industrialization, faulty economic policies of the later 1970s and also of the social and political turmoil of the early 1980s. Mass transport, municipal services (such as water works and mains, sewage disposal, and the like), and social services, in particular health services--these are underdeveloped and underinvested. Air, water, and soil pollution, both industrial and urban, is heavy and extensive, due partly to faulty location and to the antiquated technology of industries, but also to the minimal living standards of labor and the first generation of urban inhabitants. To overcome and correct all these problems will take a long time, especially under conditions of economic crisis and lack of investment funds and development potential.

## Looking Ahead

Making predictions can be a futile exercise, but still it is possible to identify some of the directions of coming change. The population transition in Poland has already passed its peak and demographic stabilization seems to be in sight, although arriving as late as the middle of the next century. This, together with the depletion of manpower reserves in the rural areas, would seem to imply diminishing rates of growth for cities and urban population. Whether this will bring urban decentralization or even dispersal remains an open question. The decentralization of industries within urban areas is paralleled by a certain concentration of population in and around the central parts of cities. Energetic efforts to preserve agricultural land and forests, as well as landscapes of natural beauty will certainly hamper desires for the eventual decentralization of urban dwellings. The decision lies, I believe, in the hands of the people, in the levels of education and culture they can achieve, and of course in their humanism.

# Chapter VI

# URBAN ISSUES IN THE SOVIET UNION

Theodore Shabad

In his classic 1970 monograph *Cities of the Soviet Union,*
Chauncy D. Harris described the Soviet Union as a "land of large
cities" vying with the United States for position as the country
with the largest number of cities of more than 100,000 population.
He also quoted a Soviet urban geographer, the late Valdimir G.
Davidovich, as having said that "the growth of urban population in
the USSR in volume and rate is without precedent in the history of
mankind." By whatever measure, there is no doubt that urban
development has been notable for its magnitude in the Soviet Union.

In the Soviet scheme of things, there has been traditionally a
heavy emphasis on industrial development, particularly the
development of heavy industry, as the most promising path to
national power. And the linkage between industrialization and
urbanization, found to be strong around the world, has been
particularly close in the Soviet Union. In fact, the economic base
can be shown to have evolved as an even more significant factor in
urbanization in the Soviet Union than such urban attributes as the
distinctive morphology of cities as forms of settlement. It is not
uncommon for populated places of rural appearance to be endowed with
urban status in the USSR in conjuction with the development of
mining or the building of a manufacturing plant. Aside from this
unususally close relationship between the economic base and what
passes for "urban" in Soviet conceptual models, there are other
distinctive features in the evolution of Soviet urban systems that
do not always conform to world patterns. These differences,
manifest in such aspects as the spatial structure of urban areas and
journey-to-work patterns, reflect both the centrally planned and
government-managed nature of the Soviet economy and the relative
isolation of Soviet society from the homogenizing forces of the
modern world economic system.

The following essay is intended to discuss some of these
distinctive features of Soviet urbanism against the background of

world patterns in modern urban change and to describe some of the trends that have been characteristic of the Soviet urban system over the last 10 to 15 years, using Chauncy D. Harris's book, whenever appropriate, as a "baseline" for subsequent changes.

## The Economic-Administrative Context

The Soviet view of what constitutes an urban place is based strictly on certain functional criteria that distinguish cities, towns, and other urban settlements from rural places. Those functional criteria serve not only as the definitional model, but also as the basis for an entire urban hierarchy that is part of the national system of governmental administration. Although the specific urban criteria vary among the 15 constituent republics that make up the Soviet Union, places are generally classified as urban if they meet two basic conditions: (1) the population must be at least 2,000 *and* (2) the majority of employment (usually two-thirds) must be in economic activities other than collective farming, which is one of the two principal institutional forms of large-scale agriculture in the Soviet Union. The central settlements of state farms, the other major form of agriculture, may on occasion be classified as urban despite the farming nature of the economic base, especially if it is the site of some form of agricultural processing. Under the Soviet definition of "urban," rural places would thus include predominantly agricultural settlements even if they exceed the population criterion of 2,000, as well as small on-farm places that do not meet the population minimum required for inclusion in the urban category.

Within this general definition of urban places, an entire urban hierarchy has been built up within the Soviet Union, consisting essentially of a smaller and economically less significant category of cities. The lesser urban settlements, which usually bear the official designation of "workers' settlement" or "settlement of urban type," tend to be associated with isolated industrial establishments such as a factory, a mine, or an electric power station, or with a major railroad station or other important economic object. Cities are usually urban places with more diversified urban functions and with a minimum legislated population of the order of 8,000 to 10,000, although some republics have set a city population criterion of as low as 5,000 and others as high as 12,000 inhabitants. Although the law classifies urban places by settlements and cities on the basis of population and economic activity, in practice the provision of urban amenities is also a factor, with the lesser urban settlements generally distinguished by a lower level of housing, municipal services, medical, educational, and retailing establishments. Finally, any unusual significance of economic activity may transcend population criteria and account for an urban place being allocated to a higher urban category.

Urban places classified officially as cities fall, in turn, into subcategories on the basis of their standing in the urban-administrative system. The lowest subcategory of cities would fall under the jurisdiction of rayons, minor civil divisions corresponding roughly to United States counties. Cities of larger population and greater economic significance would come under the jurisdiction of major civil divisions, such as the province-level entities known as oblast, krays, and autonomous republics. Finally, the largest cities, usually the capitals, of the Soviet Union's constituent republics would be administered directly by the governments of these republics. Legislation of these republics fixes threshold populations for cities to move from one subcategory to the next. In the Ukrainian SSR, for example, a populated place upon being classified as an urban settlement when reaching the lower population limit of 2,000 might *in theory* progress upward through the urban hierarchy with industrial development and urban growth, entering the rayon-city subcategory with a minimum population of 10,000, the oblast-city subcategory with a lower population limit of 50,000, and the republic-city subcategory with at least 500,000 population. In practice, such a direct ascent through the entire hierarchy would, of course, be highly unusual. It is not uncommon, however, for rural nonfarm places after being chosen as the sites of major mining or manufacturing projects to advance through the categories of urban settlement and rayon city to that of an oblast city.

Although most of the places within a given urban category are likely to fall within the legislated population limits (an urban settlement in the Ukrainian SSR, for example, between 2,000 and 10,000), the actual urban status of an industrial place would also be affected by its location (in isolation or in the suburban zone of a larger city), the level of municipal amenities, historical background, and the importance of the economic base. In the Soviet Union's Russian republic (the full dsignation is Russian Soviet Federated Socialist Republic, commonly abbreviated RSFSR), the largest and most important of the constituent republics, the legislated population range for an urban settlement is 3,000 to 12,000. In practice, however, urban settlements may be smaller or

larger because of various contributing factors. According to the
1970 census, the last enumeration for which such  detailed
information is available, urban settlements in the RSFSR ranged from
less than 1,000 (a coal-mining settlement in the east wing of the
Donets basin in Rostov oblast, for example, had a 1970 population of
868) to more than 30,000. The lead-zinc and boron mining center of
Dalnegorsk in the Soviet Far East had a 1970 population of 33,506
and is still classified as an urban settlement, presumably because
its urban services are below those qualifying an urban place as a
city. Conversely, about 15 percent of the rayon cities in the RSFSR
had 1970 populations below the statutory lower limit of 12,000.
Many of them are old historical trade centers with an established
urban infrastructure that were considered to justify city status
despite a small population. Nine "cities" in the RSFSR had
populations of less than 3,000 in 1970.[1]

### Factors and Trends in Urban Growth

The Soviet economic-administrative approach to the urban
concept becomes relevant in the analysis of urban growth patterns.
Urban growth in the Soviet context is made up of three factors: (1)
natural population increase in urban places, (2) net rural-urban
migration, and (3) administrative reclassification of rural to urban
as a result of industrialization. The weight of each factor will
tend to vary with the regional conditions, but, in virtually all
cases, straight reclassification plays a significant role. It goes
without saying that the administrative conversion of a rural place
to an urban place does not automatically transform its morphology,
services, and housing stock, and this discrepancy between the
official designation of places and their lag behind conventional
"urban" standards is an aspect that pervades the urbanization
process in the USSR.

The relative weight of the three factors in urban growth was
published in Soviet official sources for the intercensal period
1959-70, but increasing restrictions on statistical publication
beginning in the mid-1970s resulted in the announcement of less
detailed information for the 1979 census and the intercensal period
1970-79. For the latter period, urban growth in each of the 15
union republics was broken down into two components: (1) natural
population increase and (2) combined net rural-urban migration and

---

1. For more detailed discussion of the significance of the urban hierarchy
in the Soviet Union, see Theodore Shabad, "The Urban-Administrative System of the
USSR and Its Relevance to Geographic Research," in *Geographical Studies on the
Soviet Union: Essays in Honor of Chauncy D. Harris,* ed. George J. Demko and Roland
J.  Fuchs, Research Paper no. 211 (Chicago: University of Chicago, Department of
Geography 1984), pp. 93-108.

~~population increase and (2) combined net rural-urban migration and~~
administrative reclassification.

During the 1959-70 intercensal period, when the more detailed
three-factor breakdown was available, urban growth in the USSR as a
whole (from 100 million people in 1959 to 136 million in 1970, or an
increment of 36 million) was derived 45.5 percent from net
rural-urban migration, 40.5 percent from natural increase, and 14
percent from administrative reclassification. In the following
intercensal period, 1970-79, natural increase accounted for a
somewhat higher percentage (44 percent) of the urban increment of
27.6 million people, and combined migration and reclassification
played a lesser role, accounting for 56 percent of urban growth,
compared with nearly 60 percent in the previous period. The
increasing contribution to urban growth from natural increase of
city residents reflected the shift of higher birth rates from rural
to urban areas through the intermediary of migrants in the young,
reproductive age groups. The aging of the rural population, with
all that this entails for labor productivity in agriculture, has
become a serious social problem for the Soviet Union. The
differential between rural and urban rates of natural increase has
become particularly pronounced in two western republics, the Ukraine
and Belorussia, both of which are undergoing intensive
redistribution of population from rural to urban areas. In
Belorussia, for example, rural natural increase during the 1970-79
intercensal period was only 94,000 on a 1970 rural population base
of 5,094,000, or 1.9 percent, while natural increase in urban areas
was 552,000 on a 1970 urban population base of 3,908,000 or 14
percent.[2]

In general, it may be said that urbanization in the Soviet
Union, driven by whatever factor or combination of factors, has
continued at a steady pace since publication of Harris's *Cities of
the Soviet Union* (figure 6.1). The urban population increment of
27.6 million during the intercensal period 1970-79, which followed
publication of the book, represented an urban growth of 20.3 percent
over the nine-year period, and the urban population percentage rose
by six points, from 56 percent in 1970 to 62 percent in 1979.
Urbanization was such a pervasive process that every major civil
division, at the oblast level of administration, registered an
increase in urban population.

---

[2]. For urban and rural population change by Soviet republics, see Theodore
Shabad, "News Notes," *Soviet Geography* 20 (September 1979): 440-456, Belorussia is
on pp. 447-448.

106

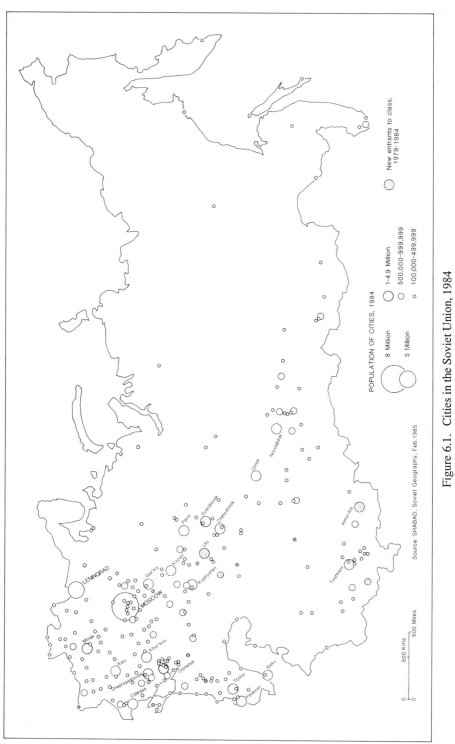

POPULATION OF CITIES, 1984

8 Million

5 Million

1-4.9 Million

500,000-999,999

100,000-499,999

New entrants to class, 1979-1984

Source: SHABAD, Soviet Geography, Feb.1985

500 Kms

500 Miles

Figure 6.1. Cities in the Soviet Union, 1984

Andrew Bond and Paul Lydolph, in an analysis of Soviet population change published shortly after the 1979 census,[3] distinguished three types of rapid urban growth during the intercensal period. The highest rates of growth were found in the new oil and gas producing region of West Siberia, which had been so slightly urbanized--in fact, so sparsely populated--that even relatively small increments of population produced large percentage gains. The principal source of urban growth in these newly developed areas was in-migration from other regions of the Soviet Union. The new oil cities of Nizhnevartosk and Surgut, both of which surpassed 100,000 population by 1979, grew by annual rates of 24 percent and 14 percent respectively during the 1970-79 period. A second type of rapid urban growth was characteristic of the western regions of the USSR, inclusing Belorussia and the western Ukraine. In this case, the driving forces, as noted earlier, were both rural-urban migration and the high rates of natural increase transferred to cities from the countryside through the intermediary of young migrants. A third type of rapid urban growth has been characteristic of the southern regions of the Soviet Union, notably Transcaucasia and Central Asia, where industrialization and urbanization levels have been relatively low. In these southern regions, rates of natural increase have been generally high and have also been a major factor in urban growth. Local rural-urban migration is a modest factor, especially in Central Asia, where indigenous rural residents, for a variety of cultural, linguistic, and other reasons, appear to have shunned migration to the largely Russianized cities.

The highly distinctive urban process in Central Asia is epitomized by the Uzbek SSR, which with a population of more than 17 million is by far the largest of the four Central Asian republics (the others have total populations of the order of three to four million each). Urban trends underwent a significant change between the 1960s, when Harris was doing his research on *Cities of the Soviet Union,* and the 1970s. In both intercensal periods, the Uzbek SSR recorded major urban population increase--58 percent over the 11-year period 1959-70 period, there was still strong in-migration of ethnic Russians and others into Uzbekistan from other parts of the Soviet Union, and these migrants moved almost entirely into Uzbek cities. As much as one-third of the urban population increment between 1959 and 1970 was derived from this largely

---

3. Andrew R. Bond and Paul E. Lydolph, "Soviet Population Change and City Growth, 1970-79, a Preliminary Report," *Soviet Geography* 20 (October 1979): 461-488.

European in-migration.  Rural-urban migration within Uzbekistan was negligible, accounting for only 1.4 precent of the urban growth. Administrative reclassification represented 14 percent, and natural increase of the urban population 52 percent.

In the 1970s, there was a sharp decline of European migration to the Uzbek SSR, and this source of urban growth dropped to 6.7 percent in the intercensal period 1970-79.  Natural increase represented 45 percent, reflecting a gradual downward trend in the high rates of natural increase characteristic of Central Asia.  As noted earlier, available information no longer made it possible to distinguish between net in-migration into urban areas and rural-to-urban reclassifiction during this period.  Both of these categories accounted for 55 percent of urban growth.  In view of the pronounced reduction of interregional migration into Uzbekistan to fill urban manpower needs, especially in large cities, it can be assumed that rural-urban migration within the republic rose in the 1970s, accounting for perhaps 20 to 25 percent of urban growth.  The administrative reclassification trend greatly increased in the 1970s and, in fact, became a matter of policy in Uzbekistan, and may have represented as much as 30 to 35 percent of urban growth.  The reclassification trend was particularly pronunced in the Fergana Valley, in Dzhizak Oblast, and in the suburban areas of Samarkand.

The Samarkand situation was unusual even in the context of Soviet urban processes.  In 1978, suburban rural areas with close to 150,000 people were included within the Samarkand city limits, so that the city's population jumped from an official estimate of 318,000 at the begining of 1978 to 475,000 at the time of the 1979 census one year later.  In the Uzbek SSR, rural-to-urban reclassification reflects a policy of introducing industry into rural areas. Rural Uzbeks, and Central Asians in general, have shown reluctance to move from rural to urban settings, and the authorities have been trying to induce rural residents to play a broader role in the industrial labor force by introducing light industry and other labor-intensive activities with low capital requirements into the countryside.  Rural places acquiring such simple factories and workshops are then arbitrarily declared urban in accordance with the principle that industrial employment is classified as urban.4

---

4.  For fuller discussion of the distinctive urban process in Soviet Central Asia, see Theodore Shabad, "Some Aspects of Central Asian Manpower and Urbanization," *Soviet Geography* 20 (February 1979): 113-123; also see Theodore Shabad, "Economic Realities and Dynamics in Central Asia," in *Conference on the Study of Central Asia, March 10-11, 1983*, ed. David Nalle (Washington: Kennan Institute, 1983), pp. 43-50.

The lowest rates of urban growth in the USSR during the 1970-79 period occurred in old, established coal-mining areas such as the Donets basin in the Ukraine, the Kuznetsk basin in southern Siberia, and the Karaganda basin in Kazakhstan. These coal basins, which also recorded relatively low rates of urban growth in the preceding intercensal period, have been feeling the effect of a general decline in labor-intensive underground mining of coal, increasing mechanization and the general shift of emphasis in the fossil fuel balance from deep-mined coal, first to oil and now to natural gas. Other low urban growth areas were the Urals and Tula Oblast south of Moscow. These regions are old metallurgical centers that were already highly urbanized by the 1960s and, in view of obsolescence, face competition from more modern industries elsewhere in the Soviet Union.

Many of these areal variations in urban growth rates were anticipated by Harris; others are more recent developments.[5] He noted, for example, the "remarkable" recovery of the western regions as an area of rapid urban development associated with local migration from densely populated rural areas and with the increasing economic interplay between the western regions of the USSR and the eastern European countries. Harris also made a point of the incipient urban explosion in the sparsely settled regions of West Siberia that developed with the discovery of oil and gas. And he noted the slowdown in urban growth in older industrial areas, such as the Donbas, the Urals, and the Kuzbas, all of which had their most rapid growth before World War II. Some of these trends have become more pronounced since he completed his study, notably the upward trend in the oil and gas regions of West Siberia and the downward trend in the older coal basins. And the remarkable use of administative reclassification in conjunction with rural industrialization of the Central Asian countryside could, of course, not be anticipated.

As might be expected, individual city growth, notably in the cities of more than 100,000 population, reflected these regional patterns. Some of the higher city growth rates between 1970 and 1979 were found in the western Ukraine, where cities like Ternopol, Rovno, Khmelnitsky, Zhitomir, and Chernigove all grew by more than 50 percent over the nine-year intercensal period. In Belorussia, five out of the 10 cities of more than 100,000 recorded increases of 40 to 47 percent, and a sixth, Minsk, with a rise of 39 percent, was

---

5. Chauncy D. Harris, *Cities of the Soviet Union* (Chicago: Rand, McNally, 1970), pp. 368-373.

the most rapidly growing city of the Soviet Union with more than one
million population. These western cities all represented examples
of sustained urban growth. During any intercensal period, a few
cities associated with priority economic projects can exhibit
extraordinary growth rates, usually based on a small initial
population preceding industrial development. Examples during the
1970-79 period were the new truck-manufacturing center of Brezhnev
(until 1982, Naberezhnye Chelny) on the Kama River and the oil towns
of Nizhnevartovsk and Surgut in West Siberia. Another automotive
center, Togliatti on the Volga, doubled its population during the
the nine-year period. Petrochemical producers also fell in the
high-growth category, notably Nizhnekamsk, near Brezhnev. Finally,
there was the new steel center of Stary Oskol in the iron-mining
district known as the Kursk magnetic anomaly, where a
direct-conversion steel plant was under construction during the
1970s. At the other end of the spectrum of urban population change,
coal-mining centers and older iron and steel towns showed negligible
growth or even continued to decline. Example were Makeyevka,
Gorlovka, and Yenakiyevo in the Donbas; Nizhniy Tagil, Serov, and
Kopeisk in the Urals; Prokopyevsk, Leninsk-Kuzsnetsky, Kiselevsk,
and Anzhero-Sudzhensk in the Kuzbas.

### The Policy of Limiting Excessive City Growth

A widely publicized Soviet urban policy has been the effort to
limit the growth of large cities. This is a highly complex issue
that has been distinguished over the years by a certain degree of
ambiguity at the policy level and by some divergence between policy
and practice. Historically, as Richard H. Rowland has pointed out
in a detailed study of the subject,[6] Marxist opposition to large
cities had ideological roots. With Friedrich Engels, Karl Marx, and
eventually Lenin opposing the "power of the large-city bourgeoisie
and the pollution and waste of large cities." However, this
anti-large-city attitude in the context of capitalism was toned down
once the Bolsheviks seized power in Russia. In the new political
setting, large cities with their industries and proletarian
population were found to be convenient centers of communist power,
to be used as bases of control and for the diffusion of the new
political and social institutions into the nonproletarian
countryside. As a result, the growth of large cities was initially

---

6. Richard H. Rowland, "The Growth of Large Cities in the USSR, Policies
and Trends, 1959-79," *Urban Geography* 4 (July-September 1983): 258-279; for
another view of the Soviet antipathy to large cities, see Robert G. Jensen, "The
Anti-Metropolitan Syndrome in Soviet Urban Policy," in *Geographic Studies on the
Soviet Union,* pp. 71-91.

favored or, at least, tolerated, and in each oblast or other major
civil division, it was usually one central city, which was also the
administrative capital, that became the focus of urban development,
often at the expense of lesser urban places. Oblast capitals were
favored by industrial investment policies, the concentration of
services, and the availability of educational and public health
institutions. They became magnets in attracting migrants from the
less favored small towns and rural areas, creating problems of urban
crowding and inadequate housing and services. The imbalance between
a highly developed oblast capital and an underdeveloped remainder of
the oblast has become a characteristic aspect of Soviet spatial
development. Oblasts and equivalent major civil divisions with a
single city of more than 100,000 have become the rule in the Soviet
Union. The imbalance has become particularly extreme in a number of
predominantly agricultural regions. In European Russia, the city of
Voronezh contains one-third of the total population of its oblast
and 60 percent of the urban population; in Siberia, the cities of
Omsk and Novosibirsk contain one-half of the population of their
oblasts and some 70 to 80 percent of the urban populations.

While this excessive development of oblast capitals was being
fostered for political reasons, the first tentative attempts to curb
the growth of the very largest cities were also set in motion. The
measures began in the 1930s with Moscow and Leningrad and were
gradually extended to other very large cities. Growth was to be
limited by restricting further industrial construction and
in-migration. However, economic planners often succeeded in
circumventing the proclaimed prohibitions on the ground of
cost-effectiveness, arguing that the infrastructure required for new
industrial enterprises was already present in large cities and would
have to be provided from scratch in other locations. The controls
on in-migration, using the so-called *propiska,* or resident
registration system, in conjuction with the Soviet institution of
internal passports also turned out not to be foolproof, and migrants
continued to move to large cities using various legal devices, for
example, marriage of city residents. Rowland has shown that net
in-migration into the largest cities during the intercensal period
1970-79 continued at a much higher rate than migration to urban
places in general.[7] Net in-migration into the largest cities--data
are available for a set of 21 cities--accounted for 66 percent of
the growth of these cities during the nine-year period, while net
in-migration *plus reclassification* (which, as noted, was quite

---

7. Rowland, "Large Cities," p. 270.

significant) represented 56 percent of all urban growth in the
Soviet Union. The effect has been for the city size class of
100,000 and more to account for a growing share of both the urban
and the total population of the Soviet Union. These cities
contained 37.6 percent of the total population in 1979, up 5.8
points from 1970, and 60.3 percent of the urban population, up 3.7
points.[8]

An equally unsuccessful policy associated with the attempt to
constrain excessive city growth has been an effort to impose some
sort of "optimum" population limit on cities. Ideally, a population
of 250,000 used to be proposed as a maximum optimum size. In fact,
however, Soviet city planners have paid little if any attention to
the concept, and the number of cities exceeding 250,000 has steadily
increased; there were 59 at the 1959 census, 80 in 1970, and 110 in
1979. In 1980, a group of Leningrad geographers pointed out that
the whole notion of an optimum size for cities in general was
oversimplified and unrealistic; they argued that the debate should
focus on optimal sizes for cities with particular functions and on
insuring that the development of social infrastructure keep pace
with industrial development.[9] This concern with the social aspects
of urbanization, and of settlement in general, has been a growing
trend in the Soviet Union, where the objectives of economic
production have traditionally overshadowed the provision of adequate
services.

With the gradual acceptance of large cities--and cities of
smaller size classes--as part of a hierarchy of urban places endowed
with particular sets of functions, there have been various attempts
to integrate cities of different sizes into urban theoretical
concepts. The prominent urban geographer Boris S. Khorev of Moscow
University has been identified with the theory of a unified system
of settlement, which conceptualizes settlement systems as consisting
of complementary functional elements such as large cities, smaller
urban places, and rural areas gravitating toward the central city or
cities of the system. The unified settlement concept, aside from
allocating a place and function to large cities, also seeks to
resolve the persistent problem of contrasting levels of living
between urban and rural areas by integrating them into the so-called
unified systems.

---

8. Ibid., p. 261.

9. Nikolay T. Agafonov, Sergey B. Lavrov, and Oleg P. Litovka,
"Contemporary Urbanization and an Optimal Size for Soviet Cities," *Soviet
Geography* 21 (October 1980): 508-514.

Another approach, focusing more directly on urban policy, has been that of urban agglomerations, for which Georgi M. Lappo of the Institute of Geography in Moscow has been the principal advocate. Urban agglomeration theory envisages the existence of urban clusters made up of a core city (or core cities) with a *minimum* population of 250,000 (once conceived as the *maximum* optimum size of cities!) and a certain number of subsidiary urban places, with the entire system interconnected by journeys to work assuming a maximum one-way travel time of 1.5 to 2 hours.[10] Advocates of the agglomeration concept, which emerged in the mid-1960s from an earlier policy of "satellite city" development, have been urging the Soviet authorities to give urban agglomerations official status as statistical and planning entities, similar to the standard metropolitan statistical areas of the United States.

So far, however, agglomerations have not been officially sanctioned, and the entire notion of urban agglomeration has not advanced beyond being a research construct. Moreover it has run into opposition within the Soviet academic community. The advocates of the unified settlement concept, integrating urban and rural forms, have accused the proponents of agglomerations of making a fetish of heavily urbanized regions, calling them "ultra-urbanists" and "agglocentrists."[11] The critics noted that, while the agglomeration approach was being advocated in the Soviet Union, the United States and Western Europe were already moving on to the stage of "deglomeration," or demetropolitanization, of population and settlement. It should be noted, in fairness, that the criticism ignores fundamental differences in urban processes between the Soviet Union and the Western world. While the flight from the city and even from metropolitan areas has become a reality in the West, the city in the Soviet Union remains a strong magnet attracting population, a dispenser of services to the surrounding region, and an organizing and management center for the regional economy.

Alternative strategies of settlement for the Soviet Union were worked out in the 1970s by the Central Urban Planning Institute, an arm of the government, projecting future settlement patterns on the basis of both the agglomeration approach and the unified settlement

---

10. For a recent discussion of the concept and application of the urban agglomeration approach, see P.M. Polyan, "Large Urban Agglomerations of the Soviet Union," *Soviet Geography* 23 (December 1982): 707-718; see also Feliks M. Listengurt, "Criteria for Delineating Large Urban Agglomerations in the USSR," *Soviet Geography* 16 (November 1975): 559-568. For an assessment of the role of satellite cities, see Gary Hausladen, "The Satellite City in Soviet Urban Development," *Soviet Geography* 25 (April 1984): 229-247.

11. Nikolay T. Agafonov, Sergey B. Lavrov, and Boris S. Khorev, "On Some Faulty Concepts in Soviet Urban Studies," *Soviet Geography* 24 (March 1983): 660-674.

concept (figure 6.2).[12] The agglomeration approach, with its heavy emphasis on urbanization, was found to be a less desirable policy than the unified settlement approach, with its emphasis on rural-urban integration, although the latter was expected to require far larger outlays for transport development, amelioration of rural settlement patterns, and other aspects. No formal strategy has been officially adopted, but research and planning on various elements continue.

One conceptual approach that has come to the fore is the notion of a basic framework (in Russian, *karkas*, akin to the English *carcass*) of settlement consisting of the nation's largest cities, interconnected by the principal transport corridors. In this construct, the settlement framework is conceived in the form of a graph, with the large cities (or their urban agglomerations) representing the vertices of the graph and the transport corridors the edges (figure 6.2). Orest K. Kudryavtsev of the Central Urban Planning Institute has traced the evolution of the framework over time. He found its basic configuration to consist of a major clustering of large cities in the European USSR, corresponding roughly to the Soviet Union's agricultural triangle of settlement, and lesser clusters in the Novosibirsk-Kuzbas region of southern Siberia and in the Tashkent--Alma-Ata region of Central Asia, with the rest of the space filled with isolated large cities, singly or in small groups.[13] Kudryavtsev operated with sets of large cities of more than 100,000 population and with a subset of cities of 500,000 or more. Lappo has conceptualized the graph as the basic framework not only for the system of settlement, but for the entire spatial structure of the Soviet economy, with agglomerations serving as the vertices that are connected by the transport-corridor edges of the graph.[14] The framework concept, in which large urban centers would serve as the foci and the transport linkages as the axes of development, is not inconsistent with either the agglomerative or the integrated urban-rural approach to settlement. In either case, large urban centers would serve as the vertices of the basic framework. The issue is whether the evolution of settlement around

---

12. A.V. Kochetkov and Feliks M. Listengurt, "A General Strategy of Settlement for the USSR: Aims, Problems, Solutions," *Soviet Geography* 18 (November 1977): 660-674.

13. Orest K. Kudryavtsev, "The Basic Framework of Settlement of the USSR: Origins and Configuration," *Soviet Geography* 24 (June 1983): 430-443: see also John Sallnow, "The USSR: New Directions for the 1980s," *Cities* 1 (August 1983): 39-45.

14. Georgi M. Lappo, "The Concept of a Support Frame for the Spatial Structure of the Soviet Economy: Its Evolution and Its Theoretical and Practical Significance," *Soviet Geography* 25 (April 1984): 211-28.

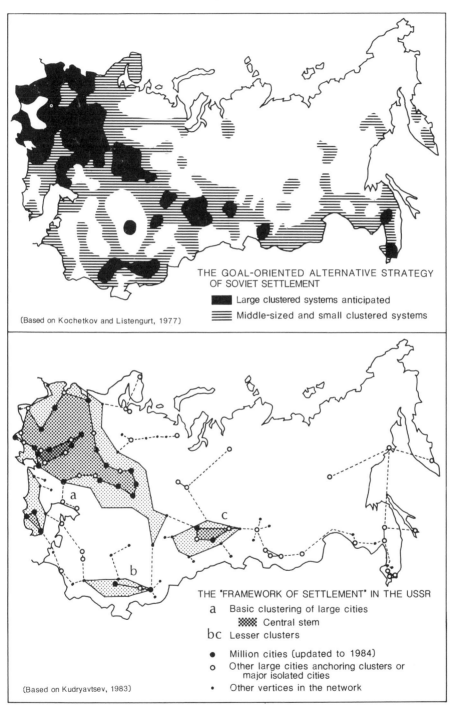

THE GOAL-ORIENTED ALTERNATIVE STRATEGY
OF SOVIET SETTLEMENT

▓▓ Large clustered systems anticipated

≣ Middle-sized and small clustered systems

(Based on Kochetkov and Listengurt, 1977)

THE 'FRAMEWORK OF SETTLEMENT' IN THE USSR

a   Basic clustering of large cities

▨▨ Central stem

bc   Lesser clusters

●   Million cities (updated to 1984)

o   Other large cities anchoring clusters or
major isolated cities

(Based on Kudryavtsev, 1983)

•   Other vertices in the network

Figure 6.2. The skeletal national planning framework for Soviet cities

each large urban center should emphasize urbanization and the development of interconnected urban systems, as in the agglomerative approach, or strive toward integration and complementarity or urban and rural systems of settlement, taking advantage both of the cost-effectiveness of modern industrial production in urbanized areas and of the positive aspects (natural landscapes, recreation land, etc.) offered by rural settings.

### The Policy of Fostering the Growth of Smaller Towns

While the emphasis in devising a strategy of settlement has been understandably on large cities and urban agglomerations as the basic support centers of the system, there has also been much discussion about the future of smaller towns of less than 100,000 population. There are more than 2,000 such urban places in the Soviet Union, accounting for a little more than 27 percent of the total urban population. (The Soviet urban literature often attaches verbal designations to city size classes, for example, medium-size to the 50,000-100,000 size class and semi-medium-size to the 20,000-50,000 size class, but these terms are often meaningless without specification of the actual population group to which reference is made.) As part of the policy of limiting excessive city growth, the smaller cities provided a potential reservoir of labor that could be usefully employed if industry were sited in these urban places, which had been bypassed by earlier industrialization drives. Accordingly, the 1961 program of the Soviet Communist Party, setting forth a number of long-range economic and social policies and objectives, called for more industrialization of smaller towns as a corollary in easing the population pressure on larger cities. In accordance with this programmatic directive, the Soviet government's State Planning Committee (Gosplan), the central planning agency, identified some 500 smaller cities as potentially suitable for the location of industry. These places were selected on the basis of what was viewed as the existence of surplus labor (meaning people in working ages who were not gainfully employed in the government-run economy) and the potential availability of a water supply, electric power, industrial terrain, transportation, housing, and construction facilities.

Although a number of smaller cities were indeed selected as sites of new industrial projects, and some in fact mushroomed into the larger-city category, the small-town industrialization cannot be said to have assumed massive proportions. While available

underemployed manpower may have been such at one time (in the late
1950s and the early 1960s, when the policy was formulated) as to
justify the siting of relatively large industrial enterprises in
selected smaller towns, this reservoir either soon became soaked up
or turned out to consist mainly of female labor, imposing
constraints on the type of industry that could be developed.
Moreover, the government's industrial ministries, which are the
channels for industrial investment, often found on closer inspection
that the construction of new projects in smaller cities would be far
more costly than in existing urbanized regions because of the lack
of an industrial infrastructure.  Accordingly, despite the
proclaimed policy, a high share of industrial investment continued
to go to large cities.[15]

Small-town industrialization remains on the agenda of public
policy in the Soviet Union, but in a modified form.  Instead of
being viewed as potential sites for major industrial enterprises,
the smaller cities, in light of their more limited labor-resource
potential, are now being treated as places suitable for the
construction of branch plants supplying intermediate products or
subassemblies to the industrial enterprises of the larger cities.
This branch-plant approach also fits in with the new form of
industrial organization that has been gradually introduced in the
Soviet Union since the 1960s--the multiplant government corporation
(Russian *obyedineniye,* literally, association).  Such a corporation
is typically made up of a major industrial plant situated in a large
city and of a number of branch plants that supply parts or
intermediate products to the head plant for fabrication or assembly
into the finished product.  The corporation structure has been
viewed by Soviet economic planners as more efficient that the
previous form of industrial organization in which the
industrial ministries directly administered each individual plant.
The branch-plant approach is being fostered especially within the
suburban zones of large cities, forming part of what is generally
defined as the urban agglomeration.  However, it is not unusual for
branch plants to be situated a greater distance away.  In more
isolated regions, smaller cities are to be developed to a greater
extent as service centers for surrounding agricultural or forestry
areas.  A growing official interest in developing so-called
agro-industrial complexes may endow such smaller towns outside
metropolitan areas with agricultural processing industries, farm

---

15. Growth trends in Soviet cities by size classes have been analyzed in
Robert A. Lewis and Richard H. Rowland, *Population Redistribution in the USSR: Its
Impact on Society, 1897-1977* (New York: Praeger, 1979), pp. 14-17 and 279-321.

equipment repair and fertilizer distribution facilities, and other activities serving the area. Finally, some smaller cities with suitable requisites may be developed as recreation centers.

One approach, considered so far only at the academic research level, and aimed to enlarge the role of smaller cities in the Soviet economy, has been the concept of *okrug* centers. Okrugs (the Russian term, used in English, is akin to the German term *kreis)* used to be middle-level civil divisions in the 1920s and early 1930s before the political-administrative system of the Soviet Union evolved into the present basic structure of oblasts as major civil divisions and rayons as minor divisions. The advocates of the okrug concept now propose the restoration of such a middle level of public administration as a means of revitalizing the economy and improving the provision of services outside the urbanized regions. Okrugs are being viewed as middle-level regions both for political administration and for economic management, and the seats of okrugs as a new middle level in the hierarchy of urban places. It goes without saying that the okrug device is also being presented as a way of stimulating the growth of those smaller cities that are selected as the administrative centers of the new middle-level entities.

One of the leading advocates of the okrug approach, Boris Khorev, also envisages the okrug centers as an element of the basic framework of settlement as part of his overall advocacy of integrated, complementary urban-rural settlement systems. In this context, Khorev has been critical of Lappo for conceptualizing the basic framework more narrowly as a network of large cities and their urban agglomerations.[16] A network of 485 okrugs, or economic microregions, was first delimited in 1978 by the Central Urban Planning Institute for the Soviet Union's Russian republic, and this network was extended by the begining of 1983 to the entire country, numbering 720 entities.[17] There have been no indications whether the proposed okrug system of middle-level administration is likely to be officially adopted. The issue is relevant to urban policy since a new system of officially sanctioned okrug centers would stimulate the growth of a selected set of smaller cities.

---

16 . Boris S. Khorev, *Territorialnaya organizatsiya obshchestva* [Spatial organization of society] (Moscow: Mysl', 1981), pp. 119-147; see also B.S. Khorev, *Problemy gorodov* [Problems of cities] (Moscow: Mysl', 1971), pp. 327-371; 2d edition, 1975, pp. 400-402.

17 . Oleg A. Kibal'chich, *Territorialnaya organizatsiya narodnogo Khozyaistva SSSR* [Spatial organization of the Soviet economy], vol. 17 of Geography of the USSR in the series *Itogi nauki i tekhniki* [State of the art of science and technology] (Moscow: Viniti, 1983), p. 145.

An interesting issue in the context of fostering the growth of smaller cities is that concerning urban places with stagnant and declining population. Available information made it possible to investigate population changes of Soviet towns with 15,000 or more people at the 1959 and 1970 censuses, with additional sets of official estimates for 1964, 1967, and 1974. A directive issued in 1976 prohibited further publication of population figures for cities under 50,000. The most comprehensive analysis of declining and stagnant towns was made by Rowland,[18] who found that more than 300 towns were in that category during the 1959-74 study period. Stagnation was defined as a growth rate of less than 5 percent over the intercensal period 1959-70, and this was prorated for the 1970-74 period. According to the analysis, about 245 towns out of a total of 700 towns in the 15,000-50,000 size class in 1959, or some 35 percent, declined or stagnated either in the 1959-70 or in the 1970-74 period. The notable aspect of these declining and stagnant towns was that virtually all of them had a narrowly specialized economic base (coal mining or other extractive industry, textiles, metallurgy, wood processing) and none was a major administrative center (above the rayon level) with the diversified economic base usually associated in the USSR with centers of government administration. The findings suggest that the proposal, implicit in the okrug concept, to endow many of the smaller cities with middle-level administrative and management fuctions may be effective in stimulating growth at that level of the urban hierarchy.

### Peculiarities of Commuting to Work in the USSR

In the very simplest terms, commuting to work in the Soviet Union may be viewed as yet another device for limiting the growth of very large cities. However, official attitudes toward the practice of commutation to central cities from outlying communities have varied over time, and urban theorists have attached different interpretations to the commuting trend to fit it into particular conceptual models of settlement. Traditionally Soviet urban planners have favored a "company town" approach to the design and location of housing, with residential areas within easy access of places of employment. This approach, which still dominates in urban design throughout the USSR, has also been fostered by the mechanism of capital investment, in which industrial ministries control virtually all the economic development funds and are responsible for

18 . Richard H. Rowland, "Recent Declining and Stagnant Towns of the USSR," *Soviet Geography* 21 (April 1980): 195-218; see also Lewis and Rowland, *Population Redistribution,* pp. 259-278.

the provision of housing and services for the workers of their enterprises. The company-town concept has been favored because it conforms with Soviet objectives of cohesion between the plant and its work force, insures a certain order in social organization, and facilitates the imposition of social controls. Not only are housing and services provided by the employer, but leisure-time activities also focus on a "company" community and social center. The so-called houses of culture, as these centers are called, are still the sites of a wide range of recreational activities in most urban places of the Soviet Union.

Against this background, commuting in the USSR has developed partly as a response to constraints imposed on the development of excessively large cities and partly because housing provision often did not keep pace with employment opportunities. In light of growing demands on limited investment resources, planners sometimes found it more economical to develop additional means of public transport to bring commuters into the cental city than to build the additional housing and service establishments near places of employment. The entire mechanism of commutation also gained increasingly official acceptance in the realm of social policy as some of the strictures of the traditional company-town straitjacket became relaxed, particularly in the context of the large urbanized areas. Changes in individual residential preferences also began to play a role as more and more people, like their counterparts around the world, came to prefer life in the quieter setting of the countryside, with a private home and garden, away from the high-rise apartment complexes and the hurly-burly of city living. Although the rise of commuting in the Soviet Union may seem to have paralleled the Western experience, at least superficially, important differences must be noted. Whereas in the West the process of suburbanization and mass ownership of private automobiles were important factors in the development of commuting, both of these aspects were absent in the USSR. Suburbanization in the Western sense, of a semiurban sprawl of single-family dwellings has never been part of the Soviet urban process; instead, on the outer margins of Soviet cities, a fringe of modern high-rise residential areas drops off abruptly to a largely rural environment, so that roughly half the commuters are in fact rural residents. Because of social and economic policies long oriented against mass use of private cars, this mode of transport has not been a factor in the rise of commuting in the Soviet Union. Most commuting is by suburban rail and bus lines, and the private automobile is only just beginnning to play a modest role.

Soviet urban geographers and planners were relatively slow to come to grips with the phenomenon of commuting compared with the voluminous research literature on the subject that has been produced in Western societies. Perhaps the main reason for this lag of interest was the fact that commuting as a process arose more or less spontaneously in the Soviet Union rather than as an instrument of social policy; it gradually imposed itself, so to speak, and had to be accepted as a fact of life. Because of the unplanned nature of the commuting process, the statistical accounting sources needed for research and analysis were slow to be developed. Many Soviet studies of commuting patterns are still constrained by data limitations and must depend heavily on time-consuming special-purpose surveys and questionnaires. Finally, urban theorists, at least initially, had problems fitting the commuting process into existing conceptual models. Some saw the emerging process simply as an extension of interacity movements or as an important lever in the formation or urbanized areas such as urban agglomerations. A normative commuting time of one and a half to two hours became, in fact, one of the definitional criteria of such agglomerations. In contrast to this stress on the urbanizing aspects of commuting, the advocates of urban-rural integration seized on commuting as a process that was likely to foster the formation of the so-called unified systems of settlement. To these analysts, it was the commuting of rural residents to cities that was of the greatest interest.[19]

Aside from the source areas of commuting in the Soviet Union and the modes of transportation used in the process, there are also remarkable differences in the characteristics and composition of commuters in the USSR and in some Western countries. These differences are largely related to the fact that cities are still a magnet of settlement and that urban residence is still a prestigious status symbol in the Soviet Union. As a consequence, the older, skilled, and established city worker, with a relatively higher educational level, is likely to be a city resident. Commuters, especially those from rural source areas, would typically be younger people, with lower educational and skill levels, with employment in blue-collar jobs. These are, of course, highly generalized observations that are subject to variation in particular situations. For example, the share of professionals, engineers, and white-collar

---

19. The various conceptual approaches and the now substantial literature on commuting in the Soviet Union have been analyzed by Roland J. Fuchs and George J. Demko in two special issues of *Soviet Geography*, June 1978 and October 1983. Each issue contains an introductory article by the two compilers and a representative selection of Soviet writings.

workers is likely to be somewhat higher among commuters to a very
large city than in the case of medium-size cities. Early Soviet
assumptions that commuting to work in the central city was a
temporary phenomenon caused by a shortage of housing and was likely
to last only until the out-of-town resident managed to find a place
to live in the city have been modified. Several surveys have found
that one-third to one-half of commuters have been journeying to work
for more than five years.[20] It is not entirely clear whether such a
prolonged commuting way of life reflects residential preferences or
the inability to obtain the coveted city apartment. However, a
number of surveys have shown that many commuters like to live out of
town, preferably in a rural locality within easy transport access to
the city. These preferences, of course, are not unlike those of
many North Americans and Europeans.[21]

### The Role of the City in Soviet Society

It will have become apparent from the preceding discussion
that the city plays an extraordinarily important, though in some
ways strangely ambiguous role in Soviet society. The Communist
movement that gave rise to the Soviet Union had its historical base
of support in the industrial working class, and the focus of its
interests has been traditionally on cities as the locus of industry.
Under Soviet rule, the force-draft industrialization characteristic
of economic policy was inevitably centered on cities, which became
the symbols of political power, the organizing and mangerial levers
of the economy, purveyors of services, and magnets attracting the
population. Soviet investment policy, by giving priority to the
development of industry, especially heavy industry, channeled
available resources mainly into cities, which thus became the
primary beneficiaries of economic growth. The combination of
political power and economic priority focused on cities, especially
on the principal centers of administrative control, was largely
responsible for the lopsided growth of the capitals of oblasts and
other major civil divisions already discussed.

The other side of the coin in this preoccupation with
industrial and urban growth has been the relative neglect of the
countryside, including not only purely rural areas, but even smaller
towns and other so-called urban places. Although the ultimate
leveling of differences in urban and rural living levels has always
been a fundamental tenet of the Soviet ideology, its realization has

---

20 . *Soviet Geography* 24 (October 1983): 605.

21 . Ibid., p. 555.

been painfully slow and a wide gulf in urban and rural life styles persists.  One major factor in this lag of rural development has been the traditional emphasis on investment in industry as opposed to agriculture, although in recent years greater efforts appear to be under way to correct this imbalance.  The availability of greater employment opportunities, cultural and educational facilities, and a wider range of services in cities have drawn a steady stream of migrants from the countryside, mainly young people.  The result has been to leave a relatively less productive, aging segment of the nation's work force in agriculture and rural economic activity in general, while the more vibrant, younger elements of society are associated with industry and cities.  The effect has been to perpetuate the rural-urban gap in living standards.  The magnitude of tha gap is probably one of the most distinctive traits of Soviet society compared with the situation in the West.

Sophisticated Soviet visitors to Western Europe or to North America are generally prepared, even on the basis of their controlled information media, for some of the features of Western living that are in sharp contrast to life in the Soviet Union: the abundance, variety, and wide availability of consumer goods, the range of services, the mass use of private automobiles, the neater and more carefully tended appearance of the human landscape, and so forth.  But if there is one unexpected aspect of Western society for which Soviet visitors are rarely prepared either by their own experience or by the information available to them, it is the remarkable leveling of life styles, in terms of service and amenities, of Western urban and rural areas.  Such a leveling of differences remains an important goal of societal evolution in the Soviet Union, but to anyone familiar with present-day reality, it appears to be a distant goal, unlikely to be attained in the forseeable future.

The practical effect of this urban-rural dichotomy is particularly evident in the realm of services.  Rural areas look to urban places for the satisfaction of the most elementary needs, whether it is a matter of shopping for food, buying a new suit of clothes, or having a television set repaired.  The shopping malls that have become a virtually ubiquitous feature of the rural and small-town environment of North America seem unimaginable in the Soviet countryside.  Regional planners in the Soviet Union make no secret of the fact that they conceptualize a hierarchical spatial distribution of service establishments, with everyday needs being filled ideally at the local level; periodic needs being filled

ideally at the seat of the rayon, the minor civil division of county
rank; and more occasional needs at the next higher level, which
would be the capital of the oblast or equivalent major civil
division. It is not much of an exaggeration to suggest that,
according to this model, the apex of this pyramid of services would
be occupied by the city of Moscow, which thus becomes the shopping
center for the nation. Soviet sloganeering does little to
discourage this notion. Moscow is being presented as a model city,
with the ultimate in urban amenities, cultural offerings, and
shopping facilities. No wonder that Soviet urban planners are
trying to use every available administrative device to fend off
migrants to the Soviet capital. As it is, even the relatively
ampler shopping facilities of Moscow are strained to capacity, not
only by the needs of the city's eight million residents, but by
hundreds of thousands of out-of-town shoppers who are likely to
travel long distances on buying sprees.

Paradoxically, despite this concentration of political power
and economic activity in urban centers, the city as a governmental
institution does not carry much weight in the organization of Soviet
society. It is by far the dominant setting in the geographic
organization of space, but this outstanding role is not being
translated into institutional authority. The reasons for this
situation can be found in the system by which government investment
is channeled into industrial, hence urban, development and in the
company-town approach to urbanization. The established channels for
investment in the economy are the industrial and other sectoral
government ministries. Traditionally, they have been responsible
not only for building up production capacity within their particular
industries and other sectors of the economy, but also the housing
and services for the work force associated with these enterprises.
Relatively smaller funds are channeled through the Soviet budgetary
system to cities and other urban places as governmental
administrative institutions. As a result, the municipal authorities
in the Soviet Union, by and large, are beholden to the management of
those large industrial enterprises that form the economic base of
the city or urban settlement. Only in the largest and most highly
diversified urban centers such as Moscow and Leningrad, the capitals
of the Soviet Union's constituent republics, and other important
cities can the municipal authorities be regarded as wielding
substantial authority in their own right and being essentially the
masters of the city. In many of the lesser urban centers the
company-town approach prevails.

This approach to urbanization has had at least two adverse consequences, one in the realm of urban planning and the cost-effectiveness of operation of urban communities, the other in the realm of housing and services. In urban planning, the Soviet Union generally prides itself on its approach to urban design in the construction of new cities or in the expansion of older established centers, the drafting of urban master plans and other aspects of goal-oriented urban develoment. Many of these plans and designs ultimatlely come to fruition, but all too often reality does not conform to the original projections. Much of this discordance is undoubtedly due to the general problems of having plans faithfully implemented, even in a so-called planned society. But in the context of the urban process, the company-town approach is an important contributory factor.

Much urban development is handled by industrial ministries in the context of providing housing and services for the work force of their plants and factories, so that traditionally many urbanized communities in the Soviet Union have grown as virtually self-contained entities focused on the place of employment. If two or more industrial ministries become involved in constructing the economic base of an urban center, two or more virtually seperate communities may arise under the nominal institutional umbrella of the particular city. Also included under that umbrella might be the original rural settlement on whose territory the new industrial and urban development proceeds and, in many cases, a so-called private settlement of single-family dwellings built by residents averse to apartment living. The urban communities developed by industrial ministries in conjunction with the construciton of large new industrial enterprises are virtually run by the ministries, which provide housing, services, transportation, and even hotel accommodations. The city administration, with its limited budget, exercises only limited authority. As a result, many new cities, especially in areas of pioneering development as in Siberia, are far from the carefully laid-out, integrated organisms envisaged by urban planners and become simply collections of disparate communities under the nominal umbrella of a municipal administration.

One of the best known new cities in Siberia, the city of Bratsk, with a population of 230,000, consists of eight settlements strung through the taiga over a distance of 50 miles and separated by long stretches of virgin forest.[22] The first settlements, named

---

22 . Paul E. Lydolph, "A Visit to Bratsk," *Soviet Geography* (November 1977): 681-689.

Padun (for the Padun Gorge on the Angara River where the Bratsk Dam
was ultimately built) and Gidrostroitel (hydro builder), arose in
1955-56 at the hydroelectric station, which with an installed
capacity of 4,500 megawatts is now one of the largest in the world.
With the Bratsk dam project serving as the initial economic base of
the future city, the ministry of electric power became the first
institutional authority, and its construction agency, bearing the
Russian acronym Bratskgesstroi (for Bratsk hydroelectric station
construction), became the main building contractor. In 1959,
construction began on a third settlement near the dam as a permanent
residential area for workers employed at the power station, and it
was called Energetik (power worker). The power station, in turn,
provided the basis for the development of two basic industries in
Bratsk, a wood-processing complex and an aluminum plant. Under the
original urban designs, the workers of the timber complex were to be
housed in a central settlement, which was conceived as the "city
center," and the aluminum workers in a southwest settlement,
provisonally designated as Tsvetnogorsk (meaning "nonferrous
mountain"). However, the idea of a separate aluminum town was
subsequently dropped and the aluminum workers were to be housed in
the central settlement, which had to be redesigned and enlarged. A
smaller aluminum settlement, ultimately named Chekanovsky, remains
as testimony to the original urban design.

Another example of this industry-by-industry approach to urban
development may be found in the city of Ust-Ilimsk, farther
downstream on the Angara River, where another hydroelectric station,
with an installed capacity of 3,840 megawatts, has given rise to an
urban center of more than 90,000 people. The construction of the
dam and power plant was associated with the building of a town on
the left bank that is virtually under the control of the Ministry of
Electric Power, and the subsequent location of a huge woodpulp mill
on the right bank was accompanied by the development of another
major urban settlement on that side of the river, which is under the
control of the Ministry of Pulp and Paper Industry. Each ministry
provides housing and services on its side of the river, which the
entire urban formation nominally combined under an Ust-Ilimsk
municipal administration.

Although the provision of consumer goods and services in the
Soviet economy had traditionally taken second place to production of
the basic sinews of industrial power, the situation may have been
further exacerbated by the practice of channeling much of the
investment in social welfare through industrial ministries. It

would seem natural for government agencies concerned with economic development and intent on meeting assigned output plans to give priority to production. The Soviet press often reports that money allocated to a particular industrial project for investment in housing and services has not been fully spent, while the industrial portion of the project is reasonably on schedule. Similarly, official press accounts frequently note the relative lack of resources for urban development that are channeled through municipal administrations and call for changes in the system. It may be idle to speculate whether greater municipal responsibility for the welfare of citizens would result in more rapid improvement on the consumer side of the Soviet economic equation. But it is evident that the established ministerial system is so deeply rooted in the whole Soviet machinery of economic development as to make significant modification difficult.

### Conclusions

The purpose of this essay has been to provide a general overview of current urban issues in the Soviet Union based on the Soviet urban literature and the daily press, seven years of residence in Moscow, and frequent study trips to the Soviet Union. The observations here are, of course, highly generalized, and they focus on only some of the dominant themes in urban policy and practice. Even though it is fair to regard the Soviet Union as an urbanized society, it is also important to be aware of the context.

One of the most distinctive aspects of the urban process in the Soviet Union is probably its rigid linkage with the process of industrial development. This linkage is evident at many levels, from the administrative definition and the national hierarchical structure of urban places to the mechanism by which investment resources for urban development are channeled through industrial ministries rather than municipal administrations. As already noted, there are, of course, many exceptions to this pattern. Moscow, as the national capital, and many of the larger, multifunctional cities of the Soviet Union display institutional authority of their own. But, by and large, it is fair to say that cities and lesser urban places are dependent on the industrial ministries that control the economic base of these urban entities.

The other basic point worth stressing about Soviet urbanism is the preoccupation with the design and planning of urban centers as such and as part of a national system of settlement. An attempt has been made here to show that urban master plans calling for integrated physical layouts and municipal organization often come into conflict with the practical aspects of urban development as masterminded by industrial planners. This is particularly true of some of the smaller cities without independent resources that are dependent on the industrial ministries responsible for building up the economic base of these urban centers. As for the role of cities in a national system of settlement, there the emphasis thus far has been on the conceptual aspects rather than on practical implementation of a concerted policy. A huge literature has been built up in the Soviet Union, with different schools of thought vying for attention. The two basic approaches that have emerged are the urban agglomeration school, which views large cities as the cores for ever expanding urbanized areas held together by journeys to work and other interurban linkages, and the the unified settlement school, which looks to greater integration of urban and rural areas within regional systems as a way to eliminate the persisting gap between living levels in town and countryside.

It should be emphasized, however, that whatever approach may ultimately prevail will be relevant mainly in the context of regional settlement patterns focused on particular large cities. Regardless of whether settlement around large cities follows the agglomerative or the integrative urban-rural trend, the outlines of the national system are likely to conform to the emerging concept of the basic framework of national settlement. This concept views large cities of 100,000 people or more as the basic nodes and transport corridors as the interconnecting pathways of a structural framework not only for a national system of settlement, but for the spatial organization of the entire Soviet economy. Large cities, which have long been viewed by Soviet planners and ideologues with a certain amount of ambiguity, would thus be given a fitting role in the future evolution of Soviet society.

# Chapter VII

# THE TRANSFORMATION OF THE URBAN LANDSCAPE IN SOUTHEASTERN EUROPE

George W. Hoffman

The five countries of Southeast Europe considered in this
essay--Albania, Bulgaria, Greece, Romania and, Yugoslavia--are
characterized by the great diversity expressed in their physical,
economic, and cultural make-up. These countries do not comprise a
demographically homogeneous region, and all their social forces and
institutions have undergone numerous transformations throughout
history. The crossroad position of the peninsula accounts largely
for this diversity since the region witnessed the movements and
conquests of many peoples. Their marks are visible everywhere: in
the form of pagan temples; pre-christian tombstones; old weathered
coins; Thracian tumuli; Roman walls, roads, baths, and forums;
Byzantine fortress walls, churches, and early frescoes; medieval
Bulgarian and Serbian castles; Turkish mosques; and Austrian baroque
architecture. The urban landscape was repeatedly molded as much by
cultural influences from neighboring regions as by their indigenous
inhabitants. This interaction resulted in regional differentiation
which in turn greatly influenced the transformation of the
settlement pattern throughout the history of southeastern Europe.
All these cultural influences have complicated relationships with
neighboring countries as well as with the various regions of the
later national states. Centuries of invasion and domination by many
powers (Greeks, Romans, Turks, Venetians, Austrians, Germans,
French, British, and Russians) have left a deep imprint on the
developments of the various regions, and nowhere is this more
visible than in the settlement pattern of the present-day urban
landscape.[1]

---

1. A large international literature exists on the topic of this essay.
Only publications specifically referred to in this essay are footnoted. In
addition, the author has touched on various aspects of the topic in earlier
writings, as follows: *The Balkans in Transition* (Princeton, N.J.: D. van
Nostrand, 1963); "Transformation of Rural Settlement in Bulgaria," *Geographical
Review* 54 (January 1964): 45-64; "The Problem of the Underdeveloped Regions in
Southeast Europe: A Comparative Analysis of Romania, Yugoslavia and Greece,"
*Annals of the Association of American Geographers* 57 (December 1967): 637-66;
"Thessaloniki: The Impact of a Changing Hinterland," *East European Quarterly* 2
(March 1968): 1-27; "Regional Development Processes in Southeast Europe: A

It seems clear that the reasons for the transformation of Southeast European cities and ultimately the growth of urban concentrations there is closely related to numerous negative and positive foreign influences over long periods of time, which produced urban processes that are considered transitional within the general European context. The long development of these cities before the birth of the modern national states in the nineteenth century brought about major differences in their ethnic composition from those of West and North-Central Europe (Poland, Czechoslovakia, and Hungary). Problems of assimilation of a largely foreign, non-traditional population, a mixture of nationalities and religions, with their emphasis on mobility, raised numerous social and institutional problems. The increased urbanization since the latter part of the nineteenth century and the expansion of towns and cities specifically have been tempered by regional differences in culture, ethnicity, social structure, and the values and perceptions of the largely rural population. The movement of people from rural to urban areas and especially from underdeveloped, peripheral regions and mountainous refuges to the fertile plains since the establishment of the national states continued through the interwar period and, in ever increasing numbers, after World War II. The varied migration streams have been strongly related to employment which in turn depends on the various locational factors of the postwar industrialization drive in Southeast Europe.

The following discussions cannot treat the origin and transformation of the urban landscape of Southeast Europe in depth. Rather the study aims at a broad-based, comparative analysis to present a series of vignettes of the most important forces which contributed to the rural-urban settlement pattern within the historical framework of socio-economic and institutional developments in the present five countries of Southeast Europe. At the same time, the goals and instruments used in accomplishing this urban transformation, as well as the relationship between the

Comparative Analysis of Bulgaria and Greece," in *Eastern Europe: Essays in Geographical Problems,* ed. George W. Hoffman (London: Methuen, 1971): 431-82; "Migration and Social Change," *Problems of Communism* (November-December 1973) pp. 16-31; *Regional Development Strategy in Southeast Europe: A Comparative Analysis of Albania, Bulgaria, Greece, Romania and Yugoslavia,* Praeger Special Studies in International Economics and Development (New York: Praeger Publishers, 1974); "The Impact of Regional Development Policy on Population Distribution in Yugoslavia and Bulgaria," (with Ronald L. Hatchett) in *Population and Migration Trends in Eastern Europe,* ed. H.L. Kostanick (Boulder, Co: Westview Press, 1977) pp. 99-123; "The Evolution of the Ethnographic Map of Yugoslavia," in *An Historical Geography of the Balkans,* ed. Francis W. Carter (London: Academic Press, 1977) pp. 437-99; "Variations in Center-Periphery Relations in Southeast Europe," in *Centre and Periphery: Spatial Variations in Politics,* ed. Jean Gottmann (Beverly Hills, Ca.: Sage Publications, 1980) pp. 111-34; and *A Geography of Europe: Problems and Prospects,* 5th edition, ed. George W. Hoffman (New York; Wiley, 1983), pp. 446-508.

villages, small and medium-sized towns, and capital cities, will be scrutinized.

## Urban Developments in Southeast Europe before the Emergence of National States in the Nineteenth Century

The functions and historical development of the earliest cities in Southeast Europe have left an important impact on the later urban pattern of the peninsula. Inasmuch as the agricultural population has dominated the cultural landscape of Southeast Europe throughout history, it was mostly the conquerors who built cities and fortresses. The Romans greatly expanded the concept and spread of the city, more widely than the Greeks, whose cities were mainly located along the coasts of the Aegean, Adriatic, and Black Seas. A network of Roman roads and settlements serving the military, administrative, and cultural needs (customs and speech) of the empire extended to the Rhine and Danube rivers, to northern England in the west and Transylvania in the east. Newly founded cities and trading stations in strategic locations were spread all over Southeast Europe, a number of them to play long and important roles: Thessaloniki, signficant in the expansion of the Roman empire to the east and north to the Danube, Serdica (Sofia), Naisus (Niš), Trimontium (Plovdiv), and Dyrrachium (Durrës), to mention only a few. Some of the Roman settlements, several sources indicate, were probably already in use in the pre-Roman period. Extensive historical research since the nineteenth century has provided a fairly reliable picture of the extent and character of Roman settlements, at least for the region south of the Danube.[2]

City founding in Southeast Europe can be accounted for by seven different historical influences.[3] First, the Roman, respectively Greek, Venetian Mediterranean type is concentrated along the Dalmatian-Albanian coast. Roman foundations serving military and administrative purposes stretch throughout the peninsula and in the Roman province of Dacia covering the western part of today's Transylvania. Second, Central European--German,

---

2. Recent studies, specifically by geographers include Norman J.G. Pounds, "The Urbanization of the Classical World," *Annals of the Association of American Geographers* 59 (1969): 135-57, and "The Urbanization of East-Central and Southeast Europe: An Historical Perspective," in *Eastern Europe: Essays in Geographical Problems,* ed. George W. Hoffman (London: Methuen, 1971) pp. 45-81. An important contribution has been made by Gavro Skiranić, "Roman Roads and Settlements in the Balkans," in *An Historical Geography of the Balkans,* ed. Francis W. Carter (London: Academic Press, 1977) pp. 115-145. Numerous works have also been published analyzing Latin inscriptions in Pannonia and the Balkans.

3. Josef Matl, "Entwicklung der städtischen Gesellschaft auf dem Balkan," in *Die wirtschaftliche und soziale Entwicklung Südosteuropas im 19. und 20. Jahrhundert, Südosteuropa-Jahrbuch* 9 (Munich, 1969): 108-09; also Jovan Cvijić, *Balkansko poluostrvo i juznoslovenske zemlje* [The Balkan peninsula and the south Slavic countries] (Zagreb, 1922), especially p. 283; and Walter Hildebrandt, "Die Stadt in Südosteuropa," *Leipziger Vierteljahrschrift für Südosteuropa* 3(1939): 153-97.

Austrian, and Magyar--influence spread via the Danube and Sava rivers from Ljubljana through Zagreb, Osijek to Novi Sad into today's Yugoslav autonomous province of the Vojvodina and the Banat of Romania in an area largely unaffected by the Turkish conqueror. Third, the so-called Balkan type of Byzantine-Oriental influence, later modified by Ottoman-Turkish characteristics, left its mark in Turkish administrative and military centers in Bosnia, Macedonia, Albania, and Bulgaria. Fourth, the Black Sea trade and shipping centers, for example, Varna in Bulgaria and--after the mid-19th century--Constanta (Romania) and Burgas (Bulgaria), show influences from Genoa and Venice. Recent archeological work in Constanta found food remnants of Greek traders. Fifth, the cities of the Carpathian basin enjoyed self-determination until they became part of Hungary (and since 1918 part of Romania). Sixth, the historic regions of Moldavia and Wallachia are of transitional type and received their urban characteristics from eastern European-Russian-Byzantine-Turkish and Central European influences (Austrian-Hungarian). Finally, a few markets and trading settlements, mostly semi-urban provincial cities, the so-called "palanka" in the Serbian region of the Šumadija, the Bulgarian Korpivstica and Gabrovo, had relatively few oriental influences, and their mainly-Slavic settlers were characterized by their patriarchal living customs. In addition, a number of settlements were located on the southern slopes of the Balkan and the foothills of the Rhodope Mountains, some of which were to become important trading cities once the lowlands were secure enough for the indigenous inhabitants to leave the protection of the mountainous refuge.

The settlements in Roman Southeast Europe and their urban life generally reached a climax in the second century and then stagnated during the last years of the western empire and on into the classical and medieval periods, though some cities were revived between the eighth and fourteenth centuries. Historically, the process of urbanization progressed very slowly and unevenly throughout Southeast Europe, with periods of growth followed by stagnation and decline. Urban historians and geographers are in general agreement that the decline between the classical and medieval periods had a catastrophic effect which was mirrored in a general population decline in this region. Varied cartographic and documentary evidence suggests that some older cities revived and a few new towns were established between the eighth and the middle of the fourteenth centuries but that the urban pattern generally declined again during the nearly 500 years of Turkish occupation.

Few new towns were established before the development of the modern industrial and commercial city. The Turkish conqueror, however, while destroying many urban settlements, did enlarge a few settlements that had their origin in the pre-Turkish period, for example, Skopjed, Novi Pazar, and others, which were mainly provincial towns serving their military and administrative needs. The development of Sarajevo in 1462 with the establishment residence (the "saray") is the best example. It became one of the important Turkish cities of Southeast Europe. By the middle of the seventeenth century, the city had a population of 50,000, but with the decline of Turkish power, the city's importance also waned.[4] Bucharest exemplifies the enlargement of an older town. It became the capital of Wallachia in 1659 and rapidly expanded. By the mid-eighteenth century, the city was described by several visitors as attractive and included about 10,000 houses. One hundred years later, it had 120,000 people (figure 7.1). Ploeşti, located on the important routes from Bucharest to Transylvania and Moldavia, is another good example of a growing trading town. Galati and Brăila were important Romanian ports for trade with Turkey and the Mediterranean early in the eighteenth century. Both ports increased in importance after the Turkish monopoly of foreign trade with Romania was abolished and Turkey agreed not to hinder Danubian traffic in 1815. This in turn permitted the shipment of goods from Austria to various Danubian ports, thereby reducing the time for transporting goods, but at the same time diminishing the role of several cities in the interior which had long served as trans-shipment points on the caravan routes. The grain trade in Brăila and other Danubian ports increased dramatically during the first part of the nineteenth century.

Other cities in Southeast Europe grew in population during the Turkish period due to their increased importance as trading centers or military outposts. Older cities, not recent growth centers, included Belgrade, Sofia, Plovdiv, Split, and especially the port of Thessaloniki. On the other hand, a number of specialized mining towns established during the late middle ages in the southern part of Serbia, using foreign miners, mainly Germans, lost their prosperity and drastically declined or even disappeared in the following century. The foreign miners mostly returned to their homelands.[5]

---

4. This information is summarized from the "comments" by Ian M. Matley to a paper by Pounds, "The Urbanization of East-Central and Southeast Europe," p. 80.

5. Oliver Davies, "Ancient Mining in the Central Balkans," *Revue Internationale des Études Balkaniques* 3 (1937-1938): 404-18; Arno Mehlan, "über

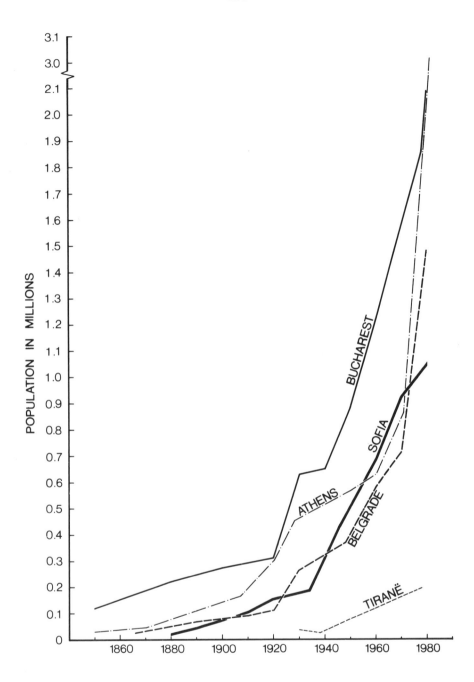

Figure 7.1. Population growth of capital cities in Southeast Europe

Many settlements in Southeast Europe, especially the larger
ones, distinguished themselves from those in Western Europe until
the late nineteenth century by their large and ethno-religiously
diverse foreign populations, that is of Greeks, Armenians, Vlachs,
Turks, Jews, Tartars in the inner parts of the peninsula, Germans
and Hungarians in the Danube and Sava region, and Italians along the
Dalmatian coast. Most of these foreign people had their own quarter
in such cities and many of the towns had only a small indigenous
population. Most of these foreign people were engaged in handicraft
and trade, the latter mainly in foreign trade, serving not only the
Turkish armies and their leaders, but also local needs.

Only warfare and the paralyzing plague retarded trade during
the later part of the Turkish occupation. Greeks, Albanians, and
Vlachs served as forwarding agents for Macedonia, Thessaly, and
Epirus towns; Thracian merchants, Armenians from Bulgaria, and later
Serbian pig merchants of the Šumadija and agents from Bosnia set up
business in the border towns of the Turkish empire, as well as in
the great trading towns of Central and Western Europe. Stoianovich
credits these small groups of Balkan merchants, mostly Orthodox,
with serving as the "human catalyst which joined the Balkan peoples
to Europe, both by their commerce and ideas" and provided their
cities of Southeast Europe with important business and contacts
beyond the Turkish empire.[6]

Increased trade with the West brought about an increased
agrarian colonization and the establishment of numerous
communications by the early eighteenth century. Many settlements in
the central Danubian plain, after the Ottomans were forced to
retreat south of the Danube, brought settlers from all over Europe
with their new techniques and new crops, such as potatoes and
tobacco. Houses duplicated the architecture of many parts of
Western Europe and the Austrian empire, and even today the
settlements in the southern and southwestern part of the Pannonian
plains (Vojvodina and Banat) are clearly distinguishable from those
of the neighboring regions. These towns are characterized by their
baroque churches and the centrally located town squares surrounded
by public buildings. These squares served as parade grounds for the
Austrian troops. The plains of eastern Wallachia and north of the

---

die Bedeutung der mittelalterlichen Bergbaukolonien für die slawischen
Balkanvölker," *Revue Internationale des Études Balkaniques* 3 (1937-38): 387-404;
and Milenko S. Filipović, "Das Erbe der mittelalterlichen Bergleute in den
südslawischen Ländern," *Südost Forschungen,* 22 (1963): 192-233.

6. Traian Stoianovich, "The Conquering Balkan Orthodox Merchant," *Journal
of Economic History* 20 (June 1960): 282; and a more general study on this same
topic, *A Study in Balkan Civilization* (New York: Knopf, 1967).

lower Danube (Moldavia) and adjacent to the Ottoman frontier, as
well as important plains of the interior of the peninsula, were
still largely uninhabited during the eighteenth century. The
Austrian settlements of the central Danubian plains were important
in part to provide agricultural supplies for their armies.
Colonization was encouraged and people from Wallachia, Serbia, and
the Transylvanian mountains provided a substantial proportion,
having migrated in part to avoid heavy taxation and the oppressive
rule of the Phanariot Romanian regimes.[7]

The development of urban centers which could become
politically powerful, including focal points for national
integration, was impossible in Turkish occupied territory, owing in
no small measure to the large foreign elements. The situation in
the urban centers of the Austrian and Hungarian dominated lands was
not very different.[8] While their administration was more efficient,
the leadership was securely in Austrian and Hungarian hands. The
objective of the newly built infrastructure in the peninsula was
clearly oriented toward the exploitation of the rich raw materials
and increasingly an important agrarian base that served the
commercial and political power centers outside the Turkish or
Austria-Hungarian occupied areas. Local centers in Turkish occupied
territory or parts of the Austrian territory such as Zagreb,
Karlovac, Split, and Novi Sad were either important command
headquarters along the military border or market towns serving a
small hinterland.[9] But the political and economic power located in
these centers left the backward peripheral regions largely
undisturbed.

In the period before the rise of national states, the
long-distance trade routes connecting regional centers were crucial
to the more intraregional flow of goods as well. They were also
needed for the military traffic of various local rulers and
conquerors throughout history and ultimately for the integration of
the individual regions and states. The efforts by those in control
of all or parts of the peninsula--Romans, Turks, Austrians--were

---

7. The Phanariotes, an administrative aristocracy of Greek laymen within
the Ottoman empire, were used by the Turks for the performance of duties for which
the conquerors had neither liking nor aptitude. They inhabited that quarter of
Constantinople (Istanbul) assigned to the patriarch known as Phanar and rose
rapidly to a position of great responsibility. Between 1711 and 1821, Moldavia
and Wallachia were ruled by a rapid succession of Greek bureaucrats, the
Phanariotes.

8. Francis W. Carter wrote an analysis, "Historical Geographies on the
Balkans," in his "Introduction to the Balkan Scene," in *An Historical Geography of
the Balkans,* ed. Francis W. Carter (London: Academic Press, 1977) pp. 10-14.

9. The military border separated the Ottoman from the Austrian empire for
several centuries and was located in the northwestern and northern parts of
today's Yugoslavia.

always directed toward the priority of a well-developed transport and communication network. The towns, mostly alien enclaves, served nevertheless as centers of a market economy at various periods of development and proved essential in forming a pre-industrial urban hierarchy.[10]

### Economic Development and the Growth of Cities

With the decline of the Ottoman empire in the later part of the eighteenth century, the struggle for national liberation became increasingly important. While the traditional urban centers slowly gained in importance, their ties with the largely primitive, peripheral, but densely settled regions exisitng in mutual isolation scarcely improved. The growing importance of a few cities was closely related to the opening of the Ottoman empire to foreign influences and subsequent establishment of the national states of Romania, Greece, Serbia, and Bulgaria during the nineteenth century. Many of the urban problems of the twentieth century must be related to the period of nation-building in the preceding century and were mostly a legacy of the Ottoman empire. This legacy of insuperable backwardness both in urbanized and rural regions among the poverty-stricken indigenous population--especially the peasantry, but also the many ethnic and religious groups living in the few cities--contributed to the great spatial differences and internal political problems in several of the present-day countries of Southeast Europe.

Ottoman Southeast Europe had only a few large inhabited places, besides the former regional capitals, which could be called cities. Examples include Plovdiv and Varna in Bulgaria, Iasi, and Bucharest, the capital of Romania, by the end of the eighteenth and the beginning of the nineteenth centuries. According to John Lampe other cities were "still located in the borderlands of the Hapsburg or Ottoman empires." These were the cities of Zagreb in Croatia, Sarajevo in Bosnia, Trieste, which served as the key Adriatic port for the Austrian-Hungary monarchy, and Cluj in Transylvania. The important Aegean port of Thessaloniki did not become part of Greece until the Balkan wars of 1912-13. Only since the close of the nineteenth century have the cities of Southeast Europe undergone rapid change, not only in population size, but also in the architecture and layout of the city centers, marking the basic transition from Ottoman to European appearance.[11]

---

10. Francis W. Carter, "Urban Development in the Western Balkan 1200-1800," in *An Historical Geography of the Balkans,* pp. 187 and 148-195.

11. John R. Lampe, "Urban History in Southeastern Europe: Recent Research

Insofar as cities are part of the total socio-economic development of a region, the political and economic change in Southeast Europe over the last two centuries from stock breeding and tribal association to agriculture, urban services, and industrial occupations connotes a very basic change in the social structure and functions of the population. This has of course transformed urban life, affecting particularly the ethno-religious structure of cities, while at the same time drawing closer the bond between city and countryside.

The appearance of the various national states also affected the spatial relations of the traditional peripheral regions, sometimes referred to as the "mountain heartland." This heartland assumed considerable importance in specific historical periods in contrast to the sparsely populated fertile plains and river valleys settled more by foreigners, often brought into the region for special purposes, like military defense and trading. The heartland, during certain periods, became a zone of security, an area of retreat, and a refuge for the indigenous population fleeing invading armies.[12] The important role of the indigenous population in the mountainous heartland after the creation of independent states and their subsequent movement to the plains meant a move to a different and usually better life for people traditionally oriented to livestock and innured to permanent insecurity. Those people, such as the Vlachs, ancestors of today's Romanians, Greeks and Vlachs in the highlands of Thessaly, Epirus, and Macedonia, the Bulgars in the mountains surrounding the fertile Maritsa basin, the Serbs in today's Yugoslavia, and the Albanians, to mention only a few, not only adopted arable farming but replaced the foreign population departing the few existing cities with the defeated conquerors. They also moved into the small regional centers, from which they often directed and participated in the struggle for liberation. All this was part of a wider complex process whose outline and impact did not reach its full expression until the second half of the twentieth century. The results have included rapid rural depopulation, massive rural-to-urban migration, often uncontrollable urban growth, extensive commutation, seasonal and long-term

on the Capital Cities," *Maryland Historian* 11 (fall 1980): 25. A most useful publication by Lampe and Marvin R. Jackson is the recently published *Balkan Economic History, 1550-1950: From Imperial Borderlands to Developing Nations,* Joint Committee on Eastern Europe Publication Series no. 10 (Bloomington, Ind. : Indiana University Press, 1982); see also *Die Stadt in Südosteuropa. Struktur und Geschichte,* ed. Klaus-Detlev Grothusen, *Südosteuropa-Jahrbuch* 8 which contains a number of contributions pertinent to the topics discussed in this paper.

12. Josip Roglić, "Die Gebirge als die Wiege des geschichtlichen Geschehens in Südosteuropa," *Colloquium Geographicum* 12 (1970): 225-39.

migrations to urban centers, and both short-term and permanent migration abroad. It is obvious, therefore, that geography and history have interacted in Southeast Europe, bringing about a complex cultural landscape with great regional differences and with a "heterogeneous grouping of cultural variables and a political system that has been in constant flux as a result of external pressures and internal instability."[13]

The extension of urban values and increased job opportunities was a slow process and tied closely to the spread of industrialization. The creation of national capitals for the newly organized states of Serbia, Bulgaria, Romania, and after World War I Yugoslavia, the growing importance of Athens in an enlarged Greece after the Balkan wars, and the new national state of Albania with its capital of Triane, made capital cities particularly strong foci of attraction. The increasingly important role of major cities organized or enlarged during the middle ages, or those whose origin lay in antiquity as economic and government centers, also helped widen the disparities between the more rapidly growing capital cities, the secondary growth centers (regional capitals), and the many smaller towns in peripheral areas.

A few urban concentrations where industrialization was beginning showed some dynamic advances. They were the potential growth poles and centers, and it was hoped that they would lead to "spread" effects of modern economic development. Mihailović, using the example of Yugoslavia, pointed out that polarization is to be expected at a low level of development simply because the volume of manufacturing is not great enough to spread over the whole territory.[14] Industry is of necessity concentrated in regions where infrastructure, a skilled labor force, and a market exist. There are few such areas in the underdeveloped countries of Southeast Europe, and for this reason a certain amount of polarization in regional development and the growth of medium-sized and smaller cities is inevitable. The original urban concentrations proved early to be zones of gravitation for people from the backward mountainous regions, but the "spread" effect had to await events after World War II. Still, these developments often served to accentuate regional differences instead of ameliorating them. The traditional countryside was little affected by industrialization

---

13. Jack C. Fisher, *Yugoslavia: A Multinational State* (San Francisco: Chandler Publishing, 1966) p. 19.

14. Among the best discussions is Kosta Mihailovic, *Regional Development: Experiences and Prospects in Eastern Europe* (Paris: Mouton, for the United Nations Research Institute for Social Development, 1972).

before World War II and often not until the 1960s. The few
medium-sized urban cities were hardly tied together with the various
regions in the individual countries and what infrastructure there
existed was in its infancy before World War II. Many regions in
1940 were still without a unified transport network, making
consistent internal migration a haphazard venture. Still,
industrialization slowly expanded, especially in the more important
towns of certain agricultural regions, for example, those of
Slavonia, and Vojvodina of Yugoslavia, the Banat of Romania, and the
Maritza Valley of Bulgaria, as it did also in the larger cities and
national capitals.

### The Role of the Capital Cities

From the late nineteenth century onward the cities that became
the new national capitals in Southeast Europe experienced, in John
Lampe's phrase, a "demographic explosion," and came to exercise
special roles in the region's urban system. Several evolved into
primate cities, and even before World War I capital city populations
often multiplied four or six-fold in three to four decades. This
increase was further accelerated in the inter-war period as new
territory was acquired, new manufacturing industries located, and
the migration from underdeveloped and often peripheral regions to
the capitals greatly increased (figure 7.1). Sofia grew from 21,000
in 1880 to over one million in 1980, Bucharest from 120,000 in 1850
to over two million in 1980, Belgrade from 26,000 in 1866 to
1,470,000 in 1981, and Athens from 31,000 in 1850 to over three
million in 1981. Even Tiranë, the capital of Albania, which became
independent only after World War I, increased from 31,000 in 1930
(the first population census) to nearly 200,000 by 1979. Obviously,
the industrial growth and the increasing centralized government
functions were the main motors behind this rapid expansion.
Increased administrative centralism, whether in Athens (where it
reflects an endemic feature of Greek society, according to a study
by Evan Vlachos) or in the capitals of the other socialist
countries, with the exception of decentralized and self-managed
Yugoslavia, has a direct bearing on the capital's population size.
Its consequences, however, reach all the way down the national urban
hierarchies. These capital cities also play an important role in
the percentage their population comprises of the national population
(table 7.1). Athens, followed by Sofia, Tiranë and Bucharest, have
the largest percentage of their respective country's population,
with Athens far in the lead. Several of the socialist countries in

TABLE 7.1

CAPITAL CITY POPULATION AS A PERCENTAGE OF
NATIONAL POPULATION IN SOUTHEAST EUROPE

|  | Population at last census ('000s) | City (agglomeration) population ('000s) | Percent |
|---|---|---|---|
| Athens (Greece)[α] | 9,706 | 3,016 | 31.1 |
| Belgrade (Yugoslavia)[α] | 22,428 | 1,470 | 6.6 |
| Bucharest (Romania)[β] | 22,280 | 2,090 | 9.0 |
| Sofia (Bulgaria)[α] | 8,889 | 1,056 | 12.0 |
| Tiranë (Albania)[C] | 2,590 | 272 | 10.0 |
| Total Country Population | 65,893 |  |  |
| Total Population of Capitals |  | 7,904 | 12.0 |

SOURCE: National statistical yearbooks

$\alpha$ = 1981; $\beta$ = 1980; c = 1979.

the post-World War II period have tried by various measures to
restrict the movement into the capital city, but these on the whole
have not been particularly successful.  Restrictive measures have
included officially designated areas with "development potential,"
mandatory residence permits in Bulgaria, the relocation of industry
in the provinces from their concentration in the primate cities,
limiting urban sprawl by encircling the city with a 'green belt,'
and deliberately inadequate housing programs.  Even so, industrial
output in the various capitals has run from 30 to 60 percent of the
country's output.  Belgrade and Tiranë represent exceptions.
Yugoslavia, with its historical capitals of Belgrade, which is both
the national and republican capital (Serbia), and Zagreb, the
capital of Croatia, has no primate city.  Its unusual position is
due to its unique historical circumstances.  An index of primacy
among Southeast European countries over the period 1960-1970 based
on the ratio of the largest city in the country to the combined
population of the next three largest cities shows that Greece ranked
3.4, Romania 2.3, Bulgaria 1.7, Albania 1.1, and Yugoslavia 0.6.[15]
The primacy indexes over time indicate that the relative population
of these largest cities has declined.  Controlling the urban
networks in Southeast Europe in their rank-size aspects has not
always been successful, and many problems have arisen as a result of
specific regulations.  These include a slower rate of economic
development, population changes from primate cities to their suburbs
and satellite towns, undesirable developments in those cities with
growth limits such as a concentration of older people, and a decline
of small and medium-sized towns and small rural villages.[16]

### Postwar Urbanization

The rapid changes in economic activity and industrialization
resulted in increased population in the larger cities, a growing
number of medium-sized towns, and a slow but steady increase in the
total urban population (figure 7.2).  Overall urbanization in the
four socialist countries increased from 8.9 to 23.7 million.
Medium-sized towns, those between 100,000 and one million, grew
between 1940 and the late 1970s from 2 to 9 in Yugoslavia, 2 to 7 in
Bulgaria, and 3 to 18 in Romania, at the same time the urban

15. Evan Vlachos, "A Comparative Analysis of Urbanization in the Balkans,"
paper presented at the Annual Meeting of the American Association For the
Advancement of Science, March 1971, p. 20; also Roland J. Fuchs and George J.
Demko, "Spatial Population Policies in the Socialist Countries of Eastern Europe,"
*Social Science Quarterly* 58 (June 1977): 60-73; and Dean Rugg, *Spatial Foundations
of Urbanism* (Dubuque: Brown, 1978) pp. 310-12.

16. Roland J. Fuchs, "The Transformation of East European Cities," in
*Urban-Rural Transformation,* IREX Occasional Papers, May 10-13, 1979 p. 18.

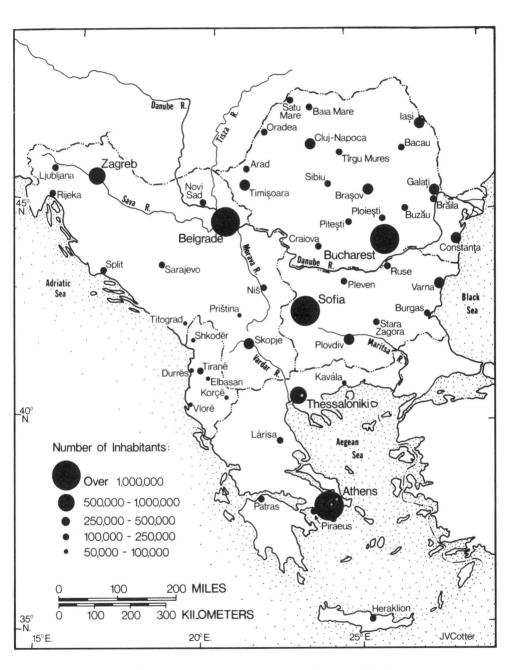

Figure 7.2. The urban pattern in Southeast Europe, 1980-81

population represented in these medium-sized towns increased from
21.8 to 35.5 percent in Yugoslavia, 28.8 to 40.2 percent in
Bulgaria, and 34.5 to 44.0 percent in Romania. Of Greece's
population in 1971 53 percent lived in places of over 10,000 and
35.1 percent in places of less than 2,000. Five cities now have
populations of over 100,000. Comparable figures cannot be given for
the other countries because of differing interpretations of the
terms urbanization, communes, cities, towns, and villages, making
comparison impossible. Latest country-wide urban percentages are 39
percent for Yugoslavia (1971), 62 percent for Bulgaria (1980
estimate), 35 percent for Albania (1970), and 49 percent for Romania
(1980), but these figures conceal wide differences between
individual regions in each country.

The basic pattern of post-war urbanization shows many
similarities among the five countries due to the rural-urban
migration and the growth of villages into towns. It is perhaps
least developed in Albania, but the size of the country influences
this development. Rapid changes in society and economy since World
War II have greatly affected rural areas, with their traditional
village structure and values based on close family ties. The
large-scale migration of younger people from the backward periphery
(the mountainous heartland in Yugoslavia) to the rapidly growing,
more viable regional centers and metropolises, and the large-scale
emigration from Yugoslavia[17] to Western Europe, have had a lasting
impact on agrarian structure and traditions of the countryside, but
especially in the peripheral lands.

Fuchs and Demko in a recent study identifying the spatial
population problems of the contemporary socialist economies of
Northeast Europe (including Hungary) group them under two headings
which demonstrate the relation between population and economic
development. Problems arise, first, from regional disparities in
rates of population and economic growth, levels of economic
development, manpower, and welfare. Secondly, there are problems
stemming from imbalanced urban networks including excessive urban
population and industrial concentrations, disproportions in the
rank-size distribution, and a lack of spatial integration. As these
writers note, "These two sets of problems are not mutually exclusive
but are interrelated through migration, transport networks,
investment allocation decisions, and other national-level

---

17. Ivo Baucíc, "Some Economic Consequences of Yugoslav External
Migrations," in *Demographic Developments in Eastern Europe,* ed. Leszek A. Kosinski
(New York: Praeger Publishers, 1974), pp. 266-283.

processes."[18]

The rapid urbanization brought about by industrialization resulted in a large-scale migration from the backward peripheral areas in all the countries of Southeast Europe. These movements, especially into capitals, but also into secondary growth centers, created in many areas the necessary conditions for an accelerated discrepancy between center and periphery. This was futher encouraged by the rapid expansion of communications, thus bringing the outlying parts of a national territory within easy reach of the growth centers. Obviously, this is simpler in some of the smaller countries with a developed infrastructure, such as Bulgaria, than in Romania or even Yugoslavia, with their long individual histories of various multiethnic, backward regions. In addition, the great economic disparities between these regions under the long Turkish and Austria-Hungarian control--roughly a north-south division--even today underlie considerable political and economic unrest.

Finally, it should also be pointed out that in recent years the dichotomy between developed and underdeveloped zones was further modified by the increased industrial dispersion into the growing centers of the underdeveloped regions, especially of labor-intensive and foot-loose industries. Considerable urban growth was thus diverted to small and intermediate-sized cities. This deliberate policy of bringing industries to many underdeveloped regions has obviated to a large degree the need for long distance travel of the working population; still, serious socio-economic problems exist for those regularly commuting to work. Initially, industrial growth enterprises absorbed surplus labor directly from agriculture and served as centers of economic growth which created additional employment opportunities. In Yugoslavia, for example, growth in the officially designated underdeveloped areas generally exceeds the national rate. In most countries this resulted in a drastic reduction of migrant labor and a corresponding increase in commuting. Its impact on a growing proportion of the rural labor force, which thus became engaged in non-agricultural activities, the so-called "peasant workers," has been dramatic.[19]

Since World War II, few regions in Europe have experienced such far-reaching structural changes in their urban-rural relationships as the five countries of Southeast Europe. Migration from rural to urban areas, or outside the immediate region and even

---

18 . Fuchs and Demko, "Spatial Population Policies," p. 62.

19 . William C. Lockwood, "The Peasant-Worker in Yugoslavia," in *The Social Structure of Eastern Europe,* ed. Bernard Lewis Faber (New York: Praeger Publishers, 1974), pp. 266-83.

to foreign countries, while already existing in earlier times, was greatly accelerated in the present century, with increased emphasis on industrialization. This became the prime vector of change in the spatial distribution of economic activities, particularly after World War II. Planners thus hoped to absorb the sizable rural surplus labor in an increasing number of new industries and provide a rapidly growing number of secondary and tertiary employment opportunities. According to the new leaders of the socialist countries, socialist development provided an opportunity by the use of planned investments to influence the location of new industries, thus contributing to a wider regional distribution and spread of economic activities, especially in the underdeveloped, peripheral regions of individual countries.

The building of heavy industries received top priority. Five new iron and steel works were built in different regions of Yugoslavia alone. As additional industries were located in underdeveloped regions, the "spread" effect began to have a variable influence on the backwards regions, particularly in medium-sized and smaller towns and villages. The spread of manufacturing has now stimulated new dispersion among smaller towns of consumer and service concentrations. Examples abound in Slovenia, the northeastern part of Bosnia and Hercegovina, Slavonia (between the Sava and Drava rivers), the region south of Belgrade to Niš, the Danubian plateau region and the Maritsa Basin and Black Sea littoral of Bulgaria, Transylvania, and western Wallachia, with a number of older industrial concentrations such as Resita and Hunedora (iron and steel works), the pre-war east-west and north-south axis from Bucharest, the Prahova Valley with Ploeşti as its center, Brasov, as well as new industrial locations in Moldavia, Oltenia, Maramures, Dubraja, and the southern and eastern sub-Carpathian regions.

Numerous economic activities in widely dispersed medium-sized towns and growing villages are an indication of the effect of the establishment of well distributed growth poles. Such activities show important spread-effects in many of Romania's backward regions. Bucharest and the twelve largest towns had 59 percent of the Romanian urban increase between 1948 and 1970. By comparison, industrial activities in Greece concentrated largely in its two most important cities, Athens, the capital agglommeration, and Thessaloniki in the north, with a number of more recent industrial developments along the south-north axis, between Athens-Piraeus-Lárissa-Thessaloniki and Kavalla. After criticism that the early growth pattern in Bulgaria resulted in concentrations in a few large cities (Sofia, Polvdiv, Dimitrovgrad, Pernik, Stara Zagora, Varna, and Pleven) more effort was made to locate new industrial activities more widely. The trend in all of these countries is to place new industrial capacity in more medium-sized towns, often regional centers, that have a high potential as development poles. Such a policy of emphasizing development poles and growth centers comprising both economic and noneconomic activities is of special importance in Yugoslavia, where investment policies are highly decentralized and the need for increased industrialization in the backward parts of the country, such as Kosovo, Montenegro, and Bosnia, is an urgent one.

In most countries of Southeast Europe regional equalization of the standard of living of the population now has top priority. To accomplish this goal the development of infrastructure has received added attention in regional policies, since industrialization per se no longer plays an exclusive role. Significant changes have occurred, especially in second-order cities, or are planned, changing the role of many regions and slowly affecting the relationship between primate cities or largest agglomerations and places of lower rank.

### Implications of the Changing Pattern of Urban Settlements

There is little doubt about the influence that differing historical development has had on the inhabitants of Southeast Europe and its effect on the patterns of urbanization and migration since the mid-nineteenth century. Regional differences have greatly influenced the intensity of economic development, and this is reflected in the speed of the movement of people from rural to urban areas and from lagging, underdeveloped, and peripheral regions to the more economically advanced regions and the rapidly growing industrial centers.

The slow absorption of these rural people resulted in official or hidden unemployment. Yugoslavia permitted emigration to foreign countries as a safety valve. Greece always had a high emigration rate. The shift of employment from the agricultural to the nonagricultural sector regardless of its location within different settlement types is therefore the best criterion of urbanization. In all five countries of Southeast Europe a sizable number of people left agriculture in the post-war period to take jobs in industry or other nonagricultural branches of the economy. It is clear that industrialization was the driving force in the development of urban places, with great pressure exerted by the sizable rural population, though other factors have certainly played an important role. The large agrarian overpopulation in most areas of the region, especially in the mountainous heartland with its large natural increases until the last few years, has strained the absorption capacity, especially of the small and medium-sized towns. Because towns themselves were underdeveloped and lacked industries, the shift from agriculture did not make important contributions to the growth of towns until the 1960s and 1970s. It has been only in the last decade that industries have penetrated regions which previously were entirely agricultural and that the number of nonagricultural jobs in rural areas have grown and new settlements have been established. It also resulted "in the transformation of compact towns into more loosely connected groupings of settlement units--urban agglomerations."[20]

Most industrial expansion occurred in the more developed parts of the countries, in and around existing towns. This precipitated a relatively quick growth of urban population and often in a spontaneous and uncontrolled expansion of towns, either by absorption of surrounding rural settlements or by creation of new residential areas. The migration of a large number of people from rural areas resulted in a number of problems, including housing shortages, insufficient utilities, poor transport facilities, strains in the work performance of commuting workers, split families, and squatter residence (often illegal) on the outskirts of some of the larger towns in Greece and Yugoslavia. Some of these constaints, it is argued, were planned deliberately to slow down this massive migration to save the huge financial outlays in building housing units in towns or even a too-rapid expansion of the transportation network, all non-economic investments at the beginning of the massive drive for industrialization in all of the socialist countries. Such a policy of underurbanization sought to achieve economies in the urbanization process.[21] It has even been argued in connection with Bulgaria and Romania that commuting was preferable to migration.

The rapid migration from rural to urban areas has also given rise to numerous purely social problems. Apart from the need for the migrants to adopt quickly to urban life, the break-up of family

---

20. L. Van den Berg, et al., *Urban Europe: A Study of Growth and Decline,* for the European Coordination Centre for Research and Documentation in Social Sciences (Oxford: Pergamon Press, 1982), p. 5.

21. Ger Ofer, "Economizing on Urbanization in Socialist Countries: Historical Necessity or Socialist Strategy," in *International Migration: A Comparative Perspective,* ed. Alan A. Brown and Egon Neuberger (New York: Academic Press, 1977), pp. 277-303.

life, if only one part of the family moved to cities--and this was usual in the early period, even if visits to their rural home was frequent--created many serious family and community problems. Foreign emigration increased such social stresses and has become a major national problem in Yugoslavia, with nearly 700,000 of its workers employed in Western Europe, most of them either single or without their full families with them.

Finally, the large question being raised, and with some insistence, is whether the rapid deagrarianization is leading to the urbanization of rural areas or rather to the "peasantization" of the city. Any visitor to a number of cities in Southeast Europe becomes aware of this problem, which is only slowly being addressed by planning authorities. Once expectations of the advantages of life in urban communities have been raised, it is difficult to slow down the rural-urban migration. As Carter and others pointed out, the significance of the role played by earlier migrants and particularly friends and relatives is in providing information on the place of designation. It is clear that the intensity of migration in the countries of Southeast Europe is difficult to slow down and, as Hägerstrand pointed out, "must be consistently in close proportion to the frequency of communicative impulses," or, put another way, that "migration is best explained by the amount of information available from relatives."[22]

Urban demographic trends in Southeastern Europe are well established and are unlikely to change substantially in the decade ahead. The process is long-term, as studies a decade ago made clear. When a population increases within fixed limits in a state, even though such an increase has slowed down, as is well shown in advanced Slovenia or the Vojvodina and backward Losovo in Yugoslavia (6.9 or 2.5 vs. 25.1 annual average natural increment per 1,000 in 1980), more people mean more houses, and more houses mean increased urbanization. Planning can retard such a development, but it cannot stop it. A greater concentration in fewer growth centers with greater specialized industrial locations, mainly for economic reasons, is another stage in the process of urbanization which can be expected for all the five countries of Southeast Europe. As elsewhere in industrializing Europe, the trend is such that "the

---

22. Torsten Hägerstrand, "Migration and Area: Survey of a Sample of Swedish Migration Fields and Hypothetical Considerations on Their Genesis," in *Migration in Sweden: A Symposium,* ed. D. Hannenberg, Lund Studies in Geography, no. 13 (Lund: Gleerup, 957); and D.S. Thomas, "Research Memorandum on Migration Differentials," *Social Science Research Council Bulletin* 43 (New York, 1938); as quoted in Francis W. Carter, "Internal Migration in South Eastern Europe, 1964-1974, Part A: Bulgaria, European Turkey & Greece," paper presented at International Slavic Conference, Banff, 1974, p. 19.

differences in living standards between rural and urban areas will decrease through a gradual assimilation by the rural population of an urban life style, its work pattern, dwelling arrangements, recreational pursuits and services."[23]

---

23 . Van den Berg, *Urban Europe,* pp. 4-5.

# REGIONS OF RECENT MODERNIZATION OF ANCIENT URBAN TRADITIONS

# Chapter VIII

# THE DEVELOPMENT OF ISRAELI URBANISM

David H. K. Amiran and A. S. Shachar

### Traditional Urbanization

There is ample evidence, both archeological and historical, for considerable prosperity in the Land of Israel during much of the first millennium B.C. and until the Byzantine period around the 7th century A.D. Many important towns emerged in those times, and the original site of many of them was occupied repeatedly by urban settlements in subsequent periods. The following twelve hundred years were centuries of decline and deterioration in general security and economy. Although the ensuing stagnation affected the cities no less than the countryside, it strengthened the role of the cities as the political and economic centers of the country. By the year 1800, 20.6 percent of the total population of Palestine, according to Bachi, inhabited the twelve towns exisiting in those days.[1]

Modern urbanization began in the second half of the nineteenth century and resulted from several factors operating simultaneously. The major one is the penetration of European powers into Palestine and the ensuing diffusion of organizational and technological innovations which stimulated urban development. The grant of semi-autonomous political power to the European consular representatives, the so-called *capitulations,* substantially eased the oppressive Ottoman rule, securing a number of basic rights and services, such as legal protection, financial transactions, and postal services. These innovations made city life more secure and opened new economic opportunities for urban entrepreneurs. The European powers, competing to extend their foothold in the major urban centers, mainly in Jerusalem and Jaffa, established various community facilities, such as schools, hostels, and hospitals, raising significantly the level of urban amenities. The extent of

---

1. Roberto Bachi, *The Population of Israel* (Jerusalem: Hebrew University, 1977), pp. 32, 33, tables 4.1, 4.9.

urban autonomy achieved by the European powers and the introduction by them of new technologies and services mark the beginning of modern urbanization in Palestine.[2] The second factor was the opening of the Suez Canal in 1869, which had a significant impact on the geographical situation of the eastern coast of the Mediterranean. The new maritime lines greatly lessened the peripheral position of this region within the Ottoman Empire. The third factor which stimulated urban development since the second half of the 19th century was the gradual influx of Jewish immigrants.

It is obvious that for many centuries Arabs and others were the prevalent population element in the towns of Palestine. Bachi mentions a steady number of twelve towns during the 19th century.[3] Eight of the fourteen top-ranking places listed for 1875 by the present authors had hardly any Jewish citizens.[4] ~~Eight of the fourteen top-ranking places listed for 1875 by the present authors had hardly any Jewish citizens'~~. Nearly all these towns can trace their origin to antiquity, being mentioned in the Bible or in slightly later Jewish sources, many of them by their present names. The one exception is Ramle, 15 km southeast of Tel Aviv, founded in the eighth century A.D.

The population of cities in Palestine before World War I consisted of a large Arab sector--traders, craftsmen, blue collar workers, and, at the top of the social pyramid, rich merchants and absentee owners of rural land, the *effendis,* who wielded much political and economic influence.[5] The leading Arab families acquired large blocs of urban property, both in the older cores of the cities and in the adjacent areas which were developed gradually in subsequent stages. This brought about a considerable increase in the wealth of this social stratum. In the later half of the nineteenth century, the Arab population underwent a gradually broadening process of modernization, both professionally and in

---

2. Ruth Kark, *Jaffa: From Village to Primate City: A Study of Transition 1799-1914* (Jerusalem: Yad Izhak Ben-Zvi Publications, 1984), in Hebrew.

3. Bachi, op. cit., p. 33, table 4.2.

4. David H. K. Amiran and Avie S. Shachar, "The Towns of Israel: The Principles of Their Urban Geography," *Geographical Review* 51 (1961): 348-369, table IV; *idem,* "Estimates of the Urban Population of Palestine in the Second Half of the Nineteenth Century," *Israel Exploration Journal* 10 (1960): 181-83. It is remarkable, however, that as late as 1931 small numbers of Jewish families, or individuals, lived in nearly every Arab town. The following towns had less than 10 Jewish citizens each in both 1922 and 1931: Bethlehem, Ramallah, Khan Yunis, Jenin, and Jericho; Shafa Amr and Beit Jala had single Jewish citizens in 1931, but not in 1922; Majdal, the predecessor of Ashkelon, was the only town with no Jews in both census years. Other towns had more substantial numbers of Jewish citizens: Hebron 430 (or 2.6 percent of the town's inhabitants), Beer Sheva 98 (4.3), and Acre 78 (1.2).

5. Many a land-owning family owned the entire lands of a village, or even of villages, with the peasants being only sharecroppers.

their way of life, especially in the commerical field. This was influenced by the activities of the various European institutions and small communities, as well as by Jewish modernization towards the turn of the century. Among the Christian communities, the French, English, Russians, Americans, Germans, Austrians, Greeks, and Italians were all influential, especially through regular and vocational schools.

The second urban element were the Jews, who changed considerably during the nineteenth century. For generations past, Jews had resided in the four "Holy Towns," Safed, Tiberias, Jerusalem, and Hebron.[6] These towns had substantial Jewish populations, as documented by the censuses of the British mandate. In 1875, the majority of Jews were of East European origin--*Ashkenazis*--who came to Palestine for religious reasons, for a life devoted to prayer and the study of the scriptures. The great majority of the families were poor, many of them elderly. They were maintained by contributions from their home communities in Eastern Europe. Their total number was minute at the beginnning of the nineteenth century, an estimated 6,700. Their number increased to 42,900 by 1890, with 93.9 percent living in towns.[7] The nineteenth and early twentieth centuries brought a considerable influx of Jewish immigrants, whose motivation ranged from purely religious reasons, to antisemitism in Europe, especially the pogroms in Czarist Russia, and to Zionism. The vast majority of immigrants of this period were town-people who brought with them the occupations and outlook of the East European small town. This found its outward expression in such architectural details as the adoption of the gabled, red-tiled roof, as opposed to the flat or cupola roof of the typical Arab town.[8]

Whereas building in the Arab sectors of the towns was essentially on an individual and private basis, construction in the Jewish quarters introduced two patterns still important to this day. The highly religious Jews who devoted their life to prayer needed assistance; their home communities not only provided them with monetary allotments, the so-called *hallukah*, but built for them public housing projects on a landsman-basis. The first of them was Mea Shearim in New Jerusalem in the early 1870s; and many others

---

6 . Yehoshua, Ben-Arieh, "Urban Development in the Holy Land, 1800-1914," in *The Expanding City*, ed. John Patten (London: Academic Press, 1983), pp. 1-37.

7 . Bachi, op. cit. p. 32, table 4.1.

8 . Note the close correspondence of buildings constructed 1866-1937 (sheet 9) with gabled, red-tiled roofs (sheet 14) in *Atlas of Jerusalem* (Berlin and New York: Walter de Gruyter, 1973).

followed.  These were the antecedents of modern condominiums and of the public housing projects of the 1950s.  The second pattern, noted in many other countries as well, consisted of construction projects initiated, financed, and executed in part by entrepreneurs, international construction firms, and bankers, who developed new neighborhoods, sometimes for specific groups of clients.  It is interesting to note that besides local citizens a number of Europeans who were temporary residents of Palestine in those days took a prominent part in these activities, such as the Swiss banker Frutiger and others.  The neighborhoods so constructed were generally of uniform style.

The early years of the twentieth century saw a very different type of Jewish immigrant.  The Zionist movement had a distinctly non-urban, not to mention anti-urban motivation,9 and was the decisive element in planning policy in Jewish Palestine until the rise of Hitler in Germany and Europe.  Its object was to bring a maximum number of Jews back to the old homeland, in which the Zionists would build a normal, "natural" society with definite preference for a productive community—first and foremost agriculturalists—who would supply the basic needs of the new community.  The hard core of these old-time "pioneers" were idealists who wanted to build a new society aiming at *social* achievement rather than wealth and at the same time restore the land of Israel to its natural prosperity, if not to the proverbial "Land of Milk and Honey."  These ideals were not always maintained later on under the pressure of a mass immigration only partly motivated by the same ideology.  The early pioneer society gave much attention to training of agriculturalists, to advancement of the backward agriculture of pre-World War I Palestine, and to planning of rural settlement.  There was but little concern with urban development and planning.  The many Jews who came to live in the towns of late Ottoman and British Mandatory Palestine up to 1932, although not considered a kind of "necessary evil" by the Zionist authorities, were certainly not regarded as deserving special consideration in national efforts and resource allocation.  In the 1930s and again in the 1950s, some publicity was aimed at stimulating migration "From Town to Village," but the results were insignificant.  The census of population taken in November 1931, however, gives a convenient picture for the end of this period.  It showed that at that time already 73.5 percent of the Jewish population were urban, and only

---

9. Erik Cohen, *The City in the Zionist Ideology* (Jerusalem: Hebrew University Institute of Urban and Regional Studies, 1970).

26.5 percent were rural.[10]

In summary, the sources of modern urbanization in Palestine were external in nature: the penetration and competition of European powers to achieve a degree of influence in a peripheral region of the crumbling Ottoman Empire, the changing geopolitical situation enhancing the importance of the region, and the gradual influx of Jews, introducing an urban and commercial tradition conducive to urban growth. Being an externally induced urbanization, it did not assume the regular process of rural-to-urban migration that fuels the growth of cities in many other regions.

### Urbanization under the British Mandate

The introduction of British Mandatory Administration in Palestine, which, under the terms of the League of Nations, had as one of its major objectives the establishment of a Jewish National Home in that country, brought a strong wave of Jewish immigration.[11] This influx enlarged the cities, mainly the large ones. The growth of the three major cities was differential, both during 1920-1947, the years of the British Mandate, and since Independence. Tel Aviv had the attraction of being the only major, purely Jewish, city during the Mandate period.[12] It developed as the main economic and banking center of the country, had the majority of daily papers, and served as the center of the arts and of Jewish culture, including all the theaters and the philharmonic orchestra. Haifa attracted many of the European immigrants, especially the professional classes. Its scenic setting on the slopes of Mount Carmel, overlooking the bay, was another attractive element. Last, but by no means least, Haifa in the Mandate period was the one important center of industry in Palestine, growing around the nucleii of the refineries and the harbor.[13] Industry was complemented by the Technion, the Technical University of Israel, founded in 1912 and thereby the nation's oldest academic institution. Haifa lost its economic primacy to Tel Aviv during the 1950s. Modern transportation and communication decreased the importance of

---

10. Eric Mills, *Census of Palestine 1931: Vol. II Tables* (Alexndria: Whitehead Morris, 1933), pp. 18-19, table VI.

11. According to Bachi, op. cit., p. 79, table 8.1, a total of 84,300 Jews immigrated to Palestine in the years 1850-1914. A further 97,316 were added in the early years of the Mandate, 1919-1926.

12. It was the only city in Palestine which had its own municipal police force, consisting entirely of Jewish policemen. All other police units were part of a national force of which the higher ranking officers were British.

13. The refineries located at Haifa constituted one of the two Mediterrranean terminals of the pipeline of the Iraq Petroleum Company. The other terminal was at Tripoli in Lebanon where a second refinery was located. See Arnon Soffer, "The Dispersion of Industries in the Haifa Bay," *Studies in the Geography of Israel* 9 (1976): 136-55, in Hebrew, with English summary.

secondary regional centers such as Haifa and strengthened Tel Aviv
as the apex of a uni-centered economic and managerial structure in
Israel.[14] Tel Aviv outgrew it around 1930. Jerusalem more than
other cities in Israel was a town of officialdom of various types;
besides government, the consular corps was located here. It was the
seat of the elaborate institutions of the three religions, and of
the many philanthropic organizations connected with them. It
contained the central organizations of the two major communities,
Jews and Arabs. In the 1920s, the Hebrew University of Jerusalem
opened its campus on Mount Scopus. From the beginning it was an
important spiritual center, but more in the quiet way of Heidelberg
or Göttingen, than of the large American university type. A
considerable part of the original faculty had been displaced from
Germany and Central Europe by the Nazis.

The main factor in urban growth during the Mandate period was
the private sector, the middle class element. This involved much
active speculation in real estate, bringing about large increases in
prices of land and housing. The needs of the lower income clases
were met by workers housing estates, some of them built on a
cooperative basis and many assisted by mortgages from the financial
institutions of the General Federation of Labor. In order to
facilitate the provision of housing at lower cost, much of it was
located at the periphery of the major cities or at some distance
from them.[15] Here houses were simpler and of cheaper construction
than those built for the private market. At the same time some had
a small garden lot, an asset at a later date when more intensive
development created considerable demand for building area.

The rise of the Nazi regime in Germany and its ramifications
throughout Europe brought about another great wave of immigration:
191,224 immigrants arrived between 1932 and 1936, more than doubling
the Jewish population of 175,031 as enumerated in the census of
November 1931. This was a most important addition to the Jewish
population professionally, giving Palestine and later Israel among
other things one of the most favorable ratios of doctors to patients
and an outstanding medical service. Many of the immigrants of the
1930s and the hard-working idealistic pioneers who had come from
Eastern Europe in the early years of the century gave Israel its

---

14. See Amiran and Shachar, op. cit., n. 4. above.

15. Examples are Givatayim (founded 1922), Bene Berak (1924), and the
relevant parts of Petah Tiqvah, east of Tel Aviv; the two Me'onot Ovdim quarters
built in the late 1920s in Jerusalem, as well as the "Workers' Quarter" of Bet
ha-Kerem in that city; the respective development in Haifa was in the northeast in
the Haifa Bay neighborhoods of Qiryat Hayim, Motzkin, and Bialik, founded in the
early 1930s. See "Housing Estates in the Early Mandatory Period," *Proceedings of
the Israel Geographical Association* (Haifa, 1979), pp. 131-36, in Hebrew.

distinctive "Western" society, deliberately distinct from the "levantism" of the Near East.

Most of the immigrants of the 1930s streamed into the larger cities bringing about a considerable expansion of their built-up area. During the years 1926-1937, the built-up area of Jerusalem grew by approximately one-third.[16] That of Haifa more than doubled between 1930 and 1948.[17] Tel Aviv increased by 135 percent during 1930-1944.[18] This immigration was a great boost to the urban element of the Jewish population. It ended the temporary relative increase of the rural population during the 1920s which had benefitted from the special planning attention of the Zionist movement.

Cities and towns in pre-independence Israel were well-ordered in distinct size groups (table 8.1). Tel Aviv, Jerusalem, and Haifa had 66.2 percent of the total urban population of Palestine in 1944, which in turn accounted for 47.37 percent of the total population (9.9 percent in Group II and 17.6 percent in Groups III and IV combined) and less than 4 percent in Group V. It is thus evident that Jewish immigration was the major source of urban growth in Israel in the twentieth century. The leading older Arab cities (Group II) grew but moderately and hardly doubled their population between 1875 and 1944, whereas in the same period Jerusalem grew more than 7 times, Haifa 30 times, and Tel Aviv-Jaffa 35 times. The slow growth of Gaza is particularly noteworthy as it had been the second-ranking city until nearly the end of the nineteenth century and held fourth rank (following Group I) to the end of the British Mandate.

The second part of the Mandate period (the 1930s and 1940s) brought about an increasing segregation between Jews and Arabs. The small Jewish minorities in middle and small-size towns almost entirely disappeared. Furthermore, those neighborhoods in the large towns, especially Jerusalem and Haifa which had a mixed residential population, experienced increasing segregation, following each wave of inter-communal strife, eventually turning either purely Jewish or purely Arab.

Neither the days of Ottoman rule nor those of the British Mandate saw the foundation of new towns. The sole exception were two Jewish towns, Netanya, founded in 1929 on the coast between Tel Aviv and Haifa, and Afula, the center of the important agricultural

---

16. See *Atlas of Jerusalem,* sheet 9.

17. Arnon Soffer and Baruch Kipnis, eds., *Atlas of Haifa and Mount Carmel* (Haifa: University of Haifa, 1980), pp. 62-65.

18. *Atlas of Israel,* 3rd edition, forthcoming, sheet 19.

TABLE 8.1

TOWNS 1944, BY SIZE GROUPS

| Group Number | Town | Population |
|---|---|---|
| Group I | Tel Aviv - Jaffa | 260,970 |
| | Jerusalem | 157,080 |
| | Haifa | 128,800 |
| Group II | Gaza | 34,170 |
| | Hebron | 24,560 |
| | Nablus | 23,250 |
| Group III | Lydda | 16,780 |
| | Ramle | 15,160 |
| | Nazareth | 14,120 |
| | Acre | 12,320 |
| | Safed | 11,930 |
| | Tiberias | 11,310 |
| | Khan Yunis | 11,220 |
| | Rehovot | 10,020 |
| | Majdal | 9,910 |
| | Bethlehem | 8,820 |
| Group IV | Rishon le-Zion | 8,100 |
| | Tulkarem | 8,090 |
| | Hedera | 7,520 |
| Group V | Beersheba | 5,570 |
| | Beisan | 5,180 |
| | Ramallah | 5,080 |
| | Jenin | 3,990 |
| | Beit Jala | 3,710 |
| | Shafa Amer | 3,640 |
| | Afula | 2,310 |

SOURCE: Official Estimate, *Statistical Abstract of Palestine*, 8, 1944-45 (Jerusalem, 1946), p. 21-22, Table 10.

NOTE: No estimate is available for Jericho, the 1931 census population of which was 1693.

inland basin of Emek Yisre-el, which although founded in 1925 had by 1944 no more than 2,310 inhabitants.

In summary, urbanization during the British Mandate was an outcome of large-scale Jewish immigration. A large proportion of these immigrants tended to settle in the gateway towns of Tel Aviv and Haifa or were attracted to the capital, Jerusalem, because of the employment opportunities in administration and education offered there. Urbanization was influenced by the emerging national conflict between Jews and Arabs, each wave of political disturbances bringing about a sharper separation between the two national groups and strengthening the emergence and maturing of two separate economies and labor markets.

### Modern Urbanization

The declaration of independence of the State of Israel on the eve of May 15, 1948, brought about a radical change in nearly every aspect of the region's life.

The pace of Jewish immigration during the nineteenth century was heightened during the Mandate period, with a strong boost in the mid-1930s as a result of Nazi persecutions in Germany. The rate of immigration changed, however, due to fluctuations in pressure, motivation, and restrictions on immigration, with a noticeable decrease in 1937 through 1945. Increasing numbers of immigrants were "displaced persons" and survivors of the holocaust in Europe had to make their way as "illegals." Public efforts in absorbing immigrants during the British Mandate were directed toward the rural sector, and some of the immigrants established new agricultural settlements in various parts of the country. But the majority who turned to the cities had to get established almost on their own. Thus, the urban sector, mainly the three large cities of Tel Aviv, Jerusalem, and Haifa, was growing vigorously during the British Mandate through the efforts of entrepreneurs and the investment of private capital both in housing and in economic activities. Urbanization in this period was carried out by the individual locational decisions of the immigrants, and the cities were shaped by the actions of land developers and speculators.

The independence of the sovereign State of Israel threw the doors wide open to anyone in quest of a Jewish homeland. The survivors of the holocaust were joined by substantial numbers of Jews from North African and Middle Eastern countries. Entire communities migrated to Israel, seeing in its independence the fulfillment of the messianic prophecy, a Jewish tradition of untold generations. Others had to leave their countries of residence on account of the hostile attitudes they encountered as a result of the War of Independence. The result was an unprecedented wave of immigration between May 1948 and the end of 1951, more than doubling the Jewish population within forty-three months (table 8.2).[19] Although this wave of mass-immigration abated considerably in subsequent years, it had far-reaching effects on the development of Israeli urbanism.

The problems of absorption were stupendous. The new citizens had to be provided with housing and work. Some of them were placed in villages, exisiting ones and especially new ones,[20] given on-the-spot training as farmers, or given employment on public works.[21] As a result the proportion of the Jewish population in rural areas reached 23.6 percent in 1954, which was, except for 1944, its highest value. But the majority of immigrants, nevertheless, had to be accommodated in towns, especially as most of them were urbanites by background.

The years 1948 to 1951 mark the major turning point in the urbanization process of Israel. From this time onward urban development began to be supported, and in many cases even initiated and implemented, by central government and other public agencies. It should be emphasized that the onset of induced urbanization to be carried out by governmental action was not an outcome of an ideological change affecting the anti-urban bias inherent in the Zionist and socialist ideologies prevailing in Israel.[22] The Israeli government launched a massive urbanization program because this was the most efficient means to achieve the two major national goals: the social goal of absorbing the mass-immigration and the political goal of securing the territorial integrity of the country by firmly occupying the peripheral areas of Israel. Absorption of the new immigrants in urban settlements did not require any prior ideological motivation, in contrast to the pioneer settlers who established the communal and cooperative rural settlements. Urban settlements were able to cater for the large numbers of new

---

19 . By the end of 1951, a total of 656,740 immigrants were added to the May 1948 population of 649,000.

20 . Israel had 326 rural settlements in November 1948, 456 at the end of 1949, 606 at the end of 1951, and 732 at the end of 1955--that is, an increase of 125 percent over 1948! See *Statistical Abstract of Israel* 9 (1957-58): 14-15, table 8. By 1958, the "New Settlements" accommodated 48.6 percent of the Jewish rural population. The number of Jewish rural settlements increased to 876 by May 1983; 628 of them were "New Settlements."

21 . These were the years when, among other things, large afforestation projects were carried out all over Israel.

22 . Cohen, op. cit.

TABLE 8.2

JEWISH IMMIGRATION FOR SELECTED PERIODS

| Years | No. of immigrants |
|---|---|
| 1882-1903 | 20-30,000 |
| 1904-1914 | 35-40,000 |
| 1919-1923 | 35,183 |
| 1924-1931 | 81,613 |
| 1932-1936 | 191,224 |
| 1937-1938 | 6,029 |
| 1939-1945 | 81,809 |
| 1946-V 1948 | 56,467 |
| 15.V.1948-1951 | 656,739 |
| 1952-1967 | 583,327 |
| 1968-1981 | 437,637 |

SOURCE: *Statistical Abstract of Israel,* 33, 1982, p. 134/5, Table V/1.

NOTE: According to Bachi, op.cit. n.l., p. 116, 272,500 Israeli emigrated in the years 1920-1975. The rate of emigration increased considerably in the late 1970s and even more than balanced immigration. Total net immigration 1919-1981 was 1,994,142.

TABLE 8.3

JEWISH IMMIGRATION FOR SELECTED PERIODS, IN PERCENT, BY CONTINENT OF ORIGIN

| | Europe | America | Africa | Asia |
|---|---|---|---|---|
| 1919-1931 | 81.2 | 2.5 | 0.7 | 8.9 |
| 1932-1938 | 86.8 | 2.3 | 0.6 | 8.3 |
| 1948-1951 | 47.6 | 0.7 | 13.7 | 34.6 |
| 1952-1959 | 32.1 | 3.4 | 51.96 | 12.4 |
| 1975-1981 | 60.1 | 24.0 | 5.2 | 10.3 |

SOURCE: *Statistical Abstract of Israel,* 33, 1982, p. 134/35, Table V/1.

immigrants and were amenable to the bureaucratic procedures of
large-scale absorption. Thus induced urbanization became the major
instrument in achieving the social goal of absorption. The unique
situation in which central government controlled both the human and
the capital resources becoming available made this effort of induced
urbanization on a national scale a feasible one and brought Israeli
urbanization rates to an extraordinarily high level.

Accommodation of immigrants was achieved in three ways.
First, large public housing estates were added to major cities, such
as the south and east of Tel Aviv, the periphery of Haifa, and the
south and south-west of Jerusalem.[23] Due to the pressing needs to
provide speedy accommodation, most of these housing projects were
highly standardized in design, medium-to-low quality in
construction, and consisted of small apartments (55 and even 35
square meters were early standards). This made for crowded housing,
particularly serious for immigrants from North African and Middle
Eastern countries, many of whom had large families (table 8.3).[24]
Only part of the mass-immigration was accommodated at the fringes of
the existing large cities. Most immigrants, therefore, never
experienced the well-known phenomena of large "favelas" or
"bidonvilles," characteristic of many large cities in developing
countries, arising from rapid rural-to-urban migration.
Nevertheless, because of the industrialized, standardized,
low-quality housing provided for the new immigrants, these newly
built areas were due for urban renewal efforts after a short span of
time. The recent national project of neighborhood rehabilitation is
therefore quite suitably allocating considerable resources to the
improvement of the housing quality of these areas.

The accommodation of new immigrants in large-scale public
housing estates in the large cities was the least desirable means
from the point of view of national planning, which had as its
primary objective the dispersal of the immigrants to the periphral
regions of Israel. Therefore, the large cities which were
undergoing a pronounced process of metropolization grew mainly by
natural increase and by positive net migration with other regions of
the country, while the settling of new immigrants was only a
secondary source of urban growth.

---

23. This enlarged the built-up area of these cities within a few years by
about 40 percent. See *Atlas of Israel,* (Jerusalem and Amsterdam: Survey of Israel
and Elsevier, 1970), sheet XI/4.

24. They amounted to 56.4 percent of the immigrants of 1948-1959, being
505,022 persons.

The diversion of new immigrants from settling in the large cities was but one strategy of limiting the cities' growth. Another comprised administrative restrictions on building on "agricultural land," which was defined very broadly to include almost all vacant land around the large cities. Constant pressure of land developers, private and public alike, "unfroze" some of this land and put it to urban uses. This restrictive policy is still in effect and contributes to checking the growth of the large cities, mainly in the central coastal plain of Israel.

Despite national urbanization policies, the three major cities, and particularly Tel Aviv and Haifa, developed into major metropolitan areas by 1960, and a distinct metropolitan structure has been evolving since (table 8.4 and figure 8.1).[25] This brought about a clear functional division into a business center, which is being increasingly drained of its residential population, and outer rings of dormitory towns around it. The population of the three metropolitan areas amounted to 57 percent of the total population of Israel in 1961, decreased to 52 percent by 1972, but rose again to 59 percent in 1983. The declining share of the metropolitan areas in the total population of Israel during the sixties represents a certain success of the national settlement policy, which encouraged urban growth at the peripheral regions of Israel and did not support it in the Tel Aviv and Haifa metropolitan areas.

The second form which urbanization took in the period after independence was the expansion of previously small settlements, either urban or rural, and the re-population of former Arab towns which were vacated during the War of Independence by their Arab inhabitants (figure 8.2). Jaffa, Lod, Ramle, and Migdal are the major examples of this process. (A similar but politically inverted case is provided by the Old City of Jerusalem which had to be evacuated by its Jewish inhabitants during the war.) The urbanization of the "private" Jewish villages, the *moshavot,* is of special interest. They are the least generally known type of Jewish rural settlement, having no novel features as do the communal *kibbuts* or the cooperative *moshav.* As in the *moshava* there is no standardization of size of landholding, private land-ownership, and no community restriction on transfer of property. These settlements

---

25. The emergence of a metropolitan area of Jerusalem was inhibited by political factors. Between 1949 and 1967, the city was partitioned between Israel with 72.4 percent of the 1961 population and Jordan with 27.6 percent repectively; the Israeli city was at the end of a cul-de-sac, the "Jerusalem Corridor." Since re-unification in 1967, Jerusalem has redeveloped its regional functions and centrality, but mainly in the economic field. By and large, the Arab municipalities concerned, Ramallah and el-Bireh in the north and Beit Jala, Bethlehem, and Beit Sahur in the south, reject cooperation with Jerusalem for political reasons, with a few exceptions, such as garbage disposal.

TABLE 8.4

POPULATION OF THE THREE MAJOR CITIES, 1910-1983

| City:<br>(Metropolitan Area) | Jerusalem | Tel Aviv | Haifa |
|---|---|---|---|
| 1910 | 70,000 | 43,400 | 18,000 |
| 1922 | 62,578 | 47,708 | 24,634 |
| 1931 | 90,503 | 97,967 | 50,403 |
| 1946 | 164,440 | 284,780 | 145,430 |
| 1961 | 227,923[1] | 386,070<br>(776,300) | 183,021<br>(259,700) |
| 1972 | 313,861 | 363,756<br>(1,029,600) | 227,200<br>(335,700) |
| 1983 | 431,800<br>(443,400) | 330,400<br>(1,564,700) | 227,900<br>(391,100) |

SOURCES: Bachi, cf. n. 1, and *Statististical Abstract of Israel*.

[1] Comprises both the Israeli and Jordanian parts of Jerusalem in 1961.

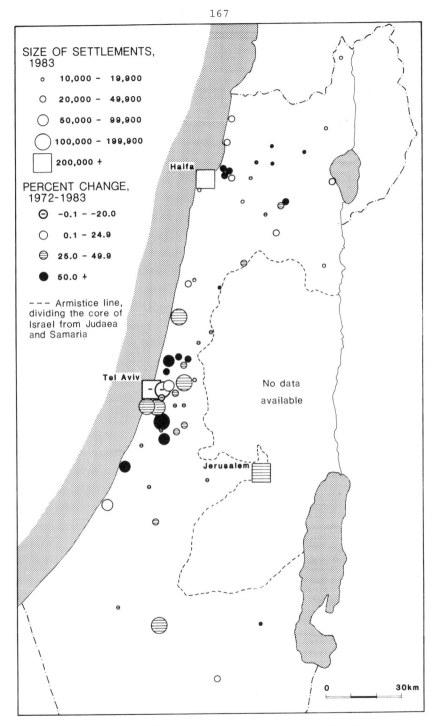

SIZE OF SETTLEMENTS,
1983

- o    10,000 – 19,900
- O    20,000 – 49,900
- ◯    50,000 – 99,900
- ◯  100,000 – 199,900
- ▢    200,000 +

PERCENT CHANGE,
1972-1983

- ⊖   −0.1 – −20.0
- ◯    0.1 – 24.9
- ⊜   25.0 – 49.9
- ●   50.0 +

– – – Armistice line,
dividing the core of
Israel from Judaea
and Samaria

Haifa

Tel Aviv

No data

available

Jerusalem

0            30km

Figure 8.1.  Changing size of urban settlements in Israel

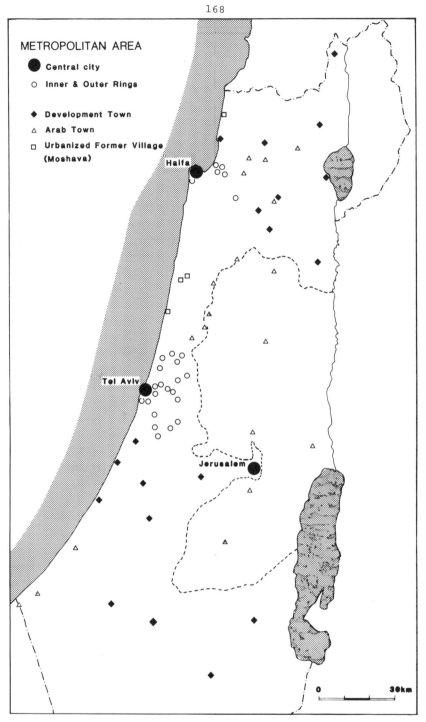

Figure 8.2.  Types of cities and towns in Israel

embarked early on a path of commercialization and urbanization, assisted by the exisiting functional and social infrastructure.[26] To a degree, the urbanization of the *moshavot,* such as with Hadera and Rehovot, helped in part to fill the missing middle strata of the urban hierarchy, which had been a conspicuous feature of the Israeli urban system prior to the establishment of the State of Israel.

The third and perhaps most interesting means of accommodating the immigrants are those New Towns which in Israel are known as "Development Towns" (table 8.5). In addition to providing housing and work to new citizens,[27] they were to serve two purposes. Some were located so as to expand, or secure, the effective area of settlement of the new state or to utilize some of its mineral resources (Group A). These include such towns as Eilat, the port at the head of the northeastern gulf of the Red Sea and Israel's southermost town (mid-1983 population: 19,200); and towns in the hitherto unsettled Negev: Yeruham (6,200), Dimona (27,800), Arad (12,600), and the small Mizpe Ramon in the Central Negev Highlands, halfway to Eilat, Israel's highest town at 850 m (2,900).

A second purpose was to serve as urban service centers for their rural hinterland, an idea consciously based on a "central place" model (Group B).[28] This group consists of towns such as Qiryat Gat (25,800), the prototype of the regional service center in Israel, founded in 1954 as the major service town of the Lachish Settlement Region with its more than fifty villages. A similar role was allocated to other new towns such as Ofakim (13,000), Netivot (8,000), and Sederot (9,500) in the northern Negev and Qiryat Shemona (15,400), Ma'alot (7,600), Beth She'an (13,100), and others in northern Israel.

To provide an economic base for these towns, in addition to providing services to their rural hinterland, heavily subsidized industry was introduced in many of them. This was essential in those places which had no hinterland to serve, such as the towns in the Negev desert. In selecting the type of industry, preference was given to labor-intensive industry which would provide work for a maximum of people with minimum investment; the textile industry was

---

26. Amiram Gonen, "Urbanization of the 'Moshavoth' in Israel," *Studies in the Geography of Israel* 10 (1978): 31-44, in Hebrew, with English summary.

27. To assist the newcomers in getting established in these new towns, a number of seasoned pioneers moved there as training personnel. They were joined by enterprising young people, some of them former kibbuts members, who were attracted by the challenge.

28. Eliezer Brutzkus, *Physical Planning in Israel* (Jerusalem: Ministry of the Interior, 1964) and *Regional Policy in Israel* (Jerusalem: Ministry of the Interior, 1970); Yehoshua Cohen, *Urban Zones of Influence in the Southern Coastal Plain of Israel* (Rehovot: Settlement Study Center, 1967).

TABLE 8.5

DEVELOPMENT TOWNS[1]

| | Period of Foundation[2] | Population 1961 | Population 1983 |
|---|---|---|---|
| Quiryat Shemona | B | 11,800 | 15,400 |
| Shelomi | B | 1,700 | 2,400 |
| Nahariyya | A | 14,600 | 28,100 |
| Ma'alot | C | 3,300 | 7,600 |
| Hazor | B | 4,600 | 6,500 |
| Zefat | A | 11,000 | 16,500 |
| Karmiël | C | - - - | 15,700 |
| Tiberias | A | 20,800 | 28,600 |
| Nazerat Illit | C | 4,300 | 23,700 |
| Migdal ha-Emek | B | 4,000 | 13,700 |
| Yoqne'am Illit | B | - - - | 5,100 |
| Afula | A | 13,800 | 21,500 |
| Or Aqiva | B | 3,200 | 8,100 |
| Bet She'an | A | 9,700 | 13,100 |
| Yavne | B | 5,400 | 14,100 |
| Ashdod | B | 4,600 | 66,700 |
| Bet Shemesh | B | 7,000 | 13,100 |
| Qiryat Malakhi | B | 4,600 | 12,300 |
| Ashkelon | A | 24,300 | 53,400 |
| Qiryat Gat | B | 10,100 | 25,800 |
| Sederot | B | 3,500 | 9,100 |
| Netivot | C | 2,900 | 8,000 |
| Ofakim | B | 4,600 | 13,000 |
| Beer Sheva | A | 43,500 | 111,100 |
| Arad | C | - - - | 12,600 |
| Dimona | B | 5,000 | 27,800 |
| Yeruham | B | 1,600 | 6,200 |
| Mizpe Ramon | B | 300 | 2,900 |
| Eilat | B | 5,300 | 19,200 |
| TOTAL | | 225,500 | 601,300 |

SOURCE: Central Bureau of Statistics: *Statistical Abstract of Israel,* and Census of Population and Housing, 1983 - Preliminary Results.

[1] North to south.

[2]
A    Before 1949
B    1949-1955
C    1956-1965

a favorite under these considerations.[29] This and similar
industries, however, have little competitiveness once custom
barriers are removed in an increasingly open market. Those
development towns depending solely or mainly on such lagging
industries (and unfortunately there are others) offer little
possibility for advancement to less routine jobs and better wages,
which serves as a disincentive to the younger generation. Many of
those having advanced schooling, or training in the army, tend to
move elsewhere.

In the classic settlement pattern, part of the village
population finds employment in a nearby town. In Israel, with its
highly developed *kibbuts* villages which by now have many medium-size
industrial plants, many of them quite sophisticated, many a "village
provides employment to the town." This, as Barkai stated recently,
"is a paradox hardly to be found elsewhere, except in Israel."[30] As
a result of the dependence of the New Towns on employment
opportunities provided by industries of the highly developed *kibbuts*
villages, a rift of a social and political nature has developed
between the New Towns and their rural hinterland. In some awkward
way, a class-based conflict emerged between the New Towns'
population and the *kibbutsim,* the former providing semi-skilled
labor, the latter performing managerial functions.[31] This class-type
conflict went even deeper as the workers of the New Towns were
mainly of "Oriental" (Middle Eastern and North African) origin or
Israeli-born. The social and cultural tensions expressed themselves
politically, when in the last national elections most New Towns
turned solidly toward the right wing parties in a strong protest
movement against the left wing political affiliation of the
*kibbutsim.*

Furthermore, the original idea according to which the
Development Towns were to provide commercial and administrative
services to their rural hinterland was itself hardly successful.
With the reduction in distance and travel time resulting from
traffic and communication of the later twentieth century and in a
country the small size of Israel with a sectoral, highly centralized
rural settlement organization, the functions of trade, banking, and
administation tend to be streamlined in a uni-centered pattern

---

29. Yehuda Gradus and Yakov Einy, "Trends in Core-Periphery
Industrialization Gaps in Israel," *Geographical Research Forum* 3(1981): 25-37.

30. Z. Barkai, "Planning of Rural and Urban Regions," *Karka* [Land] 23
(1982): 14-18, in Hebrew.

31. Shiome Hasson, "Social and Spatial Conflicts: The Settlement Process in
Israel during the 1950s and the 1960s," *L'Espace Geographique* 10 (1981): 169-179.

focused at Tel Aviv.  Even important regional centers are being outflanked, not to mention small Development Towns.  All told, some Development Towns are experiencing a crisis today.

## Urbanization in the Arab Sector

There is another group of new towns which deserves attention. They are the large Arab villages which in recent years have grown into towns.  The high rate of natural increase of the Arab population, especially the Moslems,[32] their social preference for remaining resident with the family clan, and administrative difficulties for migration to existing towns, brought about the growth of many an Arab village into a town, sizeable both by population and area.  Many of its citizens commute for work to other places, including the major cities.  In distinct contrast to the traditional pattern of the Arab village which is nucleated and densely built, these newly-grown towns spread in a loosely built pattern over a wide area, individual clusters of houses or hamlets belonging to *hamulas* or clan-groups being located on somewhat isolated spurs or hills.

A last and very different type of Arab town is just emerging, the Beduin town.  The Beduin population of the northern Negev has for some decades been undergoing an accelerated process of sedentarization.  None of the Beduin are migratory any longer in the traditional way.  They were inclined to build their houses in a pattern to which they were used in the tented encampments which they moved from time to time.  This was both extremely space-consuming and inefficient for a regular settlement.  The government, therefore, began planning a number of towns for the sedentarizing Beduin.  They are planned and serviced by modern design and facilities, organized in separate quarters, each inhabited by a different clan group.  As the Beduin are an industrious and prosperous population, the first of these towns, Rahat located some 20 km north of Beer Sheva, makes quite a modern and well-to-do impression.  Its population is already close to 10,000.

## Recent Trends in Urbanization

The pressures of dense urbanization in Israel, with 90 percent of the Jewish population being urban and 59 percent of the total population living in the three metropolitan areas, created here as elsewhere a trend of "counter urbanization" or migration of urban families into rural places.  For acceptable commuting distances, up

---

32. Natural increase of the Moslem population of Israel in the years 1960-64 was 45.3 per thousand.  It is slowly decreasing and was 34.7 per thousand in 1980.  See *Statistical Abstract of Israel* 33 1982): 76,table III/1.

to one hour of travel time, one finds villages in which individual
houses, or even the majority of them, are residences of urban
people. This trend has been spreading outward from the city for
quite some years. It caused concern especially in the case of Tel
Aviv because its rural hinterland is located on prime agricultural
land. Although the extent of land converted to non-agricultural use
by these urbanites is inconsequential, the dislocation to the proper
function of village agriculture and to its development may be
serious.

These general developments, which Israel shares with most
Western countries, were given an exra regional dimension in the last
decade. It is the declared policy of the present government to
introduce Jewish settlement into Judea and Samaria, those parts of
Mandate Palestine which in 1948 were occupied by Jordan and are
under Israeli administration since 1967. Considerable parts of it
are in convenient commuting distance from the Tel Aviv metropolitan
area and from Jerusalem, much of it no more than half an hour by
modern roads. To achieve this political purpose the government is
offering sizeable subsidies and various other incentives to people
moving into this area. As a result two types of people move there.
Some move there because they share the present government's
ideology. They are joined by others who avail themselves of the
opportunity to obtain housing at a price they can afford, which is
out of their reach in the metropolitan areas of Israel with their
expensive real estate prices. Furthermore, others who lived mainly
in the Tel Aviv metropolitan area rent their apartments there and
move to the new dormitory settlements of upland Samaria, thereby
obtaining a new house at a very reasonable cost, living in a
pleasant rural environment and having an additional income from the
rent of their apartment in Greater Tel Aviv.

For pure considerations of physical planning this might be
good procedure, as the land concerned is what in the Mandate period
was termed "rocky ground," that is, *lapies* on barren limestone rock
with but few pockets of soil. It would be reclaimable for
agriculture only with very heavy investment, definitely an
uneconomic proposition today. On the other hand, however, it would
divert further urbanization from the valuable agricultural lands of
the coastal plain.

The objectionable part in the minds of many people is that the
scores of new settlements, most of which are small but all of
definitely urban character, will make it extremely difficult to
bring about a spatial segregation between Jewish and Arab settlement

in these upland areas.  This last stage in Israeli urbanization, the
expansion of urbanite settlement into Judea and Samaria, is,
therefore, one aspect of the major political controversy in Israel
today: Israel a country with a majority of Jews and a Jewish
culture, *versus* the Land of Israel occupying the entire area
promised by the Bible.

# Chapter IX

# URBAN CHANGES IN INDIA

Rana P. B. Singh and R.L. Singh

### Introduction

With the spectacular discovery of immense urban remains at
Harappa and Mohenjo-daro in the northern and southern parts of the
Indus valley, archeologists now place the origins of cities in India
back to the third millennium BC. According to archeological
investigations these early cities contained many-storied, palatial
buildings, solidly built of well-baked bricks and supplied with
amenities, including excellent sanitary facilities. The excavation
sites show clearly that civic organization was as well developed and
complex as in the carefully planned cities of later date such as
Indraprastha (Delhi), Mathura, Kosambi, and Varanasi.[1] Carbon-14
dates suggest that by the second millennium the late-Harappan urban
culture spread from the Indus valley to the upper Ganga valley and
also into northwest coastal India. Sites at Kotla Nihang Khan,
Rupar, and Bara exemplify this dispersal of urban culture.[2]
Kalibangam and Lothal are other sites which developed at a distance
of over 300 km from the Harappa/Mohenjo-daro area. The remains of
woven cotton found there attest to the antiquity of an industry for
which in later times India has been particularly famous.[3] The
location of these ancient towns reveals clearly the early perception
of water symbolism. The plans of these ancient towns generally
shows a rectangular pattern with the longer axis running from north
to south and include remains of dockyards connected to nearby rivers
by artificial channels, such as the channel of 2.5 km at Lothal.[4]

---

1 . Damodar D. Kosambi, *The Culture and Civilization of Ancient India in
Historical Outline* (New Delhi: Vikas Publications, 1970), p. 54.

2 . Subhash C. Malik, *Indian Civilization: The Formative Period* (Simla:
Indian Institute of Advanced Study, 1968), pp. 52 and 80.

3. Bridget and Raymond Allchin, *The Birth of Indian Civilization*
(Harmondworth: Penguin Books Ltd, 1968), p. 132.

4 . Ibid., p. 241.

In the course of time, water symbolism, sustained through its endowment with religious meaning, acquired strategic and geographical suitability. The expansion of the built-up area of towns followed the needs of population pressure, defence, suitable physical conditions, and related factors. The importance of defence can be easily explained by the location of forts in the inner part of the city and the water channel or ditch on the outer side. During the Aryan penetration of India, the great perennial rivers afforded the most suitable communication and navigation routes, hence many cities have grown up along the rivers, followed by religious monuments.[5]

The generalized urban growth and internal structure of a typical colonial Indian city conforms to some degree with the "multiple-nuclei" model of contemporary functional structure identified by Chauncy D. Harris and Edward L. Ullman in 1945.[6] With this in mind this essay is written in honor of Chauncy Harris, whose early work on the functional classification of cities of the United States provided a widely noted methodological framework for the taxonomy of towns and proved influential in the study of the urban geography of India.[7] The present essay reviews the trend of urbanization in India between 1901 and 1981, focusses particular attention on cities with over one million inhabitants, and concludes by considering the future urban zones of India and some of the related problems of urbanization.

### Patterns of Urbanization, 1901-1981

Although urbanization as a process denotes a complex interplay of socio-economic, political, technological, geographical, and cultural factors, its measurement is considered mostly on the basis of demographic criteria. According to the 1981 Census of India, a settlement is classified as a town if it has:

1. A municipality, corporation, cantonment board, or notified town area committee, etc. and
2. Satisfied the following three criteria:
   a) A minimum population of 5,000
   b) At least 75 percent of the male working population engaged in non-agricultural pursuits, and
   c) A density of population of at least 400 persons/km².

---

5 . Kusum Lata Taneja, *Morphology of Indian Cities* (Varanasi: National Geographical Society of India, pub. 7, 1971), p. 23.

6 . Chauncy D. Harris and Edward L. Ullman, "The Nature of Cities," *Annals of the American Academy of Political and Social Science* 242 (1945): 7-17.

7 . Chauncy D. Harris, "A Functional Classification of Cities in the United States," *Geographical Review* 33 (1943), pp. 86-89.

This definition was first adopted in 1951. In the 1961 Census, a concept of "town group" was adopted which was refined in the 1971 Census with the introduction of certain requirements of contiguity and urban character. This is called "urban agglomeration," which consists of one or more towns (including in some cases villages or parts of a village) which can be considered as urbanized and contiguous to the town or towns concerned. It means that an urban agglomeration is by definition the continuous urban spread consisting of a core town and its adjoining urban outgrowths which may be either urban in their own right or rural.[8]

The urban population of India in 1981 was about 157 million or nearly 24 percent of the total population. The number of towns has fluctuated from decade to decade because of changes in definitions and concepts, and towns have even been declassified or new places have been classified as towns. Therefore, the trend in urbanization can more usefully be considered on the basis of the urban population and its variations over the decades.[9] In 1901, about 11 percent of the population lived in urban areas and this ratio continued until about 1931. By 1941, urbanization increased to encompass 14 percent of the nation's population, reaching 18.24 percent in 1961. Since 1971, the growth of urban population has risen fairly rapidly (table 9.1). These growth trends may be divided into three periods.

During 1901-1931, urbanization was relatively slow, due mainly to the effect of famines and epidemics, such as the plague in 1911 and influenza in 1918. These epidemics further checked the migration of rural people to urban areas. Although conditions improved after 1921, the trends of natural increase and migration were slow.

The period 1931-1961, recorded a rapid growth of urban population with the pace of industrialization increasing and relatively more migration to urban areas. During 1941-51, the highest percentage increase occurred, faster than that experienced by Japan and about two-thirds as fast as that in United States.[10] Moreover, the partition of India in 1947 brought the mass migration of displaced persons, which had a phenomenal impact on India's urban growth. Most of the migrants settled in urban areas and were responsible for the growth of very different urban conditions.[11]

---

8. Census of India 1981, Series-1 INDIA, Paper 2 of 1981, *Provisional Population Totals* (New Delhi: Registrar General Office), p. 23

9. Ibid., p. 36.

10. Kusum Lata Taneja, op. cit., p. 2, fn. 5.

TABLE 9.1

TREND IN URBANIZATION AND URBAN POPULATION GROWTH
IN INDIA, 1901-1981

| Census year | No. of urban places | Urban population (in mill.) | Percent of urban population | Decadal variation (percent) |
|---|---|---|---|---|
| 1901 | 1,836 | 25.77 | 10.96 | – |
| 1911 | 1,821 | 25.85 | 10.41 | 0.29 |
| 1921 | 1,949 | 27.96 | 11.33 | 8.16 |
| 1931 | 2,079 | 33.29 | 12.18 | 19.08 |
| 1941 | 2,240 | 43.95 | 14.09 | 31.99 |
| 1951 | 2,867 | 62.09 | 17.59 | 41.28 |
| 1961 | 2,371 | 78.16 | 18.24 | 25.88 |
| 1971 | 2,574 | 107.82 | 20.21 | 37.96 |
| 1981 | 3,301 | 157.44 | 23.71 | 46.01 |

SOURCE: Census of India 1981, Series-1, INDIA, Paper 2 of 1981.

TABLE 9.2

URBAN PLACES AND PERCENTAGE OF URBAN POPULATION BY
SIZE-CLASS IN INDIA, 1961-81

| Size Class | No. of urban places | | | Percent of urban population | | | Decadal variation (percent) | |
|---|---|---|---|---|---|---|---|---|
| | 1961 | 1971 | 1981 | 1961 | 1971 | 1981 | 1961-71 | 1971-81 |
| I. 100,000+ | 104 | 147 | 218 | 50.90 | 56.30 | 60.41 | 52.61 | 55.67 |
| (a) above one mill: | 7 | 9 | 12 | 22.84 | 25.43 | 26.69 | 53.64 | 53.25 |
| (b) below one mill: | 97 | 138 | 206 | 28.06 | 30.87 | 33.72 | 51.78 | 59.49 |
| II. 50,000-99,999 | 129 | 178 | 270 | 10.92 | 11.16 | 11.56 | 40.94 | 51.22 |
| III. 20,000-49,999 | 450 | 573 | 744 | 17.30 | 16.26 | 14.33 | 29.67 | 28.66 |
| IV. 10,000-19,999 | 736 | 850 | 1053 | 12.98 | 11.16 | 9.48 | 18.61 | 24.11 |
| V. 5,000-9,999 | 743 | 656 | 761 | 7.01 | 4.62 | 3.67 | -9.11 | 16.06 |
| VI. Less than 5,000 | 209 | 170 | 255 | 0.89 | 0.50 | 0.55 | -22.52 | 59.68 |
| TOTAL | 2371 | 2574 | 3301 | 100.00 | 100.00 | 100.00 | 37.96 | 46.01 |

SOURCE: Census of India 1981, Series-1, INDIA, Paper 2 of 1981;
and other reports.

These immigrations caused rapid growth of urban population in
general and a shift in the proportion of urban to total population.

With the rapid migration to urban areas, unemployment rates
also became high and resulted in large pools of unemployed persons.
These together further encouraged migration from rural to urban
areas.[12] Some of the evil consequences of this pattern are visible
at the outskirts of cities in the form of slum areas and *bustees*.

The period 1971-81 saw a very high growth of urban population
(over 46 percent). This growth has resulted in part from a high rate
of natural population increase (about 25 percent), which is
accelerated by the development of industries and job opportunities
in urban areas, especially in case of cities of class I (over
100,000). The impact of "pull" factors appears distinct in such
areas. Moreover, the emergence of new industrial towns and the
rapid growth of older industrialized cities played an important role
in speedy urbanization.[13]

According to the 1981 Census, there are 3,301 urban places in
India, which are grouped into six classes of population size (table
9.2). Except in 1911, there has been a continuous increase in the
number of towns of all categories, particularly notable in classes I
and II. The decline in numbers in classes V and VI suggests that
towns have continued to grow bigger in terms of population from
decade to decade. In fact, in the higher classes the increases are
due only to movement from a lower class to a higher one through
resident population increase in each decade. Nearly 60 percent of
the urban population of the country is located in cities of 100,000
and above (class I), and it is these cities that registered very
high growth rates during 1971-81 (56.7 percent). It is, however,
significant that the towns of middle-size classes (III-V) have
increased in their numbers continuously since 1961, but lost their
proportion of urban population gradually.

The socio-economic development of urban areas is reflected by
the steady increase in number of class I urban agglomerations. On
the other end, class IV units have either moved up into class III or
have become constituents or urban agglomerations formed in relation
to the 1981 census. Considering the year 1901 as 100 for all the
size classes of urban places, the growth trend of urban population

11. Donald J. Bogue et al., "Urbanization and Migration in India," in
*India's Urban Future,* ed. R. Turner (Bombay: Oxford University Press, 1962), p.
31.

12. Ashish Bose, *Studies in India's Urbanization, 1901-1971* (Bombay: Allied
Pub., 1973), p. 6.

13. C.D. Deshpande and L.S. Bhat, "India," in *Essays on World Urbanization,*
ed. Ronald Jones (London: George Philip & Son, 1975), p. 358.

may be graphically represented, showing a very high increase of
class I cities, while class IV and V towns followed a stagnant trend
(figure 9.1). Class II and III cities experienced moderate growth,
and those of class IV slow growth. In terms of the percentage of
population living in towns by size class one may notice the decline
for classes III to VI, while class II presents a slow growth and
class I, steady growth (figure 9.2 and table 9.2).

### Million Cities

In 1901, the only urban agglomeration with over a million
inhabitants was Calcutta, though by 1911, Greater Bombay was also
grouped in the same category. By 1951, Delhi, Madras, and Hyderabad
urban agglomerations had been added to the list. Between 1951 and
1961, Ahmedabad and Bangalore also crossed the threshold of one
million, thus bringing the number to seven. During 1961-71, Kanpur
and Pune were added, and in 1981 Nagpur, Luchnow, and Jaipur urban
agglomerations had also surpassed the one million mark. Thus by
1981, twelve urban units became one million cities (see tables 9.3
and 9.4).

Until 1941, Calcutta and Bombay accounted for less than 2
percent of total national population and less than 13 percent of the
total urban population. But afterwards with the emergence of other
million cities the ratios for this class of cities reached 6.39 and
26.91 percent in 1981 respectively (table 9.3). The percentage
share of urban population in 1981 is very close to that of 1971; in
actual terms there has been an addition of slightly more than 14
million in these 12 cities. It is also to be noted that these 12
million-plus cities account for 44.57 percent of the population of
all class I cities in India. That is, about half of the population
of the 218 cities in class I are living in these 12 cities. The
population statistics show that Delhi has grown very rapidly in
comparative terms; the population of Delhi in 1971 was 16 times what
it was in 1901. In the case of Bangalore in the same years it was
about 10 times.

The *presidency towns,* Calcutta, Bombay, and Madras, all
developed Western-style central business districts (CBD) with banks,
insurance offices, cinema halls, hotels, and large-scale retail
establishments at the city center. The adjacent areas were occupied
by administrative offices and transport and communication offices.[14]

---

14. Ashok K. Dutt, "Cities of South Asia," in *Cities of the World: World
Regional Urban Development,* ed. Stanley D. Brunn and Jack F. Williams (New York:
Harper & Row Pub., 1983), p. 231; see also John E. Brush, "The Growth of
Presidency Town," in *Urban India: Society, Space and Image,* ed. Richard G. Fox
(Durham, NC: University Program in Comparative Studies on South Asia, 1970), pp.
91-113.

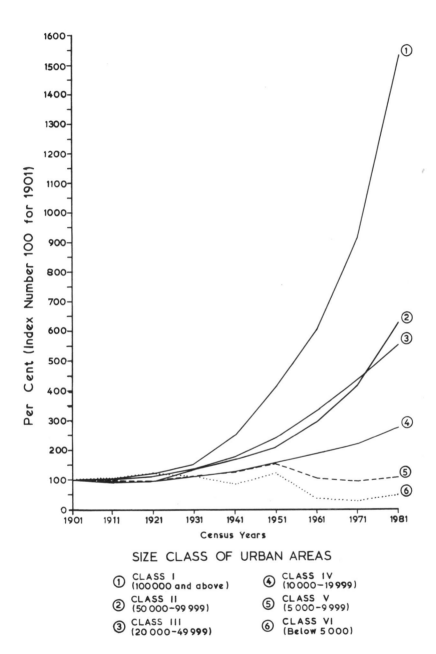

Figure 9.1. Growth rate of urban population in India, by size of urban areas, 1901-81

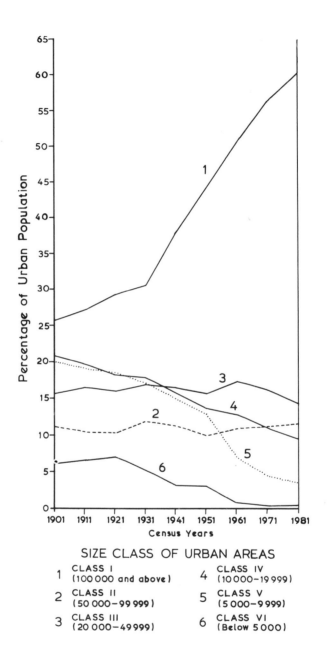

Figure 9.2.  Urban population in India, by size of urban areas, 1901-81

TABLE 9.3

INDIA:   ONE MILLION PLUS URBAN AGGLOMERATIONS

| Census year | Number | Population('000) | Percentage of Total Pop.* | Percentage of urban pop.* | Decadal percen- tage growth(+) |
|---|---|---|---|---|---|
| 1901 | 1 | 1,488.3 | 0.64 | 5.81 | - |
| 1911 | 2 | 2,736.8 | 1.11 | 10.70 | 83.89 |
| 1921 | 2 | 3,095.6 | 1.27 | 11.18 | 13.11 |
| 1931 | 2 | 3,374.0 | 1.25 | 10.23 | 8.99 |
| 1941 | 2 | 5,263.9 | 1.70 | 12.08 | 56.01 |
| 1951 | 5 | 11,662.9 | 3.33 | 18.92 | 121.56 |
| 1961 | 7 | 17,847.6 | 4.20 | 23.01 | 53.03 |
| 1971 | 9 | 27,420.8 | 5.18 | 25.63 | 53.64 |
| 1981 | 12 | 42,022.9 | 6.39 | 26.91 | 53.25 |

SOURCE:   Census of India 1981 Series-1, INDIA, Paper 2 of 1981

*
The population of Assam and J & K have been excluded.

TABLE 9.4

5)

INDIA:   POPULATION OF MILLION PLUS AGGLOMERATIONS, 1901-1981

(In Thousand)

| Rank in 1981 | 1901 | 1911 | 1921 | 1931 | 1941 | 1951 | 1961 | 1971 | 1981 |
|---|---|---|---|---|---|---|---|---|---|
| 1. Calcutta | 1488 | 1718 | 1851 | 2105 | 3578 | 4589 | 5737 | 7031 | 9166 |
| 2. Gt. Bombay | 813 | 1018 | 1245 | 1268 | 1686 | 2967 | 4152 | 5971 | 8227 |
| 3. Delhi | 214 | 238 | 304 | 447 | 696 | 1437 | 2359 | 3647 | 5714 |
| 4. Madras | 594 | 604 | 628 | 775 | 930 | 1542 | 1945 | 3170 | 4277 |
| 5. Bangalore | 159 | 189 | 237 | 307 | 407 | 779 | 1200 | 1654 | 2914 |
| 6. Hyderabad | 448 | 502 | 406 | 467 | 739 | 1128 | 1249 | 1796 | 2528 |
| 7. Ahmedabad | 186 | 217 | 274 | 314 | 595 | 877 | 1206 | 1742 | 2515 |
| 8. Kanpur | 203 | 179 | 216 | 244 | 487 | 705 | 971 | 1275 | 1688 |
| 9. Pune | 164 | 173 | 199 | 250 | 324 | 606 | 790 | 1135 | 1685 |
| 10. Nagpur | 167 | 119 | 165 | 242 | 329 | 485 | 690 | 931 | 1298 |
| 11. Lucknow | 256 | 252 | 241 | 275 | 387 | 497 | 656 | 814 | 1007 |
| 12. Jaipur | 160 | 137 | 124 | 149 | 181 | 304 | 410 | 637 | 1005 |

SOURCE:   Census of India 1981 series-1, INDIA, Paper 2 of 1981.

184

At the initial stage of historical development, forts formed the urban nuclei of Bombay, Madras, and Calcutta. In modern times, the CBDs of these cities, like their Western counterparts had little residentital population. The city of Calcutta developed a bifocal pattern consisting of a "European town" in the south and a "native town" in the north. It grew spatially around the fort constructed in 1756, which was demolished and rebuilt south of its original location. As the city grew, its northern part reflected more native characteristics, while the southern part presented a more of European look. The Calcutta Metropolitan District, spread over 1,300 km², contains India's largest concentrated manufacturing capacity, accounting for 15 percent of the country's total manufactured goods.[15]

As a consequence of the American Civil War during the early 1860s, world supply patterns of raw cotton shifted in India's favor, and Bombay was developed as a port. In 1953, the opening of railroads connected the city with its hinterland and Bombay started serving as entrepôt to the coast of India. The typical social structure of Bombay's population reflects the presence of the Zoroastrians ( *Parsis* as they are called in Bombay). They are concentrated in larger numbers here than at any other place. In terms of ethnic composition Bombay is the most diversified among South Asian cities.

Madras has a character of a typical regional city, where three-fourths of the residents speak Tamil. In general, the urban landscape of Madras reflects a combination of colonial and traditional influences. On the other end, Delhi reflects a deep-rooted historical background with colonial and modern forms. According to historical records 18 different capital sites have been chosen in the past 3,000 years in Delhi. The control of Delhi was so vital to the rule of North India that a popular saying arose: "He who controls Delhi, controls India."[16] With the shifting of the British capital from Calcutta to Delhi in 1930, a new town was planned by British architect-planner Edwin Lutyens with spacious roads, a magnificent viceroy's residence, a circular council chamber, and a Western-style shopping center (Connaught Place) at New Delhi. The main economic function of New Delhi is, however, administrative.

---

15. See Nisith R. Kar, "Economic Character of the Metropolitan Sphere of Influence of Calcutta," *Geographical Review of India* 25, no. 2 (1963): 108-37; Brian J.L. Berry and Philip H. Rees, "The Factorial Ecology of Calcutta," *The American Journal of Sociology* 74 (1969): 445-491.

16. Ashok K. Dutt, op. cit., p. 353 (fn. 14).

Bangalore has grown along the ancient banks of Dharmambudhi and Sampangi and is further oriented to the ridge and valley topography. The extensive cantonment in the east and the newly developed, planned residential colonies in the west and south have developed on the periphery of the ancient zone.[17] The establishment of heavy industry, such as Hindustan Aeronautics Ltd., Aero Engine Factory, and Bharat Electric Ltd., have together given a large boost to its growth and expansion. Similarly, at Kanpur the growth was initiated with the British cantonment, followed by industrial establishments.[18]

Hyderabad-Secunderabad, a twin city, outshone the fortress of Golconda and became the central site of the Muslim kingdom. Its growth continued east-west along the commercial highway of the kingdom until 1687. The three urban units of Golconda, the present Hyderabad, and Chaderghat (Secunderabad), which until 1931 was a separate municipality, developed in a concentric pattern. With the expansion of railroads the retail business market expanded in Hyderabad.[19]

Ahmedabad was founded in 1410 by Ahmed Shah, who expanded the already existing small town of the eleventh century.[20] Urban functions at Ahmedabad are well expressed in the forms of the incorporated residential areas, ruler's palace (Bhadra), court (Maidain-i-Shahi), and the growth of market centers and religious places (such as the Jami mosque).[21] With a rich cotton-producing hinterland, the city has attracted a textile industry, with the opening of the first mill in 1857. It developed rapidly after the introduction of a broad-gauge railroad in 1864.

Pune was initialy developed as a military center by the British. The existence of cantonments and a British civil administrative area outside the main city remain dominant characteristics. Representing the regional culture of Maharastra, the city later on expanded with the development of an engineering and textile industry.[22] In the same region, with the growth of the

17. Ram L. Singh, *Bangalore: An Urban Survey* (Varanasi: Tara Pub; 1964), pp. 15-25.

18. See Harihar Singh, *Kanpur: A Study in Urban Geography* (Varanasi: Indrasini Devi Pub., 1972).

19. S. Manzoor Alam, *Hyderabad-Secunderabad (Twin Cities): A Study in Urban Geography* (Hyderabad: Osmania University Press, 1965), pp. 128-130.

20. Jean-Elie Hamesse, *Sectoral and Spatial Interrelations in Urban Development: A Case Study of Ahmedabad, India* (Paris: Edition Herodot, Settlement Studies 1, 1983), p. 61.

21. Ibid., p. 63

22. See John E. Brush, "Spatial Patterns of Population in Indian Cities," *The Geographical Review* 58, no. 3 (1968): 362-391.

cotton-textile industry, Nagpur has similarly grown up. Nagpur's increasing role as a nodal center for railroads has been vital to its development: The Great Indian Peninsular Railway (1867), the Bengal-Nagpur Railway (1883), the Chhindwara line (1908), and the Chanda line (1913). These railroads connect the city with Bombay, Calcutta, Chanda, Hyderabad, and Madras and facilitated re-establishment of several entrepôts.[23]

During the medieval period, Luchnow developed as the provincial headquarters of the Mughal kings and later remained the seat of the Nawab of Oudh. After independence it was declared as the state capital of Uttar Pradesh; therefore, administrative functions became dominant in the city. The city has sustained an array of fine luxury crafts, from embroidered cotton goods to pottery and jewelry.[24]

Jaipur (the Pink City) was founded in 1725 by Sawai Jai Singh. During 1725-1767, nine blocks of the city were expanded. The establishment of educational institutions and the opening of a railroad connecting Delhi in 1882 together provided a base for the rapid growth of the city.[25] After independence, the city was declared as the state capitol of Rajasthan in 1949; thus, administrative functions were also added to this city.

It is expected that by 1991 nine more cities will be included among the million-plus urban agglomerations. These cities already came close to the population threshold by 1981. In descending order these are: Coimbatore (917,000), Patna (916,000), Surat (913,00), Madurai (904,000), Indore (827,000), Varnasi (794,000), Agra (770,000), Jabalpur (758,000), and Vadodara/Baroda (744,000). Patna and Surat recorded population growth of above 85 percent during 1971-81, while Indore and Jabalpur recorded over 40 percent. The rest of these cities have shown more modest growth, less than 30 percent.

Among the potential million cities, Varanasi is a particularly interesting case, for it is widely regarded as the cultural capital of India.[26] Phosphate analysis of ancient sites in Varanasi has indicated the city to be one of the "oldest continuously-occupied

23. Annapurna Kasyap, "Nagpur: A Study in City Morphology" (unpub. Ph.D. Dissertation, Nagpur University, 1961), p. 83.

24. Thomas R. Metcalf, *Land, Landlords, and the British Raj* (Berkeley: University of California Press, 1979), p. 50.

25. Ramesh K. Arora, Rakesh Hooja, and Shashi Mathur, *Jaipur, Profile of a Changing City* (Jaipur: The HCM State Institute of Public Administration, 1977), pp. 1-2.

26. See Ram L. Singh, *Banaras: A Study in Urban Geography* (Varanasi: Nand Kishore & Bros., 1955).

modern" (i.e., existing) cities in the world.[27] The religious sanctity and spatial transposition of sacred sites scattered all over India reflect the distinct character of Varanasi.[28]

## Regional Pattern of Current Urbanization

The States and Union Territories exhibited a wide range of urban growth rates during 1971-81. Mizoram in the northeast recorded urban growth of 225.1 percent, while Tamil Nadu showed 27.8 percent. With the addition of new towns, there appears to be a very high growth rate in the states of Orissa, Uttar Pradesh, and Haryana (60 percent and above). The Union Territories of Mizoram (225.1), Arunachal Radesh (129.7), Andaman and Nicobar Islands (89.3), and Chandigarh (80.8) have also seen high growth rates. Sikkim (159.9), Manipur (163.8), and Nagaland (133.8), all lying in the northeast hilly areas, all recorded change over 100 percent. A comparison of maps showing the percentage of urban population to total population in 1981 (fig. 9.3) and the changing size of urban populations of class I urban places (fig. 9.4) indicates clearly the correspondence between the location of class I urban areas and highly urbanized districts. This relationship extends also to the distribution of lesser places and the concentration of urbanization at district level. Such a pattern was already evident during the 1960s.[29]

With the growth of new towns in Dadra, Nagar Haveli, and Lakshadweep for the first time, these territories have entered in the stream of urbanization. The speedy growth of urban population in already existing cities and migration from rural areas were the factors responsible for such a trend.

Six urban agglomerations, all industrial-commercial cities, have more than doubled their population between 1971 and 1981, namely, Ondal (246.6 percent), Raniganj (156.4) in West Bengal; Bokaro Steel City (143.8) in Bihar; Ghaziabad (128.6) in Uttar Pradesh; Bhubaneswar (108.0) in Orissa; and Durg-Bhilai (100.0) in Madhya Pradesh. Apart from these six cities, Ranchi (95.9), Bathinda (95.1), and Aurangabad (91.4) have also recorded very high growth during the period--again all these cities being primarily industrial--commercial in function.

---

27. Robert C. Eidt, "Detection and Examination of Anthrosols by Phosphate Analysis," *Science* 197 (September 1977): 1332.

28. See Rana P.B. Singh, "Sacred Space, Sacred Time, and Pilgrimage in Hindu Society: A Case of Varanasi City," in *Sacred Places, Sacred Spaces: Geography of Pilgrimages,* ed. E. Alan Morinis (New York: 1984).

29. See Ram L. Singh, *Processes of Urbanization and Urban Development in Monsoon Asia* (Varanasi: National Geographical Society of India, 1977), pp. 8-9.

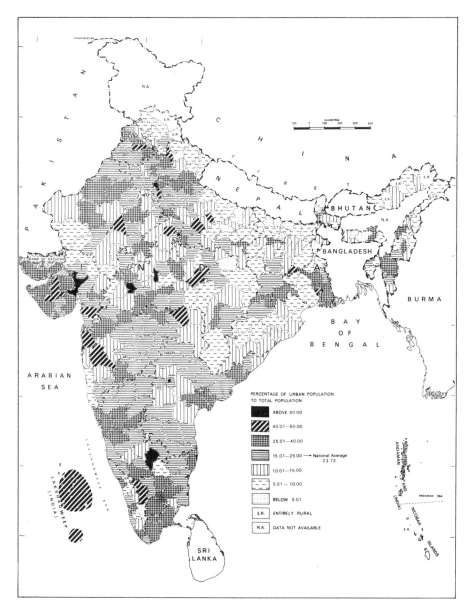

Figure 9.3. The proportion of urban population in India, by districts, 1981

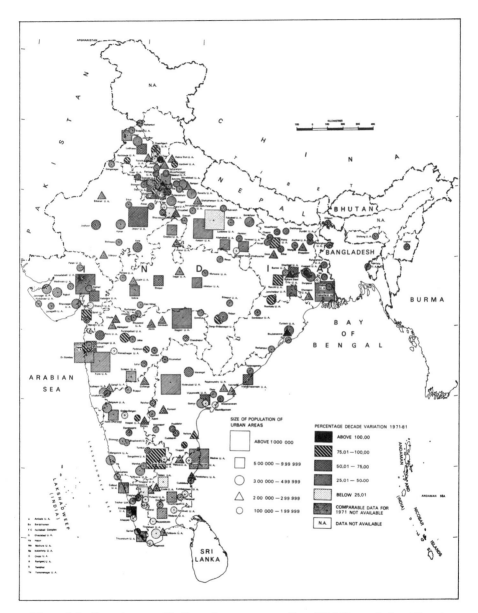

Figure 9.4.  Growth rates of Indian urban areas exceeding 100,000 population (Class I),

1971-81

The even distribution of cities in India is primarily due to the existence of a network of administrative centers from the earliest times. The spatial pattern of towns, however, could be easily grouped into two zones: the fertile Ganga valley in the north and the coastal belt of the south. The overwhelming superiority of Calcutta in the east, Bombay in the west, Madras in the south, and Delhi in the north is a composite outcome of encouragement in the form of administrative-cum-trade capitals and ports during the British period and industrialization in recent decades.[30]

### Projected Urbanization Zones

Taking topographical and topological connectivity among cities (between major cities, and between cities and their hinterlands) as a basis for predicting future urban zones and corridors, 24 urban zones have been projected, and it is expected that by the turn of the present century they will develop in actual form (fig. 9.5). It is suggested that a pre-conceived strategy needs be formulated so that these urban zones may generate maximum social and economic infrastructure without destroying the natural resources in and around these zones.[31] Crucial problems to be faced by these zones include housing, water supply, and various other amenities. The Sixth Five Year Plan (1980-85) once again recognizes that national urban policy should encompass regional problems and that urban development should be viewed in the context of its relationships with rural development in each region. Accordingly, the thrust of urban planning during the next decade will be to emphasize the provision of infrastructure and other facilities in the small, medium, and intermediate towns which have hitherto been neglected in this respect. In the Sixth Five Year Plan, in addition to continuation of these schemes, efforts toward the environmental improvement of slums has been extended to provide civic and other amenities in the slums of all urban areas, irrespective of their size.

According to one estimate, by 1991 there will be 233.8 million people in the urban areas of India, with a growth of 46.4 percent during 1981-91. Urban growth will be around 37.1 percent during 1991-2001, with the urban population projected to reach 320.5 million in 2001. It is further estimated that by 2100 there will be four distinct urban density zones: 0.3-2 persons/ha, 2-10, 10-40,

---

30. Ibid., p. 3.

31. Bhupendra K. Roy, "Population: A Major Element in Habitat Transformation," in *Environmental Appraisal and Rural Habitat Transformation,* ed. Ram L. Singh and Rana P.B. Singh (Varanasi: National Geographical Society of India, Pub. 32, 25th IGC Paris volume, 1984), p. 295.

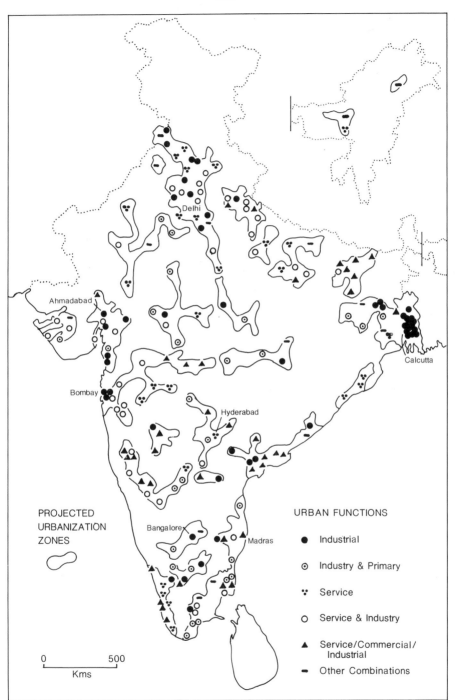

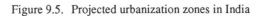

Figure 9.5. Projected urbanization zones in India

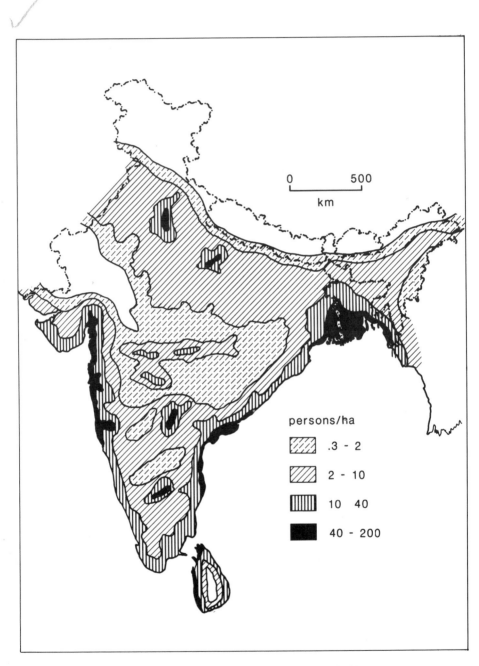

persons/ha

.3 - 2

2 - 10

10  40

40 - 200

Figure 9.6.  Urbanization in India by AD 2100

and 40-200 (fig. 9.6). The latter two density zones would be concentrated in the coastal belt, while the central part of the country would record the lowest density.

With these projects in mind, a population distribution policy is not considered to be a pressing need. For one thing, demographic implications of migration patterns have to be taken into consideration in policies relating to various sectors of the economy, such as urbanization, industrial location, provision of basic infrastructure, and so forth. Rational distribution of population within urban centers is also a concern, though this is to be handled through the development plans for important cities and towns around the country. The zonal pattern of future urban growth has also to be visualized in reference to spatial patterns of crime in Indian cities, which conform to the general regional occurrences of crime. It has been noted that cities located in north-central "subculture" regions have the main concentration of violent, economic, and group crimes, while South Indian cities show a relatively less frequent incidence of crime of all types.[32] Such issues also need consideration to make urban life more peaceful and acceptable.

### Closing Remarks

Geographers in India usually study the functional structure of general urbanization and the morphology of urban landscape in isolation and neglect cultural synthesis through a combination of these approaches. A dialectical approach to the spatial context of urban change from a full cultural perspective is needed to understand the urban scene in a more rational way.[33] In India such studies would be useful, as many ancient cities have maintained their cultural identity through traditions and customs, despite strong pressures of "Westernization."

---

32. Ashok K. Dutt and G. Venugopal, "Spatial Patterns of Crime among Indian Cities" *Geoforum* 14, no. 2 (1983), p. 288.

33. See Michael P. Conzen, "Analytical Approaches to the Urban Landscape," in *Dimensions of Human Geography: Essays on Some Familiar and Neglected Themes,* ed. Karl W. Butzer, Research Paper 186, (Chicago: Department of Geography, University of Chicago, 1978), pp. 164-165.

# Chapter X

# SOME REFLECTIONS ON URBANIZATION IN SOUTHEAST ASIA

## Norton S. Ginsburg

Planning for the future of the Asian city is planning for
change; . . . planning not only for the cities as they now are but for
the cities as they seem to be becoming; . . . planning not only at the
scale of the city and its parts but also at regional and national
scales, where the functions and the benefits and costs of urbanization
assume quite different proportions; . . . planning not only for the
physical city, but more important, for the kinds of people who will be
residing in it, . . . planning for modernization, for development, and
for urban forms that need not duplicate those of the West and which
indeed may vary significantly from country to country within the region.
Even as they are, cities are the centres for change in Asia. The
challenge and the opportunity lie in moulding that change for the
benefit of two-thirds of mankind.[1]

Asia, next to Africa south of the Sahara, appears to be
proportionally the least "urbanized" of the major world realms
(figure 10.1),[2] but in fact in terms of numbers of urban dwellers it
is the most highly "urbanized." Almost half of the world's urban
population of upward of 700 million people is believed to live in
Asia. Of these about 90 million live in Southeast Asian countries
(table 10.1), and those numbers are increasing at the rate of about
5 percent per year.

This essay looks at the Southeast Asian city as it has been
evolving since June 1969 when the University of Hongkong acted as
host for an international conference on "The City as a Centre of
Change in Asia." At that conference the concluding plenary address
attempted to generalize about some of the characteristics, problems,
and prospects of the Asian city, with emphasis on those in Southeast
Asia.[3]

---

1. Norton S. Ginsburg, in *The City as a Centre of Change in Asia,* ed.
Donald J. Dwyer (Hongkong: Hongkong University Press, 1972), pp. 281-2.

2. Figure 10.1 is based on data from the mid-1970s made available by
Richard Forstall of the U.S. Bureau of the Census for a research project at the
University of Chicago on world development patterns. Given the threshold figure
of 20,000 as a definition of "urban" population, this map may well be the most
reliable display of world urbanization available.

3. Norton S. Ginsburg, "Planning the Future of the Asian City," in Dwyer,
op. cit., pp. 269-84.

196

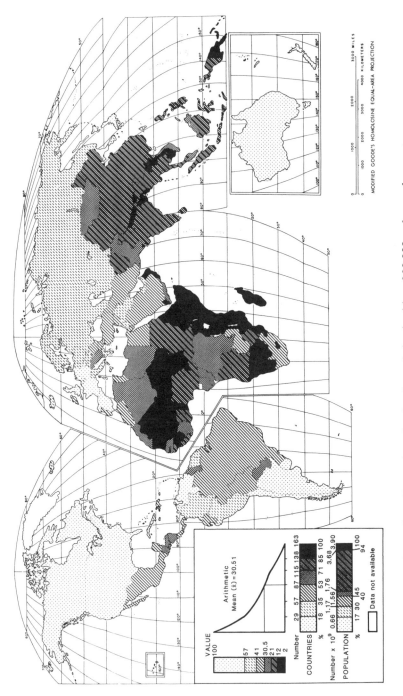

Figure 10.1.  Proportion of national population in cities of 20,000 and more, by country

TABLE 10.1

TOTAL URBAN POPULATION: SOUTHEAST ASIA, 1981[a]

| Country | Total Population (000s) | Urban Population (000s) | % Population Urban | Primacy (1970)[c] (a 4-city index) |
|---|---|---|---|---|
| 1. Brunei | 187 | 119 | 63.6 | n.a. |
| 2. Burma | 36,166 | 9,837 | 27.2[b] | 2.1 |
| 3. Indonesia | 150,520 | 33,562 | 22.3 | 1.2 |
| 4. Kampuchea | 5,746 | 799 | 13.9 | 8.7 |
| 5. Laos | 3,810 | 560 | 14.7 | n.a. |
| 6. Malaysia | 14,179 | 4,169 | 29.4 | 1.0[d] |
| 7. Philippines | 49,530 | 17,930 | 36.2 | 4.6 |
| 8. Singapore | 2,443 | 2,443 | 100.0 | n.a. |
| 9. Thailand | 47,875 | 6,894 | 14.4 | 10.0 |
| 10. Vietnam | 55,053 | 12,552 | 22.8 | 1.0 (est.) |
| TOTAL | 365,509 | 88,865 | 24.0 | |

[a] Data from Encyclopedia Britannica, based on best available sources for mid-year 1981. Most figures are estimates in the absence of recent census information. Definitions of "urban" vary from country to country.

[b] The urban proportion of Burma's population seems extraordinarily high. Other sources for 1970 and the mid-70s give estimates of 16 percent and 19 percent respectively.

[c] Population of the largest city divided by the combined populations of the next three, from D.W. Fryer, *Emerging Southeast Asia* (N.Y.: John Wiley, 1979), p. 90. The index originally developed by Kingsley Davis, et al. at International Urban Research. For index numbers based on 1950s data, see N. Ginsburg, *An Atlas of Economic Development* (Chicago: University of Chicago Press, 1961), pp. 36-7. Primacy is indicated by values larger than 2.

[d] Estimated after datum for Singapore was dropped.

A number of generalizations were posed, most of which came out of the discussions. Most Asian cities are the products of or have been influenced substantially by the expansion of Europe since the close of the fifteenth century, and almost all in Southeast Asia may be regarded as derived from Western colonialism. Most, especially the larger, are the foci of rapid change in society and economy and increasingly display the consequences of government policies. All display a basic dualism which reflects a counterpoint between traditional and indigenous on the one hand and modern, which inevitably means foreign, on the other. The larger cities seem to be growing faster than the smaller, a fact which seems to arouse great concern among planners and policy-makers. At the same time, with few exceptions, planning for the Asian city is inadequate, handicapped by ideas and concepts derived from solely Western experience[4] and by the biases of planners against the great city. However, since governments are committed to modernization, and modernization involves industrialization, and industrialization implies urbanization, it is likely that the larger cities will continue to grow. That growth will be tempered by the nature of modern manufacturing which employs fewer workers than used to be the case. Thus, employment opportunities are bound to remain constrained despite rapid urban population growth due to both natural increase and immigration. In addition, policies directed toward the development of "balanced hierarchies" were rejected, as they were at the Pacific Conference on Urban Growth in Honolulu two years earlier,[5] as being ill-founded, expensive, and, given available transportation techniques, probably counter-productive. Other propositions emphasized the importance of ethnicity in understanding urban structures, the need for rural policies which would facilitate the "urbanization of the countryside" immediately tributary to the cities, and the desirability of innovations which would assist both urban populations and potential ones still in rural areas to cope with the problems and opportunities of urban life.

Most of these generalizations appear to have stood up well in the past fifteen years. What follows will reflect on some of them in the light of fifteen years of change.

---

4. Akin Mabogunje et al. deal with this problem in *Shelter Provision in Developing Countries (SCOPE II)* (New York: John Wiley, 1978).

5. Milton Kaplan, *Pacific Conference on Urban Growth: The New Urban Debate, a Conference Report* (Washington: U.S. Aid, 1968).

## The Distribution of Cities

Most of the major cities of Southeast Asia are located on tidewater. Strung along the coasts like beads on a string, they acted during colonial times as points of entry for foreigners and as terminal points for the umbilical cords that bound the then dependent territories to the so-called "mother country." Thus, we see, including river ports, Akyab, Rangoon, Moulmein, Tavoy, Mergui, Penang, Melaka, Singapore, Belawant Deli, Palembang, Jakarta, Chiribon, Semarang, Surabaya, Makassar, Banjermasin, Menado, Sandakan, Davao, Cebu, Tacloban, Iloilo, Manila, Saigon, Danang, Hanoi, and Bangkok. To be sure, many of these had pre- or non-colonial histories or antecedents, among the more important of which are Palembang, Melaka, Bangkok, and Hanoi; but the impress of European expansion on their landscapes has proven thus far indelible, and their characters have been substantialy molded by that impact.

In addition to them are a number of non-port cities, usually smaller and less important than the larger of the ports, among which Mandalay was and Kuala Lumpur is exceptionally important. The Mandalay area has been a major area of Burmese power in the precolonial period. In peninsular Malaysia Kuala Lumpur, like Ipoh and Taiping, was developed by Chinese as a mining town immediately prior to or concomitant with the colonial impact. On Java, Surakarta and Jogjakarta reflect their status as *nagara* in the empire of Mataram.

Elsewhere in Asia, to a degree in India and largely in the Sinitic world including Korea, Japan, and northern Vietnam, interior cities and indigenous city systems provided the bases for later urban expansion and change under foreign influence. Thus, one can argue that no part of Asian Asia remained immune from the impact of European expansion on cities and urban systems.

To be sure there had been cities in Southeast Asia from very early times, the origins of which have been admirably discussed by Paul Wheatley in a recently published work,[6] but it was not until the seventh or eigth centuries that their characters can, even in part, be documented, and then chiefly on mainland locations, as in Cambodia, where massive ruins of a large sacred capital remain, and on Java. For the most part, these reflected Indian cultural influences and models. By the second half of the fourteenth century, systems of cities appear to have developed in several

---

6. Paul Wheatley, *Nagara and Commandery: Origins of the Southeast Asian Urban Traditions,* Research Paper no. 207-8 (Chicago: Univ. of Chicago, Dept. of Geography, 1983).

regions of Southeast Asia, but the character of these systems is by no means clear.[7] Apparently they were all primate in nature, with the religious-cum-administrative center at the peak of a vertically elongated pyramid, a number of regional administrative cities at a secondary level carrying out at lesser scale the plans of the primate city, and then a number of still lesser places possessed of administrative (e.g., tax-gathering) and related functions, no doubt with local market functions as well. At that time too a different species of towns, mostly coastal, also began to appear, as on the northern coast of Java, in southern Sumatra, and along the Malayan west coast, which were primarily commercial in function. These new kinds of towns were maritime, trade-oriented, and multi-ethnic and were possessed of a high degree of autonomy. Among them, Melaka (Malacca), the most important, acted as the focal point for trade between the East Indies, China, and India and the Middle East for about a century until conquered by the Portugese in 1511.[8]

Most of the major pre-colonial cities (Melaka was an exception) were located in areas that were well populated and possessed of productive agricultures. Many, though not all, of the colonial coastal cities were associated with the development of coastal lowlands under foreign rule or influence, as illustrated by Rangoon and the Irrawaddy delta, Saigon-Cholon and the lower Mekong region, Penang, Kuala Lumpur, and Singapore and the west Malaysian tin-and-rubber belt, and Manila and the central Luzon lowland. The result has been a remarkable areal coincidence between the cities of southeast Asia, especially the larger, and population in general. Even in Thailand, never under direct European domination, the expansion of the Thai into Lower Siam concentrated much of that country's population, both rural and urban, there, within 100 miles of Bangkok.

There is no way of knowing what kinds of cities and urban hierarchies might have developed in the absence of the European expansion and impact. In the case of peninsular Malaysia, the best documented case, it is unlikely that anything resembling the present urban system would have developed without Chinese and later British initiatives. Only in Tonkin and central Vietnam, unlike the rest of Southeast Asia an offshoot of the Sinitic world, would a well developed settlement hierarchy have appeared and maintained itself.

---

7. See Wheatley, op. cit., p. 426 and Paul Wheatley and Kernial S. Sandhu, eds., *Melaka: The Transformation of a Malay Capital c. 1400-1980* (Kuala Lumpur: Oxford University Press, 1982), vol. 1, p. 24.

8. Norton Ginsburg, "The Changing Meaning of Modernization in Southeast Asia," chapter 37 in Wheatley and Sandhu, op. cit., pp. 285-98.

In China, of course, a highly developed urban system, based largely
on the administrative principle, appeared long before the European
impact which became significant in settlement terms only after the
middle of the nineteenth century.

It is true, however, that the hierarchies of cities in most
Southeast Asian countries appear truncated. Primacy characterizes
the smaller and medium-sized countries, except for Malaysia for
which Singapore had been the primate city until 1965 or so, and
Vietnam which under colonialism developed northern and southern
"poles" of development. Indonesia, the largest country, has a low
primacy index, despite the very rapid growth of Jakarta in recent
years as the center of national authority in a newly independent,
very large, and fragmented country with an extended array of cities
of different sizes distributed about the archipelago but
concentrated on Java, the hub of the Indonesian universe (figure
10.2).[9]

Moreover, the smaller and medium-sized towns appear to be
growing less rapidly, though with some exceptions as discussed
below. This being the case, the argument often is made that this
phenomenon, when combined with primacy in some countries, is
undesirable and must be rectified. This is the main thrust of
Dennis Rondinelli's recent book.[10] However, the question also needs
to be raised again as to the extent to which such cities are
necessary, given the distribution of populations in national
ecumenes and the capabilities of the larger cities, especially the
capitals, of commanding even larger populous hinterlands by means of
readily available transporation and communication technologies.

### A Collection of Period Pieces

This term, coined by C.S. Chandrasekhara at the 1969 Hongkong
conference, provides a useful point of entry to describing the
internal structure of Asian cities.[11] Basically, Asian cities can be
divided into two parts, an old and a new, a traditional or perhaps
colonial and a modern; but there are great differences among
countries as to what these parts incorporate. For the most part,
none of them, with some partial exceptions in Japan, reflect sensu
stricto the trio of organizational principles presented in

---

9. Figure 10.2 was prepared by Clifton Pannell for a project at the
University of Chicago on mapping techniques in Southeast Asia under a grant from
the Southeast Asia Development Advisory Group (SEADAG). Though dated, it fairly
reflects the current distribution of Indonesian cities.

10. Dennis A. Rondinelli, *Secondary Cities, in Developing Countries:
Policies for Diffusing Urbanization* (Beverly Hills: Sage, 1983).

11. See the reference in Ginsburg, "Planning the Future," in Dwyer, op.
cit., p. 274.

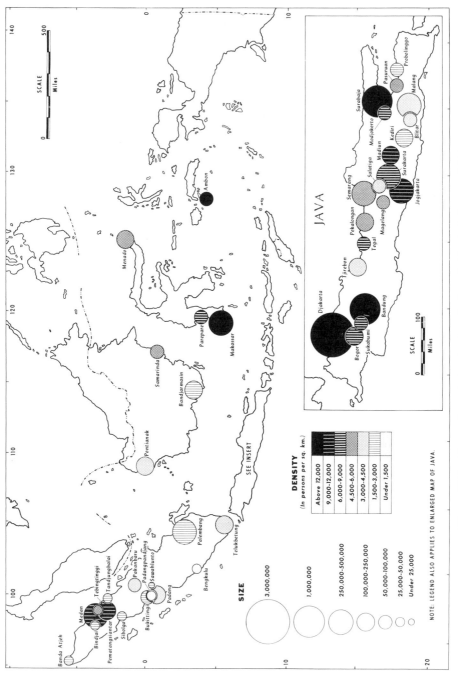

Figure 10.2.   Size and population density of selected cities in Indonesia, 1961

Harris and Ullman's classic article on the "Nature of Cities."[12]
There may be multiple nuclei, but they are associated with ethnic
diversity and governmental policy for the most part rather than
market and other social forces. There is concentricity to be sure,
but the concentric zones differ radically from what has been
postulated for Western cities--for example, the poor usually live
far from the center of things, and industrialization tends to lead
the way to suburbanization rather than primarily high quality
residential land uses. There also may be sectors which may expand
outward, but their character is little like that postulated by Homer
Hoyt and included in the Harris and Ullman schema.

Chandrasekhara's model applies best to Indian cities. In
Delhi, for example, there is, to be sure, an Old City and a New
City. The Old City is of Mughal origin, reflecting Persian cultural
influences--walled, densely populated, with irregular street
patterns, with many multiple-storied buildings of three and
sometimes more floors, often with open courtyards, dominated by a
great mosque along one side and a large market area behind it
elongated along a major commercial street running westward from the
rear of the mosque. Segregation by occupation and ethnic origin
characterizes the Old City, but the New City--New Delhi--is even
more diverse. There is an adminstrative area modelled along
European lines; residential neighborhoods of a strong European, even
garden city, cast; a primary shopping center; a military cantonment;
a railway cantonment; a series of outlying residential areas along
European lines, commonly called "colonies;" industrial exclaves
along the margins of the built-up area frequently walled and
associated with workers' housing; and clusters of squatter and other
low-income settlement in the interstitial areas. Delhi is, of
course, unique, but similar patterns are found in most cities in
northern India in greater or lesser degree.

In Southeast Asia this multiplicity of forms is diminished,
but it is still there. The basic divisions, apart from old and new,
are among indigenous where relevant, foreign Asian, and European
colonial and post-colonial. In Bangkok, for example, the "city" in
the sense of a central business district has long been an area of
Chinese shophouse settlement which also is the area of highest
population density. To the north of it is an area of religious and
governmental land uses with interstitial areas of Thai residential
structures little different from those found in rural areas.[13] To

---

12. Chauncy D. Harris and Edward L. Ullman, "The Nature of Cities," *Annals of the American Academy of Political and Social Science* 242 (1945): 7-17.

the west, across the Menam, are extensive Thai residential areas, amphibious in nature, with stilted structures oriented toward canals rather than roads.  Unlike the Mughals, the Thai, like most Southeast Asian peoples, were not great city builders.  Temples and the palace residences of the rulers and the nobility were the indigenous core of the capitals, themselves ephemeral and shifting.  The Chinese built what would be recognizably urban landscapes in their "quarters," as might other foreigners.  Thai commoners lived along the peripheries of these two core areas; but until the mid-nineteenth century the size of the urban centers was small by European standards.

The Malays also were not great city builders.  Most cities of the Malayan Peninsula were or are predominantly Chinese in population, and most were in fact founded and developed by Chinese either before or during the colonial period.  Pre-European urban centers like Melaka were extremely small in both area and population.  The contemporary Malaysian city, like Bangkok, has its "Chinatown" as the functional center of highest population density, near which is the main mosque and the residence of the ruler or administrator frequently associated in the smaller cities with a square or *maidan* similar to that in Calucutta.[14] To these basic elements, the British added administrative areas, usually near the mosque, and Western-style residential areas chiefly in peripheral locations.  Malay residential areas also were largely peripheral and have, until recently and even now, closely resembled the rural *kamong* from which most Malay urban dwellers have come in increasing numbers.

Obviously, these patterns differ in other countries, not least because the numbers of Chinese in their populations have been much smaller than in Malaysia and, until very recently, in Bangkok itself, but the three key elements of a weakly developed indigenous ceremonial urban element, a Chinese city, and a European colonial city, juxtaposed, bring order to the seemingly heterogeneous landscapes of most Southeast Asian cities.

In the East Asian Sinitic world, including much of Vietnam, the situation is quite different in that a long tradition of multiple-function urbanization has existed for centuries.  It would

13 . Sternstein describes part of this area thus: "The innermost 1.4 square kilometers between the Lot Canal and the Chao Phraya River contain little else but the Grand Palace, several large ministries, several large monasteries, the Thammasat and Fine Arts universities, the National Museum, the National Archives, the National Theatre, and the Phra Men Ground," in Dwyer, op. cit., p. 253.

14 . Norton Ginsburg and Chester F. Roberts, Jr., *Malaya* (Seattle: University of Washington Press, 1958), pp. 86-94.

not be appropriate to attempt here a description of the paradigmatic Chinese city, for example, but most also display a prominent dualism between old and new, especially in the former Treaty Ports of which there were 119 at one time, although to be sure many of these were not functional ports at all. In many cases, the indigenous urban landscape proved subordinate to that resulting from Western and later Japanese urban forms--as in the cases of, for example, Harbin, Chang-ch'un, Mukden, Tientsin, Ch'ing-tao, Shanghai, Wu-han, and even Canton; and there are some cases chiefly in Manchuria where cities like Fu-shun and An-shan were virtually modern industrial creations reflecting foreign (that is, Japanese) influence.

### The Alien Town

The history of urbanization in Southeast Asia largely as a result of the expansion of Europe into the region may be reason enough for applying the phrase, the "alien town,"[15] to Southeast Asian cities; but, as implied earlier, there is yet another justification for it. To a remarkable degree the populations of those cities are foreign, by which is meant chiefly "other Asian." This characteristic differs from country to country in the region; but it also is a characteristic of larger cities in other parts of Asia. In India, for example, each of the four largest cities--Bombay, Calcutta, Delhi, and Madras--has large minorities from regions of the country other than its hinterland. That some of these are successful in the competition for scarce jobs and entrepreneurial activities has created high tension and ethnic stress in those cities and in others. In Japan, large Korean and smaller Chinese minorities are concentrated in the larger metropolitan areas. Historically, in China, the former Treaty Ports, and earlier some of the southern ports open to trade during the Sung, Tang, and early Ming dynasties, also had foreign quarters of considerable size, though present-day populations are more homogeneous. To be sure, multi-ethnicity is a characteristic of most larger cities wherever they may be--in the developed countries as in the underdeveloped--but the importance of ethnic minorities in Southeast Asian cities is striking.

If we examine the map of Malaysian cities and towns according to the 1947 census (figure 10.3),[16] we find that, of the fifteen

---

15 . A term used by Ann Larimore in her study of Busoga, Uganda, *The Alien Town*, Research Paper no. 55 (Chicago: University of Chicago, Dept. of Geography, 1958).

16 . From Ginsburg and Roberts, op. cit., p. 91. Parenthetically, maps based upon more recent censuses would show much the same pattern as that on figure 10.3, but the predominance of the Chinese in Kuala Lumpur will have been diminished. After all, Malaysia is a Malay-oriented society, and Kuala Lumpur is

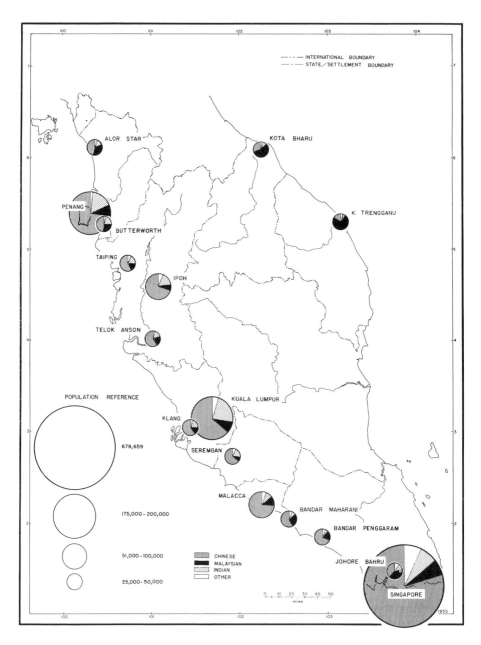

Figure 10.3.   Major cities and towns in Malaya, 1947

largest cities in the peninsula at that time, twelve had Chinese
majorities, and thirteen had non-Malay majorities, counting Indians.
Singapore, Kuala Lumpur, Penang, Ipoh, Taiping, and Melaka were
essentially Chinese cities, alien enclaves in an otherwise
predominantly Malay setting. To be sure, Malaya then and Malaysia
now are not typical of the rest of Southeast Asia in that the
proportion of the overall population that is Chinese and Indian is
well over forty percent; and Singapore is sui generis in having
three-fourths of its population Chinese and thereby meriting the
accolade (or epithet) the "Third China." In any event, urbanization
in Malaya received much initial impetus from Chinese miners'
settlements, for example, Kuala Lumpur, which the British
incorporated into an incipient urban hierarchy as they established
control over the peninsula.[17]

In other Southeast Asian countries, the proportions of Chinese
and other non-indigenous Asians are much smaller than in Malaysia
and Singapore, but the importance of them in the urban pattern was
and is still significant. For example, Bangkok in 1940 was
generally acknowledged to have been a substantially if not
predominantly Chinese city, although precise evidence for this
proposition is missing since the Thai recorded in their censuses
only those Chinese who were foreign-born, a smaller number than the
whole.[18] Rangoon at the same time was a largely Indian city, with
large Chinese and Burmese minorities. Many Indians fled before the
Japanese occupation of 1941, and others left after the end of the
Pacific War; so did many Chinese. Still their impact on the urban
landscape remains, although the population of the city is now
overwhelmingly Burmese. In Indonesia most larger cities have
sizable Chinese minorities and shophouse areas which act as the
commercial cores of the urban centers, although there are fewer than
four million Chinese in the entire country, and they have been much
persecuted by other Indonesians. Too, on Java there are some
exceptions to the rule that larger cities must be "alien towns," in
that both Surakarta and Jogjakarta, for example, are the lineal
descendants of the traditional *nagara* of premodern times. In the

---

capital where patronage is dispensed to Malays who flock in from rural areas
seeking both opportunities and handouts from a sympathetic government committed to
raising Malay living levels.

17 . Those observers who write of "dysfunctional" settlement patterns
resulting from colonialism should reflect on what alternatives would otherwise
have arisen. Rather than being "dysfunctional," the urban system in Malaya, for
example, acts as a key element in the national spatial system.

18 . Donald W. Fryer estimates the proportion of Chinese as 60 percent. In
the intervening years, as the city has more than tripled in population size, that
proportion has much diminished.

Philippines, sizable Chinese and Chinese mestizo minorities characterize the urban areas, as is or was the case in Indochina, especially in the south. The effect of the recent emigration of predominantly ethnic Chinese from Vietnam as boat people has yet to be determined, but it surely means a decline in the importance of the Chinese in Vietnamese cities throughout the country.

In any event, ethnicity is a key word in understanding the present character of Southeast Asian cities, particularly as related to the Chinese. In South Asia the word is of lesser importance, but it still is significant. Only in East Asia does the term have little current value.

### The Dynamics of Change: The National Urban System

Recent changes in the national urban systems of Southeast Asian countries have been less dramatic than might have been expected. Existing urban hierarchies basically resemble those that existed at the close of the Pacific War, but there have been changes, some of them striking.

The most important change reflects the rapid growth of urban populations in most countries. Regional demographic data, as noted earlier, are poor, but there is general consensus that urban populations are increasing at about 5 percent per annum, whereas over-all populations are increasing at less than half that rate. Southeast Asia is still a region of rather low urbanization as measured by the proportion of the national populations living in cities, but the proportions are changing significantly. More than half the population of western Malaysia consists of urban dwellers, and Singapore is, of course, almost 100 percent urban. The rate of urbanization has been much slower in economically stagnant Burma and even slower in the Indochinese states where there might even have been some decline in the urban population as many residents of Saigon-Cholon (Ho Chi Minh City) have been sent down to the countryside and thousands of others, chiefly Chinese, have fled by boat to other countries in the region. Parenthetically, although the proportion of the population urban in Vietnam is shown on table 10.1 as 22.8 percent, earlier information suggests for South Vietnam a figure nearer 40 percent as migration from insecure rural areas continued unabated in the early 1970s.

Although much of the urban population increase has been due to in-migration from rural to urban areas, it is probable that natural increase has been an even more important factor.[19] Contrary to much

---

19. In India between 1951 and 1971, immigration accounted for about 40 percent of the increase in urban population. V.L.S. Prakasa Rao, *Urbanization in*

opinion, living conditions in the larger cities are better than those in rural areas, and longevity is greater. Thus it is not strange that the populations of the larger cities tend to grow as fast or faster than those of the smaller, even though the latter have not all been falling behind.

Still, the fact that the larger cities continue to act as magnets for immigrants and increase their populations at a high rate arouses considerable concern. In fact, the argument continues to be made that middle-sized city growth should be stimulated by government policy and investment, so as to create a more "balanced" urban system.[20] It is doubtful that this concern is well-founded or that its objective of greater "balance" is achievable. The larger cities, primate or not, are growing because there is good reason for them to do so. Most of them, like Kuala Lumpur and Jakarta, are centers of administrative authority, a condition associated with swollen bureaucracies. Governmental policies tend to favor the larger places, and industry, such as it is, also tends to favor them. If smaller cities are to grow rapidly and to act as deflectors of rural migrants from the larger cities, they must have a raison d'être for doing so. As Osborn pointed out in his study of the middle-sized city in Malaysia,[21] those that do not possess comparative advantages are bound to decline, and indeed it might be to the national advantage if they do so instead of being propped up at great cost to countries which can ill-afford unnecessary, and even some necessary, expenditures.

To take an example, Chiengmai in northern Thailand has been pointed out as an example of dynamic urbanization at the middle-sized level in a study which has emphasized the seemingly crucial role of local entrepreneurship in urban growth.[22] No doubt that factor is important, but Chiengmai is sui generis even in Thailand, where other cities in a hierarchy dominated by primate Bangkok have been growing much more slowly. What the report does not make clear is Chiengmai's unusual comparative advantages among Thai cities. It is, for one thing, in the Menam basin; a raft or country boat can move directly down the Ping River in the rainy

---

*India: Spatial Dimensions* (New Delhi: Concept Publishing Co., 1983), p. 47. The proportion in the 1951-61 decade was somewhat higher; in the 1961-71 decade considerably lower.

20 . Rondinelli, op. cit.

21 . James Osborn, *Area, Development Policy, and the Middle City in Malaysia,* Research Paper no. 153 (Chicago: University of Chicago, Department of Geography, 1974), pp. 253 ff.

22 . Chakrit Noranitipadungkarn and A. Clarke Hagensick, *Modernizing Chiengmai: A Study of Community Elites in Urban Development* (Bangkok: National Institute of Development Administration, 1973).

season from Chiengmai to Bangkok. The towns of northeastern and of peninsular Thailand have no such advantage. Chiengmai has an extraordinarily salubrious climate, perhaps the best of any in Thailand. It also has a long history as a center of Thai civilization and has played a key role in the wars against the Burmese. It also acts as a regional capital for a strategically important area bounded in part by Laos, Burma, and (a distance away) China, and therefore it is of particular importance in Thai national and international policy. It is well tied to the national spatial order; in early 1951, the author went by train to Chiengmai from Bangkok on a well-maintained roadbed in a comfortable train pulled by a spanking new Japanese-built, wood-burning locomotive. Therefore, it is no mere backwater, but rather a place to which people are quite willing to be assigned, if they are government officials, or to move to if they are not. In addition, the Chiengmai basin has been one of the few areas of double-cropped irrigated paddy cultivation in the country,and this firm rural, agricultural basis for regional development has been reinforced by crop diversification, particularly tobacco cultivation, which has increased regional prosperity. The fact that the hills around Chiengmai are major teak producers also is important, as is the fact that the hill peoples of the region have long been the target for missionary activity in the area, which has resulted, before the government expanded its own school system and founded a major university there, in a number of high quality schools, colleges, and even a research center. And then, in those hills, there is the opium poppy . . . 23 In short Chiengmai is no ordinary place in the Thai scheme of things. It grows because it has the capabilities for doing so.

In any country, where such advantages do not exist, smaller cities, serving depressed rural areas with little surplus, are not likely to grow, and government investment in them will, ceretis paribus, not be productive. Thus, we see in western Malaysia, for example, the stagnation of Melaka, once a great trading emporium, now a relatively minor backwater. On the other hand, the recent development of offshore petroleum deposits along the east coast of Malaysia and improved transportation facilities associated with them, along with government interest in developing that backward

---

23. Readers will be both informed and entertained by a series of short articles in the *Far Eastern Economic Review* 126, no. 52 (December 1984), pp. 34-8 and 47-51, which deal with the opium/heroin traffic in Southeast Asia and Chiengmai's role in it. Also informative is a delightful series of fifteen essays on Chiengmai by Willard A. Hanna, "Change in Chiengmai," *Southeast Asia Series* 13, nos. 2ff. (New York: American Universities Field Staff, Inc., 1965).

region for tourism and for the benefit of the largely Malay populations of Kelantan and Trengannu, may result in more rapid and fruitful urban growth than would have been thought possible.

Meanwhile, the largest cities continue to grow and to become ever-more dominant in the national urban systems. Not all such cities are primate, however; size of country matters. Thus, Indonesia in Southeast Asia, India, and China do not display the primate phenomenon, except on a regional basis, nor does Vietnam, whereas Thailand, the Philippines, and to a lesser degree Burma do. In Malaysia, where Singapore was the primate city until 1965 when it was expelled from the Federation of Malaysia, metropolitan Kuala Lumpur has grown more rapidly than any other major place, but it still falls far short of the primacy standard. Singapore, of course, is primate by definition as the only city-state in Asia.

Whether the continuing dominance of the largest cities in the national urban systems is desirable or not remains an issue for continuing investigation and debate. There are virtually no firm quantitative data relating to the efficiencies of larger versus smaller cities, although on the basis of one study of Indian cities it appears that a city population of about 130,000 is required for the scale-economic support of modern industry.[24] When a conference on smaller cities in Asia was held at the East-West Center in 1980, the author asked Harry Richardson, an economist who has been a consultant to the World Bank, why economists have not made benefit-cost studies of urban size, he replied that it could not be done. Nevertheless, Richardson has advocated the development of smaller cities at the expense of larger under certain circumstances, as part of a useful review of concepts in urban geography and planning prepared for the World Bank, though the costs remain unknown.[25] What is certain is, first, that large numbers of people will continue to move to the larger cities from rural areas and small towns, that their numbers may well increase as agriculture is "modernized", that un- and under-employment are rife in those cities, and that their infrastructures are sadly lacking in the necessities for dignified urban living and for the creation of job opportunities. The problem therefore might be less how to keep urban population numbers down, though that may be desirable, than how to provide for those already there and about to come.

---

24. Stanford Research Institute, "Costs of Urban Infrastructure for Industry," *Ekistics* 20 (November 1969), pp. 316-20.

25. Harry W. Richardson, *City Size and National Spatial Strategies in Developing Countries,* World Bank Staff Working Paper 252 (Washington: The World Bank, 1977).

It is noteworthy in this connection that neither India nor China are experiencing a very rapid expansion of the largest cities. The Chinese case has been much publicized, but China's success in slowing large city growth has been associated with a national policy of immobilizing the population, something that only a totalitarian state could enforce.[26] On the other hand, the several largest Indian Metropolitan areas also have been growing more slowly than had been expected.[27] A more careful comparative study of the two countries in this regard clearly is called for.[28] Scale again appears to be an important dimension of the problem.

### The Dynamics of Change: Urban Patterns and Structures

Change at the individual city and metropolitan level also has been taking place. Several conditions forecast in 1969 have impressed themselves upon the urban landscapes of Southeast Asia's cities.

First, ethnicity in the larger cities and consequent segregation has been lessening as more rural peoples have moved to the larger cities. At the same time, there has been a steady trickle of emigration by Chinese, for example, to areas and countries where they are less likely to be discriminated against. Moreover, in some cases, particularly Thailand, the very large Chinese national minority has been experiencing assimilation at a rather rapid rate, and it is believed that a high proportion of the Thai government bureaucracy consists of assimilated Chinese mixed-bloods. Assimilation in Malaysia and Indonesia has been taking place for generations also, but at a very much slower pace than in Thailand, largely because assimilation means adherence to Islam the rigidity of which, unlike Buddhism, is unattractive to most Chinese.

Second, the governmental administrative areas near the old Chinese business-cum-residential districts have been expanding especially in the capital cities, and housing has had to be found for the rapidly enlarging bureaucracy. Kuala Lumpur and Jakarta are conspicuous examples, but Bangkok and Manila are not far behind.

---

26 . Chi-Keung Leung and Norton S. Ginsburg, eds., *China: Urbanization and National Development,* Research Paper no. 196 (Chicago: University of Chicago, Department of Geography, 1980). Various references.

27 . Prakasa Rao, op. cit., pp. 64-5.

28 . One comparative study has appeared recently, T. Banerjee and S. Schenk, "Lower Order Cities and National Urbanization Policies: China and India," *Environment and Planning A* 16 (April 1984): 485-509. Unfortunately, the authors attribute the seeming success China has had in restricting great city growth and encouraging small city growth to forward-looking policies, whereas in fact great city growth has continued apace despite the ban on population mobility in China, and the environmental and other problems of small cities and towns are very great. India, as usual, receives a poor press, only partially deserved.

Third, growth corridors have grown at a remarkable rate. That between Kuala Lumpur and Port Klang in the Kelang river valley is an outstanding example. Others are the corridors along highways linking the largest cities with their airports. Here the Bangkok case is notable in Southeast Asia, but similar phenomena appear also, for example, Calcutta with its Dum Dum corridor, as well as in Bombay and Delhi.

Fourth, these corridors are closely associated with industrialization. As the writer stated in 1969:

> Modern industries can find few sites within the built-up area, and they therefore seek sites on its outskirts where land is cheaper and access to raw materials (somewhat) easier. The plant locations already are generating residential-commercial developments around them, the total effect (of which) is to enlarge the areas for which urban services are required and to somewhat lessen over-all urban densities. Unlike the situation in, say, the United States, industries rather than higher quality residential land uses will lead the way to suburbanization.[29]

Like all such generalizations, there are exceptions to this one. It finds partial exception in Manila, where in the suburb of Makati modern commercial buildings, boulevards, and high-income residential areas are the norms which characterize a new suburbia. In the case of Singapore the generalization is only partly valid, since government housing policies have created vast residential estates, chiefly high-rise, around the landward margins of the built-up area.

Fifth, cities in Southeast Asia and indeed most of Asia continue to be more compact and display higher densities than their equivalents in the West, and the break between what is visually rural and urban is extremely sharp. However, the word "visually" is important here, since many residents of the villages in immediate urban hinterlands increasingly are obtaining part if not most of their incomes from employment, however modest, in the cities themselves.

Sixth, despite these developments, the cities continue to display, both in their landscapes and in their socioeconomic structures, the same conspicuous dualism that was associated with the colonial period. The so-called "informal sector" continues to account for a high percentage of employment in most cities, an estimated 40 percent in the case of Calcutta, for example.[30] Although economists appear uncomfortable in dealing with that sector, research by geographers and sociologists has cast much light on the way it is organized and functions as both an economic and a

---

29. Ginsburg, "Planning the Future of," in Dwyer, op. cit., pp. 277-78.

30. Harold Lubell, *Urban Development and Employment: The Prospects for Calcutta* (Geneva: International Labor Office, 1974), p. 25.

socializing phenomenon.[31]

Last, all Asian cities are subject to what has been called the "technological imperative." To be sure, even given the fact that the city is an artifact and therefore reflects the cultures of the societies it serves, the role of a universally distributed technology, particularly that of transportation, has become of increasing importance. To be sure, that technology can be misapplied. For example, this writer and others sought to influence the Thai government not to fill in the *klong* (canals) of Bangkok and surface them as major arteries for automotive transport but failed; witness therefore the terrible traffic jams for which Bangkok has become notorious and, even more important, the frequent floods during the rainy season which the old *klong* system usually would have mitigated. Singapore, confronted with similar traffic problems, has committed itself to an elaborate mass transit system now under construction. However, the result of the belated automotive revolution inevitably will mean expanded urban and metro areas, further separation of workplace from residence, and a lowering of the barriers which have separated the "period pieces" to which reference has been made above.

### Envoi

It is far from certain just what kinds of cities will evolve in Southeast Asia, but it seems likely that they will increasingly resemble those found in the West. Still, as cultural artifacts however complex, those cities will reflect primarily the kinds of societies that produce them. Just as the societies in Southeast Asia will continue to contain both modern (that is, Western) and indigenous elements, so will their cities; and government intervention in the urbanization process is likely to increase. Most countries in Southeast Asia have governments which seek to command development and change in ways resembling those of the centrally planned economies, whether or not they are overtly socialist in ideological cast. In this respect, Singapore is more likely to be a model than the countries of western Europe, North America, or Japan. In the Singapore case, low and middle-income housing has been sited by government planning primarily in the margins of the built-up area, something foreign to the West; but it will not be foreign to the other countries in the region.

---

31 . For example, see Terry G. McGee and Yue-man Yeung, *Hawkers in Southeast Asian Cities: Planning for the Bazaar Economy* (Ottawa: International Development Research Center, 1977).

Moreover, as urban populations increase proportionally, and especially as the capital cities and larger regional centers grow, the cities will play a greater role in determining not only the futures of their countries but also their own futures. In this connection, there is an appalling lack of understanding of the political economies of Southeast Asian cities and for that matter of Asian cities in general.[32] In addition, the nature of the relations between cities and their hinterlands is poorly understood and needs intensive study. Since the immediate hinterlands of the cities, say within 100 miles, contain a very high proportion of the national populations—given the areal coincidence between urban and gross population distributions in most Asian countries—raising the sights of urban planning strategies from the cities alone to incorporate their hinterlands would appear to be an essential ingredient of productive planning at national and regional levels. In short, the "urbanization of the countryside" would appear to be as important as increasing the efficiencies of the cities themselves.

That the cities are not efficient in a classical Western mode is indicated in part by their composition as collections of period pieces, as noted earlier. The reconciliation of the colonial patterns with the needs of the emerging new societies must have a high priority in developing productive national urban policies. Moreover, as is well known, despite the increases in manufacturing employment in most Asian countries and the larger cities, they have failed to keep pace with the growth of the urban labor force, a high proportion of which is associated with the so-called informal sector of the urban economies. The work of geographers like McGee and Yeung and of sociologists like Hollsteiner and Yeh have demonstrated that the informal sector plays valuable roles both in providing employment, however sporadic, and in acculturating in-migrants to an urban way of life. As Yeung has pointed out, "a fruitful line of enquiry can thus be an exploration and elaboration of the linkage between formal and informal sector employment, which at present is only vaguely understood."[33] Implicit in any strategy for strengthening such linkages is the assumption that appropriate and effective labor-intensive industrial techniques and organization can be developed, which will effectively compete with and interrelate with those in the more modern sector. It is worth noting that Japan succeeded in these matters during its early and middle modernizing

---

32. Norton S. Ginsburg, "Closing Session, Part II," in *Proceedings, Pacific Science, Fourth Inter-Congress 1-5 September, 1981* (Singapore: National Academy of Sciences, 1982), pp. 51-2.

33. Yue-man Yeung, "Closing Session, Part I," in ibid., p. 50.

periods, and South Korea appears to have been successfully melding the two forms of organization within the past 25 years.

Since housing is in such demand in the burgeoning cities it constitutes one of the major problems to be dealt with.[34] It also might provide one means of strengthening the informal sector and merging it with the formal sector if properly approached; yet housing in most Southeast Asian countries other than Singapore continues to have a very low priority in the general developmental scheme of things. The Singapore experience, however, is salutory. When Singapore was cast out of the Federation of Malaysia in 1965, it was cut off from a substantial part of its natural hinterland, unemployment rose to record levels, and the future of the new city-state was in jeopardy. The construction industry became a major weapon for dealing with unemployment, for training a comparatively skilled labor force, and for providing a restless and unhappy proletariat with a quid pro quo for loyalty to the new state. Howe, Yoon-chong, the first Director of the Housing and Development Board, later Director of the Port Authority and Minister of Defense, has described the government policy to build public housing on a large scale as a great gamble, so far as he knew without clear precedent elsewhere; but the gamble paid off.[35] To be sure, Singapore is unique and is possessed of great assets, not least, a population that is largely Chinese; but the lesson might yet be applied elsewhere.

A scenario which likens the great cities of Southeast Asia to a multitude of Singapores-with-hinterlands is the stuff of dreams, but it suggests the need for thinking of ways to use the cities as major resources for development. Good housing programs, potable water supplies, improved transportation both within cities and between them and their hinterlands, education for urban living, and manufacturing technologies appropriate to conditions of an abundance of labor, along with agricultural development programs in the urban hinterlands may well be the essential ingredients for productive change. To be sure, given the scarcity of capital in most countries this may mean the neglect, benign or other, of peripheral areas of relatively low population densities and productivity, with consequent costs to national purpose attractive to most of their populations; but perhaps there is some way to minimize the political risks of such neglect. There may be no other alternative.

---

34. Yue-man Yeung, ed., *A Place to Live: More Effective Low-cost Housing in Asia* (Ottawa: International Development Research Center, 1983).

35. In conversation with the author in Singapore, September 4, 1981.

# Chapter XI

# THE TRANSFORMATION OF THE OLD CITY OF BEIJING, CHINA

A Concrete Manifestation of New China's
Cultural Reconstruction

Hou Ren-Zhi

In the modern world, China is both a developing nation and a
newly emerging socialist state. Coming from an ancient cultural
tradition, she now faces a new era of unprecedented social change.
While overhauling her backward economy and actively pursuing
reconstruction and modernization, she is also rapidly developing a
new socialist culture. In the process of modernization and
reconstruction, it is necessary for China to adopt the foreign
science and technology according to her own needs. But the
development of a new socialist culture, however, entails a more
important and complex problem: how to identify and preserve the
valuable part of China's own traditional culture.

It is impossible, of course, for China's new socialist culture
to drop from the sky, or be imported intact from any particular
foreign country. It can only grow from China's own native soil.
This is not to say that all foreign cultural influence should be
rejected, but it can only contribute positively to China's new,
modern culture by being first fused with China's unique traditional
culture. Taking into account this background of great social
change, this essay attempts to describe and explain a concrete
example of the issues which must be faced in creating the new
socialist culture. In presenting the problem of transforming an
old, historical city into a modern, new one, I can only offer the
perspective of an historical geographer, not that of a specialist in
city planning, but hope this discussion has some value in that
context.

## The Relevance of Ancient Chinese Planning Theory

With the growth of world urbanization in recent times, city planning as a specialized science has become more complex and more important each day. But it is not a new science, as it was already flourishing in some of the great civilizations of antiquity. Ancient China was no exception, and Wheatley has drawn particular attention to the symbolic nature of the "ideal" planned layout of ancient China's cities, citing corroborative evidence in the *Book of Artificers* (Kao Gong Ji). One of the outstanding features of the ideal layout is the north-south axis of the whole city, and "this axial design is superbly executed in Pei-Ching [Beijing]."[1]

The *Book of Artificers* was completed around the Fifth century BC and deals primarily with manufacturing technology. It also records the plan for the construction of the imperial capital, which is somewhat ambiguous and has been subject to varying interpretations and reconstructions. The main points of the plan include the following. First, the capital should be laid out as a square, surrounded by a city wall; each side should extend nine li (Chinese mile, equal to about 1/2 kilometer) and contain three city gates. Second, within the city there should be nine longitudinal and nine latitudinal thoroughfares, or three longitudinal and three latitudinal thoroughfares, each consisting of three chariot lanes. Third, in the center of the capital is the Imperial Palace of the emperor. On the left side of the Imperial Palace is the "Tai Miao," where the emperor pays homage to his ancestors. On the right side is the "She-ji Tan," where he worships the gods of soil and grain. The front part of the Imperial Palace is the emperor's administrative center, and to the rear of the Imperial Palace is the capital's main market and commercial center.

These declarations in the *Book of Artificers* refer to the capital and largest city of the empire; "left," "right," "front," and "back" refer to the four cardinal directions (respectively east, west, south, and north). The Imperial Palace of the emperor faced true south and was located in the geometric center of the whole city. Tai Miao (the Imperial Ancestral Temple) lay to its east, She-ji Tan (the Altar of Soil and Grain) lay to its west, and the city market to its north. The city was aligned along a north-south axis, facing the south and with its back to the north. This orientation bore a close relationship to the residential traditions of the lower reaches of the Yellow River (Huang Ho), where Chinese

---

1. Paul Wheatley, *The Pivot of the Four Quarters: A Preliminary Enquiry into the Origins and Character of the Ancient Chinese City.* (Chicago: Aldine Publishing Company, 1971), p. 425.

civilization originated. The plains of the lower Yellow River, small ones such as the Jing-Wei and Yi-Lo Basins as well as the great North China Plain, have a flat and open topography. They are located in the temperate zone, characterized by strong prevailing monsoons and four distinct seasons, with hot, rainy summers and cold, blustery winters. In order to maximize ventilation in the summer, while in the winter providing maximum exposure to the sun and shelter from the cold north wind, residential structures in this area were built to open toward the south, with their backs to the north. Over time, these evolved into the *se-he-yuan* (house built around a courtyard). The *si-he-yuan* has structures facing the center on all four sides, with the principal one, called the *zheng-fang,* to the north.

The *si-he-yuan* is, in fact, the "cell" of traditional Chinese city structure. If the streets and alleys defined by rows of *si-he-yuan* are arranged in a certain pattern and surrounded by a wall, a city is formed. The emperor's palace in the national capital was simply a grand *si-he-yuan,* or a collection of them, surrounded by a palace wall and referred to as the Gong Cheng or Imperial City. The Imperial City was supposed to have a dominant position, at the center of the city's primary north-south axis, and this central location symbolized the center of the cosmos. Also, according to ancient custom the "Tai Miao" could only be built in the nation's capital.

China is an agrarian nation, and the "She-ji Tan" was an important symbol of the emperor's authority. As for the market, it was a necessity of city life. All these basic elements of the city were clearly set forth in the *Book of Artificers*. Of all the written works concerning the construction of the capital city which have been passed down from antiquity, this is the earliest and most important, and had the greatest influence on the actual design of the ancient capitals.

Of the several imperial capitals in Chinese history, the last to be built was Beijing, or more specifically, that part of modern Beijing referred to as the "Old City," and it is the actual design of this city that comes the closest to expressing the ancient principle of "palace in front, market in back, ancestral temple on right, altar of soil and grain on left." After the foundation of New China, the capital was re-established in Beijing, with its center in the Old City, and work commenced to build a "people's capital" for the new socialist era. Thus, the redevelopment of Beijing's Old City plan became an urgent task. In order to fully understand the nature of this task, it is necessary to examine the plan of Beijing's Old City in some detail.

## Early Planning and the Rise of Dadu City

Although Beijing is an ancient city with a history spanning three thousand years, it has been in its present location only since the establishment of Dadu city by the Yuan Dynasty (1271-1368) in the 13th century. The previous location was in what is now the southwest suburbs of the city. The last, and largest, city built in this old location was Zhongdu, the capital of the Jin Dynasty (1126-1279). The establishment of Zhongdu marked the beginning of Beijing's emergence as a national political center.

To the northeast of Zhongdu City there was a scenic area with a natural lake, which was utilized by the Jin emperor. The lake was expanded on its southern part and two islands were created and an imperial retreat, called the Da-ning Palace (Palace of Great Tranquility) was built (figure 11.1). In the year 1215, the army of the Mongolian leader Genghis Khan swept down from the north, occupying Zhongdu City and razing the Imperial Palace. But Da-ning Palace outside the city was spared. Forty-five years later, Genghis Khan's grandson, Kublai Khan, in order to consolidate his rule over China, decided to establish his capital in Zhongdu. But the Imperial Palace there was in ruins and would have been extremely difficult to rebuild. Worse yet, Zhongdu had but a meager water supply from a small lake (West Lake, now called Lotus Lake) just west of the city. The complex problems of providing water for the city, and especially channels for water transport, became more critical day by day.

Man-made canals were needed, primarily to ensure that the capital could be supplied with the large quantities of grain it required. During the Jin Dynasty, an aqueduct had been constructed to divert the water of the Yongding River (then called the Lu-gou River) eastward, following the natural topography, to the north moat of Zhongdu City. From there a canal continued eastward to Tong-zhou (east of present-day Beijing). The plan was to bring together river shipments of grain and other material at Tong-zhou for transshipment to Zhongdu. But when the Yongding River flooded, however, it could not be effectively controlled, and the scheme proved to be unworkable.

Kublai Khan therefore decided to abandon old Zhongdu City and commissioned the Han Chinese scholar Liu Bing-zhong, who was acquainted with the ancient classics as well as experienced in city

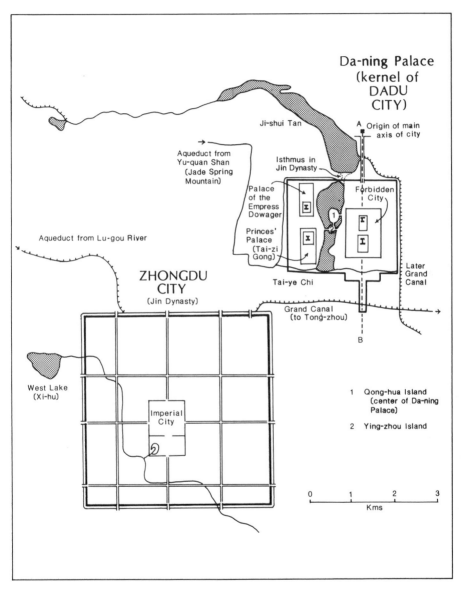

Figure 11.1. Beijing's early urban nuclei: Zhongdu City, Da ning Palace, and the kernel of Dadu City

construction, to draw up plans for a new city centered on the lake by Da-ning Palace. Liu Bing-zhong and his student Guo Shour-jing, an expert astronomer and hydraulic engineer, began directing the construction of the new city and its canal system in 1267, but the work was not completed until 1285. What they created was the historically renowned Dadu City. It was during the construction of Dadu that Marco Polo visited China and became an official of the Yuan Dynasty. Later, after his return to Italy, he recalled the grandeur of Dadu and the splendor of the palace in his account of "Khanbalig" in *Marco Polo's Journal*.

This account of the founding and initial construction of Dadu City is well enough documented, but the decisions concerning planning and design of the city are more obscure since no official papers or other accounts have been passed down. The only direct evidence for the city's internal organization consists of a restored map of Dadu City and some incomplete historical records. My own reconstruction of the city's plan development is as follows.

First, it was decided that the north-south axis of the city would be located close by the east bank of the northern part of the lake, which at that time was called Ji-shui Tan (figure 11.1). The north end of this axis was set at the northeast bank of Ji-shui Tan. The emperor's palace, surrounded on four sides by a palace wall (which became known much later as the "Forbidden City"), was located on the east bank of the southern part of the lake and centered on the city's north-south axis.

On the west bank were two palace complexes, the southerly one being the palace of the crown prince and the northerly one the palace of the emperor's mother, or "empress dowager." These two complexes, also surrounded each on four sides by a palace wall, and the emperor's palace faced each other from afar across the lake (figure 11.1). In the middle of the lake, equidistant from the three palaces, was a small island, which remained from the old Da-ning Palace complex, called Ying-zhou. Bridges extending from Ying-zhou Island to the east and west shores of the lake connected the three palaces together. North of Ying-zhou Island was a larger island, called Qiong-hua Island, upon which was the main concentration of buildings of the Da-ning Palace. Surrounding the three palace complexes was a city wall, which defined what was known as the "Royal City." Henceforth the south lake was surrounded by the Royal City, and according to tradition, was given the name "Tai-ye Chi" (Supreme Liquid Lake). Around the shore of Tai-ye Chi an imperial park was planted.

Since the northern part of the lake now lay outside the Royal City, and being separated from the southern part, a canal was constructed to divert its outflow around the east wall of the Royal City and on toward the south suburbs (figure 11.1). At the same time, a new source of water was found for the Royal City's Tai-ye Chi; an aqueduct was dug connecting the lake to a spring at the foot of Yu-quan (Pearl Spring) Hill northwest of the city. The outflow from the lake passed along the front of the Imperial Palace, then out to join the canal which drained Ji-shui Tan.

A large secular city was constructed around the Royal City. The plan for the large city placed its geometric center at the north end of the axis of the Royal city. At that site a platform was built, and on it were inscribed the four characters "Zhong Xin Zi Tai," meaning "Central Platform." This shows clearly the careful measurement that went into the city's layout.

From the Central Platform on the east to its western end, Ji-shui Tan is about 3.3 kilometers in east-west extent. The location of the west wall of the enlarged city was set a little farther than this from the city center. Ideally, this should have been the standard distance determining the location of the east wall of the enlarged city. The land at that easterly location, however, was swampy and unsuitable for heavy construction, so the east wall could not be placed that far out. The south wall of the enlarged city was located about 3.75 kilometers from the Central Platform, that being the distance which allowed the Royal City to be included within the enlarged city. It was then decided that the north wall should be placed at the same distance. Consequently, the shape of the enlarged city after the construction of the four walls was that of a slightly elongated rectangle.

The east, west, and south walls of the enlarged city each had three gates, but the north wall only two. Inside the southernmost gate of the east wall was built the Tai Miao, and inside the southernmost gate of the west wall was built the She-ji Tan. Spanning the area between the eleven city gates, which were spaced at approximately equal distances from one another, were wide avenues. Including the "wall streets," which ran along the insides of the city walls, there were nine aligned north-south and nine east-west. Many smaller lanes were laid out running east-west between the primary north-south avenues. Thus, the basic layout of all of Dadu City was accomplished (figure 11.2).

At this point, it is important to note the special significance of the location of the central gate of the south city

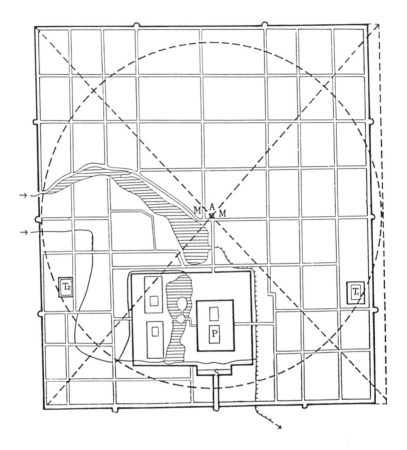

A   Central Platform
P   Forbidden City
M   Market
$T_1$   Imperial Ancestral Temple (Tai Miao)
$T_2$   Temple of Land and Grain
S   Imperial Square

Figure 11.2.   The layout of Dadu City (Beijing)

wall, at the south end of the city's north-south axis. Along the sides of the "Imperial Road" which connected this city gate to the south gate of the Royal City, a T-shaped square was built. This was equivalent to the so-called "Wai Chao" (Outer Court) of antiquity. Precisely located along the central axis of the whole city were the chief buildings of the emperor's palace, as well as the emperor's throne. The purpose of this was to demonstrate that the emperor was "number one under heaven," a concept with great symbolic meaning.

The last major project in the construction of Dadu was the tapping of the springs of the mountains to the northwest to provide the city's water supply (figure 11.3). All these springs, except for those of Yu-quan Hill which were used exclusively to feed the Royal City's Tai-ye Chi, were brought together into a single channel which flowed into Dadu City's Ji-shui Tan. From there, these waters were channeled southward around the east wall of the Royal City, joining the old Jin Dynasty canal in the southern suburbs which led to Tong-zhou. At Tong-zhou this joined with the historically renowned Grand Canal, which linked the area to China's southern regions. The northern terminus of the Grand Canal system therefore was Ji-shui Tan, which became a bustling port, crowded with boats laden with grain and goods from the lower valley of the Changjiang (Yangtze River). An area on its northeast shore, including the vicinity of the Central Platform and a street along the north side of the lake, became the most prosperous commercial center of the city (figure 11.4).

The Yuan Dynasty's construction of Dadu City required eighteen years from beginning to end. If the design of Dadu is compared to the elements of ideal city layout set forth in the *Book of Artificers,* such as "palace in front, market in back, temple of ancestors on right, altar of soil and grain on left," and the street plan, it can be seen that these principles were completely realized in the construction of the city. Thus, the design of Dadu City without question had its origins deep in Chinese culture. But it was not just a machine-like copy of the ancient ideal form; its sides were not built in the form of a perfect square, but rather the ideal was modified to meet the requirements of reality to produce a creative work. By building the city around a wide body of water and extending its north-south dimension, it was possible to create a great city which combined grandeur with beautiful scenery. Moreover, the main elements of the ideal plan were still strongly represented, and this was no mean achievement.

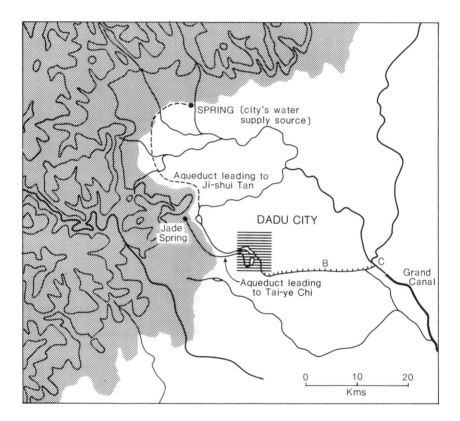

Figure 11.3. Waterways in the vicinity of Dadu City (Beijing)

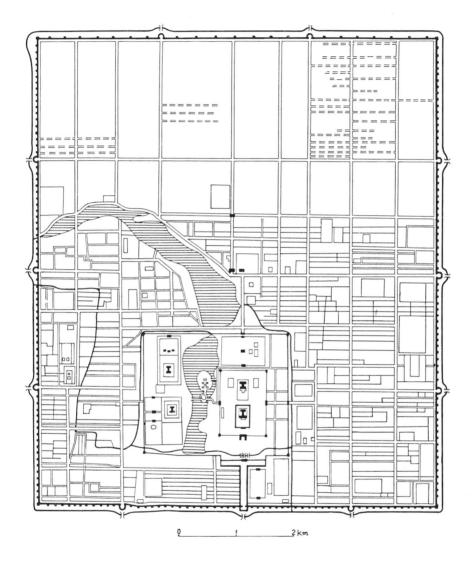

Dashed double lines indicate street locations established by archeological evidence;
In empty areas, archeological evidence is lacking.

Figure 11.4.   Reconstruction of the layout of Dadu City (Beijing) during the Yuan Dynasty

## Planning Changes in the Ming and Qing Periods

Less than a century after Dadu City was built, an uprising in the lower reaches of the Changjiang (Yangtze River) resulted in the establishment of the Ming Dynasty (1368-1644), which eventually extended its rule over the whole of China. The Ming Dynasty originally had its capital at Nanjing. After it occupied Dadu, it changed that city's name to Beiping or "North Pacification." During the reign of the third emperor, who intended to rule from Beiping, to begin with the name was changed to Beijing, or "Northern Capital," and then the capital function itself was moved from Nanking to Beijing. Concurrently, a major reconstruction of the city was begun (figure 11.5). First, the north city wall was moved about 2.5 kilometers to the south, leaving the northwest part of Ji-shui Tan outside the city. Then both the south city wall and the emperor's palace were rebuilt a little to the south. This reconstruction produced the new emperor's palace, or the Forbidden City, which has been passed down to the present, and is today's Palace Museum. Within the Ming Dynasty's Forbidden City, the most important buildings were a row of six great palaces, built along the city's main axis, which symbolized the supreme power of the emperor. The geometric center of the whole city was no longer at the Central Platform, but had shifted south to a point just north of the new Forbidden City. In order to clearly mark the new city center, soil excavated from a new artificial lake at the southern end of the Tai-ye Chi and from a newly constructed moat of the Forbidden City was used to build a hill about seventy meters high. This was named Wan-sui Shan (Long Life Mountain) and symbolized the eternal ruling power of the emperor.[2] In addition, the Tai Maio and She-ji Tan were moved from their old locations inside the east and west walls to new locations just outside the south gate of the Forbidden City. They were still placed on the left and right sides of the meridional axis, respectively, in keeping with the tradition of "Tai Miao to the right and She-ji Tan to the left." At the same time, the south, north, and east walls of the Royal City were extended a bit, so the Tai Miao, She-ji Tan, and the new lake south of Tai-ye Chi were all contained within them.[3]

---

[2]. Later the name was changed to Jing Shan (Scenic Mountain) and also Mei Shan (Coal Hill).

[3]. During this period, the canal formerly outside the Royal City's east wall was incorporated into the Royal City, and shipping on the Grand Canal was thus unable to reach Ji-shui Tan. The lower part of Ji-shui tan was connected with Tai-ye Chi to the south, and the aqueduct which had been specifically created to supply water to Tai-ye Chi was abandoned. Altogether, the city's water system regressed while under the Ming Dynasty's management.

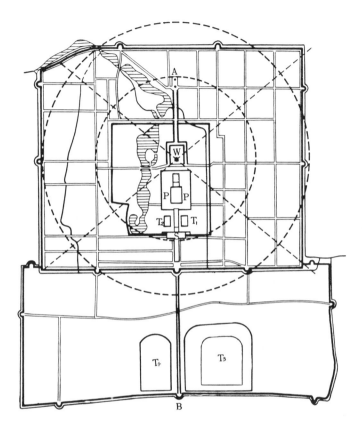

| P | Forbidden City |
|---|---|
| W | Long Life Mountain |
| T1 | Imperial Ancestral Temple (Tai Miao) |
| T2 | Temple of Land and Grain (She-ji Tan) |
| T3 | Temple of Heaven (Tian Tan) |
| T4 | Temple of Mountains and Rivers (Shan Chuan Tan) |
| A | Bell Tower and Drum Tower |
| B | Outer City's Mid-South Gate |
| AB | Central axis of the city |
| S | Imperial Square |

Figure 11.5.  Dadu City's transformation into Beijing City under the Ming dynasty

More importantly, two major new groups of buildings were
constructed in the southern suburbs, one east and one west of the
meridional axis.  To the east was the Tian Tan (Temple of Heaven),
where the emperor paid homage to the gods of heaven, and to the west
was the Shan Chuan Tan (Altar of Mountain and River), where he paid
his respects to the gods of mountain and river.[4] Up until 1553, this
southern part of Beijing was outside the city wall; then an "outer
wall" was built to formally incorporate the above-mentioned temple
and altar into the city.  The middle gate of this new outer wall was
situated on the center axis, between these two groups of buildings.
The main north-south road within the gate was built along the axis.

At the northern end of the axis, where the old Central
Platform was located, two new buildings were constructed; the Bell
Tower to the north and the Drum Tower to the south.  The newly
extended north-south axis had a full length of almost eight
kilometers.  The Forbidden City occupied the most important location
on the axis; to its north, standing like a picture screen, was
Wan-sui Shan; to its south, on the left and right, were the Tai Miao
and the She-ji Tan.  Between these two temples was the Central
Imperial Avenue, which started at the Wu Men (Meridional Gate) at
the center of the south side of the Forbidden City and extended to
the Tian-an Men (Gate of Heavenly Peace) at the center of the south
side of the Royal City.[5] After passing through the Tian-an Men, the
avenue widened into a T-shaped palace square.  The square was
bounded on three sides by red brick walls.  Inside the east and west
walls, long corridors called the "Corridor of a Thousand Steps" were
built.  Outside the south central gate of the square was the south
central gate of the inner city wall.  This gate was known as the
Zheng-yang Men, or Front Gate, and the part of Beijing which lay
beyond it was called the outer city.  Along the main axis of the
city, which had been extended, the fundamental principles of the
design of Dadu City were further developed, and a higher aesthetic
level was achieved.

The Qing Dynasty (1644-1911), the last imperial dynasty in
China's history, also established its capital in Beijing.  Besides
erecting more palace buildings in the Forbidden City and in the
imperial park around Tai-ye Chi, it did not do much to change the
layout of the city.  Thus Beijing City--or as we now call it,
Beijing's Old City--was preserved until the eve of the birth of New

---

4. The name "Shan Chuan Tan" was later changed to "Xian-nong Tang" (Altar
of the God of Agriculture).

5. During the Ming Dynasty, the Tian-an Men was called the Cheng-tian Men.

China. Starting with the principles set forth in the *Book of Artificers* with adjustments made to accommodate local geographical characteristics, and then having gone through numerous reconstructions, Beijing has finally come down to us as the ultimate expression of the ideal traditional Chinese city.

It is just this Beijing City which has been the object of high praise from Western urban planners. For example, the renowned Danish architect Steen Eiler Rasmussen, in the preface to his book *Towns and Buildings,* wrote:

> There are excellent German and Japanese guide books giving detailed information about every single palace and temple in Peking. But they do not contain a single mention of the fact that the entire city is one of the wonders of the world, in its symmetry and clarity a unique monument, the culmination of a great civilization.[6]

Another example is provided by the distinguished American city planner Edmund Bacon, who was Executive Director of the Philadelphia Planning Commission for twenty years and made an important contribution to historic preservation and restoration in that city. In his book *Design of Cities* he wrote this regarding Beijing's Old City:

> Possibly the greatest single work of man on the face of the earth is Peking. This Chinese city, designed as the domicile of the Emperor, was intended to mark the center of the universe. The city is deeply enmeshed in ritualistic formulae and religious concepts which do not concern us now. Nevertheless, it is so brilliant in design that it provides a rich storehouse of ideas for the city of today.[7]

Bacon's comment is noteworthy. As a center of imperial rule, he said, it was a great design achievement and should be studied by city planners today. At the same time, he points out that it contains much that does not serve the needs of the present. This clearly reveals the dilemma we face today.

### Plan Changes in the New China Era

Following the progress of history and the passage of time, old cities--especially those of intricate design--unavoidably face the necessity of continuous redevelopment. This is especially true in the case of Beijing's Old City, since the single underlying motif of all its splendid architecture and ingenious design--namely, symbolizing the supremacy of a medieval sovereign--stands in such sharp contrast to the spirit of the present time. The establishment of New China represents the beginning of a new, socialist era. As Beijing is the nation's capital in this new era, the reconstruction of the city should reflect the fact that the people are now the true masters of their country.

---

6. Steen Eiler Rasmussen, *Towns and Buildings,* Paperback Edition. (Cambridge, Mass.: First M.I.T. Press, 1969), Preface, p. v.

7. Edmund N. Bacon, *Design of Cities,* revised edition. (London: Penguin Books, 1980), p. 244.

How can this reconstruction effectively be carried out? First, it must be seen that this is not simply a matter of engineering and technology, but also a problem concerning our custodianship of a venerable historical and cultural inheritance, as well as the challenge of creating a new socialist civilization.

All of Beijing's Old City is part of China's historical and cultural inheritance. It is a symbol of the magnificent development of China's culture in imperial times. As Rasmussen pointed out, it is a significant monument to the highest achievements of a great civilization. The new Beijing City, as the people's capital and a symbol of the new socialist culture, can only rise from this historical foundation. But as we assume our charge over this historical and cultural legacy, we must adhere to the principle of maintaining a critical perspective. We can neither totally deny the legacy nor totally accept it. It is important to distinguish between the "wheat" and the "chaff;" we must accept and make full use of the wheat, while criticizing and giving up the chaff. In this way we can follow the principles of "making the past serve the present" and "weed through the old to bring forth the new," in order to use our historical foundation to create something new. We must note, however, that the standards for distinguishing the "wheat" from the "chaff" have changed through time. Today, we place a high value on all things which benefit the masses or fully express the people's creative abilities. That which truly embodies this populist spirit should be accepted and developed. That which does not should be criticized and given up. Today, this principle must be applied to the reconstruction of Beijing's Old City.

Some reconstruction work affecting the layout of Beijing's Old City has already been done since the establishment of New China. The most notable example of this is the reconstruction of Tian-an Men Square. As noted earlier Tian-an Men was originally fronted by a T-shaped square. This was designed to serve as an imperial square--a place where the emperor performed important ceremonies (figure 11.6). On its east, west, and south sides were red walls which totally shut off public access. It was thus a great obstacle to east-west communications within the city. Viewed from the south end of this imperial square, the Tian-an Men loomed to the north as a lofty, ornate palace built upon a red platform. In old times, this sight served to create an impression of grandeur and solemnity. In 1911, after the overthrow of the last dynasty, Tian-an Men Square was opened and people were allowed to pass through, but the red walls were kept as before. On October 1, 1949, the declaration of

233

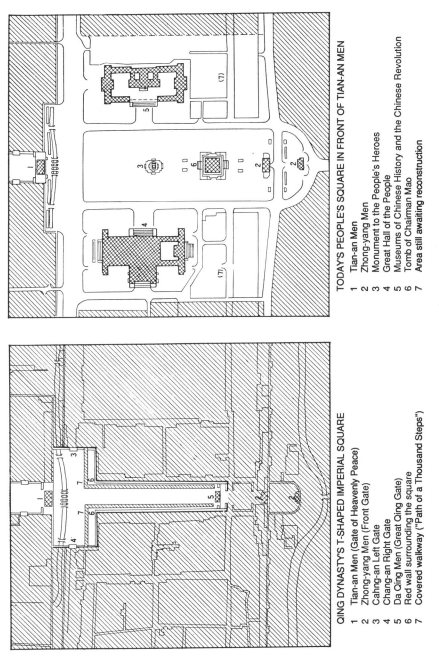

QING DYNASTY'S T-SHAPED IMPERIAL SQUARE

1 Tian-an Men (Gate of Heavenly Peace)
2 Zhong-yang Men (Front Gate)
3 Cahng-an Left Gate
4 Chang-an Right Gate
5 Da Qing Men (Great Qing Gate)
6 Red wall surrounding the square
7 Covered walkway ("Path of a Thousand Steps")

TODAY'S PEOPLE'S SQUARE IN FRONT OF TIAN-AN MEN

1 Tian-an Men
2 Zhong-yang Men
3 Monument to the People's Heroes
4 Great Hall of the People
5 Museums of Chinese History and the Chinese Revolution
6 Tomb of Chairman Mao
7 Area still awaiting reconstruction

Figure 11.6. From imperial square to people's square at the Tian-an Men, Beijing

the establishment of New China took place there.  An important
reason for this was that Tian-an Men Square was the site of the
outbreak of the May 4th Movement of 1919, which set the stage for
the New Democratic Revolution.  Thus it is one of the places in
Beijing's Old City with an honored revolutionary tradition.

The Tian-an Men, which stands above the square, expresses the
full talent and intelligence of China's working people in the art of
construction.  It could be considered a masterpiece among the
ancient structures of Beijing.  As for the red walls on the east,
west, and south sides of the square, they still obstructed the
movement of people and were actually a public nuisance.  Therefore,
on the tenth anniversary of the founding of the nation, the red
walls surrounding the square were totally demolished, and a new
square appeared which was several times larger than the old one.  On
the west and east sides of the square, two modern buildings were
constructed.  On the west arose the Great Hall of the People, and on
the east was built the structure containing the Museum of Chinese
History and the Museum of the Chinese Revolution.  In the center of
the square stands the Shrine to the People's Heroes.  On the eve of
the 30th anniversary of the revolution, the Memorial Hall of
Chairman Mao was built on the south side of the square, just inside
the Zheng-yang Gate.  The transformation of Tian-an Men Square to
the center of political activity was essentially complete.  Although
its location remains the same, its nature and function have totally
changed, and it has an entirely new appearance (figure 11.6).[8]

At the beginning of the reconstruction of Tian-an Men Square,
its left and right wings extending along Chang-an Street (the
street's name was derived from the former left and right Chang-an
Gates on either side of the old square) were widened and extended to
become a broad, tree-lined thoroughfare.  This thoroughfare extended
to the east and west suburbs and created a major new axis for the
whole city (figure 11.7).  On one hand this reinforced the primacy
of Tian-an Men Square's location in the layout of the whole city,
and on the other hand it relegated the location of the old Forbidden
City to "back yard" status.  That ancient symbol of imperial primacy
thus lost its exhalted position relative to the rest of the city.

Although work remains to be done in the reconstruction of
Tian-an Men Square, its position as the center of political activity
in the city has been established.  The old buildings on the square,

---

8 . The actual work, of course, was not without problems.  For instance, in
the cases of the demolition of the old city wall and most of the old gates and the
filling of the moat, there was serious disagreement in the beginning.  From
today's point of view, these are simply irretrievably lost.

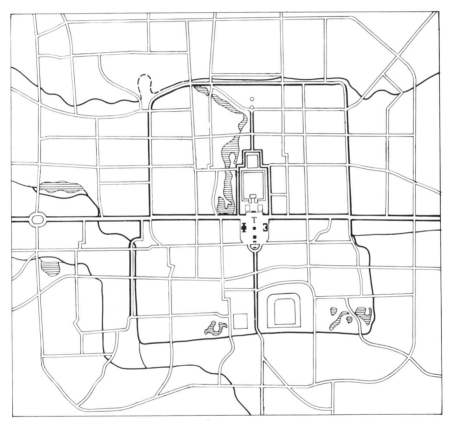

Figure 11.7.  Chang-an Street, Beijing, extending east and west from Tian-an Men

such as the Tian-an Men and the Zheng-yang Men, and the modern
buildings, such as the Great Hall of the People and the Museums of
History and the Revolution, all go together very well, showing at
the same time continuity with the past and the new spirit of the
present. The principle of "weed through the old to bring forth the
new" has been fully realized. With regard to the improvement of the
layout of Beijing's Old City, it cannot be said that this was not a
success.

There are still many opportunities for today's city planners
to apply their creative talents, in accordance with this principle,
to the reconstruction of Beijing's Old City. For instance, one such
case is the question of what to do with the old Ji-shui Tan. Should
we consider it an obstacle to the city's development and fill it in
to create land for buildings? Or should we consider it a place of
historical significance in the development of the city and protect
and improve it?

The Ji-shui Tan of antiquity, as discussed earlier, had a
great influence on the location and layout of Beijing's Old City.
The city's main axis was set next to the eastern shore of Ji-shui
Tan, and the width of the lake determined the location of the east
and west city walls. It could be said that had Ji-shui Tan not
existed, Beijing would not exist in anything like its present form.
In Dadu City of the Yuan Dynasty, Ji-shui Tan was of great
importance as the northern terminus of the Grand Canal. After the
early period of the Ming Dynasty, when the north city wall was moved
southward 2.5 kilometers, the northwest part of Ji-shui Tan was
excluded from the city, and the area of the lake inside the city was
greatly reduced. Subsequent reconstruction of Beijing's Old City,
while further developing the primary themes of the original city
plan, resulted in the filling of the Grand Canal's bed within the
city and the elimination of its upper reaches. All that remained
was the spring from Yu-quan Hill, which flowed into Ji-shui tan and
thence on to Tai-ye Chi. After this rearrangement of Beijing's
water system, Tai-ye Chi, which was inside the Royal City, was again
enlarged by the addition of a new lake at its southern end. The
trees and structures around it increased in number, and it developed
into the most scenic park district in the city. The lake became
known as the "Three Seas"--the "South Sea" (Nan-hai), the "Middle
Sea" (Zhong-hai), and the "North Sea" (Bei-hai). The "North Sea"
has now been opened to the public; known as the Bei-hai Park, it is
renowned for its most beautiful scenery. This was the location of
the Jin Dynasty's imperial retreat, Dan-ning Palace.

Ji-shui Tan, which lay outside the Imperial City, has a much different fate than the "Three Seas," with their imperial parks and gardens. Throughout the Ming and Ching Dynasties and up to the establishment of New China, it never received much attention from the highest rulers. Thus it has not benefited from any definite plan or development, and has quite naturally become a neglected backwater. The lake shrank into three parts, and only the northwesternmost part was still called Ji-shui Tan. A larger part of the lake, to the southeast, was called Shi-cha Hai. The area remained, however, one of the most scenic parts of the city. Especially lovely was the view looking west from the east shore of Shi-cha Hai; the reflected peaks of West Mountain seemed like part of the city landscape. Therefore this region in old times, especially during the Qing Dynasty, attracted some of the imperial nobility. They built great houses near the lake shore and channeled lake water into their private gardens. In addition, a number of large, wealthy temples were established around the lake. But, apart from the nobles' houses and temples, the greatest part of the lake region became a public recreation place for the common people. The southern part, especially, evolved naturally into a real "people's park." Concurrently there arose in that place a common people's market, where prices were low and merchandise was good. Because of a profusion of lotus growing along the lake shore there, this market came to be called the "Lotus Market." Up to the eve of the birth of New China, this region remained a haven for the common people, where they could relax and enjoy life in a rustic setting. This informality contrasted sharply with the detailed planning and arrangement of Tai-ye Chi and its imperial gardens.

Now, inside Beijing's Old City, this overlooked lake is still there, and along its shores there are still patches of greenery and glimpses of its former beauty.

Further planning and reconstruction of the Ji-shui Tan district has already been scheduled as part of the effort to improve and reconstruct Beijing's Old City, in coordination with the overall plan for greater Beijing (figure 11.8). As this process goes forward, we must consider the historical importance and value of this region. We must consider the strong association of the common people with this place and the present necessity of creating more spacious, pleasant and culturally meaningful recreation areas for our citizens. We must consider the potential for improving the natural environment and making the city a more beautiful place. We must also build our plan upon the historical base we have inherited,

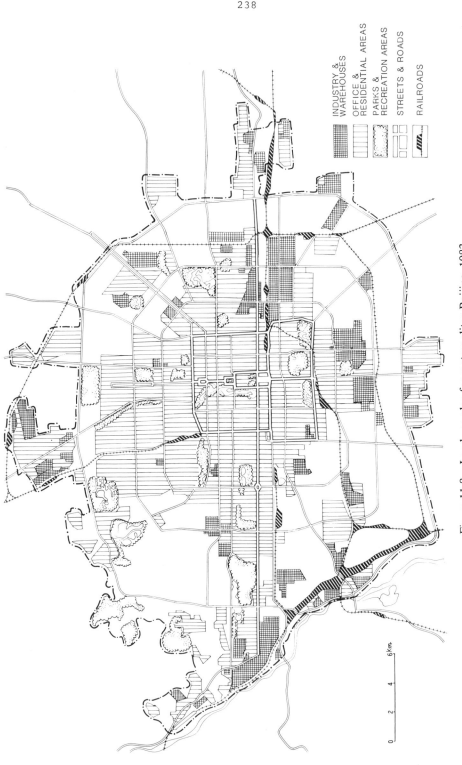

Figure 11.8. Land use plan for metropolitan Beijing, 1983

INDUSTRY &
WAREHOUSES

OFFICE &
RESIDENTIAL AREAS

PARKS &
RECREATION AREAS

STREETS & ROADS

RAILROADS

0    2    4    6 Km.

all the while maintaining a critical attitude and doing our best to realize the principle of "weed through the old to bring forth the new." Ji-hui Tan is waiting for us to make this effort.

## Conclusion

This essay examines only two examples, from the geographical perspectives of city location and design, in an attempt to assess what attitude we should have and what basic rules we should observe in the process of reconstructing Beijing's Old City.

In July of 1983, the Chinese Communist Party Central Committee and the State Council approved in principle the Master Plan for the City Construction of Metropolitan Beijing. This plan clearly evaluates Beijing's Old City, and while pointing out those strengths and notable traditional characteristics which should be preserved in the process of reconstruction, it also emphasizes the creation of a new style characteristic of the people's capital in the new era.[9] Thus, we have reason to believe that by the end of this century a new Beijing City will emerge; one which will maintain its ancient cultural tradition, but with a new face reflecting a prospering, new socialist culture. At the same time we also hope that this new culture, which is still developing, can make an important contribution to the civilization of all mankind.

---

9. See "The Beijing Daily" (Beijing Ribao), August 3, 1983, and "The Beijing Evening News" (Beijing Wanbao), August 5, 1983.

## Chapter XII

# RECENT CHANGES IN DOWNTOWN AREAS OF JAPANESE GREAT CITIES

### Shinzo Kiuchi

This essay considers recent changes in the core areas of
Tokyo, with comparative reference to Japan's ten other great
cities.[1] Core areas can be demarcated in relation to the
administrative division known as *ku* (ward), so that the geographical
extent of the urban functional core may be located in some part of a
*ku,* or extend across one or more adjacent *ku*.  In addition, there is
an historical reason to define and delineate what in Japanese cities
can be called "lower-town" *(shitamachi)* and "upper-town" *(yamanote)*
areas, for the lower-town, while it shares some functional
characteristics with the modern American "downtown," nevertheless
differs from the latter in crucial ways.[2]

#### Lower-Town and Upper-Town Areas of Japanese Cities

In Japan, cities in the pre-industrial era were often located
on the margins of hilly terrain for defense, and particularly where
a hill lay adjacent to a low plain where commercial activity could
prosper through access to water transportation.  Most often, such
towns were castle towns *(jokamachi),* and they developed a
"double-decker" spatial structure.  In the upper-town resided most
of the *samurai* (high-ranking warriors), while the lower-town was
allocated to merchants and artisans.

---

1. Only a few studies out of the voluminous literature on Japanese urban
geography can be cited here.  Among the general works, see Association of Japanese
Geographers, *Japanese Cities* (Tokyo: The Association, 1970); Eiichi Aoki et al.,
*Gendai Nihon no toshika* [Urbanization of contemporary Japan] (Tokyo: Kokon Shoin,
1979) [in Japanese]; Shinzo Kiuchi, *Toshi chirigaku kenkyu* [Urban geography:
structure in development of urban areas and their hinterlands] (Tokyo: Kokon
Shoin, 1956) [in Japanese; English table of contents]; Shinzo Kiuchi, *Toshi
chirigaku genri* [Principles of urban geography] (Tokyo: Kokon Shoin, 1956) [in
Japanese; English index]; Fumio Takano et al., *Toshi keisei no chiriteki kiban*
[Geographical foundations of urban development] (Tokyo: Taimeido, 1980) [in
Japanese].

2. For some general views of Japanese urban core areas, see Hiroko Fujioka,
*Kobe no chushingai* [Central areas of Kobe] (Tokyo: 1983) [in Japanese]; Keijiro
Hattori, *Daitoshi chiiki ron* [The study of the metropolitan area] (Tokyo: Kokon
Shoin, 1969) [in Japanese]; Ken'ichi Tanabe, *Toshi no chiiki kozo* [Regional
structure of the city] (Tokyo: Taimeido, 1979) [in Japanese; English table of
contents].

After the Meiji Restoration, most castle towns continued as centers of regional administration and trade and often acquired new industrial functions. Major social changes flowed from this watershed in Japanese history and in an urban context found expression in the functional transformation of these towns' double-decker pattern, though its broad physical distinctiveness was not erased. With the soldiers gone, the upper-town evolved not surprisingly into a general residential area for upper class residents, while the lower-town concentrated even more than before on commercial and manufacturing activities--a district of densely built-up character, containing a high population density which represented a disproportionate number of nonwealthy residents. The lower-town in many cases developed on a delta site as *shitamachi,* that is, the center of commercial activity and less wealthy residence.

*Shitamachi* connotes also a socio-economic concept of a town which has preserved a traditional way of life in the lower, core area of the city. People live and work in the same multi-functional area, deriving satisfaction from this active human environment and communal life in closely shared space--an observation clearly confirmed on festival days. Comparable "*shitamachi*" characteristics can also be discerned in the core areas of Paris and London, and other old continental, European cities. In American cities, the commercial core, or "downtown," is similarly situated in the center of the urban or metropolitan area but in modern times has largely lost its resident population. Some downtown districts preserve adjacent, old immigrant neighborhoods, but mostly the periphery of the commercial cores have been substantially redeveloped or at least partially cleared. There is little to compare with this in Japan.

The upper-town in Japanese cities, the *Yamanote* of Tokyo and *Yamate* of Yokohama and Kobe connotes a residential district situated on a hillslope or hilltop, usually of well-to-do character. In contrast to the crowded life of the *shitamachi,* that of *yamanote* is more expansive, with abundant greenery. It is also more private, with less of the incessant human contact of communal living.

Population increases, urbanization, industrial development, and planning have substantially altered the character of traditional *shitamachi* and *yamanote.* The rebuilding after World War II, metropolitan growth, national and regional planning (especially after 1950), the revolution in transportation and communication technology, economic growth, and Westernization have all contributed to a profound alteration of the Japanese urban environment and general urban way of life. The processes and outcomes are not the same from city to city, though they can be generalized somewhat. The great cities of Japan are transforming quickly to accommodate the information age, and their core areas will reflect these changes with rapidity.

### The Withdrawal of Population from Core Areas of Major Japanese Cities

Between 1975 and 1980, most core areas of the eleven major cities of Japan lost population (table 12.1).[3] Based on the census of night-time population, 81 out of 131 *ku* (61.8 percent) lost population. Nine of the eleven *shi* (administrative urban areas, equivalent to metropolitan areas) increased population on the whole, although their core areas declined. The two largest metropolitan areas, Tokyo and Osaka, experienced more widespread population loss, since the central city of Tokyo *(kubu)* and Osaka-*shi* (city) registered absolute decline, representing 3.4 and 4.7 percent respectively. In Osaka-*shi* 21 of the 26 *ku* lost population, and 19 of the 23 *ku* did the same in metropolitan Tokyo. These declining *ku* were not all in central locations but were distributed even among peripheral, residential *ku*. This phenomenon is now spreading beyond the confines of the early twentieth-century built-up area.

The profile of the population growth rate approximates a wave, pushing from the city center towards the suburbs (figure 12.1). The trough at the center gets deeper and wider, while the maximum growth rate crest moves higher and further out from the center. The crest reflects metropolitan expansion, which abuts a zone of slight population withdrawal at the rural fringe--in anticipation of the urban spread. Tokyo's crest of growth stood at about 30 km from the metropolitan core in the period 1935-40 but by 1975-80 had reached 50-80 km. The declines in and near the center (figure 12.1) represent a loss of night-time residents who have presumably become commuters over the years. In Tokyo, the day-time density of commuters and shoppers now exceeds 100,000 people.

Population growth rates offer the clearest measures of urbanization. The largest rate of increase was registered by Sapporo, regional center for the island of Hokkaido in the north. Sapporo grew by 161,000 inhabitants between 1975 and 1980 (13.0

---

3. Statistics in this discussion are drawn from *Population of Major Metropolitan Areas,* 1980 Population Census of Japan, Reference Report Series no. 4 (Tokyo: Prime Minister's Office, Statistics Bureau, 1980) and *Japan Statistical Yearbook* (Tokyo: Japan Statistical Association, 1980). For useful studies of population change and urban growth, see Minoru Kishimoto, *Jinko chirigaku* [Population geography] (Tokyo: Taimeido, 1968) [in Japanese]; and Kenji Kitagawa, *Koiki chushinchi no kenkyu* [The regional central places of Japan] (Tokyo: Taimeido, 1976) [in Japanese].

TABLE 12.1

POPULATION GROWTH RATES OF JAPAN'S ELEVEN GREAT CITIES

| City | Population, 1980 (in '000) | Increase (1975–80) | | No. of *ku* | |
| | | No. (in '000) | Percent | Increased | Decreased |
|------|------|------|------|------|------|
| Tokyo-*kubu* | 8,349 | -297 | -3.4 | 4 | 19 |
| Osaka-*shi* | 2,648 | -131 | -4.7 | 5 | 21 |
| Yokohama | 2,774 | +152 | +5.6 | 9 | 5 |
| Nagoya | 2,088 | +8 | +0.4 | 6 | 10 |
| Kyoto-*shi* | 1,472 | +18 | +5.6 | 4 | 7 |
| Kobe | 1,372 | +7 | +0.5 | 3 | 6 |
| Sapporo | 1,402 | +18 | +13.0 | 6 | 1 |
| Kawasaki | 1,041 | +26 | +2.5 | 2 | 3 |
| Hiroshima-*shi* | 899 | +47 | +5.5 | 5 | 2 |
| Kita-kyushu | 1,065 | +7 | +0.6 | 2 | 5 |
| Fukuoka-*shi* | 1,087 | +86 | +8.6 | 4 | 2 |

TABLE 12.2

MIGRATION PATTERNS WITHIN THE URBAN SETTLEMENT SYSTEM

OF JAPAN, 1981

| Migration Type | | Percent |
|------|------|------|
| A. Intra- and inter-metropolitan areas | | 42.1 |
| Intra-metropolitan | 38.1 | |
| Inter-metropolitan | 4.1 | |
| B. From metropolitan areas to hinterlands | | 13.1 |
| To regional centers | 4.6 | |
| To local cities | 4.4 | |
| To rural towns and villages | 4.1 | |
| C. To metropolitan areas from hinterlands | | 9.6 |
| From regional centers | 3.6 | |
| From local cities | 3.3 | |
| From rural town or village | 2.7 | |
| D. Local and regional intra- and inter-regional moves | | 35.2 |
| Within the same prefecture | 18.8 | |
| Between different prefectures | 16.4 | |
| TOTAL | | 100.00 |

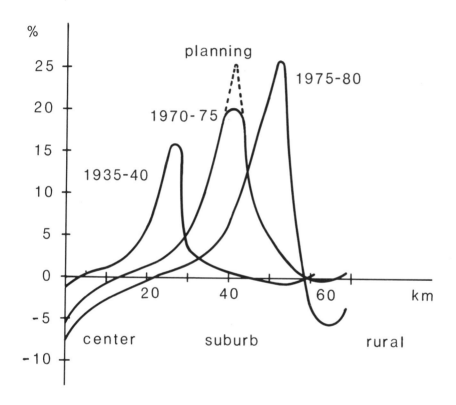

Figure 12.1.   Tokyo's population growth rate

percent increase), which comprised 68 percent of the total
population growth of the island. The next most impressive case was
Fukuoka-*shi*, regional center of the island of Kyushu in the south,
with an 8.6 percent increase. By contrast, the overgrown cities of
Osaka-*shi* and Tokyo-*kubu* experienced significant decline, reflecting
a negative effect of urbanization. Expensive land, environmental
degradation, and traffic congestion acted as "push" factors, while
housing projects, cheaper land, and better environmental conditions
elsewhere represented "pull" factors.

## National Urban Residential Mobility

In Japan, 7,160,000 people changed their place of residence in
1981. The Land Agency surveyed a sample of 7,000 adult movers, with
a 74.4 percent response rate.[4] Moves were classified among four
hierarchical groups of settlement types and on this basis into four
major types of migration. The four settlement groups were: (a)
three major metropolitan agglomerations (Tokyo-Yokohama,
Chukyo [Nagoya], and Kyoto-Osaka-Kobe); (b) regional centers
(Sapporo, Hiroshima-*shi*, Kita-kyushu, Fukuoka-*shi*, and other
prefectural capitals); (c) local cities; and (d) rural towns and
villages. The proportion that each type of migration accounted for
is presented in table 12.2.

The main reasons for moving were also tabulated and vary, of
course, by age, sex, occupation, and region. Most moves were made
for occupational or professional reasons (37.6 percent), followed by
family reasons (14.6 percent), housing or living reasons (13.9
percent), with a large residual (33.9 percent) for other reasons.
Most notable among motives when broken down by migration type was
the large proportion of type III movers (that is, those making
centripetal moves to metropolitan areas)--61.9 percent. Housing
scored low with this group (1.6 percent), while other reasons
accounted for 30.9 percent, such as school or college entrance (14.0
percent) and marriage (9.8 percent).

Perceptions among migrants to large metropolitan areas about
the urban conditions they were accepting by making their moves,
compared with what they had known, were predictable enough. They
cited better facilities for transportation, shopping, culture,
educational services, and recreation and on the debit side noted
poorer environmental conditions, traffic safety, greater likelihood
of urban disasters, higher crime, higher prices (including housing
costs), and weaker sense of community (type III). The perceptions

---

4. Data on residential mobility are drawn from the *Survey of Population
Migration* (Tokyo: Prime Minister's Office, Land Agency, 1982).

of migrants moving in the opposite direction (type II) were
generally the reverse of the foregoing.

### Population Change in the Central City of Tokyo (*kubu*), 1950-1981

It is possible to study the population changes of central
Tokyo every five years from census data and pinpoint the periods of
population maxima for individual *ku*. As noted earlier, the climax
was found earlier in the center and later in the periphery. The
effects of urban change were strongest in commercial and business
districts (table 12.3).

Chiyoda-*ku*, the core of central Tokyo, and Chuo-*ku*, the heart
of Tokyo's CBD, reached their population maxima in 1955.
Surrounding these are inner wards of "upland" character, containing
the traditionally better residential milieux, in the modern period
much redeveloped for blocks of apartments or flats and modern shops.
In these wards, Minato-*ku*, Shinjuku-*ku*, and Bukyo-*ku*, the
residential climax came in 1960.

Taito-*ku*, the old lower-town center, saw its climax in 1960
also. The decade of the 1960s was a turning-point in postwar
reconstruction and high economic growth, and the "lowland"
industrial *ku,* such as Sumide and Koto, as well as mixed-use areas
such as Ohta, generally reached their maximum population in 1960-65.
The western "upland" residential districts experienced a late
maximum.

The central city as a whole *(kubu)* grew by 49,858 people
during 1980-81 as a result of natural increase (44,370 deaths
offsetting 94,228 births). The city's population change was more
influenced, however, by the effects of migration: 365,927
in-migrants were out-balanced by 415,156 out-migrants. With a net
out-migration of 49,232, the net population change for the city was
a loss of 15,755 during this one year alone.

### Industrial Structure and Changing Central Tokyo

Population decline in central Tokyo did not presage a negative
influence on industrial development, as it has in many other great
cities.[5] The city of Tokyo *(kubu)* reported a 7.8 percent growth in
the number of industrial establishments and a 4.0 percent growth in
people employed in them for 1975-78, and 5.8 percent and 4.6 percent
respectively for the period 1978-81. By the latter year, Tokyo's 23
*ku* contained 665,000 industrial and service establishments,

---

5. Earlier studies of the changing urban core include: Nobuji Sugimura,
*Chushin shotengai* [Central retail districts] (Tokyo: Kokon Shoin, 1974) [in
Japanese]; and Nobuji Sugimura, *Chushin shogyochi* [Central business districts]
(Tokyo: Kokon Shoin, 1977) [in Japanese].

TABLE 12.3

POPULATION GROWTH OF TOKYO *KU*, 1950-1981 (in '000s)

| Year: | 1950 | 1955 | 1960 | 1965 | 1970 | 1975 | 1980 | 1980-81 | | |
|---|---|---|---|---|---|---|---|---|---|---|
| | | | | | | | | X | Y | Z |
| Chiyoda A | 110 | 123 | 117 | 93 | 74 | 62 | 55 | + | − | + |
| Chuo | 162 | 171 | 161 | 128 | 104 | 90 | 83 | + | − | − |
| Minato(B) | 216 | 255 | 267 | 242 | 229 | 209 | 201 | + | − | + |
| Shinjuku(B) | 246 | 349 | 414 | 414 | 391 | 367 | 344 | + | − | − |
| Shibuya | 181 | 243 | 283 | 284 | 275 | 262 | 247 | + | − | + |
| Toshima | 217 | 301 | 363 | 373 | 354 | 321 | 289 | + | − | − |
| Bunkyo C | 191 | 237 | 259 | 253 | 234 | 216 | 202 | + | − | − |
| Taito D | 262 | 310 | 310 | 286 | 244 | 208 | 186 | + | − | − |
| Koto* E | 182 | 278 | 351 | 360 | 346 | 355 | 362 | + | + | − |
| Edogawa | 209 | 255 | 317 | 405 | 447 | 473 | 475 | + | − | − |
| Ohta* F | 400 | 568 | 706 | 756 | 735 | 691 | 661 | + | + | − |
| Setagaya*G | 408 | 524 | 653 | 743 | 787 | 805 | 797 | + | − | − |

360 = maximum population

A-G = regional classification of *ku* (wards); see Fig. 2.

\* = single *ku* example from this classification type (A-G)

X = natural increase

Y = net migration within Tokyo

Z = net migration with other prefectures

TABLE 12.4

INDUSTRIAL GROWTH OF TOKYO'S CENTRAL *KU*, 1975-81

| Region(*ku*) | Establishments (percent growth) | | Persons engaged (percent growth) | | Density (sq.km.) 1981 | Day/night population 1980 |
|---|---|---|---|---|---|---|
| | '75-78 | '78-81 | '75-78 | '78-81 | | |
| *Kubu* | 7.8 | 5.8 | 4.0 | 4.6 | 10,993 | 127 |
| A. Chiyoda | 11.9 | 8.6 | 2.2 | 4.1 | 73,289 | 1710 |
| Chuo-*ku* | 11.4 | 8.4 | 1.2 | -0.4 | 68,710 | 794 |
| Minato | 12.6 | 10.8 | 7.5 | 8.3 | 33,238 | 353 |
| B. Shinjuku | 11.6 | 6.4 | 11.2 | 7.0 | 25,445 | 201 |
| Shibuya | 3.5 | 18.4 | 13.5 | 7.0 | 20,584 | 187 |
| Toshima | 5.0 | 6.0 | 8.0 | 7.2 | 16,352 | 128 |
| C. Bunkyo | 6.6 | 3.3 | 3.0 | 3.8 | 15,553 | 160 |
| D. Taito | 4.7 | 2.8 | -1.5 | 3.3 | 28,210 | 181 |

employing 6.5 million people.[6]

The density of these workplaces in 1981 amounted to 1,123 establishments per square km and a city-wide density of 10,993 workers per square km. Their distribution was uneven, as might be expected (figure 12.2). Central *ku* showed high densities, peripheral ones the opposite, while the growth rate was highest in the middle band of *ku* as regards employment. In general, their distribution varied by region and industry. To illustrate this, eight centrally-located *ku* are isolated for comparison (table 12.4), demonstrating the industrial structure of Tokyo's urban core.

It is assumed that central and near-central districts of great cities will show higher industrial employment densities than for the city as a whole—at least, this is presumed for Tokyo. Since Tokyo's figure is 10,993 persons per square km, the critical density for distinguishing between "central" and "peripheral" *ku* will be 10,000 persons per square km. Of all privately held land in Tokyo-*kubu* 91 percent was in use in 1981, and notwithstanding the recent increase in high office buildings and apartment blocks (buildings of more than four stories now number about 65,000), the vast proportion of this land is occupied by low wooden houses.

Tokyo's 23 *ku* may be grouped by industrial character and location into seven regions. Four of them exemplify central and near-central *ku* (table 12.4). The full seven industrial district groupings are as follows:

1. Urban core districts (Chiyoda-*ku*, Chuo-*ku*, Minato-*ku*). These are centrally located, around the Imperial Palace, and include such specialized streets as Kasumigaseki (government), Maronuchi (CBD), Kabutocho (stock exchange), and Ginza (shops). This group contains the highest employment densities.
2. Near-center "upper-town" districts (Shinjuku-*ku*, Shibuya-*ku*, Toshima-*ku*). These are located on the Yamanote Loop line, developed since the great 1923 earthquake. The Nishi-Shinjuku subcenter and Ikebukuro are the most recently developed areas.
3. Inner Yamanote (Bunkyo-*ku*). This is an "upland" residential and cultural district and includes the University of Tokyo.
4. Subcenter of Shitamachi--"lower-town" (Taito-*ku*). This area contains traditional lower-town functions, including temples and railway terminals.

---

6. Statistics are drawn from the *Establishment Census* (Tokyo: Prime Minister's Office, Statistics Bureau, 1981).

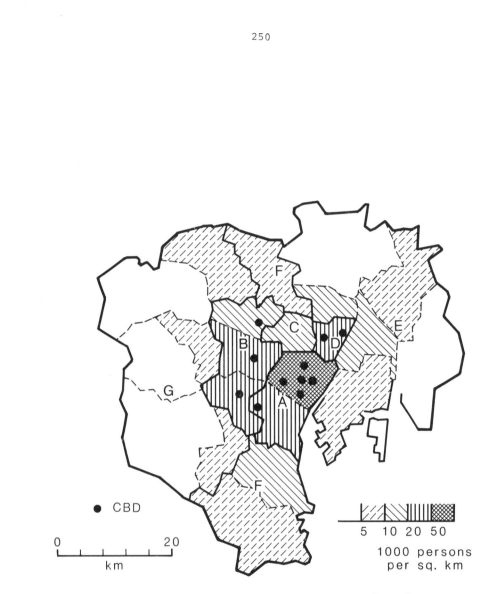

Figure 12.2.   Density of establishments in Tokyo in 1981 (by *ku*)

5. Eastern "Lowland." Six *ku*, mostly industrial.
6. "Upland/Lowland." Three *ku*, of intermediate character.
7. Western "Upland." Six *ku*, mostly residential.

At the broad scale, these groupings produce a coherent and orderly pattern of metropolitan spatial organization, with the oldest, functionally and morphologically most complex districts anchoring the pattern in the center (figure 12.2).

## Closing Remarks

Contemporary cities are changing rapidly. Their encircling metropolitan areas are the battlefield for innumerable decisions about future growth. But it is the city core in Japan that is still the "engine room" of urbanization. Crucial planning decisions are made about the functional structure and shape of the urban core, the effects of which then diffuse throughout and transform the rest of the metropolis. Consequences flow out even beyond the single metropolis and cascade with variable impact throughout the world urban system at large, affecting each regional and local system sympathetically or adversely according to prevailing cultural values.

REGIONS OF RECENT URBANIZATION
AND MODERNIZATION

# Chapter XIII

# BACKWASH URBANIZATION: THE PEASANTIZATION OF CITIES IN SUBSAHARAN AFRICA

## Akin L. Mabogunje

> Nowhere in the world have other classes risen to power without making
> the many small and independent rural producers subordinate to their
> demands . . . Africa is the only continent where the peasants have not
> yet been captured by other social classes.[1]

The rapid tempo of urbanization has been perhaps the most
visible, most dramatic manifestation of changing conditions in
Africa especially in the second half of this century. From a mere
eleven millions in 1950, the inhabitants of cities in Africa have
increased to over 37 millions in 1970 and over 72 millions in 1980.[2]
These give rates of urban growth of some 6.3 percent per annum
between 1950 and 1970 and some 6.9 percent per annum in the period
since 1970. These rates, particularly in the more recent period,
are regarded today as the fastest in the world. Even allowing for
the smaller base to which they relate, the annual addition of over
three million individuals to the urban population of Africa since
1970 is a phenomenon of considerable relative significance. This is
more so because of the fragile and febrile economic circumstances
against which these rapid growth rates have to be viewed.

The invitation to contribute to this special volume provides a
most suitable opportunity for reflecting on what the current
patterns of urbanization in Africa really signify. Over the past
three decades, starting with the monumental UNESCO volume on *The
Social Implications of Industrialization and Urbanization in Africa
South of the Sahara,* various attempts have been made to interpret
this phenomenon.[3] Viewed from the vantage point of 1985, it may not
be unconscionable to regard most of these attempts as not only
premature but in some cases quite superficial. Why, the question

---

1. Göran Hydén, *Beyond Ujamaa in Tanzania: Underdevelopment and an
Uncaptured Peasantry* (London: Heinemann Educational, 1980).

2. See *Growth of World Urban and Rural Population up to Year 2000* (New
York: United Nations, 1973).

3. International Africa Insititute, *Social Implications of
Industrialization and Urbanization in Africa South of the Sahara* (Paris: UNESCO,
1956).

remains, have large numbers of African rural folks been rushing into the cities? What have the cities made of them? What have they made of the cities?

It is the contention of this essay that until recently, the phenomenon of urbanization in Africa has tended to be observed and interpreted in a benign and optimistic manner, characterized as either the rural African reaction to the "bright lights" of Western modernization or as a concomitant by-product of economic and social development. Without doubt, the process is in part a response to these novel conditions in the life of the masses of these countries. But increasingly, the failure of the process across the continent to seriously improve the lot of the majority of the population either in the urban or the rural areas calls for a re-examination and a deeper insight into the nature of the complex social forces which urbanization represents in the peculiar circumstances of the African continent today.

Such a re-appraisal, in my view, would gain considerably if positioned against the wider background of the political economy of most African countries. Such a stance requires recognizing the fact that the urbanization process in Africa has been taking place in societies which are still heavily involved in the peasant mode of production and over which the heavy arm of modern statehood still rests rather lightly. In the circumstance, the peculiar characteristics of contemporary African urbanization must be seen as reflecting the current stage in the resolution of what looks like a game of "hide and seek" between, on the one hand, the masses of peasant producers and, on the other hand, the state apparatus operating in the shadow of international capitalism.

This essay is divided into five parts. The first considers the nature of African urbanization within the framework of the colonial political economy. It relates the somewhat restrained pattern of urban growth during this period to the more determinate nature of colonial control over the urban economy and social life, and especially the minimal demands made on peasant producers while integrating them somewhat into the global capitalist economy. The second part examines the indeterminate nature of the political economy of the post-colonial era, the rise of "modern" African states, their urban economic policies and programs, and their rather ambivalent relation to the masses of peasant producers in their countries. The third part then evaluates the extent to which current patterns of urbanization in most African countries must be seen as the backwash effects of policies and programs which have

been pursued over the last three decades by states whose agencies
and organs are only minimally "engaged" with the predominantly
peasant producers in their countries.  The fourth part assesses the
implications of this type of backwash urbanization with respect to
other aspects of social and economic life in these countries whilst
the fifth and concluding part considers the future of backwash
urbanization in Africa.

### Urbanization within the Colonial Political Economy

The period 1884-1960 may properly be characterized as the
colonial period in Africa.  Starting with the British Conference of
1884 when various European powers met in Berlin to agree to share
out the continent in exclusive spheres of trading influence, this
period saw the beginning of a more systematic attempt to integrate
the economies of various African communities into the global sway of
international capitalism.  The instrument of this integration was
colonialism, and its particular strategy of operation had
significant consequences for both the contemporary and later
patterns of urban growth and development in this part of the world.

Since, with few important exceptions in Francophone Africa,
the basis of colonial domination over a large part of the continent
was not outright conquest but various forms of skillful political
manipulations centered around so-called "treaties" of concession or
protection, the important consideration was how to exploit the
economic potential of the different territories at minimal
administative costs.  The British solution in the form of the famous
"indirect rule" system was perhaps the most ingenious of them all.
It was indeed most economical, given the fact that the country came
to control some of the relatively more populous areas of the
continent.  Nonetheless, even the "direct rule" systems of the
French, the German, and the Portuguese were not noted for
excessively high administrative costs as "forced labor" was made a
concomitant of each of these systems.  Relatively high cost was
incurred, however, wherever colonialism was made the prelude to the
establishment of a substantial settler population from the
metropolitan country.  The demand of such groups for living and
working conditions not too dissimilar from what they were used to in
their home country led to major investments especially in urban
infrastructural equipment.  Thus, settler cities in sub-Saharan
Africa such as Dakar, Abidjan, Nairobi, and Luanda have
characteristics which set them sharply apart from such other centers

as Lagos, Kumasi, Freetown, and Mombasa.[4]

However, in considering the major factors in the political economy of the period that influenced the pattern and process of urbanization, it would be useful to examine them under broad headings such as the pattern of economic activities, the nature of the social relations, and the level of political mobilization. Over most of Africa, the dominant character of economic activities was the exploitation of natural resources whether agricultural, forestry, or mineral. Export agricultural production, in particular, dominated much of economic life in western and eastern Africa. In the former, much of this was left in the hands of native small producers whose efforts were encouraged by the introduction of new and more profitable crops such as cocoa, coffee, and bananas or the dissemination of improved varieties of traditional crops such as cotton and groundnuts (peanuts). Although there were a few plantations managed by foreign settlers in western Africa, it was in eastern Africa for much of the colonial period that the latter dominated the export agricultural economy. Mineral production was of more consequence in central Africa where the exploitation of copper and tin overshadowed most other production.

All over the continent, however, the major investment of the colonial administration to stimulate the colonial economy was in the railways and ports. In one territory after another, a skeletal rail line went from a port center into the interior to facilitate the collection, bulking, and evacuation of the various produce, and the complementary distribution of cheap manufactured commodities being imported in exchange for the former. It was thus not without reason that colonial urbanization came to develop around the ports and major nodes on the rail line.

These facts about colonial urbanization are already well known and need not concern us here.[5] What is, however, more critical and less often explored are the patterns of colonial social relations and the effect this had on the character and trends of urbanization then and now. Essentially, the colonial social relations, especially with regard to the native population, was predicated on two basic principles: first, the extraction of surplus value from their productive activities to make colonialism profitable, and secondly, artificial depression of wage levels for the Africans so

---

4 . See William M. Hailey, Baron, *An African Survey,* (London: 1957), pp. 261-379 for a comparison of colonial systems of government in the various territories.

5 . See, for example, William A. Hance, *Population Migration and Urbanization in Africa* (New York: Columbia University Press, 1970), pp. 209 and 297.

as not to excite unwarrantable expectations. Up to the Second World
War, surplus value extraction took various forms. It included
systems of converting traditional units of exchange to monetary
specie introduced by the colonial administration in a manner biased
in favor of the latter, low pricing policies for agricultural and
mineral commodities, and a poll tax payable in the newly introduced
monetary specie. The last was of special significance since it
defined specific obligations by individuals to the colonial
administration and thereby forced many into the money-exchange
economy.

For the members of the local population who had to help run
the economy, both their status and their wages were kept low. A
policy of segregation from colonial officials and the settler
population meant that the style of life of the latter was not meant
to be copied or easily reproducible by the colonial population.
Even in the French and Portuguese colonies which operated so-called
policies of cultural assimilation, the number of Africans who were
allowed to pass the stiff test of education, marriage system, and so
on was so small as to make little difference to the overall
segregationist thrust of colonial relations.

In some ways, this pattern of social relations suited the
masses of peasants since it placed minimal burdens on their
shoulders. Various adjustment and survival strategies were devised
in order to be able to meet the major burden of the poll tax. Where
there was inadequate surplus to sell to earn the required amount,
various forms of short-term migrations--to richer rural areas, to
the mines, and to the city--were embarked upon. The causes and
characteristics of these short-term migrations dominated much of the
literature of social conditions in the colonial periods. Most of
these publications emphasized the circulatory nature of many of
these movements and the target character of their objective. What
they did not usually grasp is that the African peasant was not very
interested in the cities of the colonial powers. He was prepared,
however, to come in, work to earn enough to discharge his duties to
the colonial administration, and return as soon as practicable to
his farm.

Trouble could therefore be expected wherever the colonial
administration frustrated these processes of adjustment, either
through the imposition of prestation or forced labor or through
expropriation of land for the use of settlers. The former was the
vogue in most colonies of France, Belgium, Portugal, and Spain as
well as in British colonies in eastern, central, and southern

Africa. It began to be challenged as a means of extracting colonial surplus as far aback as the 1930s, although it continued in many territories right up to the 1950s.[6] Land expropriation for settler agriculture and occupance was more characteristic of the higher and cooler areas of eastern and central Africa. The problems they posed were not resolved until real violent encounters occurred, such as the Mau Mau rising in Kenya and the war of liberation in Zimbabwe.

In short, the colonial cities in most of sub-Sahara Africa were centers called up to perform particular tasks and their attraction for the masses was consequently limited. This was made more so by various legislative provisions meant to make such centers more conducive to the health and safety of the colonial civil servants by enforcing stringent rules of environmental sanitation relatively irksome to the prevailing disposition of the African population. In Nigeria, for instance, the Township Ordinance of 1917, apart from classifying the cities and imposing on them certain building regulations, paid considerable attention to issues of sanitation, household hygiene, refuse disposal, and so on.[7] Part of the essential duties of the Colonial Police Force was to help maintain this high standard of environmental sanitation and inflict swift and stiff penalties for the slightest infractions. Having few political rights, the masses had no easy recourse for changing these conditions of urban life. The only escape was to "vote with their feet" and keep away as much as they could from the colonial city.

By 1950, the percentage of the tropical African population living in cities of 100,000 and above was no more than 2 percent, compared with a world average of 13 percent. Even if the definition of urban was brought down to 5,000 inhabitants, less that 8 percent of the African population were to be found in such settlements. Not only did the colonial economy have no need for many people living in the cities but the colonial administration operated regulations and by-laws which made urban centers not so welcoming to the masses of rural inhabitants. All these were to change drastically within two decades of political independence in most of these countries.

### Indeterminacy in the Post-Colonial Political Economy

To understand what happened to urbanization in the period following the political independence of most African countries, it is important to appreciate the somewhat tenuous social relations

---

6 . See *Report on Forced Labour* (Geneva: International Labour Office, 1929), leading to the Convention of 1930.

7 . Frederick J.D. Lugard, Baron, *Instructions to Political Officers on Subjects Chiefly Political and Administrative, Memorandum No. XI-Townships* (London: H.M. Colonial Office, 1919).

that existed between the mass of peasant producers and the "genre" of political leadership that took over power from the colonial administrations. In his recent study of the situation in Tanzania, Hydén has provided perhaps the most incisive understanding of the socio-economic matrix in which these peasants live and have their being.[8] For him, the primary concern of peasant producers in Africa is not only to meet the needs of the present generation households for subsistence in a reliable manner but also to provide the means of subsistence for the next generation in the form of land, for example, or modern education. As such, within the context of the household economy, the planning perspective relates less to productive than to socially reproductive needs. In other words, it is the needs of man rather that those associated with the development of the means of production that take precedence in the calculus of socially productive activities. Consequently, paradoxical as it may seem, agricultural modernization appears more often than not as a threat to the domestic orientation of the peasant household economy in many African countries.

This peasant mode of production Hydén calls an economy of affection. This is an economic system within which work, or improved productivity, is not an end in itself. Or as he puts it,

> In the economy of affection, economic action is not motivated by individual profit alone, but is embedded in a range of social considerations that allow for redistribution of opportunities and benefits in a manner which is impossible where modern capitalism or socialism prevails and formalized state action dominates the process of redistribution.[9]

It is from this perspective that one can better appreciate what happened after political independence when African political leaders tried to impose on this mode of production a state apparatus which for all practical purposes was simply an extension of international capitalism. This state apparatus was meant to serve as a regulatory and developmental instrument. In the African context, as country after country became independent in the 1960s, this instrument was translated to imply the articulation of so-called medium-run national "development" plans which were often no more than shopping-lists for large-scale importation of goods and commodities from industrialized countries.

Of particular interest in this post-colonial economy was the attention paid to academic counselling by Western or Western-trained scholars as to the best way to put a pre-capitalist economy on the path of self-sustained growth. Perhaps the most seductive advice

---

8 . Hydén, *Beyond Ujamaa.*

9 . Hydén, *Beyond Ujamaa,* p. 19.

was that of import-substituting industrialization. The logic of
this strategy has been elegantly argued in many publications of the
late 1950s and 1960s and need not take too much of our time.[10] Put
briefly, this strategy counselled African and other developing
countries to substitute for their exigent importation of the
consumers goods which they need within a given time period, the
importation of the capital equipment, machinery, raw material, and
technical know-how in the tenuous hope that over time and through
the operation of backward-linkage effects they will internalize the
whole production process and became industrialized.

Too many variables were, of course, held constant in these
intellectual projections. The reaction of multinational
corporations to the costing and transfer of their technological
properties, the international terms of trade (especially the pricing
of manufactured goods as against raw materials), the evolving
pattern of international financial markets, and so on--all these
were given rather scant attention in propagating this development
gospel. The impact of these factors on African countries has been
to make this strategy of import-substituting industrialization not a
means to self-sustaining economic growth, but rather the mechanism
for pushing their fledgling economies deeper and deeper into
stagnating international indebtedness, and making them more and more
exposed and dependent on external economic conditions.[11]

The fact of international indebtedness has indeed become a
salient feature of economic life in virtually all countries of
sub-Saharan Africa today. As the International Monetary Fund (IMF)
itself noted, much of this indebtedness was due not so much to
increases in oil prices (since oil is not as important in the
poorest countries), as it was to the collapses in the primary
commodity markets and the substantially increased cost of borrowed
capital. This includes loans from the IMF, the World Bank, and
other banks and suppliers, many of whom have added significant
surcharges in recent years to repayments which have lately fallen
into arrears.[12] This situation has led to a serious deterioration in
the terms of trade of most African countries of some 25 percent and
more in recent years and has given rise to an "import strangulation"

---

10. The best known publication on this is that by Albert O. Hirschman, *The
Strategy of Economic Development* (New Haven: Yale University, 1958).

11. For a detailed critique of this strategy, see Henry J. Burton, "The
Import Substitution Strategy of Economic Development," *Pakistan Development
Review*, 10 (1970); see also Michael Roemer, "Dependence and Industrialization
Strategies," *World Development* 9 (1981): 429-434.

12. International Monetary Fund, *Annual Report, 1982*, (Washington, D.C.:
IMF, 1982), pp. 22,29.

of no mean proportion. Indeed in 1981 import values fell by 40
percent in Madagascar, 36 percent in Sierra Leone, 29 percent in
Ghana, 20 percent in Zambia and 12 percent in Tanzania.[13] Import
substitution industrialization strategy has led African countries to
this state of "economic strangulation" through import restrictions.
As Helleiner observed,

> Without crucial imported inputs and spare parts, much of the capital
> stock--in transport, industry, agriculture and, even social
> infrastructure such as schools and hospitals--cannot function
> adequately. This results frequently in long-term physical
> deterioration, often accelerated in tropical conditions. In some
> instances, the unavailability of fuel, inputs and spare parts has
> severely reduced the capacity to move potential foreign exchange earning
> export products to the port.[14]

This galloping international indebtedness would have been more
bearable if the impact of foreign capital, while it lasted, had been
felt positively in all sectors of the economy. But this in fact had
not been the case. The primal and primary economic sector, namely
peasant agriculture, suffered tremendous discrimination and its
viability was seriously undermined in many countries of sub-Saharan
Africa. There were four ways in which peasant agricultural
production was negatively affected in the post-colonial political
economy.

First, the need to provide appropriate infrastructural
equipment for the new industries led to a highly exaggerated bias of
government expenditures in favor of urban centers and a
complementary sharp neglect of rural areas. Road construction,
water supply, power production, residential estates, office blocks
and industrial premises, educational institutions, and health
services, all commanded immediate and substantial attention and led
to heavy capital investment in the cities. By the same token,
resources available for rural roads, rural water supply, rural
housing, rural cooperatives, and other complementary rural
development activities were much reduced. Even where some effort
was focussed on rural electrification and rural water supply, the
lack of priority was so evident that these serve only to underline
further the strong discrimination of policies and programs against
rural areas.

Second, the better organization of urban workers into trade
unions served to force labor wages up and in some countries to
encourage the establishment of a national minimum wage. This
relatively high urban wage level came to pose real difficulties for

---

13. International Monetary Fund, *World Economic Outlook 1982* (Washington
D.C.: IMF 1982), p. 97.

14. Gerald K. Helleiner, "The IMF and Africa in the 1980s," *Canadian
Journal of African Studies* 17 (1983): 20.

hired rural labor supply. Peasant farmers thus had to compete for unskilled labor at wage levels which in terms of prices being offered for agricultural commodities were clearly uneconomic.

Thirdly, much of the urban industrial activities could take place only behind high walls of tariff protection. This means, of course, a substantial rise in the cost of home-produced industrial goods and a situation in which consumers, largely farmers, have to subsidize a large number of inefficient industries in circumstances in which their income from export agricultural production suffers from considerable fluctuations in the world market.

Finally, as if this negative impact on rural producers were not enough, the urban labor force came to develop dietary tastes and habits which increasingly prefer imported food items, notably wheat, rice, milk, and beverages, to local staples. The result is the weakness in the mutual interaction between urban and rural economic growth. The rise in per capita urban income, rather than fuel significant growth in rural economic activities and income, simply results in increased importation from abroad with consequent worsening of international debt.

In short, the most striking feature of the post-colonial political economy in many sub-Saharan African countries is the unequal nature of the exchange between the urban and rural sectors of national production. This inequality provides the backdrop against which to position social movements and tendencies within African countries. The asymmetry in urban-rural relations is, however, not simply a function of internal social forces. It also results to a large extent from the impact of external forces, such as the multinational corporations. This connection with the outside world lends a certain poignancy to the difficulties behind efforts to correct the asymmetry and make for a more stable and determinate national economy. Against such a background, urbanization in many African countries is today more a measure of the despair, than of the hope, that had accompanied the process of so-called economic development during the last three decades.

### Current Urbanization as a Reactive Strategy

To understand how policies formed in the economic context just discussed translate into rural-urban migration streams, it is necessary to consider how the masses of the rural population react to state apparatus. For all its deleterious impact on their economic well-being, it maintains only a grip on the means of their reproductive existence. This state apparatus, as Hindess and Hirst observed, would seem to have no necessity but is "suspended over society as a given without conditions of existence in society."[15] As a result, when this apparatus intrudes so insiduously into the peasant economy, the peasants evolve various strategies to minimize the net effect of its disruptive impact. This resistance to being "captured" by the state apparatus takes various forms, from open indifference to collaborative subversion. The main argument of this present essay, then, is that the current pattern of urbanization in many African countries can only be understood in the light of the reactive strategy.

Principal in this strategy is the search for a niche within the peripheral capitalist economy of the post-colonial city which still leaves the peasant producer master in his own house or controller of the means of his productive activity. In other words, if the state improves urban areas to the severe detriment of life in the rural areas, one reactive strategy is to "refuse to die on one's feet" and move *into* the city without becoming *of* the city. This means that the peasant continues to hang on to his rights in rural land (which often he continues to exploit simultaneously) while participating in the urban economy on his own terms. Those terms include involvement in what has come to be referred to as the "urban informal sector." Indeed, it is not for nothing that this sector became sufficiently prominent as to gain academic recognition only in the 1970s. It was Hart, reporting from Ghana in 1971, who first called attention to the increasing significance of so-called informal activities in the economy of a number of Ghanaian towns.[16] Later, in its report on employment in Kenya, the Labour Office described this sector in detail. It is characterized by ease of entry, reliance on indigenous resources, family ownership of enterprises, small-scale operation, labor intensity, and adaptive technology, skills acquired outside the formal school system, and unregulated and competitive markets.[17] Informal sector activities are largely ignored and rarely supported, by government, which does, however, sometimes attempt to regulate and discourage them. But by the 1970s this sector represented a significant proportion of total employment in most African cities. In the 1972 survey of employment

---

15. Barry Hindess and Paul C. Hirst, *Pre-Capitalist Modes of Production* (London: Routledge and Kegan Paul, 1975), p. 197.

16. J.K. Hart, "Informal Income Opportunities and Urban Employment in Ghana," paper presented at a conference on "Urban Unemployment in Africa" at the Institute of Development Studies, University of Sussex, September 1971; subsequently published in revised form in *Journal of Modern African Studies* 11 (1973): 61-89.

17. International Labour Office, *Employment, Incomes and Equality: A Strategy for Increasing Productive Employment in Kenya* (Geneva: ILP, 1972), p. 6.

in urban centers in Kenya, the informal sector accounted for between 28 and 33 percent of those employed.[18]

A considerable literature has grown up in the last decade on the theoretical and policy implications of this budgeoning economic sector in African cities. That it is the refuge of rural migrants and the urban poor is hardly ever disputed. What is often questioned is whether its relationship with the formal sector is generally "benign" or "exploitative." A benign interpretation usually derives from a social-democratic political perspective on development. By contrast, Marxist scholars see this relationship as essentially exploitative. The informal sector is seen as no more than petty commodity production the "underdevelopment and backwardness [of which] . . . are necessary conditions for the development and advancement of the organized, formal sector dominated by a few, oligopolistic houses."[19]

What is inadequately appreciated, however, is that participation in the urban informal sector may be a continuation of a preferred peasant reactive strategy against being captured by a highly impersonal state apparatus. Anthropologists, studying urban societies in developing countries, have noted the persistence within them of a peasant mode of production. This had led Franklin to suggest that urban centers in developing countries contain three main systems of production--peasant, capitalist, and socialist--in which,

> . . . the fundamental differentiator is the labour commitment of the enterprise. In the peasant economy, the individual entrepreneur is committed to the utilisation of his total labour supply--that of his family who may and do often find alternative or additional sources of employment. This accounts for the diversities of the historical peasant societies, but if these sources are not available the *chef d'entreprise* must employ his kin . . . In the capitalist and socialist systems of production, labour becomes a commodity to be hired and dismissed by the enterprise according to changes in the scale of organisation, degree of mechanisation, the level of market demand for products. It is for this reason especially, not so much because of the introduction of mechanisation and the factory system that the capitalist system of production has been disruptive of traditional societies. It introduces a hitherto unheard of scale for the evaluation of the human individual.'[20]

The point, then, is that, while governments in many African countries have in various ways undermined the vitality of peasant agricultural production in the rural areas, the peasants have reacted by moving into the city to take some advantage of resources

---

18 . ILO, *Employment, Incomes and Equality,* p. 225.

19 . A.N. Bose, *The Informal Sector in the Calcutta Metropolitan Economy* (Geneva: ILP-WEP Working Paper, 1974), p. 1. See also Caroline O.N. Moser, "Informal Sector or Petty Commodity Production: Dualism or Dependence in Urban Development?," *World Development* 6, no. 9/10 (1978), pp. 1041-1064.

20 . Samuel H. Franklin, "Systems of Production, Systems of Appropriation," *Pacific Viewpoint* 6 (1965): 148-49. See also Terry G. McGee, "Peasants in the Cities: A Paradox, a Paradox, a Most Ingenious Paradox," *Human Organization* 32 (1973): 135-42.

disproportionately allocated there by the state. In so doing, they have had to change their habits little and remain relatively uncaptured by the state apparatus.

This "backwash" effect of inappropriate development policies applied to essentially precapitalist economies is better appreciated when one considers whether the inner dynamism of the urban informal economic sector supports an evolutionary or an involutionary interpretation. The school of thought which sees the interrelationship between the formal and informal sector as benign assumes an evolutionary path of growth for the latter. It believes that the adoption of a positive attitude by government towards its promotion--through such measures as ceasing the demolition of informal sector housing, reviewing trade and commercial licensing procedures, and intensifying technical research and development work on products suitable for its production process--would enhance the evolution and modernization of this informal sector.[21]

In opposition to this, it is argued that the only possible outcome for the informal sector is involutionary, or "self-inflationary" as McGee has called it.[22] If enterprises in this sector became more efficient and profitable, they would lose their intrinsic character as an "informal" organization. They would have to be more capital rather than labor intensive, they would pass out of the category of being small-scale, relying only on family labor or purely indigenous resources, and would increasingly need to "catch the eye" of formal authorities, for instance, as a result of their enhanced requirement for credit. Therefore, to preserve their intrinsic character, informal sector activities can develop only through an "involuntary" process exhibiting "an increasing tenacity of basic pattern, internal elaboration and ornateness, technical hairsplitting and unending virtuousity."[23] Involution, in effect, allows more and more people (or migrants) to be absorbed into informal sector enterprises through intensive sub-division (or elaboration) of tasks, often involving unproductive technical hairsplitting, but all at a cost of reducing per capita returns to labor. The system is geared to survival rather than progress.

---

21. Moser, "Informal Sector," p. 1045.

22. Terry G. McGee, *The Urbanization Process in the Third World: Explorations in Search of a Theory* (London: Bell, 1971).

23. See Clifford Geertz, *Agricultural Involution: The Processes of Ecological Change in Indonesia* (Berkeley, Calif.: University of California Press, 1963), p. 82.

Given the worsening economic conditions of rural Africa, the
continued growth in the size of cities results more from the
unexhausted potential of occupational and trade involution than from
the conventional type of economic growth arising from functional
specialization and higher labor productivity. Current urbanization
trends, then, represent the backwash effect of inappropriate
economic policies in many of these countries, policies which
continue to destroy the vigor of rural areas and suffocate the
cities with the burden of human casualties the process creates.

### Implications of Backwash Urbanization

Perhaps the most visible manifestation of this "backwash"
urbanization is the environmental condition of many African cities.
This is dominated by the vast sprawl of slum dwellings or
bidonvilles whose tenure within the city area may be legal or
illegal. In western African cities, for instance, most of these
dwellings are perfectly legal, even though they are constructed
haphazardly and need to satisfy no municipal regulations.[24] Half of
Lusaka's inhabitants now live in squatter housing.[25] Muench observed
that around Kampala for several kilometers there are, apart from the
rather grand landowners' villas with cars parked beneath banana
trees, extensive areas of simple structures of mud and wattle or
rusty metal sheets which are somehow divided up into several
"bedspaces" for the poorest migrants to the city.[26] Similarly, Stren
noted that in Dar-es-Salaam, Tanzania, the in-migration of the 1960s
so outpaced the municipality's ability to provide even surveyed
building plots that by 1972 there were some 28,000 squatter
dwellings housing about 220,000 people; and by 1980 these figures
had doubled.[27]

That most of the slums and squatter settlements in African
cities are poorly supplied with urban services of any kind--roads,
water, sewage, refuse disposal, electricity, schools, health and
recreation centers--are facts too well known to need emphasis.
Given the level of income of the majority of urban residents and

24. See, for instance, Josephine O. Abiodun, "Urban Growth and Problems in
Metropolitan Lagos," *Urban Studies,* 11 (1974): 341-47; and Margaret Peil, *Cities
and Suburbs: Urban Life in West Africa* (New York: Africana Publishing Co., 1981).

25. Ann Schlyter and Thomas Schlyter, *George: The Development of Squatter
Settlement in Lusaka* (Stockholdm: Swedish Council for Building Research, 1980).

26. Louis H. Muench, "The Private Burden of Urban Social Overhead: A Study
of the Informal Housing Market of Kampala, Uganda" (Ph.D dissertation, University
of Pennysylvania, 1978).

27. Richard E. Stren, *Urban Inequality and Housing Policy in Tanzania: The
Problem of Squatting* (Berkeley: University of California Institute of
International Studies, 1975); see also his "Underdevelopment, Urban Squatting, and
the State Bureaucracy: A Case Study of Tanzania," *Canadian Journal of African
Studies* 16 (1982): 67-91.

rather poorly organized or non-existent tax systems, it is easy to appreciate why environmental conditions in most African cities are in such a parlous state. For instance, except in those cities where European settlers have been dominant, few African cities have developed a system of property valuation and rating as a means of generating much-needed revenue to underwrite urban infrastructural equipment. The problem, in fact, becomes rapidly more intractable as the slums or shanty towns settlements become ever more prominent components of the urban landscape.

Faced with this situation, initial governmental responses have aimed at preventing the multiplication of such slums and squatter settlements rather than devising schemes to integrate them properly into its system. Slum clearance and demolition of squatter settlements were often the preferred policies of officials in many African countries, and Hake has described the extent of the demolitions in Nairobi, for example, between 1968 to 1972.[28] There were similar instances in Lusaka, while the authorities in Harare stood up squarely against squatting--at least up to the end of the period of the unilateral declaration of independence. That these policies proved futile is demonstrated by the continued vigorous growth of such substandard housing areas in many African cities.

This gulf between what governments would like to do with such areas and what they are actually able to do underscores the extent to which African cities have been "peasantized." This reflects both the "peasant" or rural origins of the in-migrants as well as their use of "peasant-type" strategy to survive, albeit now within an urban environment. This strategy involves minimizing bureaucratic interference in their affairs through the political process. Post-colonial politics in many African countries has played into the hands of the "peasants" by its emphasis on "one man, one vote." By putting the "peasants" in the vaunted position of patrons to be wooed by politicians (as clients) for their votes, often by means of "largess," it made it possible for them to treat politics largely as a superstructural phenomenon with little or no relationship to their production but providing possibilities for manipulating the administration for limited advantages.

Thus, in the urban as in the rural areas, when government officials advocate policies based on capitalist and so-called "modernizing" considerations, it has often been easy to defeat or ignore them by manipulating the inverted "patron-client"

---

28. Andrew Hake, *African Metropolis: Nairobi's Self Help City* (London: Chatto and Windus, 1977).

relationship between them and the politicians. The result has been that such "spontaneous" or "self-help" settlements are being increasingly accepted as part of the city through a process of benign indifference, and efforts are even made sometimes to accord them formal, legal status. In Dar-es-Salaam, for instance, legal rights have been granted to many who built illegally in the 1960s whilst basic services have been extended to some formerly squatter areas.[29] Similarly, in Lusaka the government has embarked upon a massive program of upgrading squatter settlements, involving both granting legal occupancy rights and providing services such as roads, water supplies, schools, and clinics.[30]

This accommodation of peasant-produced housing within so-called modern or modernizing cities has gained some orthodoxy through its acceptance since the early 1970s by the World Bank. According to its Sector Policy Paper, "The analysis of the housing situation and of the Bank Group's experience both suggest that the upgrading of squatter housing to ensure the retention and improvement of existing housing stock and the provision of serviced sites on which lower-income families may construct new housing for themselves by self-help methods are prime lending instruments for more equitable urban development."[31] Thus, from a single such project in 1972, the Bank's involvement rose to 12 projects worldwide by 1976, six of which were in Africa. Presently, the Bank is also collaborating further with various African governments, notably Nigeria, to extend this program to their major urban centers. In every instance, however, the Bank insists each project be seen not as a social welfare scheme but as an economic proposition. Hence, much attention is paid to pricing and cost-recovery, both for the site development of residential plots and for the urban services provided. Although it advises that proposals allow prospective housing to be affordable by the lowest income groups, the Bank requires full recovery of allocated capital and recurrent expenditure.

The question remains whether intervention by so august an organization as the World Bank can really help the plight of the poor moving into African cities, or whether it simply serves to compound and further distort their problems. Burgess, for instance,

---

29. See, for instance, Richard E. Stren, "Urban Policy," in *Politics and Public Policy in Kenya and Tanzania,* ed. Joel D. Barkan and John Okumu (New York: Praeger, 1979), p. 196.

30. David Pasteur, *The Management of Squatter Upgrading: A Case Study of Organisation, Procedures and Participation* (Farnborough, Eng.: Saxon House, 1979).

31. *Housing Sector Policy Paper* (Washington, D.C., World Bank, May, 1975), p. 45.

emphasizes the difficulties and ultimate futility of establishing this type of housing policy in isolation from more general development strategies.[32] Indeed, there is little doubt that, given the heavy hand of bureaucracy likely to accompany state-assisted self-help schemes, the majority of those in need of low-cost housing are bound to meet their requirements outside such a framework, and often in defiance of it.

### Conclusion: The Future of Backwash Urbanization

This essay has tried to call attention to a grand irony noted by many writers on post-colonial urbanization in Africa. Urbanization, far from being a correlate of economic development, is today the very symbol of the failure of strategies aimed at achieving that goal. To understand how this has come about in many African countries, the urbanization process needs to be seen, not simply within the context of the political economy of these countries, but also their politics. Central to this is the influence which peasants exert on decision-making and how this has been used both in rural and urban settings to mimimize the disastrous and deleterious consequences of wrong-headed or inappropriate development strategies for peasant survival capabilities.

Peasant influence on the politics of many African countries was not difficult to distinguish in the colonial period because it was usually explicit, entailing either active resistance or participation. Since independence, however, it has been more difficult to recogize because it was hidden behind popular concepts such as African socialism or democracy. As Hydén puts it:

> Peasant power was manifested by their influence on the political process itself. They were not influential in the sense of shaping policies. They were influential, however, in terms of determining what issues the political system was likely to take up. Moreover, they were often able to divert the direction of government policies by frustrating their implementation . . . Peasant influence was also exercised through patron-client relations. The patrons were by no means independent of the clients. Peasants had a hold on them because these relations were initiated by the bigger men who wanted to make some gains from them. Given lack of economic control over their clients, they could only secure their support by offering something tangible in return. Thus, patronage politics reflected peasant perceptions, cognitions and preferences.[33]

One major factor in the inability of most African governments to deal effectively with the continued spate of rural migrants into cities and the economic and environmental problems of cities is the strength of patronage politics in these countries. The persistence

---

32. Rod Burgess, "Petty Commodity Housing or Dweller Control? A Critique of John Turner's Views on Housing Policy," *World Development* 6, no. 9/10 (1978), pp. 1105-1133.

33. Hydén, *Beyond Ujamaa,* pp. 91-92.

and vigor of this type of politics is explained in turn by the limitation of state power in these countries arising from political timidity in confronting and transforming the peasant mode of production. The arena for such a confrontation is clearly in the rural areas and specifically in the field of agriculture. But it is absolutely clear that the outcome of that confrontation will be decisive for conditions in the urban centers.

Clearly, then, the future of backwash urbanization currently affecting most African countries can be influenced only to the extent that governments are willing to deal with declining productivity in agriculture and worsening social conditions in the rural areas. This essay has tried to show the wider ramifications of this problem. It has stressed that economic development strategies not focussed on directly enhancing the productive capacity of the majority of a nation's population will surely lead to economic collapse. This is the lesson of the last three decades of so-called African development, and conditions in urban centers all over the continent offer the most visible and compelling testimony of the misdirection and mismanagement of their economies.

# Chapter XIV

# URBAN CHANGE IN ARGENTINA: HISTORICAL ROOTS AND MODERN TRENDS

Herbert Wilhelmy

More than thirty years have passed since the publication of my book *Südamerika im Spiegel seiner Städte*.[1] It is now possible to recognize fundamental changes in modern Argentine urbanization that were perceptible then only in embryo. The urbanization process in La Plata region, facing the Atlantic, has differed historically from that in countries lying on the Pacific side of South America. In western South America, the primary stimulus for urbanization was provided by internal migration, but in Argentina this role until the Second World War was played by European immigration. Since that time, however, a fundamental transformation has occurred, and its place has been taken by rural-to-urban migration. This essay places that transformation in the context of long-term processes of Argentine urbanization and examines some of its geographical consequences.

The Republic of Argentina occupies an area of 2.8 million square km, making it the second largest state in South America. Argentina is eleven times as large as the Federal Repubic of Germany, although the latter has more than twice its population. Spanning 33 parallels of latitude (about 3,700 km), the country extends from the subtropical zone north of the Tropic of Capricorn, with its hot summers and mild winters, to the cool regions of Tierra del Fuego. The economic opportunities are similarly diverse. In the north sugar cane, rice, cotton, and even subtropical fruits thrive, while the climate of Patagonia encourages only sheep raising on an extensive scale. River valleys there can support productive orchards only with artificial irrigation.[2]

---

1. Herbert Wilhelmy, *Südamerika im Spiegel seiner Städte* (Hamburg: de Gruyter, 1952).

2. Franz H. Kühn, *Das neue Argentinien: Eine wirtschaftsgeographische Analyse mit Betriebs- und Verbrauchskunde* (Hamburg: C. Behre, 1941).

The Pampas, the large central portion of Argentina, enjoys a moderately warm climate, where the use of the upland rivers for irrigation agriculture (wine and fruit) compensates for the decreasing precipitation towards the west at the edge of the Andes and in the area of the Pampine Sierras. The Pampas is the economic core of Argentina. It contains 66 percent of the country's arable land. About 60 percent of Argentina's agricultural produce comes from this region, including 90 percent of the grain, 78 percent of the rape-seed, 75 percent of the stock farming production, and 20 percent of the fruit and vegetable production. The cultivation of sunflowers is limited almost exclusively to the "Fertile Crescent" on La Plata. This economic wealth of the Pampas is the result of agricultural exploitation introduced when the Spanish took possession and vigorously maintained since the middle of the last century, above all through the participation of Europeans of many different nationalities. All this has made Argentina into a larder and granary for the world.

### Early Spanish Town Founding

The broad grasslands were inhabited by the Querandi when the Spanish arrived on La Plata, at the beginning of the sixteenth century. The Querandi were wandering hunters, gatherers, and fishermen, who quickly mastered the horses introduced by the Spaniards and transformed themselves into feared horsemen. In 1529, they attacked and destroyed the first Spanish stronghold, Fort Sancti Spiritus, about 50 km north of the present-day city of Rosario, founded by Sebastian Cabot two years earlier on a tongue of land jutting out into the Rio Paraná. This fort had been planned as the harbor, depot, and jumping-off point for future expeditions to the legendary "Sierra de La Plata." The first founding of Buenos Aires on the high right bank of La Plata by Pedro de Mendoza in 1536 similarly miscarried. In the Pampas, peopled as they were only by nomadic Indians, these early fortified settlements lacked an economic base, for agricultural settlers did not immediately accompany the soldiers into the area. Famine broke out among the Spaniards in Buenos Aires even before the close of the first year which might have doomed the whole enterprise, had not Juan de Ayolas and Salazar de Espinosa a few months later found an indigenous agricultural people farther upstream. There, in the homeland of the Guarani, Asunción was founded in 1537, and this town, in the heart of a fertile agricultural area, then became the base from which further colonization of the eastern lowlands by the Spanish conquerors proceeded.

In 1541, Buenos Aires, which had been under constant attack from the Querandí, was evacuated and demolished by the Spaniards. Its surviving Spanish inhabitants were resettled in Asunción. There the conquistadores joined with the Guaraní to create a rapidly increasing mixed race population, which formed the actual basis of subsequent Spanish expansion in eastern South America. Asunción became the center of Spanish power in the basin of the Paraguay and Paraná rivers. Early settlement impulses fanned out from this city toward the northwest as far as the eastern slopes of the Andes, where in 1559 Nueva Asunción and later Santa Cruz de la Sierra were founded, toward the east as far as the area of the Guairá Falls, where several cities were laid out (only to be abandoned later under the pressure of the Paulistine slave hunters), and toward the south as far as the mouth of La Plata. From Asunción daughter settlements were founded at Santa Fé in 1573, at Buenos Aires for the second time in 1580, and at Corientes in 1588 at the confluence of the Paraguay and the Paraná (figure 14.1).

During the entire colonial period, the *frontera,* the boundary between the pacified, colonized area and the unpacified Indian land, remained completely stable in the Pampas. A series of forts--primitive fortifications with ditches and palisades--formed tight defensive perimeters around the only two large Spanish settlements, Buenos Aires and Santa Fé (figure 14.2). Santa Fé remained until the end of the eighteenth century a true frontier town. The frontier line between the Spanish settlements and the region dominated by the Pampas and Chaco Indians ran from west to east not far north of the town, from Quebracho Herrado on the post road to Córdoba to Fort San Javier, founded on the Paraná in 1734. Around 1860, the frontier was pushed northwards, to the other side of the Rio Salado. The southern frontier was three hours' ride away from Buenos Aires in 1744. It ran from San Nicolás on the Paraná via San Antonio de Areco and Lújan to Magdalena on La Plata, denoting a very narrow river margin along the right bank of the Paraná that could properly be considered as pacified in the eighteenth century. Not until 1815 did the culture boundary advance to the southern Rio Salado. By 1826, the frontier reached the line from Mar del Plata to Mar Chiquita, and finally by 1876, a line from Bahía Blanca to the southern edge of the Sierra de Córdoba.

That established the link with the second important area of early colonial Spanish town founding within the present area of Argentina. The string of towns along the "Litoral," including Buenos Aires, Santa Fé, Corrientes, and Asunción, comprised the

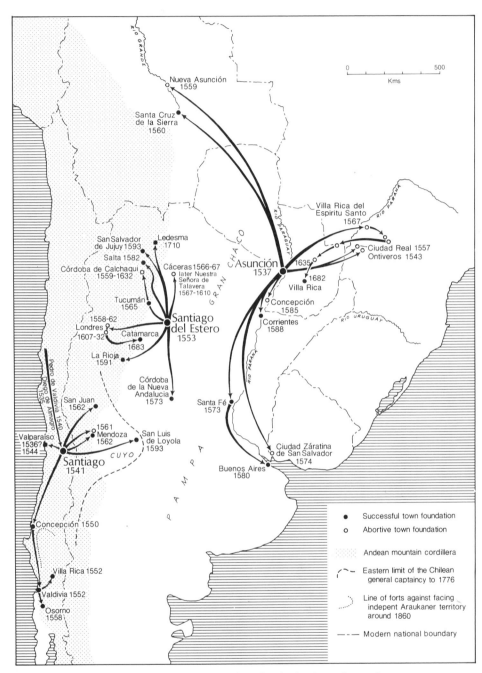

Figure 14.1.  Spanish town founding in the Argentine region

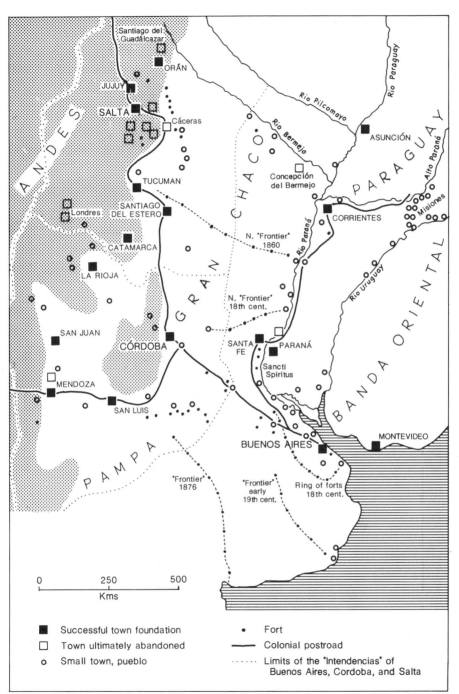

Figure 14.2.  Spanish frontiers and town foundations in the La Plata region

eastern settlement axis along the Río Paraná. These towns' most important function was political and military, asserting Spanish claims on La Plata and checking further penetration of the Portuguese toward the south. Beyond that, Buenos Aires, as the first Spanish ocean harbor on the Atlantic, had the task of securing the line of communications from Spain to Asunción.

The second string of towns developed in the west, on the edge of the Andes, and fulfilled other purposes. Northwest Argentina was conquered from the Peruvian highlands, and the first town foundations there took place from the west. It soon became evident that the valley regions on the eastern slopes of the cordillera, thickly settled by sedentary Indians and well cultivated, formed ideal supply areas for the mining regions of the Andean highlands. The possiblity of drawing the foodstuffs and pack animals (mules and horses) lacking in the mountains from northwestern Argentina made this region an important perimeter of High Peru. Hence the Spaniards gradually increased their interest in the further economic evolution of this area, building on the inheritance of Indian irrigation agriculture. Santiago del Estero arose as early as 1533 in the eastern Andean foreland. From this point of initiation on the western edge of the Chaco, many other towns were subsequently founded (figure 14.1). Some were located on the main road into the mountains, which gained increasing importance as the *camino al Peru;* some on its branch roads into the uplands, as were Tucumán (1565), Salta (1582), and Jujuy (1593); and later, on a branch of the great valley road, others like Ledesma (1710) and Orán (1794). Córdoba (1573) and La Rioja (1591) were also daughter foundations of Santiago del Estero. In addition, there were other larger and smaller places, some of which, like Metán (1665) survived. Altogether there were about 25 places established by the Spanish in this area. Many of them were added to already existing settlements in the valley oases; they received new names or took over the old Indian ones. Since Quechua had become the official trade and colloquial speech with the inclusion of northwest Argentina in the sphere of influence of the Incas, Quechua place names can be found as far as the area of Santiago del Estero and even in the north of the province of Córdoba. These names have compounded forms with pampa (plains), -yacu (water), -oro (mountain), -huasi (house), -mayu (river), -gasta, -marca (place). Today Quechua is still in use in northwest Argentina, even if only among the peasant sections of the population.

In a time when the interior of the continent was still unknown, the Spanish Crown set the eastern administrative boundary of Chile in ignorance of topographical patterns at an arbitrary 100 miles. Thus a piece of territory on the eastern flank of the Andes also legally belonged to Chile, and there in the area of the Coyunche Indians after the conquest by the troops of the Governor Hurtado de Mendoza in 1562, two towns were founded from Santiago, namely Mendoza and San Juan (figure 14.1). Several decades later San Luis de Loyola (1593) followed as a third settlement. As late as 1776, the province of Cuyo with these three most important towns was a part of the General Captaincy of Chile. But then in the course of administrative reform the area was united with the Vice-Royalty of Rio de la Plata, so that subsequently the fate of these towns was closely bound up with that of the other La Plata cities.

The numerous town foundations that resulted from Santiago del Estero reflect the economic importance of northwestern Argentina in the second half of the sixteenth century. The colonizing impulse emanating from Santiago del Estero was second only to that radiating from Asunción at exactly the same time. Both towns were centers of important agricultural areas, the only ones that now lie within the present-day political boundaries of the three La Plata nations. Only this economic basis gave them the strength to form so many daughter settlements, a strength which other towns, founded only as political-military strongholds without agricultural support, lacked.

The two town networks that focussed on Santiago del Estero and Asunción regarded one another with mutual jealousy as they extended their economic catchment areas. As the trade of Asunción began to extend to the Pacific coast, it encountered the resistance of the towns in the northwest. Their opposition was especially provoked, however, by the second founding of Buenos Aires in 1580. They foresaw their existence seriously threatened by the creation of a harbor on La Plata. The citizens of Córdoba predicted that transandean trade would cease and that goods produced in La Plata area would be exported through the new harbor. This concern was quite justified, but it would take a full two hundred years before Buenos Aires actually received the right to export goods directly to Europe.

Immediately after Buenos Aires was reestablished, both groups of cities began to compete bitterly for political and economic hegemony along La Plata. In 1587, the city council of Santiago del Estero proposed to the Spanish Crown the transfer of the harbor to the province of Tucumán, citing the city's closeness to Córdoba and its great distance from Asunción. When this application to alter territorial relations was nevertheless rejected by the crown, the cities of the northwest changed their tactics and began to fight Buenos Aires economically. Córdoba was forbidden to send any more flour to Buenos Aires, a prohibition which was, however, circumvented by merchants through intermediaries in Santa Fé. In 1598, several other cities officially demanded a limit on deliveries of goods from Asunción to Buenos Aires to the benefit of their own products. All these efforts, dictated by a ruthless self-interest of the individual towns, certainly hindered the development of Buenos Aires, but could not negate the young city's long-term potential.

Before the sixteenth century drew to a close, the interior towns were successful in one decisive move: they secured a royal decree prohibiting direct exchange of goods between Buenos Aires and the mother country by skillfully exploiting the danger of attack by foreign naval powers that existed on the Atlantic coast. And there was more to come. An interior tariff barrier was erected in Córdoba in 1622 thereby largely cutting off the coastal area from its hinterland with high tariffs. A duty of 50 percent of their value was levied on all goods coming from Buenos Aires, and Buenos Aires began to stagnate. The consequences for Asunción also became gradually evident. The former center of Spanish power in eastern South America, lying deep in the interior, lost its connection to the outside world and did not prosper in the seventeenth century as had once been hoped. Santiago del Estero, Tucumán, and Córdoba, however, flourished. The successful founding of the University of Córdoba as early as 1613, the first institution of higher learning of La Plata countries, clearly demonstrated the shifting focus of energy from Paraguay to northwestern Argentina.

Contests for regional power like those at the turn of the sixteenth century between the urban networks of Santiago del Estero and Asunción were characteristic for their time. As with early university foundations (in the western part of the colonial empire Lima and Bogotá received privileged universities in 1551 and 1610 respectively after the model of Salamanca), these contests were an expression of the great importance that accrued to strategic cities in the early colonial period.[3]

---

3. Herbert Wilhelmy and Wilhelm Rohmeder, *Die La Plata-Länder* (Braunschweig: G. Westermann, 1963), p. 152.

## The Modern Era of Argentine Urbanism

Around 1810, when the total population of Argentina numbered a little more than 400,000 people, about a quarter of them lived in the 50 places with more than 2,000 inhabitants that might be considered urban. Seven larger centers anchored the western chain of towns, stretching from Tucumán in the north to Mendoza in the south, while eight centers anchored the "littoral" band of settlement on the Paraná.[4] The broad central plain between the two chains lacked towns altogether, as did the entire southern part of the country. By 1869, the number of Argentine towns and cities had increased only to 56, but their aggregate number of inhabitants (497,000) had increased almost five-fold since 1810, reaching 28.6 percent of a total population of 1.7 million. The eastern and western town systems still remained separated from one another by the broad empty spaces of the Pampas. The great change came with the construction of the railroad from Rosario to Córdoba (1863-1870) and the extension of the line from Rosario to Buenos Aires in the course of the following decade. By about 1880, the line was in full operation. Up to this point the evolution of Argentine urbanization was dependent entirely on ship traffic on the Paraná and overland traffic on unimproved wagon roads. The onset of railroad construction, therefore, meant a "cultural-geographical transformation of the first order, a modern Conquista."[5]

During the colonial period, three main lines of traffic had emerged. The *camino al Peru* ran from Buenos Aires via Córdoba, Santiago del Estero, and Tucumán (transshipment center for the mountainous portion) to Jujuy. The post road to the west branched off from it at Villa Maria southeastwards from Córdoba and ran via San Luis and Mendoza to Chile. A third route, supplementing the water route, followed the western bank of the Paraná as far as Santa Fé, and crossing to the eastern bank reached Asunción via Corrientes. These "roads" passed through the countryside as broad ribbons of traffic grubbed up by countless wagon tracks. Their only foci were the watering places and stations for changing horses. The term *carretera,* which is still used today even for modern highways (for example, Carretera Panamericana) is a reminder that "road" and "cart way" were once one and the same thing.

---

4. Patricio H. Randle, N. Gurevitz, and R. Gonzalez Pelazzo, "Tendencias demograficas de la urbanización Argentina 1810-2010," *GAEA: Anales de la Sociedad Argentina de Estudios Geograficos* 16(1974): 339-358.

5. Franz H. Kühn, *Grundriss der Kulturgeographie von Argentinien* (Hamburg: Friederichsen, de Gruyter and Co., 1933).

The railroad line from Buenos Aires via Rosario to Córdoba was quickly followed by the construction of additional routes. From Córdoba a line reached Tucumán in 1876. In 1883, a line from Buenos Aires reached Bahía Blanca, and a year later Mendoza likewise became linked with the capital. These first lines pushing forward into the interior were genuine pioneer railroads. They did not have to take into consideration existing traffic needs but were to create them as a consequence of the settlement that was stimulated by their construction. By 1914, when the rail net encompassed about 30,000 km, the number of cities with more than 2,000 inhabitants had increased to 332. By 1914, when the rail net encompassed about 30,000 km, the number of cities with more than 2,000 inhabitants had increased to 332. By then 4.16 million people lived in them, already more than half of the total population of the country at the time (7.89 million). In the capital city alone there were 1.58 million inhabitants, more than a third of the entire urban population. But the other urban centers had also grown strongly, both in the east and the west, where the population concentrated especially in the districts surrounding Mendoza and San Juan with the development of irrigation agriculture.

The modern urbanization process in Argentina, which had begun earlier than in all other South American countries, made unusual progress up to 1960. In this year, there were 734 cities with 14.8 million of the total national population of 20 million, 73 percent of the total. Some 8.3 million of the 20 million inhabitants, or 40 percent lived in large cities with more than 100,000 inhabitants. There were ten of these, including Buenos Aires, which with its metropolitan suburbs had grown to a world class city of 6 million persons. Seven of these large cities were in the littoral area (Buenos Aires, Rosario, La Plata, Santa Fé, Mar del Plata, Bahía Blanca, and Paraná) and three (Córdoba, Tucumán, and Mendoza) in the western interior. In addition to its large cities Argentina in 1960 had 75 places with over 20,000 inhabitants and hundreds of smaller country towns with populations between 2,000 and 20,000.

Since the 1960s, there have been no new urban foundations in any numbers worth mentioning, but rather a continuous growth, especially in places of medium to small size, so that the category of towns with 8,000 to 15,000 population has become newly significant. Many of these have developed as satellite towns in the neighborhood of important central places, such as around Mendoza and Tucumán or the smaller San Juan. Another new trend in this period has been the formation of twin-city conurbations, that is, the spatial and functional amalgamation of double-cities spanning river courses that had previously strongly divided them, as in the case of Santa Fé/Paraná, which were connected in 1969 by a tunnel; Corrientes/Resistencia by a 3km-long Paraná bridge; or Viedma/Patagones. Finally it is notable that the urban development impulse that stemmed from railroad building has again retreated in favor of that stimulated by roads, as in the colonial period, although clearly these are no longer cart tracks cut to pieces by traffic, but well constructed automobile highways.

The network of modern asphalt roads has rectified in part a problem of accessibility brought on by the particular priorities of railroad construction. Since the early colonial period traffic routes were chiefly oriented from east to west and west to east, and railroad building emphatically reinforced this pattern of transverse traffic corridors, providing practically no meridional routes whatsoever. Many of the branch lines ended blindly in the western sections of the country. This was particularly true of the lines that ran from Buenos Aires in grid-like fashion to the edge of the Pampas. Several lines connected the capital with important harbors, like Rosario, La Plata, Mar del Plata, and Bahía Blanca, from which in turn smaller traffic grids radiated out, but most Pampas railroads had no continuation into the interior. Now roads provide important cross connections, enabling settlements previously quite isolated to participate in the general growth process.

### The Pace and Character of Contemporary Urbanization

The modern evolution of Argentine urbanization set in motion by the great railroad construction wave after the middle of the last century would have been inconceivable without the heavy stream of European immigrants that poured into the country at the same time and enabled Argentina's population to grow by leaps and bounds, from 1.3 million to 1860 to 4 million around 1895 and a doubling of this number to 7.9 million at the beginning of the First World War.[6] The first great wave of emigration reached Argentina after the outbreak of the American Civil War (1861-65), when the path to North America was barred to European emigrants. In the decade between 1861 and 1870, almost 160,000 persons arrived, and after 1880 over a half million in every decade, with an absolute peak between 1901 and 1910 of 1.7 million. In 1914, almost a third of all "Argentines" were foreigners. Buenos Aires became the great magnet for immigrants

6. Juan C. Elizaga, "La evolución de la población de la Argentina en los ultimos cien años," *Desarrollo Economico* 12, no. 48 (1973): 795-806; Zulma L. Recchini de Lattes, *La población de Argentina* (Buenos Aires: 1975).

from overseas, who concentrated to an overwhelming extent in the
capital and in the Pampas district near the coast (in 1895, 62.3
percent of all newcomers were in the province and city of Buenos
Aires). The European immigration extended only weak offshoots
across the margins of the Pampas. The newly arriving Europeans
strongly influenced the character of present-day Argentines, and in
the eastern part of the country led to the submergence of the Indian
part of the population, which had been only weakly represented
there.

The First World War brought a halt to immigration--and even
resulted in a small loss of population--but from the war's end until
1930 some 120,000 to 160,000 people arrived each year. The 1930s
and the Second World War years brought reverses, with periods of
emigration and a complete cessation of immigration. Immigration
surpluses were registered for the last time around 1950.

In the hundred years between 1857 and 1957, a total of 7.6
million Europeans made Argentina their goal, of whom, however, only
4.2 million were "real" immigrants. Italian agricultural workers
comprised 3.4 million; they took advantage of the half year's
displacement of the harvest period between the northern and southern
hemispheres to "commute" semi-annually across the ocean until
Mussolini prohibited the practice.[7] Their preference for Argentina
as an immigrant country gave the population a far-reaching European,
especially south European, stamp.

There has been a virtual balance between immigration and
emigration since the mid-1950s and further population growth has
rested upon natural increase. With a declining birth rate (1914-70,
3.6 to 2.0 percent), a long-stable death rate (1970, 0.8 percent),
and a now very modest yearly migration surplus of 0.12 percent,
population growth presently amounts to 1.3 percent per annum. This
exceptionally low rate in comparison with other South American
countries (except for Uruguay with a similar rate of 1.2 percent),
must be explained by reproductive behavior linked to generally high
standard of living expectations in modern Argentine society, on the
European model.[8] The high level of urbanization, the replacement of
the extended family by the nuclear family, and family limitation
have worked in the same direction. After decades of comparatively
high annual growth rates between 2.5 and 3.5 percent early in the
century, the strongest of any country then,[9] its current low growth

---

7. Herbert Wilhelmy and Wilhelm Rohmeder, *Die La Plata-Länder*, p. 126.

8. James R. Scobie, *Argentina: A City and a Nation* (New York: Oxford
University Press, 1964, 1971).

rate of 1.3 percent already approaches that of the highly
industrialized countries (U.S.A., 1.2 percent; Japan, 1.1 percent;
and the Federal Republic of Germany, 1.0 percent). Correspondingly,
the growth tempo of the total population of Argentina steadily
slowed since 1950, from 7.9 million (1914) to 15.9 million (1947),
and to 20 million by 1960. In 1970, 23.4 million were counted, and
the estimate for 1980 lay at 27 million.

Argentina remains a thinly settled country with 9.7
inhabitants per square kilometer, although with great local
differences. In the city and province of Buenos Aires 50.1 percent
of the population crowds onto 11 percent of the land area and in
rural areas on the urban periphery of the capital reaches a density
of 1,400 inhabitants per square kilometer. By contrast, there are
only 34 inhabitants per square kilometer in the province of the
Tucumán, 16 in Santa Fé, 12 in Córdoba, and in the southern
Patagonian provinces of Santa Cruz and Chubut only one per square
kilometer (1970).

These density figures dramatically illustrate the major shift
in population concentration since colonial times from the western
part of the country to the east. At the beginning of the nineteenth
century, population still clustered almost entirely in the interior
of the country. About 150,000 persons lived in the provinces of
Santiago del Estero and Córdoba in comparison with only 75,000 in
Buenos Aires and Santa Fé. For three hundred years, the economic
life of Argentina was aligned with the northwest of the country and
its cities. The reversal of this relationship since the middle of
the last century can be attributed to the large proportion of the
European immigration that remained in the eastern part of the
country, and secondly to the attraction of metropolitan Buenos Aires
and the eastern regions in general for internal migration once
European immigration dropped off after 1950. In addition to this,
the criminal neglect of agriculture in the preceding decade was a
major impulse for the rural-to-urban movement. While in 1914, 49
percent of the population of Buenos Aires still consisted of
overseas immigrants and only 11 percent were from the Argentine
interior, this relationship had by 1957 reversed itself; 36 percent
were internal migrants while 22 percent were drawn from abroad.[10] In
the interior, only the province of Córdoba, owing to the
industrialization of its capital (45,000 in-migrants in ten years),

---

9. Wolfgang Eriksen, "Bevölkerungs und Stadtentwicklung," in *Argentinien,*
ed. Francisco Zapata (Tubingen: 1978), p. 68.

10. Wolfgang Eriksen, "Bevölkerungs und Stadtentwicklung," p. 77.

as well as the still sparsely populated provinces of Patagonia, could show significant gains from internal migration. All in all, the development gradients in the country have steepened through internal migration.

Thus throughout Argentina's modern period of development there have been abundant sources for urban growth.[11] Before the First World War, overseas immigration fed this growth, which largely benefitted the cities of eastern Argentina, and particularly Buenos Aires. More recently, the growth has come from heightened internal migration after the Second World War.[12] In 1869, 28.6 percent of the population lived in cities with more than 2,000 inhabitants; by 1914, the proportion was 52.7 percent; and by 1970, it had already reached 78.9 percent. A total of 18.5 million urbanites faced only 5 million people living in the countryside in 1970, which actually represented a loss of one million since 1947. Whereas nearly three quarters of all Argentines lived in the countryside in 1869, urban and rural people by 1914 were in balance, and today almost four-fifths of all the country's people are city dwellers.

Argentina's level of urbanization (at 85 percent) is the second highest in South America, just below that of Uruguay (84 percent), above that of Chile (76 percent) and Venezuela (82.5 percent), and far beyond that of Columbia (70 percent), Peru (67 percent), and Brazil (68 percent). Paraguay (39 percent) and Bolivia (33 percent) today still have not attained the level of urbanization that Argentina already had reached by 1914.[13] Even if we restrict the definition of "urban" to places over 25,000 inhabitants Argentina before the First World War contained 36 percent of the total population in towns and cities of at least this size, and 63 percent by 1970. By comparison, the degree of urbanization of Argentina far exceeds that of the Federal Republic of Germany, in which 56.5 percent of the total population lives in cities of more than 20,000 inhabitants.[14]

Buenos Aires continues preeminent among Argentine cities. The census of 1970 counted 8.4 million in the metropolis, representing 36.1 percent of the nation's whole population and 45.7 percent of

---

11. Zulma L. Recchini de Lattes, "El proceso de urbanización en la Argentina, distribución, crecimiento y algunas carateristicas de la población urbana," *Desarrollo Económico* 12, no. 48 (1973), pp. 867-886.

12. Roberto Combetto, *Las migraciones internas en la Argentina* (Buenos Aires: 1968).

13. Jürgen Bähr, "Gross Buenos Aires: Zur Bevölkerungsentwicklung der argentinischen Metropole," *Innsbrucker Geographische Studien* 5 (1979): 154.

14. Wolfgang Eriksen, "Bevölkerungs und Stadtentwicklung," p. 78; Jürgen Bähr, "Gross Buenos Aires: Zur Bevölkerungsentwicklung der argentinischen Metropole," *Innsbrucker Geographische Studien* 5 (1979): 155.

the inhabitants of all cities.[15] Three million of these are found
within the limits of the capital itself and 5.4 million in the 19
peripheral cities lying in the surrounding province of Buenos Aires.
It is precisely these heavily industrial satellite cities that have
taken in and continue to absorb a large share of the rural migrants
streaming towards Buenos Aires, whose yearly numbers have swelled to
100,000. The most recent estimates, made in 1980, suggest a total
population for the entire metropolitan area of 10.13 million
inhabitants. With more than a third of all Argentines living in the
capital city, Buenos Aires has taken on the character of a
"hydrocephalus," grown out of all proportion.

However, the trend of increasing urban primacy may be
disappearing. Since the 1960s, Greater Buenos Aires' share of the
total urban population of Argentina has remained almost constant at
45.7 percent probably even declining in the very recent period.[16]
While early in this century the capital's annual rate of increase
was somewhat over 5 percent, it has now fallen to 2.3 percent and is
exceeded by that of all the other "million cities" of South America,
with the sole exception of Montevideo (0.5 percent). The annual
growth rates of Caracas (6.7 percent), Lima (6.2 percent), Bogotá
(5.9 percent), São Paulo (5.7 percent), Rio de Janeiro (4.1
percent), and Santiago (3.4 percent) all surpass that of Buenos
Aires. Even many provincial cities in Argentina exceed the
capital's rate growth, such as Mendoza (3.6 percent), Mar del Plata
(3.6 percent), and Córdoba (2.9 percent). At the forefront of such
provincial urban growth are the annual rates of population increase
of Comodoro Rivadavia (7.3 percent), Jujuy (6.5 percent), and
Formosa (5.3 percent).[17] Even Ushuaia, the capital of Tierra del
Fuego and the southernmost city in Argentina, grew from 3,000
inhabitants in 1970 to 5,000 inhabitants today.[18]

Just as with the massive concentration of population on La
Plata, all the other cities of Argentina, especially the industrial
cities of Rosario, Córdoba, La Plata, Tucumán, Santa Fé, Bahía
Blanca, and Mendoza, owe their rapid expansion during the last

---

15 . Ibid., p. 153.

16 . Ibid., p. 155.

17 . Ibid., p. 155.

18 . To be sure, growth rates, which are relative values, for places with
small absolute population figures say nothing—beyond the developmental tendencies
recognizable in them—about the real significance of the settlement involved and
its drawing power for rural in-migrants. At an annual growth rate of 5 percent, a
city of 20,000 inhabitants grows only by 1,000, in comparison with a super center
with almost 10 million inhabitants like Buenos Aires, which grows by 500,000.
Even a comparison with "smaller" million-cities remains problematic; more
justified is comparison with São Paolo (7.2 million) or Lima (5 million).

decade to internal migration.[19] Beside the 10-million city of Buenos Aires and the three cities of Rosario, Córdoba, and Mendoza, which have surpassed or just reached the five hundred thousand level, twelve other large cities boast over 100,000 inhabitants. It is predicted that by the year 2010 there will be 20 such centers.[20] The number of cities with 25,000-100,000 inhabitants climbed from 12 in 1914 to 33 in 1947, and to 54 by 1970, less through new foundings than through the growth of originally smaller country towns into this category. There is a total of 447 places of more than 2,000 population.[21] The province of Buenos Aires demonstrates the highest degree of urbanization; outside of the metropolitan area with its 19 peripheral cities, it has an additional 8 cities with more than 50,000 inhabitants. Other cities in this size class are distributed evenly (two each) throughout the provinces of Córdoba, Entre Rios, Mendoza, and Santa Fé.

## Structure and Change in the Large Cities

The physical transformation of older Argentine cities has been progressing by the same rules operating in all the cities of Spanish South America.[22] The old city cores have been rebuilt with modern structures, in the course of which the skyscraper, at first in embryonic form, made its initial appearance in Buenos Aires during the late 1920s and from there gradually diffused, particularly after the Second World War, to the larger provincial cities. Some of the narrow streets of the inner city dating from the colonial period have been widened, when opportunity arose through the clearance of whole rows of Cuadra between parallel streets, to widths exceeding 100 m, as in the case of the Avenida 9 de Julio in Buenos Aires. Other major traffic arteries have been created by diagonal "breakthrough" streets intersecting the older urban grid pattern which had proven unsuited for modern movement. These, as well as freeway-like ring roads, have helped alleviate chronic and chaotic traffic problems. Since most large Argentine cities lie on level building ground, urban expansion has usually occurred through the simple extension of street grids, changing direction only when

19. Roberto Cortes Conde, "Tendencias en el crecimiento de la población urbana en Argentina," *Verhandlungen 38. Internationaler Amerikanistenkongress Stuttgart-München 1968, Pt. IV* (München, 1972), pp. 259-273; César A. Vapnarsky, *La población urbana argentina* (Buenos Aires: Centro de Estudios Urbanos y Regionales, Instituto Torcuato di Tella, 1968).

20. Patricio H. Randle, et al., "Tendencias demográficas," p. 355.

21. Graziella Schneier, "L'Impact spatial de l'industrie. Essai méthodologique: Le Cas de la localisation de la sidérurgie en Argentine," *Annales de Géographie* 87 (1978): 159.

22. Paul-Yves Denis, "La Structure urbaine en République Argentine: Le Cas de Buenos Aires," *Cahiers de Géographie de Québec* 11, no. 22 (1967): 43-53.

encountering a differently oriented coordinate system of an earlier
suburb or an originally independent community.

Some of the first modern residential suburbs in the cities of
the east, especially in Buenos Aires, consist of the villa quarters
of merchants, entrepeneurs, and representatives of other independent
professions who had immigrated from Europe and who preferred to
settle in districts defined by closed landscapes. This way of
living in villas surrounded by gardens, previously unknown in
Argentina, began to appeal to the well-to-do indigenous upper class,
who increasingly foresook their patio houses in the old city and
moved to the new quarters. The old urban core districts were
progressively transformed into business and service centers, which
encouraged the further displacement of the residential population
from the older, central districts. Only the cities of the old
northwest remain relatively undisturbed by such processes of change.

Along the margins of older upper-class residential quarters
public housing developments have arisen often close to industrial
districts and above all adjacent to the *barrios* of rural in-migrants
that encircle the core cities. Frequently one can read from the
several rings of such slum quarters the chronological sequence in
which they arose. Right on the edge of the urban periphery lie the
most recent shanties, erected spontaneously on public and private
parcels of land. Further in toward the center of the cities follow
zones of older *villas miserias,* which--to the extent that legal
ownership has been granted and incomes have improved--have acquired
more permanent habitations connected to municipal service
installations. Since Argentine cities expand areally with much more
rapidity than do European cities (bound as the latter are by strict
planning requirements), the extension of municipal infrastructures
to outlying portions of the urban fringe occurs generally only after
years of settlement.[23]

### Portraits of Argentine Small Towns

Concern for the large and middle-sized cities with their
problems ought not to obscure our understanding of the
quintessential Argentine type of smaller central places--the country
towns and the *pueblos.*[24] The form of the country towns, especially
in the Pampas, reveals simple, unvarying characteristics. Most of
these towns are barely a hundred years old. Some arose in

---

23. Pierre George, "Problèmes urbains de la République Argentine," *Annales de Géographie* 77 (1968): 257-277.

24. Jorge E. Hardoy and Maria E. Langdon, "Cities and Regional Thought in Argentina and Chile, 1850-1930," *Urbanization in the Americas,* ed. W. Borah et al. (Ottawa: Museum of Man, 1980), pp. 45-56.

conjunction with fortifications *(fortines)* of the earlier Indian
frontier and others around railway stations and other traffic nodal
points.

These towns all share standardized ground plans no different
from those of their colonial predecessors. Around the square *plaza*
that serves as the point of origin for streets that cross one
another in grid fashion stand churches, the city hall, court
buildings, one or two hotels, several stores, and the Social Club.
If the town is large and prosperous enough, the square may be
planted with trees and flowers, and in the middle stands a music
pavillion and a monument to San Martín or some other hero of
Argentine history. A plaza is essential equipment for any town with
even the slightest urban pretensions. There the inhabitants gather
after sunset amid the strains of a military band. Just as with any
larger city, the public life of a town in the Argentine *campos*
without the ritual *corso* every evening is unthinkable.

Churches dominate the townscape. At the railroad station at
the edges of the towns rise the towers of the grain elevators and
mills. Multistory residential buildings are beginning to appear,
but single-story patio and half-patio houses remain predominant even
in the larger towns. Without front gardens they stand with smooth
walls, narrow entrance doors, railed window balconies, and blind
facades deceptively suggesting greater height, on the bare, treeless
streets. Further away from the town center the brick houses become
shabbier, stucco is lacking, and the courtyard becomes a vegetable
garden and chicken yard. Often there will be a second plaza, but it
remains empty and neglected. Here and there on the edge of town
stand scattered villas of merchants, officials, and managers with
front gardens and several trees. Nearby, often erected without
regard for building lines, lean the crooked huts *(ranchos)* of the
casual laborers and the poor, built of air-dried clay bricks. Here
and there a shade-giving *ombu* marks a spot where the perimeter of an
*estancia* or some other rural *rancho* once stood. And then, rather
abruptly, after a few vegetable gardens and huts of dairy cow
keepers, begin the *campos*--the open countryside.

Even more abrupt is the transition in the case of the smaller
settlements with no urban character, the *pueblos,* which cannot be
regarded as "villages" in the European sense, since they lack an
agriculturally employed population. They fulfill central place
functions at the lowest level in the broad agricultural landscape,
in which the distance to the next larger place can amount to dozens
of kilometers. The wide *campos* roads reach into the town, dust

blows on the unpaved streets, mud and puddles cover them after rain showers. These pueblos are little more than a row of a dozen or so houses to the right and left of the railroad station, often on both sides of the tracks, with adjoining cross streets. The plaza, occasionally cordoned off with a wire fence, is "decorated" with several half-dried trees. The small church or chapel stands to one side. Here the stores and taverns on the street corners dominate the local scene, places where the *campos* worker and the town residents find all the necessities of everyday life. The *almacen* is a general store, which passes on to the rural resident the goods of civilization from the large cities. There he can buy everything from nails to a suit of clothes, from salt to canned goods.

The tavern *(boliche)* generally has a small retail store attached. As long as there is no *almacen,* the *bolichero* completely dominates local business. He provides his customers with foodstuffs and commodities on credit until the harvest is brought in and later balances his accounts against their products. Above all, however, the *boliche* is tailored to the socializing needs of the men. At twilight every day, the men of the town assemble there, and on weekends also the agricultural laborers from the surrounding area, for political discussion, friendly conversation, social drinking, games, and occasional rowdiness. The horses stand bound to the hitching post, adorned with the best saddles and bridles, waiting patiently until their masters ride home late in the evening.

Certain kinds of change come even to the *pueblo.* Gradually there appear the offices of government officials, schools, churches, branch offices of banks, offices of larger trading companies, gas stations and auto repair firms. But the social nexus reigns supreme. A prime meeting place, particularly for the youth of the town, is the railroad station, if the pueblo lies on a railroad line. The station is dominated by the iron framework of a water tower and here and there by the massive construction of a grain elevator. The passage of the train is the event of the day and the excuse for afternoon or evening assignations.

## Conclusion

Argentina's contemporary system of cities has evolved from two separate nuclei. One lay in the country's eastern region and embraced the early coastal settlements, the other extended as a chain of settlements in the west along the foothills of the Andes. Asunción in the one case and Santiago del Estero in the other were original centers from which a large number of daughter towns were established, a process that established Spanish power at the outer and inner margins of La Plata lowlands. The broad interior plains remained long unsettled. Only with the building of the railroads in the last century was a firm link achieved between the two settlement nuclei and a basis created for gradually peopling the Pampas and stimulating new agricultural settlement and continued urban growth.

In contrast to North America the assertion of political control and the process of agricultural colonization in South America were not synchronous processes. While in North America the extension of territorial power, farming settlement, and town founding occurred generally together, a lapse of fully three centuries in South America separated political conquest from genuine colonization of the plains. Towns accompanied the advancing settlement frontier in North America, while in South America towns long preceded the coming of rural settlers. Here, towns were Spanish strongholds in the colonial period, whereas agricultural settlement has been post-colonial and largely the result of extensive European immigration since the middle of the nineteenth century. In Argentina this population flow in the first instance benefitted coastal towns, although it also had a stimulating effect on the urbanization of the interior.

The growing importance of the eastern cities led necessarily to a relative decline of those in the west, an imbalance that conscious decentralization policies are now trying to ameliorate. Córdoba and Mendoza have been able to maintain their position as important regional centers in western Argentina, but the persistent rural-to-urban migration which has led to explosive growth of coastal cities, especially Buenos Aires, works against this decentralization effort. Achieving a better balance between the inland cities and the national capital must be a top goal of the Argentine government in the future.

# Chapter XV

# BRAZIL'S URBAN SYSTEM IN 1980: BASIC DIMENSIONS AND SPATIAL STRUCTURE IN RELATION TO SOCIAL AND ECONOMIC DEVELOPMENT

Speridião Faissol

This essay considers the geographical structure of the Brazilian urban system in 1980 in terms of broad issues of social and economic development, based largely upon the population census of that year. Statistical evidence is drawn from the one-percent sample of census returns that are available for cities over 100,000 inhabitants. Any conclusions, therefore, will refer only to the upper levels of the urban hierarchy, although this portion of the urban system is certainly the leading segment of the system as a whole (figury 15.1). This examination focusses upon the distribution of occupations, income, and like characteristics, gives only limited consideration to industrial characteristics, and none at all to commercial and service activities.

## Brazilian Development and Urban Structure

Brazil provides an excellent example of a country showing marked economic, social, and regional inequalities. It is particularly important not just for its population size and economic strength--Brazil now has the eighth-largest gross national product in the world--but because its rapid rate of development is accompanied by an increasing gap between rich and poor, problems of intense urban industrialization, as well as most of the difficulties of a modernizing society, including dual circuits in the economy.

Urbanization has advanced so quickly that the urban proportion of the population has increased between 1970 and 1980 from 56 to almost 67 percent. Growth in some urban areas has been much higher: while the national increase in population annually during the decade was 2.5 percent, yearly population growth in all urban areas has been just over 4 percent, composed of a rate of just under 4 percent for metropolitan areas in general and nearly 5 percent for the metropolitan agglomerations.

Differences between rural and urban places in social achievements are striking. Among people over 10 years of age about

294

Figure 15.1. Brazil's urban system, 1980

40 percent in the countryside are illiterate and another 40 percent have but 1-4 years of schooling. By rough comparison, among the total urban white population aged 18-54 (a privileged group in Brazil) only 9 percent are illiterate. In terms of income, 55 percent of the rural population is classified as having no income and another 25 percent as receiving less than the first minimum wage category, leaving only 20 percent distributed among all other income categories. There are of course other differences but these suffice to stress the enormous gaps in the social structure.

Conceiving regional development essentially as a diffusion process centered upon the urban sector--though with a rural component, of course--urban change becomes the pivotal driving element within the whole development process. Hence, poverty can best be understood by examining strategies of survival among the urban poor, and the ostentatious display of wealth is likewise best seen in the context of large cities. Diffusionary development processes are associated with zonal divisions of space into "core" and "periphery" character at all geographical scales. Such distinctions apply well in Brazil, both at the national level and at the level of metropolitan regions, distinguishing between richer regions such as São Paulo for example and poorer ones like Fortaleza. For this reason, the core-periphery concept will guide the remainder of this study.

### Brazil's Economic and Social Development

The urban system of Brazil changes in relation to the nation's general socio-economic and regional composition. Brazilian society is stratified by social and economic distinctions into sharply contrasting segments of rich and poor which through processes of spatial separation are reflected in clearly rich and poor regions. Broadly speaking, the poorer areas comprise the Northeast, the North, and the Central-West regions of Brazil.[1]

Poor people, for the purposes of this essay, are those who earn less than the minimum wage. While this level ought to be considered too low in absolute terms because it represents very low buying power, the poor in Brazil have a number of ways of augmenting total family income through additional work by family members and the informal economy. Thus, the minimum wage may be considered at least in relative terms a reasonable dividing line in considering personal income.

---

1 . A more detailed division of the country into rich and poor regions, indeed into core and periphery zones, is presented in Speridião Faissol, "Regional Inequalities in Brazil," paper presented to the 19th International Geographical Congress, Commission on Quantitative Methods, Moscow, 1976.

The distribution of income among Brazilians is strikingly uneven (table 15.1). The poorer half of the entire urban population accounted for only 16 percent of urban income in 1970, and the proportion slipped slightly to 15 percent by 1980. In rural areas the poorer half's proportion was somewhat higher but declined more precipitously during the decade. By contrast, the wealthiest 10 percent of the urban population accumulated 44 percent of the income in 1970 and 46 percent in 1980, showing that the marked patterns of inequality were on the increase. As such, these proportions illustrate the classical pattern of income distribution in developing countries.

While not of central concern here, the progressive concentration of wealth in the rural areas is notable, and undoubtedly reflects economic policies aimed at enhancing exports as well as highly commercial and technically advanced agriculture during this period. In such advanced agriculture there is less opportunity to earn non-monetary income, such as through subsistence production, and hence this wealth concentration is particularly perverse. What happened in the urban sector during the late 1960s and early 1970s--namely, accelerated modernization and consequent income concentration through scale economies--is now occuring in the rural sector through similar processes.

The proportional distribution of income needs to be seen in relation to comparative measures of real income. To avoid problems of comparing current values over time, subject as they are to high rates of inflation, a measure based on multiples of the minimum wage provides a better guide, since it is adjusted every six months. Long ago the minimum wage was established as the amount of money an individual person needs for simple subsistence. There are some difficulties nevertheless in comparing this measure over time and in translating it into dollar terms. Notwithstanding these limitations it is evident that a very high concentration of people exists in the sub-minimum category with a rather small share of the income (table 15.2). Simple comparison between 1970 and 1980 is tricky because the apparent decline from 61 to 33 percent, while it would be socially desirable, does not seem reasonable and does not square with the trend associated with the poorer half of the population indicated earlier (table 15.1).

In a preliminary study of income distribution in 1980 Cezar Medici found an increase in real income over the preceding decade only for those earning less than half the minimum wage and those earning over twenty times the minimum wage. There was a decline of

TABLE 15.1

BRAZIL'S RURAL AND URBAN INCOME DISTRIBUTION IN 1970 AND 1980,
FOR SELECTED PROPORTIONAL GROUPS *(percent of total income)*

| Proportional Groups | 1970 | | 1980 | |
|---|---|---|---|---|
| | Urban | Rural | Urban | Rural |
| Poorest 20 percent | 3.4 | 7.5 | 3.5 | 4.5 |
| Poorer 50 percent | 16.0 | 23.0 | 15.0 | 19.0 |
| Richest 10 percent | 44.0 | 34.0 | 46.0 | 43.0 |
| Richest 5 percent | 32.0 | 24.0 | 33.0 | 33.0 |
| Richest 1 percent | 12.0 | 10.0 | 14.0 | 17.0 |

SOURCE: Fundação Instituto Brasileiro de Geografia e Estatistica (IBGE), *Population Census of Brazil, 1970 and 1980*. Statistics by the Superintendency of Geographical and Socio-Economic Studies (SUEGE), 1982.

TABLE 15.2

BRAZILIAN INCOME DISTRIBUTION IN 1970 AND 1980,
BY MULTIPLES OF THE MINIMUM WAGE CATEGORY

| Multiples of the minimum wage (MW) category | Persons | | | Income share | |
|---|---|---|---|---|---|
| | 1970 | 1980 | 1982 | 1970 | 1980 |
| Less than 1 x MW | 61.0 | 33.0 | 40.8 | 22.0 | 7.0 |
| Between 1 to 2 | 21.5 | 30.4 | 27.5 ) | 44.0 | 41.0 |
| Between 2 to 5 | 12.5 | 24.6 | 21.4 ) | | |
| Between 5-10 | 3.3 | 7.2 | 6.5 ) | 26.4 | 33.0 |
| Between 10 and 20 | 1.3 | 3.2 | 2.8 ) | | |
| More than 20 | 0.4 | 1.6 | 0.9 | 7.7 | 19.0 |

SOURCE: IBGE, *Population Census of Brazil, 1970 and 1980*; IBGE, *Household Survey, 1982*, special tabulations. Data refer to persons aged 15 or more.

2-5 percent in income for most of the groups in between, and for the group between twice and thrice the minimum wage the income decline was -5.98 percent--a serious erosion considering the large size of the group.  By contrast a rise of 9.18 percent for those earning twenty times the minimum wage (recalling that the index holds the effects of inflation constant) represents a substantial increase in the national concentration of wealth.[2] The aggregate value of income earned by those earning less than five times the minimum wage was spread among 95 percent of the population in 1970, but only 88 percent in 1980, representing a greater decline in income share than that of the size of the group.  There is no question that between 1970 and 1980 relatively speaking the poor generally got poorer.

This picture of wealth distribution, it should be stressed, applies to the census year 1980.  Figures for 1982 and 1983 are likely to show further concentration patterns and decreasing real wages for the poor and middle class.  The Brazilian gross national product has been declining continuously since 1981 and the level in 1984 is expected to fall below that of 1980, a significant change in the light of the larger national population.  The proportion of poor people has clearly grown *since* 1980, which runs counter to the notion of an expanding middle class supporting a vigorously growing economy.  The problem seems particularly acute among those earning between one and five times the minimum wage since the group's size increased dramatically from 34 to 55 percent of the employed while its share of income dropped from 44 to 41 percent--a considerable impoverishment of the lower and middle strata of the middle class. These shifts are troubling in a society that is trying to make social progress.  At the top end of the continuum 1.6 percent of the employed controlled 19 percent of the income in 1980, and the top 12 percent together controlled 52 percent (up from 5 and 34 percent respectively in 1970).  It is towards this group in particular that most of the durable consumer and luxury goods of all kinds are directed and raises serious questions about the potential size of the market that exists for this type of production.

A proportional decrease in the poverty group seems obvious from the statistical evidence, a trend already noted during the decade in question.  (This is of course independent of the presumed difficulties arising after 1980 because of declining real wages.) The decrease is problematical because it seems more apparent than

---

2. Andre-Cezar Medici, "Considerações sobre a distribuição does Rendimentos da População Económicamente Ativa no Brasil em 1980," I.B.G.E., D.E.S.P.O. (Department of Population Studies, Instituto Brasileiro de Geografia e Estatística), 1982, mimeo, p. 32.

real, although there are no data to specifically contradict the change shown in table 15.2. In terms of recent economic history the census years have not been ideal ones for measurement. Economic recovery from the late 1960s was well under way by 1970, and wages were generally growing though still depressed by long years of recession. By 1980, the economy had been affected by the oil crisis and a new recession was under way. Nevertheless, these conditions are insufficient to explain away the ten-year decrease of those in poverty shown in the statistics (from 61 to 33 percent). A real diminution in the size of the poverty group must be acknowledged, though accompanied by significant losses in real income at this level. The middle class appeared to be expanding in size during the period, while splitting into two levels, the lower part becoming poorer while the upper part increased its share of income. Overall, however, a general pattern of upward social mobility seems clear, something already under way in the 1960s and confirmed by numerous studies focussed on this issue.

The newest conjectural trends since 1981--of serious income erosion--threaten to set back the record of progress for an indeterminate period of time. Evidence from the Household Survey of 1982, two years after a new wage law took effect, suggests serious slippage in all income categories: an increase in the poverty group at the expense of declining middle income groups, including the upper middle class (table 15.2). Whether this latter group is retaining the same share of income it had in 1980 is unclear because the effect of the wage law has been either to redistribute income within the wage groups or simply to diminish their buying power, with recessionary consequences.

### Regional Differentiation

The social and economic differentiation just reviewed is almost perfectly matched by a regional pattern of inequalities (table 15.3). Although the general pattern constitutes one of Brazil's most widely known problems and has been amply discussed, it is worth noting that poverty is not basically a regional problem; it is more a feature of the stage of development and thus a problem for the whole society. It can be found to some extent in all regions, though certainly more concentratedly in the poor regions. The national "core" region with 60 percent of the total population accounts for 90 percent of industrial output and so highlights the importance of industrialization in regional inequality. Variations within the core and periphery zones are also significant: within

TABLE 15.3

SELECTED MEASURES OF PROPORTIONAL REGIONAL DISPARITIES
IN BRAZIL IN 1950 AND 1970

| Territorial Units | 1980 /1950 | | | 1970 | | |
|---|---|---|---|---|---|---|
| | Popula-tion | Industrial production | Tertiary revenue | Popula-tion | Industrial production | Tertiary revenue |
| Brazil | 100 | 100 | 100 | 100 | 100 | 100 |
| National core* | 59 | 90 | 84 | 61 | 92 | 85 |
| National periphery** | 41 | 10 | 16 | 39 | 8 | 15 |
| São Paulo State | 18 | 47 | 37 | 19 | 55 | 41 |
| Metropolitan regions | 18 | 46 | 58 | 25 | 52 | 61 |
| São Paulo metrop. reg. | 5 | 29 | 21 | 9 | 39 | 27 |

SOURCE: IBGE, *Population and Industrial Census of Brazil, 1975.*
*Core=South and Southeast regions;
**Periphery=remainder of the country.

TABLE 15.4

CUMULATIVE INCOME DISTRIBUTION IN THE RICH AND POOR
REGIONS OF BRAZIL, 1976

| Income categories (multiples of the minimum wage) | Rich region | | Poor region | |
|---|---|---|---|---|
| | Persons | Income share | Persons | Income share |
| Less than 1 | 24.59 | 4.69 | 53.69 | 15.76 |
| Between 1 and 5 | 83.69 | 40.60 | 92.91 | 55.76 |
| Between 5 and 10 | 93.29 | 53.37 | 97.31 | 71.12 |
| Between 10 and 20 | 97.89 | 75.94 | 99.29 | 85.20 |
| More than 20 | 100.00 | 100.00 | 100.00 | 100.00 |

SOURCE: IBGE, *Household Survey, 1976,* special tabulations.

the core, for example, the State of São Paulo already by 1970 contained a fifth of the population but over half of the industrial output, and at its heart the São Paulo metropolitan area itself boasted almost 40 percent of national industrial capacity. This concentration was up sharply from 1950 and led to some policy measures designed to encourage deconcentration. Similar trends were evident in the other metropolitan areas (table 15.3) and clearly delineate the unequal core-periphery structure of development, fueled by economies of scale, reflected in such basic attributes as industrial production, income distribution, and consumption of durable goods.

This leading characteristic of regional economic structure is further accentuated if cumulative income distributions are aggregated by specifically "core" and "periphery" zones, as data for 1976 show (table 15.4). The greater degree of income concentration among the higher groups in the "peripheral" zone than in the "core" zone at that time is notable, particularly since the upper class was proportionately smaller there. The extent of poverty was much greater in the poor region with over half of the population earning less than the minimum wage, whereas in the rich region only a quarter of the population was in this bracket, although conditions were improving over 1970.

These regional inequalities are the spatial consequences of development processes operating within a broad capitalist system. The Brazilian economy is in some ways part of the international capitalist "periphery," and thus within the country Brazil's own peripheral regions are particularly removed from the dynamic sources of development and especially prone to suffer the expropriation of profits by a small minority--the rich and privileged, however defined statistically, and irrespective of their rural or urban sphere of operations.[3]

Key to these regional differences is the spatial concentration of industrial activity. Two-thirds of the nation's industrial employment and three-quarters of value added by industry are located in the southeastern region, indicating clearly where modernization is most advanced. The State of São Paulo alone contains 48 percent of national industrial employment and 56 percent of the value added by industry. Even more concentratedly, the São Paulo metropolitan area accounts for 32 percent and 39 percent respectively in these

---

3. Speridião Faissol et al., "The Underprivileged of the Brazilian Society: A Spatial and Socio-Economic View of the Problem," *Brazilian Geographical Studies,* vol. 1 (Rio de Janeiro: International Geographical Union Regional Latin American Conference, 1982).

categories, representing the highest per capita value added in the country (Cr$97.00, compared with a national figure of Cr$80.00). Even outside São Paulo, strong concentration in these measures occurs in the remainder of the metropolitan system. São Paulo and Rio de Janeiro together account for almost half (47 percent) of the nation's value added by industry.

The development process while clearly driven by industrialization does not necessarily involve the entire manufacturing sector. The dichotomy between modern and traditional manufacturing, although hard to define in terms of the threshold of transition, results in different patterns of productivity. Food industries, for example, achieve per capita value added of about Cr$70.00 compared with Cr$56.00 for textiles--one of the most traditional--and Cr$309.00 for chemicals, among the most modern, including oil and petrochemicals (table 15.5). Within the metropolitan sub-system of the national economy the difference between São Paulo and Rio de Janeiro is striking: São Paulo has three times as much industrial employment and three-and-a-half times the value added by industry, implying a much more modernized industrial base.[4]

### Brazil's Urban System in Recent Decades

Urbanization in Brazil reflects the functioning of the peripheral zones within the global economic system and is thus tied to various developments in the "core" economies of the world. Hence urban developments represent the expansion and local penetration of the global economy, turning regional and local economies increasingly toward and making them dependent upon international markets. This interdependence is asymmetrical as local economies are necessarily dependent upon, rather than independent of, the powerful markets of the global core regions and suffer a lack of control over the terms of trade within the international market as a whole. Export prices, for example (if we exclude oil from the comparison, though this is hardly necessary nowadays), are set by the core economies and are low by comparison with import prices, resulting in escalating foreign debts. The significance of this lies in the orientation of urban economic expansion towards building exports (in conjunction with the rural sector, of course), both to earn the income to pay for imports as well as to satisfy the demand for costly consumer goods, especially among those in the top 10 or 20 percent income bracket.

---

4. Pedro Pinchas Geiger, "A Special Study Report for the World Bank," mimeo, 1980-81.

TABLE 15.5

INDUSTRIAL STATISTICS FOR SELECTED BRAZILIAN
ECONOMIC SECTORS AND TERRITORIAL UNITS, 1975

| Manufacturing sectors /Territorial units | Employment ('000s) | Production Cr$ (millions) | Value added Cr$ (millions) |
|---|---|---|---|
| Metalurgical | 443 | 104,440 | 38,800 |
| Mechanical | 390 | 61,680 | 31,644 |
| Automotive | 222 | 70,352 | 19,522 |
| Chemical | 126 | 120,140 | 38,956 |
| Textiles | 334 | 52,480 | 18,800 |
| Food | 500 | 126,800 | 34,700 |
| Southeast | 2,585 | 597,320 | 234,150 |
| São Paulo State | 1,815 | 438,200 | 171,530 |
| São Paulo metropolitan region | 1,238 | 288,930 | 119,201 |
| Rio de Janeiro metrop. region | 378 | 78,290 | 34,250 |
| National Total | 3,816 | 782,800 | 306,900 |

SOURCE: IBGE, *Industrial Census of Brazil, 1975.*

TABLE 15.6

POPULATION AND GROWTH RATES FOR SELECTED
METROPOLITAN REGIONS, 1970-1980

| Metropolitan region | Population (000's) | | Growth Rate (in percent) |
|---|---|---|---|
| | 1970 | 1980 | |
| São Paulo | 8,100 | 12,600 | 43 |
| Rio de Janeiro | 7,100 | 9,000 | 27 |
| Belo Horizonte | 1,600 | 2,600 | 60 |
| Recife | 1,700 | 2,400 | 37 |
| Salvador | 1,200 | 1,800 | 50 |
| Guarulhos | 240 | 540 | 125 |
| São Bernardo | 200 | 420 | 110 |
| Contagem | 110 | 280 | 150 |
| Diadema | 80 | 230 | 190 |
| Paulista | 70 | 166 | 140 |
| Camaçari | 16 | 60 | 260 |

SOURCE: IBGE, *Population Census of Brazil, 1980.*

This emphasis on luxury consumer goods at the expense of cheaper alternatives commanding a broader market is certainly questionable, for it highlights the contrast in patterns of spending and saving between developed and developing societies. Peripheral, developing economies tend to imitate the consumption habits of advanced economies but are unable to reproduce their savings habits--not only unable but also unwilling.[5]

The urbanization of Brazil has been advancing apace since mid-century. In 1950, a little over one-third (36 percent) of all Brazilians lived in cities, and by 1960, this proportion had risen to 45 percent; by 1970, to 56 percent; and by 1980, to 67 percent, two-thirds of the entire population. Related to this, the rural population by 1980 had for the first time declined absolutely from the level of a decade before. This urban growth has been far from regionally uniform, so that in 1980 a mere 300 counties (out of 4,000) account for about half the national population. In 1960, only São Paulo and Rio de Janeiro had more than a million inhabitants each, but in 1980 even Nova Iguaçu--a municipality within the Rio metropolitan region--had exceeded a million in population. Several other urban agglomerations in the metropolitan sub-system are close to the million mark. Metropolitan status was defined in the late 1960s as beginning at 400,000 inhabitants, and now a number of additional areas qualify by this criterion (table 15.6).

If one accepts that national development is accompanied by a shift in a country's urban size structure from a primate to a rank-size distribution, then Brazil's urban system has made some movement in that direction; no longer primate, it has some of the characteristics of both types. The structure of the system is also influenced by the international market-oriented pressure of mass consumption which affects the system through diffusionary mechanisms that are strong in the core and decrease in intensity towards the periphery (both at the regional scale and within individual metropolitan areas). These gradients of declining intensity well describe patterns of income and urban infrastructure; they are not so characteristic for durable goods, especially television, and run counter to patterns of population growth--particularly in mature

---

5. To satisfy curiosity on this point, actual patterns of urban access to and purchase of goods and services ranging from basic to luxury were correlated with a hypothetical pattern based on a quality of life continuum in which water and sewage services are given far greater priority over such items as automobiles. The resulting correlation between expected and observed distributions, regardless of geographical scale, was 0.2, in other words nonexistent. It reminds us that consumption, far from adhering strictly to biological priorities, follows the siren call of mass marketing so well inculcated by television and other mass communications.

metropolitan areas--which spill over into the fringe zone creating
higher growth rates there than in the center. This is the physical
expression of the process of "peripheralization," different from
suburbanization in developed economies because the suburban and
fringe areas are the poor areas of Brazilian metropolitan regions,
and seemingly so for large cities in many of the developing
countries.

The legal definition of a metropolitan region in Brazil today
rests on the existence of a metropolis to begin with (thereby
differing from the American Standard Metropolitan Statistical Area),
and this means a certain size and population density, representing
to a large extent the size threshold that Thompson has suggested as
a minimum to maintain a productive complex of sustained growth.[6] It
also connotes a surrounding zone of urban expansion, including
settlements of specialized character such as dormitory towns, in
which population attracted to the metropolis would locate thanks to
cheap land and housing and where new industries would spring up or
be relocated. When metropolitan regions were officially designated
in the early 1970s the only criterion then was that they should
encompass more than a single county. Now it is apparent that the
criteria should be modified to allow inclusion of broad fringe areas
with clearly urban population so that these areas can be understood
as part of the metropolitan complex.

Some of Brazil's present-day metropolitan regions have only
small proportions of their total population in the fringe areas, but
others, notably the most important ones, have as much as half of
their population in the surrounding fringe areas. This spread of
population lies at the heart of the process of "metropolization" and
significantly transforms the nature of the periphery; the higher the
proportion in the fringe the more intense and advanced are the
changes. Given the heavy demographic, economic, and political
weight attached to these metropolitan regions they have successfully
attracted a major portion of general public investment in urban
infrastructure, and in a circular fashion this has brought them more
and more migrants. Households with water and sewage service provide
a ready index of this infrastructural investment. Of the 16 million
households with these amenities about 8 million are located in
metropolitan regions, which are therefore responsible for half the
population. This is an important indication of their relative power
and should be taken into account in the formulation of urban policy.

---

6. Wilbur Thompson, *A Preface to Urban Economics* (Baltimore:  Johns Hopkins
University Press, 1965).

The same can be said for urban agglomerations, and several of these qualify for designation as metropolitan regions if only their qualification were formally recognized. There are some striking differences between the rates of growth of some peripheral towns compared with the central cities, for example the 27 percent rate for Rio de Janeiro, the lowest growth for any central city, and the rate of 190 percent for Diadema, one of the industrial towns in the São Paulo metropolitan region (table 15.6).

This manifestation of peripheral expansion is bound to affect the general quality of life, because it is too much to hope that investment in public services such as water and sewage will keep pace with peripheral growth. It is clear that fringe areas harbor impoverished social conditions (table 15.7). Migrants, already poor, flock to the urban periphery from rural areas or small interior towns and end up forming large poor sectors within the metropolitan areas. Once again, there are variations in the city-periphery contrasts from region to region. In Recife, an important center in the less developed part of the country, only 42 percent of the city's households have sewage whereas in the periphery the proportion is a mere 16 percent. This very low value is common for the fringes of most other towns in similarly less developed regions in Brazil--perhaps characteristic for developing countries in general. Even in the São Paulo metropolitan region the situation is similar owing to the lack of public funds to cope with the high rates of population growth in the peripheral towns. Clearly, from the evidence shown, there is great inter- and intra-metropolitan differentiation as far as consumption is concerned.

The productive sector displays similar patterns. Industrialization, in precipitating many of the changes in the urban system and the development process generally, is bringing about sharp contrasts in the balance between traditional and modern production. It is not easy to define industrial modernization, because modern industry is based on particular establishments rather than representing a sector as such, and there are some sectors which need modernizing more than others. However, an attempt has been made here (following Geiger's study) to classify industrial activities--defined by their offical 3-digit industrial codes, as distinct from the conventional method relying upon 2-digit codes--into five large groups that, for Brazil, suitably reflect the key relationships between the "traditional" and "modern" sectors (table 15.8).

TABLE 15.7

SOME CHARACTERISTICS OF SELECTED METROPOLITAN REGIONS

| Characteristic (in percent) | Metropolitan region | | | | | | | |
|---|---|---|---|---|---|---|---|---|
| | São Paulo | | Rio de Janeiro | | Porto Alegre | | Recife | |
| | C* | P** | C | P | C | P | C | P |
| Housing with sewage | 84 | 48 | 86 | 63 | 88 | 63 | 42 | 16 |
| Persons in manufacturing | 34 | 45 | 16 | 19 | 13 | 43 | 15 | 19 |
| Households earning: | | | | | | | | |
| Less than the MW† | 8 | 11 | 11 | 18 | 11 | 12 | 35 | 34 |
| Between 1 and 3 x MW | 46 | 54 | 45 | 56 | 42 | 65 | 37 | 47 |
| More than 10 x MW | 10 | 6 | 12 | 4 | 13 | 2 | 9 | 2 |

SOURCE: IBGE, *Population Census of Brazil, 1980,* special tabulations, 1982. *City **Periphery †Minimum wage

TABLE 15.8

VALUE ADDED FOR INDUSTRIAL SECTORS IN SELECTED METROPOLITAN REGIONS

| Metropolitan Region | Value added | | | | |
|---|---|---|---|---|---|
| | Combined sectors | Modern sector | Traditional sector | Ratio ~~Modern/tradl.~~ sectors | Percent concentrated in 4 largest establishments |
| São Paulo | 119,202 | 78,385 | 40,817 | 0.52 | 22.2 |
| Rio de Janeiro | 34,256 | 17,912 | 16,344 | 0.91 | 33.5 |
| Porto Alegre | 11,970 | 6,838 | 5,132 | 0.75 | 54.8 |
| Bel Horizonte | 7,740 | 5,784 | 1,956 | 0.34 | 61.1 |
| Salvador | 5,041 | 3,636 | 1,405 | 0.38 | 65.8 |
| Recife | 4,896 | 2,532 | 2,364 | 0.93 | 53.6 |
| Curitiba | 3,992 | 1,932 | 2,068 | 1.01 | 36.3 |
| Fortaleza | 1,603 | 432 | 1,171 | 2.71 | 32.2 |
| Belém | 1,124 | 266 | 858 | 3.22 | 49.4 |
| Total/Mean Value | 189,824 | 117,725 | 72,099 | 0.61 | 30.4 |

SOURCE: IBGE, *Industrial Census of Brazil, 1975.* Special tabulations, 1982.

Although the total value added by all industries (column 1, table 15.8) varies among the metropolitan regions (which collectively account, as noted earlier, for 60 percent of the whole country), in aggregate about 60 percent of this value added is contributed by the modern sector. This represents an important concentration in these metropolitan regions. Two-thirds of this modern sector is concentrated in São Paulo alone. The modern sector is notably comparable to the traditional one in such places as Rio de Janeiro, Recife, and Curitiba, while in Porto Alegre the modern sector is somewhat larger (column 4). In Salvador and Belo Horizonte, where industrialization is more recent, the prominence of the modern sector (particularly chemicals in the former and steel in the latter) is correspondingly evident. The situation in São Paulo is peculiar because the modern sector is twice the size of the traditional. Not surprisingly, the contribution to value added by the four leading industrial establishments in each metropolis (column 5) is much lower in São Paulo and Rio de Janeiro than most other places because of their great diversity of firms.

The development process is represented through a combination of several of these indicators, either by some absolute value which might measure the size and economic strength of towns or by relative values showing comparative levels of development. It is now appropriate to turn to a detailed, multidimensional analysis of the nation's urban system.

### The Brazilian Urban System in 1980

This examination is based on the evidence of the 1980 Census of Population relating to cities over 100,000 inhabitants. The basic data series, then, is a matrix of 82 variables for 93 urban places drawn from the population census. These variables were selected to highlight aspects of urban poverty, although they do include measures covering the wealthier segment of the population too. The core of the examination is a factor analysis (with varimax rotation) of 52 of the 82 originally selected descriptive variables for the 93 places, with frequent reference to data from the 82-variable set for substantiation and greater detail.[7] Absolute values have been used for the variables describing aggregated functional strength in order to preserve a clear measure of contrasting size across the urban system, while relative values have been used for all the remaining variables.

---

7. The 52 variables of the core analysis are listed in appendix 1.

The fundamental dimensions expected in the urban system are threefold. First, there should be a size component, functional and aggregated, measured by the 11 variables of absolute value. A second dimension should reveal levels of economic, social, and political development, measured by variables relating to income, occupations, employment, and durable goods production. Given the variables used this dimension should in fact consist of a general development factor as well as one or two further ones characterizing the upper and lower portions in particular of the development scale. A third dimension should reflect occupational structure as shown in manufacturing, commercial, and service activities, highlighting degrees of specialization and association with other facets of development.

The most important dimension is clearly that representing development in its major economic, social, and regional aspects. Its spatial structure should conform to a core/periphery pattern, though inequalities should be common at several levels from the regional to the local. Social stratification can be anticipated as an underlying characteristic of this differentiation as well as the distinctions between districts within individual metropolitan areas and central cities. Even city size distributions should display a different range within the development core than in the periphery, showing a strong rank-size order at the national scale, while primate regional capital cities dominate at the regional level. São Paulo bids fair, as Brazil's economy integrates further with the international capitalist system, to increase its role as a center of world trade, gaining further in population size and becoming more heterogeneous. The deviation-amplifying process working in São Paulo's favor, fuelled by the concentration of industrial capacity there, is relegating Rio de Janeiro to an increasingly distant second place as a national metropolis, and might even reduce it to the status of a mere regional metropolis, at least in economic terms.

In essence, the three predicted dimensions did emerge from the factor analysis. In a certain light these basic dimensions are generally independent, both theoretically and statistically; in another sense, however, they may be correlated and this problem will be reviewed as each dimension is interpreted.

### The Size Dimension

Size of place is such an obvious dimension as to need no special justification, but it needs defining, describing, and

relating to the other dimensions. Eleven of the 52 variables loaded
on the size dimension. They are highly intercorrelated and thus
somewhat redundant, but each variable adds some special ingredient
to the aggregate measure of value. Simple population size,
expressed as the number of households in a place, constituted one of
the variables. Two others, the number of television receivers and
automobiles, measure consumer buying power and index the strength of
the upper middle class. Besides households, the size of the
"economically active population" (EAP) was included, and in a large
country like Brazil this measure varies widely from region to
region.

In order to cover additional facets of the economic potential
inherent in size the total income of the EAP was also included,
since this varies with the level of development, together with the
EAP income earned in manufacturing, which should reinforce the
representation of the more developed towns where industrial activity
is not only important but directly underlies the greater levels of
development. Balancing these are variables included to reflect
urban size in the less developed regions: the absolute number of
illiterates (since the relative proportion is higher in less
developed areas, the absolute figures better indicate this aspect of
urban size) and total number of migrants of all types, which should
emphasize the larger towns. All these variables are intended to
describe and measure the size dimension without any attempt to
explain it. A distance-decay function, for example, could be
introduced later for that purpose, in a revision of this analysis.

While the effect of each of these variables will be bound up
in the factor scores for each town, it is desirable to consider some
of the individual indicators as they contribute to the overall shape
of the dimension. Some of these are shown for selected metropolitan
regions--representing different development regions--in table 15.9.
In this instance material is presented from the initial 93x82 matrix
to cast further light on urban size, particularly to show the
additive properties of highly intercorrelated variables despite the
statistical opaqueness of this fact. The number of households
(rather than individual persons) in a town well reflects the basis
for assessing local quality of life and will be taken as the
yardstick of urban population size against which to measure the
other related variables.

Regional differences are evident when household size is
compared with water service: Porto Alegre has about 17 percent more
households than Recife but 35 percent more households with running

TABLE 15.9

CHARACTERISTICS RELATED TO URBAN SIZE

FOR SELECTED METROPOLITAN REGIONS

| Variables | Metropolitan regions | | | |
|---|---|---|---|---|
| | São Paulo | Rio de Janeiro | Porto Alegre | Recife |
| Number of housholds ('000s) | | | | |
| Total | 2,000 | 1,350 | 277 | 236 |
| With running water | 1,935 | 1,282 | 258 | 185 |
| With automobile | 1,170 | 483 | 130 | 70 |
| With color television set | 1,094 | 627 | 134 | 104 |
| With stove | 2,021 | 1,320 | 266 | 218 |
| Persons (in '000s) earning: | | | | |
| Less than the minimum wage | 474 | 241 | 50 | 135 |
| More than 10x the min. wage | 425 | 251 | 60 | 36 |
| Employees in manufacturing ('000s) | 1,936 | 346 | 61 | 59 |
| Self-employed (<40hrs./wk) ('000s) | 110 | 79 | 15 | 23 |
| Total income of EAP* (Cr$ millions) | 71,996 | 45,836 | 10,742 | 6,592 |

SOURCE: IBGE, *Population Census of Brazil, 1980,* preliminary results, special tabulations, 1982. *Economically active population

TABLE 15.10

SIZE AND DEVELOPMENT IN THE CENTRAL CITIES

OF SELECTED METROPOLITAN REGIONS

| Central city | Factor scores | | |
|---|---|---|---|
| | Size | Development | Low-level development |
| São Paulo | 88.6 | 22.3 | -8.2 |
| Rio de Janeiro | 47.2 | 16.8 | -5.1 |
| Porto Alegre | 8.7 | 16.4 | -6.4 |
| Belo Horizonte | 12.4 | 4.7 | -3.2 |
| Salvador | 8.7 | -0.9 | 0.4 |
| Recife | 5.6 | -2.0 | 1.7 |
| Curitiba | 5.4 | 11.5 | -7.6 |
| Fortaleza | 6.0 | -10.5 | 6.0 |
| Belém | 0.6 | -5.7 | 2.6 |

SOURCE: Author's factor analysis.

water.  Contrasts are greater with respect to cars and television
sets.  Among the 2 million households of São Paulo almost 1.2
million have a car, whereas fewer than half a million do in Rio de
Janeiro; compared with Recife, São Paulo has something like nine
times the households and about 17 times the number of cars.  While
São Paulo boasts more than twice as many cars as Rio de Janeiro, it
contains merely 70 percent more color television sets--does this
reflect the smaller size of Rio's middle class or a consumer
preference for television?  A similar pattern emerges when comparing
Porto Alegre and Recife, with the former having twice as many cars
but only 30 percent as many more television sets as the latter.
When it comes to income, São Paulo has 60 percent more than Rio
generally and four times that in manufacturing, whereas Porto Alegre
shows the same gap over Recife in general income though not in
manufacturing income.

What all this indicates clearly is that, although in the
aggregate all these variables are highly intercorrelated and
seemingly redundant, in reality they are necessary, not so much in
the factor loadings where their existence is identifiable but in the
factor scores which define the position of each town on the
dimension.  It is the need for these complicated distinctions in the
hierarchy of urban size that justifies this reasoned violation of
the statistical redundancy principle.

It was supposed that the size of the workforce is also an
important additional aspect.  A large number of persons engaged in
manufacture would add to urban size and without it some of the most
important industrial centers would be understated.  Consequently the
*number* of persons occupied in manufacturing, commerce, and services
(the *proportions among* these categories would of course indicate
occupational structure) was included in the analysis.  Previous work
has shown that at least in the Northeast of Brazil, the less
developed part of the country, there is some correlation between the
urban size dimension and the level of development; in such
situations the larger towns are expected to be more developed.

Several results are presented from the factor analysis
comparing the size dimension with two other factors describing
complementary aspects of the development dimension for selected
towns (table 15.10).[8]  It should be stressed again that these data
relate to the central cities in the metropolitan regions, not the
whole metropolitan regions themselves.[9]  This fact explains, for

---

8 . Factor loadings for all variables are given in appendix 2.

9 . Two other analyses were done, though not described here for lack of

example, the lower scores of Recife compared with Fortaleza and
Salvador, because in the former case the process of metropolization
is further advanced and the critical population growth is now
occurring in the metropolitan fringe rather than in the central
city. The significant difference in the scores on size between São
Paulo and Rio de Janeiro represents, of course, all the differences
evident in the variables contributing to this dimension. It would
be smaller if income, income from manufacturing, or other variables
indexing São Paulo's economic structure alone were considered. A
similar comparison can be made between Recife and Porto Alegre or
Belo Horizonte.

Although discussion of the development factor will follow, a
few remarks can be made at this point in comparing urban size with
the development factor. Even though these dimensions need to be
assumed independent for purposes of statistical analysis they are in
reality not functionally unrelated, much less so in terms of cause
and effect. Porto Alegre, for example, scores far above Recife on
the development dimension, a much wider gap than on the size
dimension, while on the other hand its development score is much
closer to that of São Paulo than its size score. In this latter
instance, São Paulo's large population growth keeps its development
level, relatively speaking, low. At the other extreme, Fortaleza
scores very poorly on the development factor; indeed, all the cities
in the less developed regions show negative scores on this
dimension--in Fortaleza's case because poor migrants are ending up
within the metropolitan boundary of the city, rather than outside
those of more developed cities.

Functional size, as this urban size factor may be termed,
describes more about composite size and some of the interrelations
between different determinants of size than isolated indicators such
as simple population totals do. This is well illustrated in the
case of the twenty largest towns, ranked by score on the size factor
(table 15.11). Not surprisingly the metropolitan central cities
appear in the list, though Belém places last, but also several towns
within the two largest metropolitan regions: São Bernardo, Santo
André, and Guarulhos near São Paulo; and Nova Iguaçu, Niterói, and
São Gonçalo near Rio de Janeiro. There are other unusual
differences, such as between Recife and Fortaleza, but these
instances are largely accounted for by the stage of metropolization

---

space. The first involved two sets of towns, those in the developed and in the
less developed zones, and confirms the higher correlation between urban size and
development level in the Northeast than elsewhere; a finding replicated by a
secondary analysis involving oblique rotation of the varimax solution.

TABLE 15.11

SIZE SCORES AND POPULATION OF THE TWENTY LARGEST TOWNS

| Town | Factor score | Population ('000s) |
|------|------|------|
| São Paulo | 88.6 | 8,239 |
| Rio de Janeiro | 47.2 | 5,094 |
| Bel Horizonte | 12.4 | 1,764 |
| Salvador | 8.7 | 1,550 |
| Fortaleza | 6.0 | 1,303 |
| Nova Iguaçu | 5.4 | 1,158 |
| Brasília | 6.5 | 1,136 |
| Recife | 5.7 | 1,096 |
| Porto Alegre | 8.7 | 1,012 |
| Curitiba | 5.4 | 877 |
| Belém | 0.6 | 805 |
| Goiânia | 1.3 | 669 |
| Manaus | 0.7 | 616 |
| São Gonçalo | 0.8 | 601 |
| Santo André | 4.4 | 524 |
| Campinas | 3.4 | 511 |
| Guarulhos | 1.6 | 483 |
| São Bernardo | 2.2 | 451 |
| Niterói | 1.1 | 362 |
| Santos | 2.6 | 320 |

SOURCE: Author's factor analysis; IBGE, *Population Census of Brazil, 1980,* preliminary results.

and the degree to which population growth occurs beyond the central
city. Thus, in the advanced case of Porto Alegre metropolitan
region Novo Hamburgo and São Leopoldo are important industrial
towns, whereas with Salvador the petrochemical industry and the
industrial district of Salvador (Polo de Aratu) are generating
growth outside Salvador itself.

Underlying this discussion is the conviction that urban "size"
is a dimension which, above a certain threshold (*vide* Thompson's
notion of a "size ratchet") becomes irreversible and affects the
system in many ways. It generates several kinds of scale economies
that directly influence development, especially creating local
markets of great importance for local products, and a large labor
pool that stimulates new industries and allied economic activities
without extra cost. Size, of course, has negative attributes too,
attracting more migration than can be absorbed in the workforce, and
creating a labor surplus typical of the large metropolises of less
developed countries. Worse are the consequences of poor housing on
the urban periphery, low quality of life, poor working conditions,
and a high incidence of casual labor and participation in the
informal economy.

### *Development Dimensions: Economic, Social, and Political*

The development dimension is very complex not only in its
theoretical relation to factor analysis but also in the composite
patterns of factors that emerge from the statistical model. An
independent, general development factor clearly emerged based on a
wide range of variables describing the broad characteristics of
development. In addition, however, another factor appeared which
describes a distinctly lower level of development and it is
desirable to clarify whether or not this represents a parallel
process--maybe not an autonomous driving force in the system but
with its own characteristics.

In a large country like Brazil it would seem likely that the
urban system could be described in terms of center-periphery
structure, with various towns classified as either developed or less
developed. Before considering the detailed picture, the Porto
Alegre-Recife contrast in development scores may again be cited
(table 15.10) in which the former scored 16.4 and the latter -2.0
(with zero as the statistical mean for all towns). Further, while
Porto Alegre and Salvador are similarly sized, they differ markedly
in development level.

The assumption behind the idea of describing this lower-level development phenomenon is the notion that it represents in some way the informal, poor market--the lower circuit of Milton Santos--existing, to be sure, in the central city, but extremely enlarged in the urban periphery. It is difficult to specify this lower circuit/informal market statistically. The "self-employed" variable does capture some of the participants in this informal market, but it also includes the liberal professions and various types of clerical and white-collar occupations, and they certainly do not participate in the type of informal markets being considered. To improve on the measurement an additional variable--persons in the tertiary sector earning up to but no more than the minimum wage--was included in the analysis. This improves the representation in the model of the informal market, which in the present context should be understood as underpaid.

The factor describing what is considered here "the poor side of the development process" is composed of several variables, which include self-employed tertiary workers earning less than the minimum wage (0.79 loading), other types of subminimum-wage self-employed, employees earning less than the minimum wage (-0.90 loading), and employees in the tertiary sector (-0.65 loading). Clearly, self-employment goes far in capturing the character of this dimension.

Towns in the Northeast scored highly negative on this dimension--predictably, given previous discussion--and the extreme cases have been singled out (table 15.12). Complicating the picture, however, are some of the larger, more developed towns in that region which scored highly positive on the same factor. The central city of Recife shows a score of 1.7 compared with 14.9 for Caruaru in the same state. When one compares Campinas (-5.9) with São Paulo (-8.2), the difference is quite large, and it suggests how the diffusion of development is far more advanced in São Paulo than in the Northeast. The evidence points to a clear distance decay effect in terms of Northeastern development, with a much steeper slope than around São Paulo.

The development process, largely a natural one, does suffer from the influence of political and administrative policies--the effect of political power. Regional development policy in Brazil has been largely governmental, exemplified by the Superintendency for the Development of the Northeast (SUDENE) and fortified with a number of incentives, fiscal and otherwise. The chief decision-making body of this organization comprises the governors of

TABLE 15.12

SCORES OF SELECTED TOWNS ON THE LOW-LEVEL
DEVELOPMENT DIMENSION

| Towns | Score |
|---|---|
| Petrolina | 17.3 |
| Caruaru | 14.9 |
| Crato | 12.9 |
| Campina Grande | 9.0 |
| Maceió | 3.1 |
| Uberlândia | -0.3 |
| Juiz de Fora | -0.7 |
| São Bernardo | -4.4 |
| Sorocaba | -5.4 |
| Campinas | -5.9 |
| Jundiaí | -10.3 |
| Santo André | -10.3 |

SOURCE: Author's factor analysis.

TABLE 15.13

SCORES OF SELECTED TOWNS ON THE CAPITAL CITY DIMENSION

| Town | Score |
|---|---|
| Recife | 7.4 |
| Teresina | 6.7 |
| São Luiz | 6.6 |
| Fortaleza | 5.5 |
| Caruaru | 5.3 |
| João Pessoa | 4.4 |
| Salvador | 4.3 |
| Belém | 3.9 |
| Uberlândia | 3.2 |
| Goiânia | 0.6 |
| Jundiaí | -2.5 |
| Vitória | -3.9 |
| Imperatriz | -6.2 |
| São Carlos | -8.2 |

SOURCE: Author's factor analysis.

the states involved, and consequently it must necessarily accept decisions clearly political in nature. Unsurprisingly, then, the state capitals themselves benefit from such policy-making and might display evidence of this bias in the analysis.

An interesting combination of elements is displayed in Factor 3, in which personal services, public administration, and social activities are inversely correlated with manufacturing employment and the lower middle class (income between one and three times the minimum wage), government employees (those working less than 40 hours a week), and moderately correlated with such variables as the frequency of color television sets and households earning more than ten times the minimum wage. This set of characteristics is very likely to occur in state capitals, particularly those associated with governmental actions and incentives. These capital cities are sufficiently numerous (20 of the 93 places selected) and distinctive to influence the appearance of a separate factor in the analysis, which may thus be called simply the "capital city" factor. These cities, it should be stressed, play not only an administrative role in Brazilian life but also an economic and socio-political role, given the strong participation of the state in social and economic policies. Not surprisingly, some capital cities score very positively on this dimension (table 15.13). By the same token, some towns score highly on the negative side that lack the relevant attributes: the industrial town of Jundiaf and also São Carlos, both in São Paulo state.

The capital city dimension is clearly shown through high positive scores for places like São Luis, João Pessoa, and Teresina, medium-sized cities where these functions are a dominant feature of their make-up. Even in large places like Recife, Salvador, and Fortaleza the scores are high because this function is important in these Northeastern metropolises. Caruaru, a significant regional capital, scores higher than São Paulo or even Belo Horizonte because the importance of their regional capital functions are overshadowed in part by their large overall size and industrial function.

A last factor reflecting development, though least powerful in descriptive terms, is Factor 6, which characterizes the upper levels of the income distribution. Variables describing households earning more than ten times the minimum wage as well as those with sewerage and high rates of car ownership load high on this factor. Interestingly, several towns in the underdeveloped part of the country have high positive scores on this factor (table 15.14). For the most part, however, the same core-periphery distinctions seen in

TABLE 15.14

SCORES OF SELECTED TOWNS ON THE
UPPER DEVELOPMENT DIMENSION

| Town | Score |
|------|-------|
| Juàzeiro | 13.4 |
| Carapiquíba | 7.5 |
| Gov. Valadares | 5.3 |
| Petrolina | 5.3 |
| Cariacica | 3.4 |
| Osasco | 3.4 |
| Nova Iguaçu | 1.1 |
| Fortaleza | -1.0 |
| Recife | -1.2 |
| Uberlândia | -1.3 |
| Vitória | -2.0 |
| Rio de Janeiro | -3.3 |
| Taubaté | -3.6 |
| São Paulo | -3.7 |
| Campinas | -3.9 |
| Florianópolis | -4.1 |
| Americana | -5.0 |
| Santo André | -5.0 |

SOURCE: Author's factor analysis.

the geographical pattern of scores appear also with this factor. Campinas in the core, for example, scored high while Recife showed low values; even within the periphery Recife as a major metropolis scored higher than some interior towns like Petrolina and Juàzeiro, indicating a kind of "core-within-the-periphery" structure. This latter phenomenon can also be discerned within metropolitan regions, by comparing the values for São Paulo, Santo André, and Carapicuíba in the São Paulo metropolitan region or Nova Iguaçu in that of Rio de Janeiro. Such differences well illustrate how useful the core-periphery concept is in refining our understanding of regional variations.

## Occupational Structure

There were two aims in selecting variables to reflect occupational structure. One was to distinguish and define towns with different occupational functions, especially those of industrial centers. The other was to explore correlations between occupational structure, urban size, and level of development. Variables such as the percentage of people engaged in manufacturing, commerce, and services were included specifically to detect such specializations.

Considering all the debated relationships between industrialization and levels of economic development, only two correlations were found in this analysis, a negative correlation for persons engaged in manufacturing and positive for persons occupied in commerce and transportation. Thus, high negative scores highlight industrial centers and high positive scores indicate service and commercial towns (table 15.15). The concentration of industrial towns in São Paulo state is notable--26 out of 29 places in the state included in this analysis scored negatively on this factor; the only 3 with positive scores are Santos (which is mainly a port), São José de Rio Preto, and Araçatuba (which are mainly commercial and service centers).

## Conclusion

In this study of the structure of the Brazilian urban system, the size dimension emerges very clearly as an independent characteristic of great importance, defined as it is by no less than eleven of the selected statistical variables. While the intercorrelation among these variables is often substantial, which is methodologically unwelcome, the cumulative power of these variables where they do not overlap is sufficient justification to accept their combined explanatory contribution. The highly unequal

TABLE 15.15

SCORES OF SELECTED TOWNS ON THE
OCCUPATIONAL STRUCTURE DIMENSION

| Town | Score |
|------|-------|
| Petrolina | 6.9 |
| Uberlândia | 1.3 |
| João Pessoa | 1.0 |
| Recife | 0.9 |
| Rio de Janeiro | 0.2 |
| Petrópolis | -0.2 |
| Porto Alegre | -1.0 |
| Campinas | -2.0 |
| São Paulo | -2.2 |
| Nôva Hamburgo | -3.8 |
| Jundiaí | -4.7 |
| São Bernardo | -5.9 |
| Mauá | -6.1 |
| Americana | -7.3 |

SOURCE: Author's factor analysis.


process of development (and related urbanization) produces great
variations in industrial capacity in towns of otherwise very similar
hierarchical position, and further varies between regions in the
economic core and periphery. Recife and Porto Alegre have
comparable urban populations (1.095 and 1.012 millions), but the
former contains an economically active population of only 185,000 in
contrast with 258,000 for the latter. Core-periphery differences
are responsible for such an imbalance. Similarly, 23.5 percent of
Campina's 511,000 inhabitants are economically active, while
Goiania, with 669,000 people, claims only 10.3 percent in that
category.

   In all cases size by itself clearly differentiates towns in an
urban system, but a better measure, considering the severity of
regional inequalities, is a composite one such as that drawn from
the factor analysis considered here. What remains unclear are the
limits of this measure. For example, in what ways do some variables
like illiteracy reinforce the size of certain towns in the periphery

while others like income do the same for some industrial towns in the core. Creating balance between them is the problem in the absence of a solid theoretical foundation.

The other obvious dimension is development, which shows up clearly in the analysis. A much larger set of variables was used to describe this dimension, and regardless of expectations resulted in several factors, the most important of which was a general development factor that provided a basic delimitation of the nation's core and periphery.

From the outset, however, the purpose of the analysis was to describe the low and high sides of the development process. Understandably in an economically and socially diverse system, even viewed within the framework of a core-periphery dichotomy, development does not proceed in a smooth fashion and lags in the development process are inevitably to be found. At the same time, paralleling the "natural" process of development are several mechanisms of intervention--political pressure, for example--that can either reinforce or even counterbalance the uneven natural development process. With these complexities it is not surprising that the development process should be represented by more than one statistical factor in the model, leading among other things to the dichotomy between rich and poor in the general factor. Certainly the poor side of the process is better represented, both because poverty is so critical to the whole social fabric of Brazilian society, and because of a concern to measure the extent of that poverty--finding income and occupational structure biased towards casual workers and the informal market, self-employment and the lower exchange circuit, family survival strategies, malnutrition, and a higher priority given to television sets than a balanced diet.

Following the general development factor (which accounted for 24 percent of the statistical variation in the 52 variables) and the size factor (21 percent), the factor representing the poor side of the development process came out as the third most significant factor and accounted for 12 percent of the total explained variance. Since the bulk of the territory and population classify on the poor side and the variables that describe this have positive correlations, the higher positive scores represent the poorer sector. Thirty-five of the 93 urban places have positive scores, and another 9 score below 1.0 which is just around the average (which in the model is transformed into a zero value). The rich side shows 26 places with values between 1.0 and -1.0. Forty-three places have negative values above -1.0, that is, above the average in terms of the variables involved (color television sets and income more than ten times the minimum wage). This leaves 24 towns below the average, the smallest of the three categories just reviewed.

What this subdivision points to is that the process of unequal development seems to penetrate deeply into the internal organization of towns. A number of social area analyses in developing countries suggest clearly that social segregation in large urban agglomerations of the Third World is much more strongly unidimensional, rather than the three-dimensional structure of classical urban models presented in the literature.

This fractioning of development along more than one dimension is consistent with the dual-circuit concept. The importance of political power in development, particularly in countries geared to fiscal and other incentive policies such as Brazil, inevitably heightens the differences between towns that especially benefit from this power and those that do not. This is true for Brazil, and particularly for the Northeastern region--so much so that a "capital city factor" emerged in the study as an autonomous factor. More and more, regardless of the prevailing forms of government in the countries of the Third World, the spatial distribution of political power exerts a more profound influence on the urban system than any other single factor. This should prove the most critical link, both for nations as a whole and for their internal regions, in examining the interrelations between the changing urban system and the development process.

# APPENDIX 1. VARIABLES USED IN THE ANALYSIS

1.  Number of permanent households owned
2.  Number of permanent households with a television set
3.  Number of permanent households with an automobile
4.  Number of economically active population (EAP)
5.  Number of urban EAP occupied in manufacturing
6.  Number of urban EAP occupied in commerce
7.  Number of urban EAP occupied in transportation and services
8.  Number of migrants 10 years of age or more
9.  Total income of the EAP with income
10. Total income of the EAP occupied in manufacturing
11. Urban population over 10 years old that is illiterate
12. Percent of urban households with running water
13. Percent of urban households with sewage
14. Percent of urban households with refrigerator
15. Percent of urban households with television
16. Percent of urban households with color television
17. Percent of urban households with stove (gas or electric)
18. Percent of urban households with an automobile
19. Number of urban residents in permanent households per household
20. Percent of households with a car and income over 10 x minimum wage
21. Percent of households with a television and income over 3 x minimum wage
22. Percent of households with a color television & income over 10 x minimum wage
23. Percent of households with running water and income below 3 x minimum wage
24. Percent of households with sewage and income above 10 x minimum wage
25. Percent of urban EAP with income at or below minimum wage
26. Percent of urban EAP with income between 1 and 3 x minimum wage
27. Percent of urbn EAP with income between 3 and 5 x minimum wage

28. Percent of urban EAP with income between 5 and 10 x minimum wage
29. Percent of urban EAP with income above 10 x minimum wage
30. Percent of urban EAP working less than 40 hours weekly
31. Percent of urban EAP classified as self-employed
32. Percent of urban EAP classified self-employed & working less than 40 hours per week
33. Percent of self-employed with income below minimum wage
34. Percent of self-employed iwth income between 1 and 3 x minimum wage
35. Percent of self-employed occupied in tertiary activities
36. Percent of self-employed occupied in tertiary activities with income below minimum wage
37. Percent of urban EAP classified as employee
38. Percent of urban EAP classified as employee with income below minimum wage
39. Percent of urban EAP classified as employee with income between 1 and 3 x minimum wage
40. Percent of persons classified as employee occupied in tertiary activities
41. Percent of female urban EAP in tertiary activites with income below minimum wage
42. Percent of male urban EAP in tertiary activities with income below minimum wage
43. Percent of female urban EAP with income
44. Percent of urban EAP occupied in manufacturing
45. Percent of urban EAP occupied in civil construction
46. Percent of urban EAP occupied in commerce
47. Percent of urban EAP occupied in transport and communications
48. Percent of urban EAP occupied in personal services
49. Percent of urban EAP occupied in social activities and public administration
50. Percent of urban EAP occupied in other activities
51. Percent of migrants over 10 years old with less than 10 years of residence
52. Percent of population over 10 years old that is illiterate

# APPENDIX 2. MATRIX OF FACTOR LOADINGS IN THE ANALYSIS

| Variables | | | Factors | | | |
|------|------|------|------|------|------|------|
| | 1 | 2 | 3 | 4 | 5 | 6 |
| 1. | | 0.98 | | | | |
| 2. | | 0.99 | | | | |
| 3. | | 0.98 | | | | |
| 4. | | 0.99 | | | | |
| 5. | | 0.96 | | | | |
| 6. | | 0.99 | | | | |
| 7. | | 0.99 | | | | |
| 8. | | 0.99 | | | | |
| 9. | | 0.98 | | | | |
| 10. | | 0.97 | | | | |
| 11. | | 0.96 | | | | |
| 12. | 0.49 | | | | | |
| 13. | 0.63 | | | | | -0.56 |
| 14. | 0.85 | | | | | |
| 15. | 0.80 | | | | | |
| 16. | 0.84 | | 0.43 | | | |
| 17. | 0.70 | | | | | |
| 18. | 0.81 | | | | | |
| 19. | -0.73 | | | | | |
| 20. | | | | | | -0.57 |
| 21. | 0.50 | | | | | |
| 22. | 0.49 | | 0.59 | | | |
| 23. | 0.71 | | | | | |
| 24. | | | | | | -0.84 |
| 25. | -0.88 | | | | | |
| 26. | | | -0.80 | | | |
| 27. | 0.83 | | | | | |
| 28. | 0.79 | | | | | |
| 29. | 0.62 | | 0.59 | | | |
| 30. | | | 0.75 | | | |

| | | | |
|---|---|---|---|
| 31. | -0.55 | | 0.60 |
| 32. | | | 0.76 |
| 33. | | | 0.93 |
| 34. | -0.67 | | 0.46 |
| 35. | -0.42 | | 0.79 |
| 36. | -0.63 | | 0.53 |
| 37. | 0.42 | | -0.56 |
| 38. | | | -0.90 |
| 39. | | | -0.45 |
| 40. | | | -0.65 |
| 41. | -0.79 | | |
| 42. | | 0.43 | |
| 43. | | 0.60 | |
| 44. | | -0.63 | -0.46 |
| 45. | -0.55 | | |
| 46. | | | 0.66 |
| 47. | | | 0.80 |
| 48. | | 0.55 | 0.39 |
| 49. | | 0.79 | |
| 50. | | | |
| 51. | | | |
| 52. | -0.75 | 0.45 | |

# Chapter XVI

# URBANIZATION TRENDS IN MEXICO

Maria Teresa Gutiérrez de MacGregor

Until the beginning of the nineteenth century, Mexico City was the most important urban center of the New World. Only in 1830 did New York begin to surpass it in population size. During the course of the nineteenth century, other major cities emerged in the Western Hemisphere, so that by 1900 Buenos Aires, with a population of 800,000, and Rio de Janeiro, with 690,000, came to have more than double the inhabitants of Mexico City. At that time several South American cities achieved substantial growth rates. Buenos Aires boasted an annual rate of population increase of 5.2 percent, São Paulo 12.5 percent, and Bogota 7.5 percent.[1] By comparison, Mexico City between 1895 and 1900 grew annually by only 1 percent, although by the third decade of the twentieth century her growth rate had caught up with those of other South American cities with an annual rate of 5.8 percent. However much Mexico City may have served as a unique symbol of urban growth and status in Mexico's past, the urban pattern in Mexico today is substantially more complex.

Modern urbanization in Mexico is a most recent manifestation appearing quite suddenly and intensely in a very short span of time.[2] Its characteristics have been a faster growth rate in urban areas than in rural ones (a difference becoming more apparent by 1940), a mushrooming of new urban centers, particularly since 1940 (with a generally more complex urban network developing), and spatial concentration of urban population in the central part of the country--a pattern distinguished by a marked degree of urban primacy.

---

1. Alan Gilbert, *Urbanization in Contemporary Latin America: Critical Approaches to the Analysis of Urban Issues* (New York: John Wiley and Sons, 1982), p. 29.

2. A recent overview of urban trends in Mexico is Ian Scott, *Urban and Spatial Development in Mexico* (Baltimore: Johns Hopkins Press, 1981).

## Measures of Urban Growth

Mexico exhibits demographic contrasts which have sharpened owing to complex economic and social changes that have transformed the country from a rural state at the turn of the twentieth century to a state where the population in the cities greatly exceeds that in the rural areas. The latter is characterized by marked dispersion, so that in 1980 there were 110,000 settlements of less than 2,500 inhabitants, accounting for 34 percent of the total population in the country. Furthermore, half of these places have less than 100 inhabitants,[3] and since they are so spread apart it has been difficult to provide them with utilities and cultural services. On the other hand, urban population is highly concentrated in cities of over 100,000 inhabitants. In 1980, 75 percent of the urban population, or a total of 30,549,000 people, dwelled in such large cities. Almost half of these people--13,937,000--lived in a single conurbation, the Metropolitan Area of Mexico City.[4] Urban population is also growing at a high rate, which has brought about increasingly difficult problems, solutions to which, if at all effective, have been of only limited scope. There is not true long-term urban growth policy, and for the most part actions have been guided by spur-of-the-moment decisions.

The growth of Mexico's urban population between 1900 and 1980 (defined as that proportion of the population living in towns of 10,000 or more inhabitants) falls into two clear-cut periods, from 1900 to 1940 and from 1940 to 1980 (figure 16.1). During the first period urban population growth was relatively slow. It grew two and a half times, from 1.6 million to 4.2 million inhabitants. Several characteristics of this period may be noted.

From 1900 to 1920, rural population decreased owing to casualties during the Revolution. Urban population experienced a slight increase largely because people from the country sought refuge in the cities. From 1930 to 1940, urban population growth slowed because thousands of peasants remained in the countryside, motivated by President Lazaro Cardenas' policy. His administration showed a great concern for a more direct government involvement in the economic development of the nation. Investments were made in dams and highways, credit institutions were founded, and land distribution was three times larger than in former post-revolutionary administrations.

---

3. Secretaría de Asentamientos Humanos y Obras Públicas, Mexico (State), *Plan Nacional de Desarrollo Urbano 1982* (Mexico City, 1982), p. 16.

4. Nacional Financiera, Mexico (State), *La Economía Mexicana en cifras* (Mexico City, 1981), p. 12.

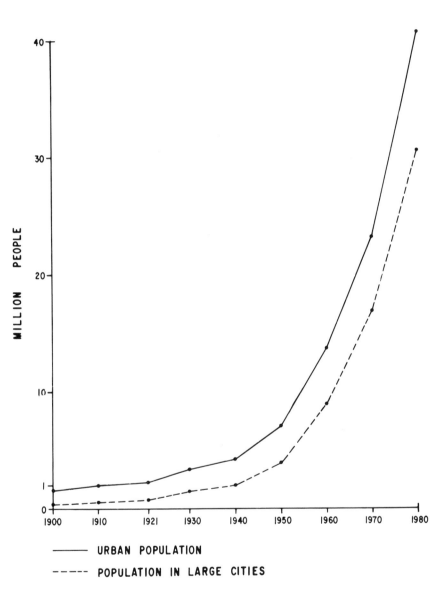

Figure 16.1.   Mexico's urban population, 1900-1980

The second period, from 1940 to 1980 (also four decades long), witnessed an urban growth rate that was nine and a half times greater, raising the urban population from 4.2 to 40.6 million inhabitants. From 1940 to 1950, the major cause of such growth was migration from the country to the cities, as a result of increased industrialization. From 1950 to 1970, the factor was mainly a natural growth and only secondarily internal migration towards industrial centers.[5] This was fostered in particular by the gradual increase of public investment in industrial development which, by 1950, was one and a half times greater than that allocated to agriculture. By 1979, federal public investment applied to industrial development had grown three times larger than that devoted to farming.[6]

Whereas the annual rate of increase of the total population had been 1.1 percent during the 1900-1910 (2.1 for urban and 0.9 for rural), a notable change had occurred by 1970-1980, with a total annual rate of increase of total population over that period of 3.2 percent (5.5 for urban and down to 0.6 percent for rural). These figures do not, of course, imply any reduction in absolute values (figure 16.2). While at the beginning of the century urban population accounted for 12.1 percent, in 1980 it had increased to 60.2 percent of the total population of the country--the first time in which urban population has exceeded rural population (figure 16.3).[7] In 1900, for every 100 persons living in rural areas, 14 were found in urban areas. On the other hand, for every 100 rural inhabitants in 1980, there were 151 in urban areas.

The rapid growth rate of the urban population is partially due to the natural growth in the nation, arising from a high-birth rate which has remained almost constant. From 1931 to 1975, the birth-rate was over 40 per thousand, the death-rate went down from 29.9 in 1931 to 7.2 per thousand in 1975, and child mortality decreased from 145 per thousand in 1930 to 49 per thousand in 1975.[8] Such trends are the partial result of improvements in hygiene and medical care (particularly mother-child care), which have increased life expectancy from 36.8 in 1930 to 64 in 1975.

---

5. Luis Unikel, *El Desarrollo Urbano de México: Diagnóstico e impicaciones futuras* (Mexico City: Colegio de México, 1976), p. 45.

6. Nacional Financiera, México (State), *La Economía Mexicana en cifras,* pp. 320-24.

7. Nacional Financiera, México (State), *La Economía Mexicana en cifras,* p. 5.

8. Subsecretaría de Planeación, Dirección General de Bioestadística, Mexico (State), *Compendio de Estadísticas Vitales de México, Serie Bioestadística 1* (Mexico City, 1975).

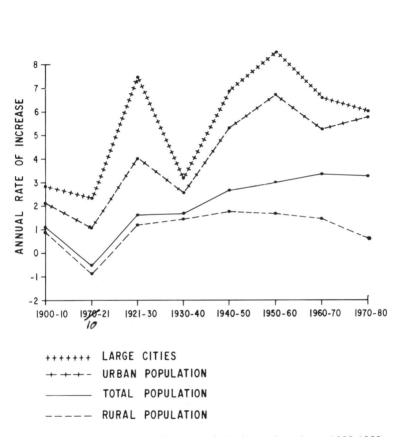

Figure 16.2. Annual rate of increase of Mexican urban places, 1900-1980

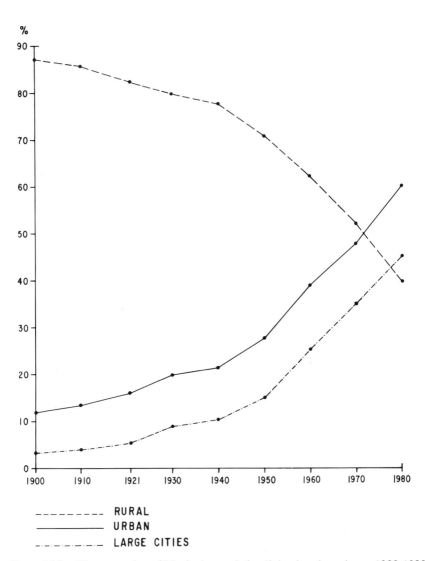

Figure 16.3.   The proportion of Mexico's population living in urban places, 1900-1980

The Mexican government, concerned by such a population boom, has implemented educational programs and, since 1977, a definite policy to attempt to curb the rapid population growth rate, called "National Family Planning Program." This program has brought about a slight reduction in annual mean growth: from 3.4 percent in the 1960-1970 period to 3.2 percent in the 1970-1980 period. Actions taken have included suggestions for changes in family behavior, by means of a mass advertising in all media, using the motto, for example, that "smaller families live better."

Significant decreases in natural growth are contemplated, since the fertility rate has diminished, and there would be a slight decrease in mortality if the programs to provide health services to the community materialize as planned. The National Development Plan 1983-88 points out that population growth has come down to 2.5 in 1982; in spite of that, the fast population growth of the recent past year will be reflected in the problems faced by the country, at least during the next ten years.

Another important reason for urban population growth, as already noted, is migration. In 1970, 31.3 percent of urban population living in cities of 100,000 or more inhabitants was made up of migrants. Some 4.5 million people during the 1950-70 period moved from the rural to the urban sector.[9] Despite variations in the rate of urban population growth, since the 1940s the annual mean has always been over 5 percent and is expected to continue at this level.

The rural population of Mexico will decrease in relative size, since it shifted from 87.8 percent of total population in 1900 to 39.8 percent in 1980.[10] Furthermore, from 1940 to 1980, the annual rural growth rate showed a constant reduction of 1.8 percent at the beginning of this period, down to 0.69 at its close. In Mexico, the rural population required to sustain one urban inhabitant is very high, because most crop lands (80 percent) are rain-fed, depending therefore on rainfall for irrigation. This is not helped in many areas by technological backwardness. In some regions, ancient pre-Spanish systems, such as the "coa" are still in use. One of the major problems in the future will be supplying foodstuffs to such a disproportionately large urban population.

The Mexican urban network greatly increased in size and complexity between 1900 and 1970. Improvements in transportation and communications contributed not only to an overall increase in

9. Luis Unikel, *El Desarrollo Urbano de México*, p. 213.

10. Nacional Financiera, México (State), *La Economía Mexicana en cifras*, p. 5.

the size of urban populations but also to an increase in the number of settlements which shed their rural nature and became urban places. In 1900, there were only 52 urban centers, but by 1970 they had increased to 278, more than a fivefold increase. For simplicity, urban centers have been classified into three sizes: small (10,000 to 49,999 inhabitants), medium-size (50,000 to 99,999), and larger centers (100,000 or more).[11] This classification differs from that used by the author in a former paper and represents an improvement.

Considering urban population distribution in terms of the various sizes of towns and cities, there was a substantial change over the period under study. At the turn of the century, a majority of the urban population, more than 56 percent, was found in small communities. By 1930, there had been a transformation in the urban structure of the nation, which increased the population living in large cities to 73 percent of total urban population in 1970. However, the remaining small-town population was distributed among 218 places, up from 46 in 1970, representing a decline from 17 to 9 percent of the urban population. Most of them grew rapidly and many climbed into the classification of large cities, particularly those that are border cities, oil-boom towns, and tourist resorts. By 1970, 30 medium-sized towns had become large ones and accounted for between 9 and 17 percent of the population living in large cities, depending on which census year is considered (table 16.1). It is evident that, with the exception only of Mexico City and Guadalajara, large cities in Mexico have grown substantially only in the last 40 years.

Between 1900 and 1970, the number of cities with more than 100,000 inhabitants increased from two to 32 in number. Considering only cities with a million or more residents, there were none at all in 1900; it was not until 1930 that Mexico City surpassed that mark. Another 40 years elasped before two more cities, Guadalajara and Monterey, reached that status. It can be inferred that an unbalanced urban network will prevail, with a huge conglomeration in just one city. Large cities will be far more numerous than medium-sized cities, and small cities will abound.

### The Progress of Urbanization and Primacy

According to Guyot, the terms "urban growth" and "urbanization" are often used interchangeably. This terminological confusion is unfortunate since urbanization must not be considered

---

11. United Nations Economic Commission for Latin America (CEPAL), *El Estado de los asentamientos humanos en América Latina y el Caribe de México* (Edición SAHOP, 1979), pp. 31, 37-38.

TABLE 16.1

RECLASSIFICATION OF PLACES WHICH CHANGED FROM MEDIUM TO
LARGE SIZE BETWEEN 1900 AND 1970
THROUGH POPULATION INCREASE

| Date | Number of places | Absolute population | % all large cities |
|------|------------------|---------------------|--------------------|
| 1910 | 0 | 0 | 0 |
| 1921 | 0 | 0 | 0 |
| 1930 | 2 | 247,730 | 17 |
| 1940 | 0 | 0 | 0 |
| 1950 | 6 | 744,004 | 19 |
| 1960 | 6 | 827,324 | 9.2 |
| 1970 | 16 | 2,209,223 | 13 |

more than just one of the factors underlying urban growth.[12] Urban
growth in Mexico is characterized not so much by the increase of
urban population resulting from the appearance of new cities, as by
the huge percentage of urban population dwelling in very large
cities. Mexico is going through the first of five urbanization
phases defined by Guyot,[13] in which the urbanization index follows
an upward trend (figure 16.4).

This process has been affected by imbalances between town and
country, as well as industrial development supported by government
policies affecting agriculture in recent years. This in turn, has
decreased job opportunities in the countryside, increased internal
migration, and encouraged unequal income distribution, producing a
lopsided economic development. According to 1979 estimates by
Nacional Financiera,[14] of the 19 million gainfully employed
population (29 percent of total inhabitants) 6 million were devoted
to agriculture and yielded only 8.7 percent of the gross national
product (GNP). In contrast, some 5 million people were employed in
industry and contributed 38.8 percent, almost four and a half times
more than agricultural workers.

On the other hand, the degree of urbanization has increased
constantly since the volume of urban population has experienced a
growth rate larger than the total. The degree of urbanization by
itself is not sufficient to provide detailed knowledge of population
distribution. Distribution is quite scattered in a great number of

12. Fernand Guyot, *Essai d'économie urbaine* (Paris: Librairie Générale de
Droit et de Jurisprudence, 1968), p. 187.

13. Ibid., p. 205.

14. Nacional Financiera, México (State), *La Economía Mexicana en cifras*, p.
42.

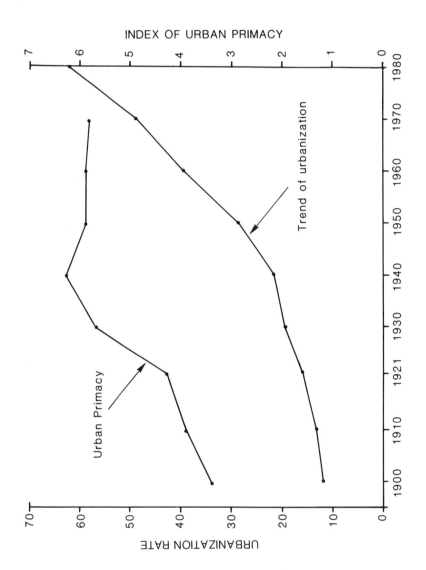

INDEX OF URBAN PRIMACY

Trend of urbanization

Urban Primacy

URBANIZATION RATE

Figure 16.4. Urbanization and primacy in Mexico, 1900-1980

small urban sites or concentrated in a handful of large cities. An
index of concentration, relating the population living in cities of
100,000 or more inhabitants to the total population of the nation,
reveals the pattern in Mexico, which in 80 years had increased more
than thirteen times, from 3.3 percent in 1900 to 45.2 percent in
1980. This change is explained by the strong demographic boom in
the three major cities of the country, just discussed, and the rise
in the number of places with more than 100,000 inhabitants.

This strong concentration is even more exacerbated if we
relate the population of Mexico City Metropolitan Area in 1980, not
with the total population of the nation, but rather with that living
in locations of 100,000 or more inhabitants. This relationship
indicates that 45.6 percent or nearly half of large-city population
dwells in the Mexico City Metropolitan Area, the nation's capital.
This proportion matches forecasts for Latin America in an ECLA
report, which states that "there is a high geographic concentration
of population in one of the most dynamic urban centers;" it goes on
to state that "the macrocephalic nature of systems and primacy
indexes have increased substantially, and they tend to reflect modes
of hierarchic distribution of settlements which are growing farther
apart from the rank-size rule."[15]

Based on trends over the last 40 years the urbanization index
will likely grow, because urban population tends to increase at a
faster rate than the total population. Furthermore, urban
population concentration in cities of 100,000 or more inhabitants
will also grow, based on past trends noted earlier. Population
concentration will continue to grow in the most dynamic urban area,
Mexico City Metropolitan Area, which will probably reach 31 million
inhabitants.[16]

The primacy index for Mexico City varies significantly (figure
16.4). In 1900, the capital was almost three and a half times
larger than the second-ranking city, Guadalajara. By 1980, the
ratio had grown to 5.5 times greater. The highest primacy index was
attained in 1940 (six times greater), and thereafter it began to
diminish between 1940-1950, a period of sound growth for Guadalajara
(4.9 percent a year, twice as much as in the former decade). Such a
high primacy index reflects once again the progress of the spatial
concentration of urban population. While industrial development
since 1940 helped Guadalajara and Monterrey both surpass one million
inhabitants by 1970 and spurred Guadalajara to a faster growth rate

15. United Nations Economic Commission for Latin America (CEPAL), *El Estado
de los asentamientos humanos,* pp. 31, 37, and 38.

16. Consejo Nacional de Población, *Boletín Informativo 5 (*March 1981): 11.

than Mexico City, thereby causing the primacy index to dip slightly, it still remains high.

Mexico City's primacy is not only based on population, but also economy as well; it has been the chief center for amassing wealth within the country, to the detriment of other states. It captures the largest part of production and consumption, as well as most administrative, economic, political, educational, and cultural functions of the nation.

Ignacio Ovalle, Secretary to the Presidential Office, in his report submitted in 1975 to the Honorable House of Representatives, stated that Mexico City in 1970 employed 43 percent of all processing industry workers in the country and accounted for 33 percent of all service establishments, 50 percent of the commercial activity of the country, 82 percent of the wholesale business, 90 percent of the commerce in industrial materials, 52 percent of all automobiles, 54 percent of all telephones, 45 percent of vocational schools and high school institutions, 46 percent of teachers' schools, and 45 percent of technical and professional schools.[17] No significant decline is foreseen in the general index over the next 20 years, in spite of the rapid and constant population increase in the second largest city of the country.

### The Urban Settlement Pattern

Urban population distribution within the national territory is highly irregular, due mainly to the influence of physical, political, and socio-economic factors. Even if historical settlements and physical resources were important at the time of modern city founding, it was not the only reason for growth, since other political and economic factors acquired a greater relevance later on.

### *Cities and Altitude*

Analyzing urban population in relation to altitude, there is a direct relationship. Most of the territory is located in low latitudes within the tropical area; thus altitude favors a better climate and consequently people have preferred to live in high places.

The overall vertical distribution pattern of urban population has not changed much (table 16.2). A large part of the population is concentrated at an altitude of more than 1,000 meters in a percentage varying from 82 percent in 1900 to 70 percent in 1970.

Also, urban population tends to grow at a higher rate over 2,000 m. In fact, Mexico City is situated at this altitude, and

---

17. Confederación Nacional de Colegios y Asociaciiones Profesionales de México, *Asentamientos humanos en México* (Mexico City: The Confederation, 1976), p. 49.

TABLE 16.2

DISTRIBUTION OF URBAN POPULATION BY ALTITUDE

| YEARS | TOTAL URBAN POPULATION | 0-200 m | | | 201-1000 m | | | 1001-2000 m | | | + 2001 m | | |
|---|---|---|---|---|---|---|---|---|---|---|---|---|---|
| | | ABSOLUTE | No. of localities | % | ABSOLUTE | No. of localities | % | ABSOLUTE | No. of localities | % | ABSOLUTE | No. of localities | % |
| 1900 | 1,651,512 | 166,915 | 9 | 10.1 | 119,151 | 5 | 7.2 | 742,589 | 28 | 25.0 | 622,857 | 10 | 37.7 |
| 1901 | 2,035,828 | 242,988 | 11 | 11.9 | 177,801 | 8 | 8.7 | 892,428 | 34 | 43.8 | 722,611 | 8 | 35.6 |
| 1921 | 2,288,156 | 295,641 | 10 | 12.9 | 227,411 | 10 | 9.9 | 920,877 | 33 | 40.2 | 844,217 | 8 | 37.0 |
| 1930 | 3,269,578 | 445,291 | 16 | 13.6 | 276,014 | 10 | 8.4 | 1,217,371 | 43 | 37.3 | 1,320,902 | 10 | 40.6 |
| 1940 | 4,214,655 | 603,033 | 23 | 14.3 | 362,226 | 11 | 8.6 | 1,440,493 | 48 | 34.2 | 1,805,903 | 11 | 42.9 |
| 1950 | 7,098,685 | 1,232,460 | 40 | 17.4 | 691,518 | 17 | 9.7 | 2,403,347 | 68 | 33.9 | 2,771,360 | 17 | 39.0 |
| 1960 | 13,703,538 | 2,296,106 | 59 | 16.8 | 1,400,158 | 25 | 10.2 | 4,103,870 | 90 | 30.0 | 5,903,404 | 25 | 43.0 |
| 1970 | 23,108,317 | 4,357,231 | 94 | 18.9 | 2,461,740 | 39 | 10.6 | 6,439,083 | 107 | 27.9 | 9,850,263 | 38 | 42.6 |

being the seat of the nation's political power has thus spurred the centralization of most activities. In this wealth concentration center, 20 percent of the country's total population have made their homes and generate 44 percent of the GNP, 52.1 percent of industrial production, and 54.7 percent of all services;[18] furthermore, this giant city absorbs 60 percent of national grants in higher education, and its budget exceeds all of the states' budget combined.[19]

The lowest population percentages are found between 200 and 1,000 m altitude, accounting for 7 percent of the urban population in 1900 and 10 percent in 1970. None of the urban centers within these altitudes has 100,000 inhabitants, except Monterrey which has reached the one million mark, almost half of the urban population living at these altitudes.

In 1900, 10 percent of the population in cities was found at altitudes of less than 200 m, on the coastal plains, while in 1970, the figure had increased to 18.6 percent. This rise is due partly to a demographic development in the northern border cities, fostered by the border national program launched in 1961, to the development of cities in the commercial agriculture areas of the Northwest and Northeast, to the creation of the national fund for the development of tourism, which mainly benefitted resort centers along the Pacific coast, and to the increase of the oil-boom which has helped some towns gush with prosperity along the Gulf of Mexico.

In relation to population distribution by altitude with regard to natural resources, the National Program for the Territorial Deconcentration of Federal Public Administration indicates: "Under the 500 m mark, where only 15 percent of the population dwells, we find 80 percent of irrigation lands, 85 percent of available water, 90 percent of power generation resources, and 100 percent of oil fields."[20]

### Cities and Climate

Mexico has three major climatic zones: the northern arid zone, the central temperate zone, and the southern tropical zone. The distribution of urban population is related only in a very general way to certain favorable climates.

The overall urban population distribution pattern in the three main climate zones has varied little during the 1900-1970 period, in spite of a substantial increase of urban population.[21] The temperate

---

18. Secretaría de Asentamientos Humanos y Obras Publicas, México (State), *Programa Nacional de Desconcentración Territorial de la Administración Pública Federal* (Mexico City, 1978), p. 34.

19. Ibid., p. 6.

20. Ibid., p. 6.

21. See Maria Teresa Gutiérrrez de MacGregor and Carmen Valverde, "Crecimiento de la población urbana en México en 1900-2000, con énfasis en las zonas climáticas," *Anuario de Geografía, 1980,* (Mexico City: Universidad Nacional Autónoma de México, Facultad de Filosofía y Letras, 1983).

zone has a greater amount of urban population than both the arid and tropical together, since it has better weather conditions, fertile volcanic soil good for the development of agriculture, more and better communication networks, concentration of industry, commerce, culture, and the capital of the country (table 16.3 and figure 16.5).

The arid lands, located mainly in the northern part of the country, were inhabited by nomad tribes before the Spanish period. During colonial times, population growth was due to the importance that mining had at the time. By the beginning of the twentieth century, some half a million people had settled, accounting for 34 percent of the total urban population, unevenly distributed over a region that comprised 58 percent of the national territory. Irrigation works and the strengthening of the northern border area brought sharp increases in population by mid-century. By 1970, although urban population increased in absolute values to more than 7 million, in relative terms, there was a slight reduction to 30 percent.

The temperate zone, located in the center of the country, has long boasted large population concentrations, even in pre-Spanish times. With the arrival of the Spaniards, its importance was confirmed, and currently it has become the area with the highest urban concentration. It is the smallest zone territorially, only 16 percent of the total land area of the country. In 1900, it bore the highest urban population, almost one million inhabitants (54.6 percent). In 1970, urban population in this area had reached almost 13 million inhabitants, or 56 percent of total urban population.

During pre-Spanish times, important population centers once thrived in the tropical area. In colonial times and during most of the independent period, this area was scarcely populated, however, and communications were minimal. Its demographic development has taken place recently. The tropical zone had the lowest urban population, within an area that represented about 26 percent of the country's total. In 1970, its population climbed to more than 3 million inhabitants, 14 percent of total urban population.

Since the beginning of the century, the temperate zone has had a substantial population living in large cities, while the arid lands experienced this phenomenon only after 1930, and the tropical areas after 1950 (figure 16.6).

The geographical evolution of the urban pattern shows striking regional differences between 1900 and 1970 (figures 16.7 and 16.8). At the beginning of the century, the temperate zone--at more than

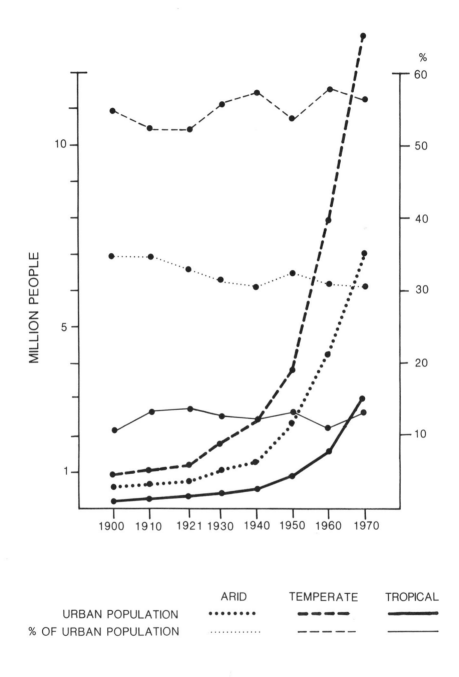

Figure 16.5.  Urban population growth in Mexico, by climatic zones

TABLE 16.3

DISTRIBUTION OF URBAN POPULATION BY CLIMATE ZONES

| YEARS | TOTAL URBAN POPULATION | ARID | | | TEMPERATE | | | TROPICAL | | |
|---|---|---|---|---|---|---|---|---|---|---|
| | | ABSOLUTE POPULATION | No. of localities | PERCENTAGE OF URBAN TOTAL | ABSOLUTE POPULATION | No. of localities | PERCENTAGE OF URBAN TOTAL | ABSOLUTE POPULATION | No. of localities | PERCENTAGE OF URBAN TOTAL |
| 1900 | 1,651,512 | 572,061 | 20 | 34.6 | 902,218 | 23 | 54.6 | 177,233 | 9 | 10.7 |
| 1910 | 2,035,828 | 694,987 | 24 | 34.1 | 1,065,418 | 24 | 52.3 | 275,423 | 13 | 13.5 |
| 1921 | 2,288,156 | 774,991 | 28 | 33.9 | 1,196,848 | 22 | 52.3 | 316,317 | 11 | 13.8 |
| 1930 | 3,269,578 | 1,029,804 | 35 | 31.5 | 1,822,674 | 31 | 55.7 | 417,100 | 14 | 12.8 |
| 1940 | 4,214,655 | 1,282,218 | 40 | 30.4 | 2,411,365 | 35 | 57.2 | 521,072 | 18 | 12.3 |
| 1950 | 7,098,685 | 2,335,764 | 57 | 32.9 | 3,818,529 | 50 | 53.8 | 944,392 | 35 | 13.3 |
| 1960 | 13,703,538 | 4,243,606 | 74 | 31.0 | 7,916,522 | 72 | 57.8 | 1,543,410 | 53 | 11.3 |
| 1970 | 23,108,317 | 7,059,563 | 104 | 30.5 | 12,981,809 | 85 | 56.2 | 3,066,945 | 89 | 13.3 |

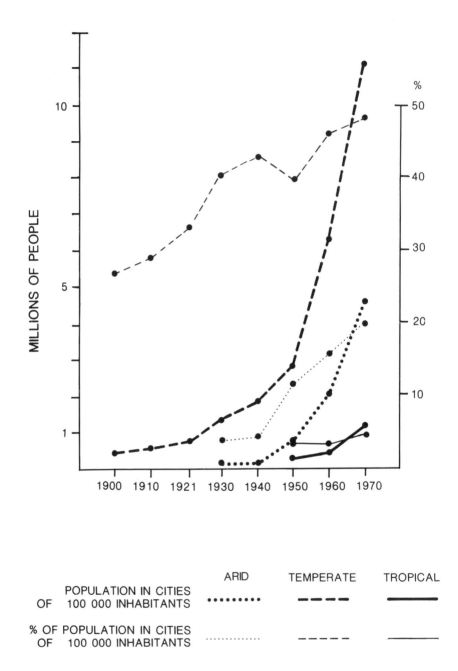

Figure 16.6. Population growth in cities of 100,000 or more in Mexico, by climatic zones

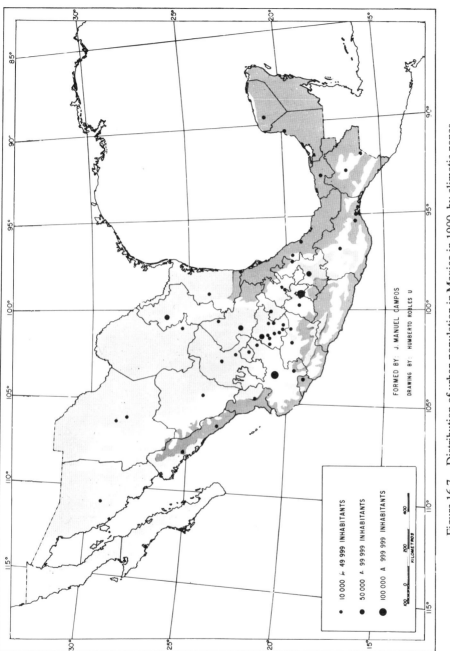

Figure 16.7.   Distribution of urban population in Mexico in 1900, by climatic zones

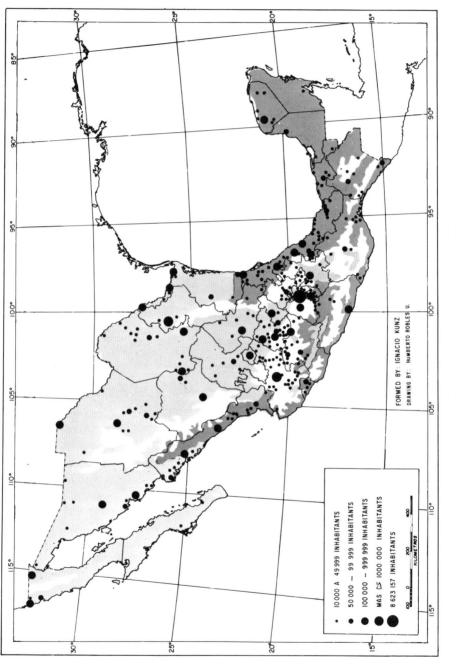

Figure 16.8.   Distribution of urban population in Mexico in 1970, by climatic zones

1,000 m altitude and in the southern portion of Mexican high
plateau--concentrated most of the urban population in 23 cities.
The two large cities of the country at that time were quite
outstanding: Mexico City, in the central region with 344,721
inhabitants, and Guadalajara, west of Mexico City, with 101,208
inhabitants. In the eastern region, Puebla was the only medium-size
city, with 93,521 inhabitants. For the rest, there were about 20
small villages scattered throughout the zone. By 1970, the number
of cities had increased to 85, including Mexico City with 8,632,157
inhabitants and Guadalajara with 1,480,472 inhabitants. Besides
these six other large cities evolved: Jalapa, Puebla, Toluca,
Morelia, and Irapuato (from east to west) and Heroica Matamoros (in
the northeast). There were also six medium-sized towns and a
mushrooming of small villages, that had reached 71 in number.

The arid zone had only 20 urban locations in 1900, and there
was no large city. The three most important medium-sized towns
were, from south to north, Leon, San Luis Potosi, and Monterrey,
accompanied by 17 small villages. By 1970, a substantial increase
in the number of urban places had occurred, totalling 104, out of
which 16 were large ones. The most outstanding cities are
Monterrey, with 1,213,474 inhabitants and in the northern border
strip (from west to east) Tijuana, Mexicali, Ciudad Juarez, Nuevo
Laredo, and Reynosa; three in the northwest of the Pacific coastal
plains--Hermosillo, Ciudad Obregon, and Culiacan--from north to
south; eight in the Mexican high plateau--Chihuahua, Torreon,
Saltillo, Durango, San Luis Potosi, Aguascalientes, Leon, and
Queretaro (from north to south). Some 13 medium-sized towns and 74
small villages completed the network.

The tropical zone in 1900 had the smallest number of cities:
only nine small villages, five of them located on the coastal plains
of the Gulf of Mexico and four on the Pacific coast. For 1970, the
increase in the number of cities is dramatic: they jumped up to 89,
exceeding in number those in the temperate zone. Seven large cities
appeared; four of them in the coastal plains of the Gulf of Mexico:
Tampico, Poza Rica, Veracruz, and Merida (from north to south), and
Cuernavaca in the central region. Also, nine medium-sized towns and
73 small villages provided lower levels to the urban hierarchy.

In 1970, the arid and tropical zones had more cities each (104
and 89, respectively) than the temperate zone, which had 85 (table
16.3). The latter's urban network had a greater density because it
covers less territory, has a larger population, and more and better
communications networks.

Consequently, we can deduce that the pattern will continue with an increasing geographic concentration of the urban population in the center of the country, in the temperate zone, and at altitudes over 1,000 m. This trend may be modified partially by the implementation of modern technology, which will stimulate development of both the arid and tropical zones. Aside from that, population preferences will continue to be high for oil towns of tropical zones, at less than 200 m altitude, on the Gulf of Mexico's coastal plains, and for industrial ports.

## National Urban Policy

Political and administrative decisions of successive governments have played a decisive role in the development of the three zones, and at the same time, they have arbitrarily altered human settlement patterns. For several centuries, all decisions focussed on the development of Mexico City; hence, the temperate zone achieved dominance in view of its administrative, economic, demographic, political, and cultural concentration. Two major concerns of the Mexican government are high population concentration in Mexico City Metropolitan Area, and the great dispersion of rural population. Because of this, it has launched several policies aimed at ameliorating this stark gap. Such policies are set forth in the National Program for Territoral Deconcentration of the Federal Public Administration.

There is little confidence in the capability of such programs to solve problems of growth and distribution of population in the country. In this regard, Garza states:

> The State must relinquish the hesitant nature of its actions, and assume the political responsibility of acting upon social relations which produce a deformed and unfair space hindering an equitable distribution of the fruits of growth among all Mexicans.[22]

Unikel offers an interesting comment on the government's urban-regional policy:

> [although] . . . politically, it was important to achieve a spatial decentralization of the economy, at the level of dominant economic groups, this objective did not get the necessary approval in order to be attained. Such a situation is reflected as a lack of control over industrial locations located there (since they do not have to pay for the social expenses that they create) and the centralization of public expenditures......[23]

The plans and projects of one government are generally changed by the next, many times without particular reason. This can be seen by comparing "The Global Plan of Development 1980-1982" with the

22 . Gustavo Garza, "Desarrollo económico, urbanización y políticas urbano regionales en México, 1900-1982," *Demografía y Economía* 17,2, no. 54 (1983), p. 180.

23 . Lius Unikel and Allan Lavell, *El Problema Urbano: La Universidad Nacional y los problemas nacionales. Volumen VII, Tomo II: Sociedad y Cultura* (Mexico City: Universidad Nacional Autónoma de México, 1979).

"National Plan for Development 1983-1988" published by the present government, both showing different plans. For that reason it is very difficult to say what any future trends in our country will be.

In conclusion, dispersion of rural population is expected to continue, as well as migration towards the three main cities (Mexico City, Guadalajara, and Monterrey), and to the northern border cities, oil towns, and industrial ports. Besides, the trend of population concentration in the Metropolitan Area of Mexico City will continue an upward swing, which will exacerbate problems of unemployment, housing shortage, water and utilities scarcity, traffic bottlenecks, and environmental pollution. From all these signs concerning the future it is clear that processes of concentration and dispersion, so characteristic of human settlement structure in Mexico, will carry the system into even greater turmoil.

# Chapter XVII

# FOUR DECADES OF CHANGE IN URBAN NORTH AMERICA

## Harold M. Mayer

The conclusion of World War II in 1945 marked the beginning of an era of rapid change in the urban areas of the United States and Canada. It also was the year of publication of one of the most widely cited, reprinted, and anthologized articles in the entire English-language literature of urban geography: the paper entitled "The Nature of Cities" by Chauncy Harris and Edward Ullman.[1] Less than a decade later, another important article by Chauncy Harris, "The Market as a Factor in the Localization of Industry in the United States," appeared.[2] Together, these two articles presented a clear picture of the external and internal spatial aspects of American cities at the beginning of the postwar period.

The spatial patterns of North American cities are, in numerous and significant respects, different from those of the 1940s. How, and to what extent, are the differences evident, and how--if at all--do the classic models of urban growth, function, and internal structure require modification in order to be applicable to contemporary American cities and metropolitan areas? A recent article has appeared that surveys briefly some of the major changes that have taken place; it demonstrates the role of various social, economic, and technological changes in North America which have catalyzed and facilitated important transformations in the spatial patterns of urban America.[3] This essay highlights some of these forces and attempt to assess, albeit subjectively, a number of the relationships between social, economic, and technological trends on the one hand and the external and internal spatial patterns of American cities and metropolitan regions on the other over the last four decades.

---

1. Chauncy D. Harris and Edward L. Ullman, "The Nature of Cities," *Annals of the American Academy of Political and Social Science,* 242 (November 1945): 7-17.

2. Chauncy D. Harris, "The Market as a Factor in the Localization of Industry in the United States," *Annals of the Association of American Geographers* 44, no. 4 (December 1954): 315-348.

3. Michael P. Conzen, "American Cities in Profound Transition: The New City Geography of the 1980s," *Journal of Geography* 82, no. 3 (May-June 1983): 94-101.

## Changing Concepts of "Urban" and "Metropolitan"

So numerous and profound have been the changes in the characteristics of the urban and metropolitan areas of the United States and Canada since the period of World War II that the definitions of those terms have been changed by the respective governmental statistical agencies, in order to conform more nearly to the realities of the late twentieth century. It is generally recognized that diffusion and deconcentration of the urban population have resulted in spatial patterns which, in large measure, render the traditional concepts of the city obsolete. Rarely, if ever, do the physical and functional boundaries of a city coincide with the administrative boundaries of the municipalities. "Overspill" and "underbounding" are almost universal. Statistics relative to the population of cities, therefore, are commonly misleading, because they refer generally only to the population resident within the municipal boundaries. In metropolitan areas, the population of the "central city" commonly represents a relatively small and decreasing proportion of the total metropolitan population.

The definition of "urban place" in the United States has not significantly changed since the first federal census, in 1790. At that time, the urban population--the population resident in places of 2,500 or more--was only 5.1 percent of the national total. Of the 24 such "urban places" at that time, none had a population of as much as 50,000, the minimum for designation now as a metropolitan area. Only two places had over 25,000. The census of 1920, following World War I, was the first to reveal that the urban population of the nation exceeded the rural. Of the 105.7 million people in the United States at that time, 54.2 percent lived in places of 25,000 or more. Subsequently, in the six following decades the population of the nation increased by over 114 percent, to 226.5 million, while the population resident in urban places increased to 167.1 million, or 73.7 percent of the total population. During the period the actual population increase in urban places was 112.9 million, a number greater than the entire population in 1920, and an increase of 208.4 percent.[4] Thus the population resident in urban places increased at a rate more than double that of the total national population.

---

4. All population figures in this article, unless otherwise noted, are compiled from two publications of the U.S. Department of Commerce, Bureau of the Census: *Historical Statistics of the United States, Colonial Times to 1970* (Washington: U.S. Government Printing Office, 1976), and *Statistical Abstract of the United States 1982-83* (Washington: U.S. Government Printing Office, 1983).

Thus, within a relatively short interval, the United States was transformed from a rural to an overwhelmingly urban nation. With rising affluence, the balance between the centripetal attractions of proximity in areas close to the cores of the cities and the centrifugal attractions of peripheral areas shifted.[5] Although suburbanization was taking place in the nineteenth and early twentieth centuries, principally along the railroad lines which provided commuter train service, the increasing use of the automobile accelerated the outward movement of population at a more rapid rate than the expansion of the areas under jurisdiction of the central city governments. Around the larger cities, land was converted from rural to urban use, especially between the earlier radial corridors aligned along the railroad lines, and later, to some degree, along the electrical interurban railway lines which were in many instances important during the first four or five decades of the twentieth century.[6] The virtual ubiquity of the automobile, however, made possible the conversion to urban uses of vast areas of land not near the rail lines, and at much lower densities than was previously feasible. Between 1920 and 1980, the number of passenger automobiles increased from 8.1 million to 122.6 million.[7]

The increased accessibility of land on and beyond the peripheries of the urban areas of the United States as a result of the automobile was reinforced by a number of changes in population trends and "life styles," resulting in a rapid spatial expansion of the urban areas. During the depression decade of the 1930s, the annual average rate of population increase was 0.74 percent. It reached 1.38 percent during the war and immediate postwar period of the 1940s and 1.71 percent during the 1950s. Then it declined rapidly; during the 1960s it was 1.26 percent and in the seventies the annual rate of population increase in the nation had almost reached the low level of the 'thirties.[8] In spite of continued

---

5. Charles C. Colby, "Centrifugal and Centripetal Forces in Urban Geography," *Annals of the Association of American Geographers* 23, no. 1 (March 1933): 1-20.

6. Marion Clawson, *Suburban Land Conversion in the United States* (Baltimore and London: Johns Hopkins Press); Louis H. Masotti and Jeffrey K. Haddon, eds., *The Urbanization of the Suburbs* (Beverly Hills, Cal., and London: Sage Publications, 1973); Harold M. Mayer, *The Spatial Expression of Urban Growth,* Association of American Geographers Commission on College Geography, Resource Paper no. 7 (Washington, D.C.: 1969); George W. Hilton and John F. Due, *The Electric Interurban Railways In America* (Stanford, Cal.: Stanford University Press, 1960).

7. *MVMA Motor Vehicle Facts & Figures '81* (Detroit: Motor Vehicle Manufacturers Association of the United States, Inc., 1981), p. 16.

8. U.S. Department of Commerce, Bureau of the Census, *Social Indicators III*

increase in population although at a decreasing rate during the sixties and seventies the number of household units increased rapidly. This was due in large measure to a decrease in the number of persons occupying a housing unit: from an average of 3.67 in 1940 to 3.14 in 1970 and 2.75 in 1980.[9] This decrease in size of housing units was reflected in a sustained demand for more units and thus for urbanized land, although at decreasing density. At the same time that the newly-urbanized peripheral areas were being developed at lower densities than those previously urbanized, the inner portions of most central cities were experiencing a decline in density due to voluntary out-migration, relocation resulting from urban renewal, highway construction, and other programs involving land clearance, and rising affluence resulting in "undoubling" of families formerly forced by economic circumstances to live together.

These shifts in urban population within the United States--and Canada as well--rendered the conventional definitions of "city" and "urban" obsolete, except in the former instance with regard to administrative areas of municipalities. New definitions were required.

### Urbanized Areas

In 1950, the U.S. Census recognized the disparities between the municipal boundaries on the one hand and the extent of the built-up urban areas on the other. It designated a series of "urbanized areas" around each of the central cities of 50,000 or more population, defined in terms of density of population and development. Both because of the increase of population within the expanding urban areas and because of the addition of newly-recognized urban areas (as central cities passed the 50,000 population threshold), the population resident in such areas increased from 69.2 million in 1950 to 118.4 million in 1970 and 139.0 million in 1980, at which time the urbanized area population constituted 61.4 percent of the total population of the nation. It is noteworthy that during the 1970s the urbanized area population, though increasing, was increasing at a slower rate than during the two previous decades, as the urban fringe areas expanded more rapidly than the urbanized areas themselves.

---

(Washington: U.S. Government Printing Office, 1980), p. 41.

9. U.S. Department of Commerce, Bureau of the Census *Provisional Estimates of Social, Economic, and Housing Characteristics, States and Selected Standard Metropolitan Statistical Areas PHC80-S1-1* (Washington: U.S. Government Printing Office March 1982), p. 3.

Because of the use of a density threshold definition, the urbanized areas changed following each census, as a result of the outward expansion of the urban population. The comparison of changes within given areas was difficult because of the shifting urban area boundaries. There was thus a need for delimiting areas with more constant boundaries, in order to permit inter-censal comparisons of functionally analogous areas through times and to utilize the more numerous statistical series which are based upon counties.

### Metropolitan Areas

Along with the urbanized areas the U.S. Census in 1950 recognized another statistical definition of urban areas: the Standard Metropolitan Area (SMA), which in 1960 and subsequently was identified as the Standard Metropolitan Statistical Area (SMSA). These areas consist of whole counties which are areas related to one or more "central cities" with a minimum population of 50,000. Each SMSA consists of the county containing the central city or cities, together with contiguous or adjacent counties having a high degree of social and economic integration with the central counties, as evidenced by such criteria as non-agricultural employment and commuting across the county boundaries. Such a definition has the advantage over the Urbanized Area definition of less frequent shifting of the outer boundaries, inclusion of lower-density but urban-oriented areas on the urban fringes, and utilization of much more numerous statistical series than those available for the urbanized areas. The principal disadvantage is that in including only whole counties, non-urban portions of counties are also included. As central cities pass the 50,000 population threshold and as peripheral expansion of urban-oriented population takes place beyond the SMSA county boundaries, new SMSAs are added, and additional counties are included in previously-delimited SMSAs. In a few instances, SMSAs have been divided, along county boundaries.

The number of Standard Metropolitan Areas in the United States increased from 168 in 1950 to 212 in 1960, 243 in 1970, and 318 in 1980, in addition to five in Puerto Rico. The population resident in such areas increased from 84.5 million in 1950 to 169.4 million in 1980: a doubling in thirty years. The metropolitan population constituted 55.8 percent of the national population in 1950 and rose to 74.8 percent in 1980; thus within three decades the proportion of U.S. residents in metropolitan areas rose from slightly over half to just under three-fourths. In Canada, the proportion of the

population in metropolitan areas is only slightly less than in the
United States: in 1976, just over three-fourths lived in urban
centers, while 55 percent were resident in 23 Census Metropolitan
Areas (CMAs).[10]

### Standard Consolidated Statistical Areas

Although cross-commuting between and among central cities of
nearby metropolitan areas was not uncommon during the era when
railroad transportation was the dominant passenger mode, the advent
of modern highways, and especially the limited-access interstates
and other express highways, accelerated the dispersion of
population. Such highways often created new axes of urban expansion
away from railroad lines or where they did not provide commuter
service. In other instances they were constructed parallel to
existing rail lines and thus reinforced and expanded the earlier
axes. Many medium-sized and smaller cities became foci for the new
highways, which, to a large extent, replicted the earlier role of
the commuter railroads in directing the spatial patterns of urban
expansion. The greater flexibility of the highways and the greater
distance, in many instances, that could be traversed within a given
time accelerated the outward movement of the urban periphery. Many
urbanized areas reached outward along the transportation axes toward
one another and sometimes overlapped with the cross-commuting in
both directions. There thus became evident a need for an additional
definition of urban areas in order to recognize the cross-commuting
and the communality of adjacent metropolitan areas.

Accordingly, the U.S. Office of Management and Budget, which
had previously identified the SMSAs, delimited, in 1975, thirteen
multi-metropolitan areas, called Standard Consolidated Statistical
Areas (SCSAs), each of which consists of two or more Standard
Metropolitan Statistical Areas (SMSAs), one of which must have a
population of at least a million. Following the 1980 census, an
additional four such areas were identified. In 1980, the Standard
Consolidated Statistical Areas had a population of 71.6 million, or
42.3 percent of the total metropolitan population and 31.7 percent
of the national population.

### Intermetropolitan Coalescence and Growth Corridors

The tendency for urban nuclei to develop along lineal
corridors has long been recognized.[11] Coastal and river ports tend

---

10. Richard E. Preston, "The Evolution of Urban Canada: The Post-1867
Period," in *Readings in Canadian Geography*, ed. Robert M. Irving (Toronto: Holt,
Rinehart and Winston of Canada, Ltd., 1978), p. 28.

11. Harris and Ullman, "Nature of Cities," 9-10; John R. Borchert,

to have a lineal alignment. When railroads made accessible the inland areas and reduced or eliminated dependence upon water transportation, urban settlements tended to develop along the railroad routes, at division points and at more-or-less regular intervals where stations and often townsites were established. In the Midwest and the prairie provinces of Canada, town plats were developed at regular intervals around collection and delivery points established by the railroads, typically six miles apart, one in each township along the rail routes.[12] By the 1930s, highways were rapidly supplanting the railroads as the dominant intercity transportation mode for merchandise--freight other than bulk commodities--and for personal movement. In general, the burgeoning network of highways did not result in significant modifications in the spatial distribution of urban places, in spite of the fact that thousands of small urban places depended entirely upon automobiles, buses, and trucks for their external transportation. On the other hand, the highway system, before and after World War II, was responsible for many new strip developments along the radial routes, as well as along the circumferential and by-pass routes that were established primarily to permit "overhead" or through traffic to avoid the congestion of the central areas of intermediate towns and cities.

These commercial developments, along with numerous industrial clusters, including industrial "parks" or organized districts, were accompanied by, and often preceded by, residential developments on and beyond the urban peripheries. In many instances, the suburban and exurban expansion was the result of activities by large-scale developers. Freed from the need for proximity to the previously established rail routes, "leapfrogging" of these developments beyond the earlier edges of the built-up urban areas was common. Thus, vacant areas remained between these new developments and the older main urban mass, to be filled in later. In many instances, premature land subdivision took place, with subsequent development awaiting later swings of the real estate cycle.[13]

---

"American Metropolitan Evolution," *Geographical Review,* 57, no. 3 (July 1967): 301-332.

12. Paul Wallace Gates, *The Illinois Central Railroad and Its Colonization Work* (Cambridge, Mass.: Harvard University Press, 1934); Richard C. Overton, *Burlington West: A Colonization History of the Burlington Railroad* (Cambridge, Mass.: Harvard University Press, 1941).

13. Homer Hoyt, *One Hundred Years of Land Values in Chicago* (Chicago: University of Chicago Press, 1933); Herman G. Berkman, "Decentralization and Blighted Vacant Land," *Land Economics* 33, no. 3 (August 1956): 270-280.

Such developments, on and beyond the urban peripheries, were in some instances within the commuting areas of two or more metropolitan agglomerations. Typical examples include the "New Town" of Columbia, Maryland, whose residents commute to employment in both the Baltimore and Washington metropolitan areas, and the multinucleated urban complex of northeastern Ohio.[14]

Somewhat analogous are multi-nucleated complexes of medium-sized cities located within the overlapping automobile commuting areas of several central cities, wherein each of the cities lacks or has fewer of the urban functions than would be expected in cities of comparable size. In order to receive the goods and services of a typical city, residents must travel to two or more of the cities in the connurbation. A notable example is the complex of cities on the Piedmont of North Carolina, which has been called a "dispersed city."[15] As expansion takes place around such cities, it results in the filling in of formerly rural areas along the interconnecting highways, eventually tending to produce a more-or-less continuous multi-nucleated urban mass.

In many instances where the commuting zones and service areas of medium-sized or larger cities overlap, major new traffic generators tend to be located in the intermediate areas, thus resulting in attraction for many other land uses in their vicinities, thereby accelerating the process of inter-metropolitan coalescence. Industrial areas, such as those between Dallas and Fort Worth, Texas, in formerly rural locations, as well as major airports serving more than one metropolitan area, are examples. Among the latter are the twin-cities airport serving Minneapolis and St. Paul and inter-metropolitan airports located between Dallas and Fort Worth, Akron and Canton, Scranton and Wilkes Barre, and Baltimore and Washington, and the five major airports serving the Los Angeles-Long Beach metropolitan area. Other examples of important traffic generators--"magnets"--located within commuting zones of more than one metropolitan center are the Disney complex in central Florida, the Great America amusement park located exactly half way between the centers of Chicago and Milwaukee, and Chicago's O'Hare International Airport--the world' busiest--which attracts

---

14. Gurney Breckenfield, *Columbia and The New Cities* (New York: Ives Washburn, Inc., 1971); Harold M. Mayer and Thomas Corsi, "The Northeastern Ohio Urban Complex," chap. 3 of *Contemporary Metropolitan America, Vol. 3, Nineteenth Century Inland Centers and Ports,* ed. John S. Adams (Cambridge, Mass.: Ballinger Publishing Company, 1976), pp. 109-179.

15. F. Stuart Chapin, Jr. and Shirley F. Weiss, eds., *Urban Growth Dynamics in a Regional Cluster of Cities* (New York: John Wiley and Sons Inc., 1962); Charles R. Hayes, *The Dispersed City: The Case of Piedmont, North Carolina,* Research Paper no. 173 (Chicago: University of Chicago, Department of Geography, 1976).

substantial patronage from the Milwaukee area, thus reducing air service at Milwaukee's Mitchell Field to a level substantially below that which would be expected at the main airport of a city with comparable population and commercial-industrial activity. Large regional shopping malls represent another typical intermetropolitan function located along the axes connecting adjacent and nearby metropolitan centers.

Around these major traffic generators, other developments typically occur, attracted by the initial development, which acts as a catalyst, precipitating symbiotically related functions and land uses.

The United States Census reports on commuting patterns have made it possible to delimit and map what some geographers term the "Daily Urban System" (DUS), an area within which there is daily commuting to a central city or its metropolitan area. Well over ninety percent of the nation's population resides within a "DUS," while a substantial proportion is within the daily commuting radius of two or more metropolitan centers.[16]

Although multi-nucleated lineal corridors have long been recognized as distinctive patterns of urban occupance, the concept was given prominence following publication by Jean Gottman of his "Megalopolis," identifying the Boston-Washington axis along the "Fall Line" contact between the Appalachian piedmont and the Atlantic coastal plain.[17] Other studies soon followed the 1961 publication of Gottman's work. Among them are those of the Chicago-Milwaukee corridor,[18] the corridors across southern Michigan west of Detroit,[19] and the "Main Street" of Canada paralleling the St. Lawrence River, Lake Ontario, and Lake Erie.[20]

The Boston-Washington megalopolis contains the densest traffic by railroad, highway, and air in North America. During peak commuter hours each weekday, congestion in the vicinities of the

16. Brian J.L. Berry, *Metropolitan Area Definition: A Re-Evaluation of Concept and Statistical Practice,* Working Paper no. 28 (Washington, D.C.: Bureau of the Census, 1968).

17. Jean Gottman, *Megalopolis: The Urbanized Northeastern Seaboard of the United States* (New York: Twentieth Century Fund, 1961).

18. Irving Cutler, *The Chicago-Milwaukeeeee Corridor: A Geographic Study of Intermetropolitan Coalescence,* Studies in Geography no. 9 (Evanston, Ill.: Northwestern University, Department of Geography, 1965).

19. Constantinos A. Doxiadis, *Emergence and Growth of an Urban Region: The Developing Urban Detroit Area, Vol. I: Analysis* (Detroit: Detroit Edison Company, 1966).

20. Maurice Yeates, *Main Street: Windsor to Quebec City* (Ottawa: Macmillan Company of Canada, Ltd., 1975); Alexander S. Leman and Ingrid A. Leman, *Great Lakes Megalopolis: From Civilization to Ecumenization* (Ottawa: Ministry of State, Urban Affairs Canada, 1976); Mason Wade, ed., *The International Megalopolis* (Toronto: University of Toronto Press, for the University of Windsor, 1969).

public transportation terminals, at airports, and on the main
highways reaches saturation and delays are frequent. Senator
Claiborne Pell of Rhode Island, a frequent traveler to and from
Washington, inspired by Gottman's book, introduced and secured
passage by the Congress of a program for experimentation and
development of transportation facilities to relieve congestion and
facilitate interaction between and among the cities of
Megalopolis.[21] One significant result was improvement of the
principal railroad axis of the corridor, consisting of the former
New Haven Railroad northeast of New York City and the former
Pennsylvania Railroad between New York and Washington, both now
owned and operated by Amtrak, the National Railroad Passenger
Corporation. Improvement of the trackage and introduction of the
famous "metroliners" (high-speed trains) speeded up the rail service
and made it more competitive with the other transportation modes.
It stimulted, in turn, numerous studies of high-speed ground
transportation elsewhere in the United States. Most noteworthy
among them, in the early 1980s, is a feasibility study, in which
various interests, including Amtrak, are seriously considering
development of a high-speed rail line exclusively for passenger
traffic, similar to the *Shinkansen* intercity lines in Japan, for the
Los Angeles-San Diego corridor.

It became increasingly evident, especially after the 1980
census, that the definitions of urban and metropolitan areas in the
United States were once again becoming inappropriate. Metropolitan
areas of 50,000 population are, in significant respects other than
size, different from those of 500,000 or five million; further
differentiation was required. In 1983, therefore, a Federal
Committee on Standard Metropolitan Statistical Areas modified the
previous definitions and criteria in several respects. In addition
to changes in terminology (SMSAs, with some changes in criteria, are
designated as Metropolitan Statistical Areas or MSAs and SCSAs
become Consolidated Metropolitan Statistical Areas or CMSAs) the
metropolitan areas are subdivided into categories in accordance with
their respective populations. The new MSA definition includes areas
with a city of at least 50,000 population or an urbanized area of at
least 50,000 and a total MSA population or an urbanized area of at
least 100,000. The four MSA population levels, designated as levels
A, B, C, and D, include areas with populations of one million or
more, 250,000 to one million, 100,000 to 250,000, and less than

---

21. Senator Claiborne Pell, *Megalopolis Unbound:  The Supercity and the
Transportation of Tomorrow* (New York: Praeger, 1966).

100,000 respectively. A new designation was added: metropolitan areas included within CMSAs are designated as Primary Metropolitan Statistical Areas (PMSAs) (figure 17.1).

Under the revised definitions the number of metropolitan areas is somewhat less than those designated in accordance with the 1980 census: 257 rather than the previous 318 while the consolidated metropolitan areas number 23 in contrast to the 18 which were previously identified.[22]

## Slowing of Urban Growth

After the post-war "baby boom" of the late 1940s and the 1950s, the rate of growth of the urban population in the United States was less than the preceding period in each successive decade, both in absolute numbers and relative to the rate of growth of the national population, which itself was slowing up (table 17.1).

The census of 1980 revealed that, for the first time since the beginning of the nation, the rate of increase of the population of rural areas and small communities exceeded that of the large cities and metropolitan areas.[23] The latter, however, continued to grow, both because of the population growth of some of the metropolitan areas and because of the designation of new areas and of counties added to pre-existing metropolitan areas as the threshold requirements for metropolitan designations were reached.

Although the general trend since World War II has been for a slowing up in the rate of urbanization in the United States--and in Canada--there are numerous instances in which individual cities and metropolitan areas have not conformed. From decade to decade, urban areas which formerly showed rapid growth subsequently slowed down or even declined, while others, particularly in the South and West, increased their rates of growth, in some instances by several hundred percent.[24] The trends of earlier post-war decades generally continued in the 1970s. The national population increased by 11.4 percent during the 1970s, but there were substantial differences between the states and the several regions. During the decade, the West increased by 24.6 percent, greater than in any previous period, while the South also showed a greater increase than in earlier

---

22 . Federal Committee on Standard Metropolitan Statistical Areas, "The Metropolitan Statistical Area Classification: 1980 Official Standards and Related Documents," *Statistical Reporter* (December 1979): 33–45; "Documents Relating to the Metropolitan Statistical Area Classification for the 1980s," *Statistical Reporter* (August 1980): 335–383; U.S. Office of Management and Budget, Executive Office of the President, Press release, June 27, 1983.

23 . Philip M. Hauser, "The Census of 1980," *Scientific American* 245, no. 5 (November 1981): 53–61.

24 . John R. Borchert, "Instability in American Metropolitan Growth," *Geographical Review* 73, no. 2 (April 1983): 127–149.

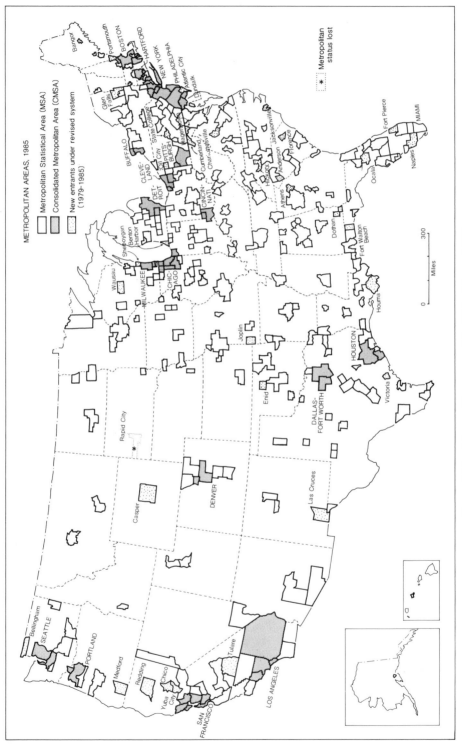

Figure 17.1.   Metropolitan areas of the United States, 1985

TABLE 17.1

URBAN POPULATION CHANGE IN THE UNITED STATES

1940-1980

| Year | Urban Population ('000) | Percent Change | U.S. Population ('000) | Percent Urban | Rate of Change in Urban Per- centage |
|------|-------------------------|----------------|------------------------|---------------|--------------------------------------|
| 1940 | 74,424 | - | 131,699 | 56.51 | - |
| 1950 | 96,468 | 29.62 | 150,697 | 64.01 | 13.27 |
| 1960 | 125,269 | 29.86 | 179,323 | 69.86 | 9.14 |
| 1970 | 149,325 | 19.20 | 203,235 | 73.47 | 5.17 |
| 1980 | 167,051 | 11.87 | 226,546 | 73.73 | 0.36 |

SOURCE:  Compiled from various reports of the U.S. Census.

decades: 20.0 percent. On the other hand, the traditional "core region" of the nation, the Northeast and North Central regions, reversed the upward trend in growth rates which preceded 1960 and subsequently lagged by increasing margins behind the national rate of population growth; during the 1970s the population of the Northeastern region increased by only 0.2 percent and the North Central region by 4.0 percent. By the late 1960s, California had overtaken New York as the most populous state, while numerous projections indicate that Texas and Florida will also overtake New York during the nineties if not sooner. Of all fifty states, California in 1980 had the highest proportion of its residents in urban areas, 91.3 percent; and both Florida and Texas substantially exceeded the national average of 73.7 percent urban.[25] The metropolitan area of Los Angeles overtook the Chicago metropolitan area as the nation's second most populous during the early 1960s, while the City of Los Angeles surpassed the City of Chicago as the second most populous city of the United States during the early 1980s. Many other cities of the South and West experienced rapid population growth: Houston, for example, increased its metropolitan population from 1.43 million in 1960 to 2.91 million in 1980, more than doubling in twenty years. The inter-regional differentials in growth rates of cities and metropolitan areas are accompanied by rapid transformations of the nature of urban America; the "sunbelt" cities, in general differ in major respects from the older cities of the Northeast and Midwest.

### Causes of Interegional, Interurban, and Intraurban Population Shifts

Migration occurs in response to differences in opportunities from place to place and region to region. These opportunities are economic, social, and cultural. Changes in social conditions, such as earlier retirements, which prevailed during most of the postwar period, have been reflected in migration of retirees to more favorable climates than that of the Northeast and Midwest. Social security and more liberal pension payments have facilitated this movement, as has, also, the increasing emphasis upon the quality of life, both for retirees and for those employed. The amenities--cultural, social, and recreational opportunities--became increasingly important.[26] In spite of the fact that most

---

25. David C. Perry and Alfred J. Watkins, eds., *The Rise of the Sunbelt Cities* (Beverly Hills, Cal.: Sage Publications, 1977); Larry Sawyers and William K. Tabb, eds., *Sunbelt, Snowbelt: Urban Development and Regional Restructuring* (New York and Oxford: Oxford University Press, 1984).

26. Edward L. Ullman, "Amenities as a Factor in Regional Growth," *Geographical Review* 44, no. 1 (January 1954): 119-132.

metropolitan areas in the United States and Canada with large
populations grew less rapidly in recent decades than did
medium-sized cities and metropolitan areas, the newer cities of the
South and West generally experienced rapid growth if their base was
already large. Economic opportunities are cumulative, because
increased population represents expanding markets and at the same
time creates demand for, and labor force to produce, goods and
services required by the increased population. Specialized
services, specialized workers, and industrial and commercial
linkages proliferate. The "multiplier effect" has been the subject
of numerous studies by geographers, economists, and others.[27] The
variety and diversity of opportunities, economic and otherwise,
varies with the size of the urban population; thus the gravitative
pull of large cities with increasing population is in large measure
a function of the population size.[28] Many urban functions require a
high minimum threshold of population in order to be present at all.

Technological changes have facilitated the shift of urban
population from the "core region" long identified by geographers in
the northeast and midwest to the south and west. Air conditioning
made the warm areas more comfortable and habitable; improvements in
transportation made them more accessible. The automobile and modern
highways facilitated the areal spread of the rapidly-growing cities,
resulting in increasing amenity through lower densities both in the
"sunbelt" cities and in the peripheral areas of the older
metropolitan complexes which expanded rapidly once the wartime
constraints upon building were eliminated. Technological advances
in telecommunications and the increasing use of computers also
tended to result in lower urban densities.

The virtual ubiquity of the automobile has exerted a dominant
influence upon the internal structure of American cities during the
past four decades, although its influence was already evident before
World War II. Until then, mass transportation dominated both
inter-city and intra-city movement. Many metropolitan areas, and
smaller cities as well, had commuter railroad service, and during

27. Theodore Lane, "The Urban Base Multiplier: An Evaluation of the State
of the Art," *Land Economics* 42, no. 3 (August 1966), pp. 339-347; Koichi Mera, "On
the Urban Agglomeration and Economic Efficiency," *Economic Development and
Cultural Change* 21, no. 2 (January 1973): 309-313; George J. Papageorgiou,
"Spatial Externalities: I, Theory; II. Application," *Annals of the Association of
American Geographers,* vol. 68, no. 4 (December 1978): 465-492.

28. Harris, "Market as a Factor;" Gerald A.P. Carrothers, "An Historical
Review of the Gravity and Potential Concepts of Human Interaction," *Journal of the
American Institute of Planners* 22, no. 2 (Spring 1956): 94-102; Fred Lukermann and
Phillip W. Porter, "Gravity and Potential Models in Economic Geography," *Annals of
the Association of American Geographers* 50, no. 4 (December 1960): 493-504; Peter
F. Colwell, "Central Place Theory and the Simple Economic Foundations of the
Gravity Model," *Journal of Regional Science* 22, no. 4 (November 1982): 541-546.

the first few decades of the twentieth century, the inter-urban electric railway also was important in influencing the spread of the cities.[29] Urban development tended to be axial and radial, and the characteristic pattern of the built-up areas consisted of a series of wedges of older high-density development.[30] Not only did the rail lines stimulate axial development in the peripheral and suburban areas; they also, in the form of rapid transit elevated and subway lines in the larger cities and street railways in most cities of all but the smallest size, encouraged internal axial development of high-density residential and other land uses.[31]

The motor vehicle resulted in significant change in the internal land use and functional area patterns of American cities, superseding the fixed-route mass carriers in most instances. In 1940, the United States had 27 million motor vehicles--automobiles, trucks, and buses--or one for every five persons, while in 1980 the number was 123 million, or well over one for every two persons.[32] To accommodate these vehicles, the nation had nearly four million miles of roads and streets, providing an average of 56 yards of roadway for each. Between 85 and 90 percent of all passenger miles of intercity travel is on the highways. The motor vehicle has also transformed the life-styles of the smaller communities by enormously increasing mobility and accessibility. The former dichotomy between urban and rural life-styles has considerably less significance now than in the past.[33] Radio, and subsequently television, together with the accompanying spread of mass merchandising, has largely homogenized the American culture. More than 90 percent of the population lives within one hour or less commuting time of the employment, social, and cultural resources of a metropolitan area. Thus, not only has cultural diffusion been facilitated, but concentration has also resulted since establishments have improved access to a wider area from which to draw their labor force. In some instances, employers and institutions in two, three, or more

29. Sam B. Warner, Jr., *Streetcar Suburbs: The Process of Growth in Boston 1870-1900* (Cambridge, Mass.: Harvard University Press and MIT Press, 1962); Hilton and Due, *Interurban Railways*.

30. Homer Hoyt, *The Structure and Growth of Residential Neighborhoods in American Cities* (Washington, D.C.: Federal Housing Administration, 1939).

31. Edwin H. Spengler, *Land Values in New York in Relation to Transit Facilities* (New York: Columbia University Press, 1930); Charles Lockwood, *Manhattan Moves Uptown* (Boston: Houghton Mifflin Company, 1976); Hoyt, *One Hundred Years of Land Values*; James Leslie Davis, *The Elevated System and the Growth of Northern Chicago*, Studies in Geography no. 10 (Evanston, Ill.: Northwestern University, Department of Geography, 1965).

32. *Motor Vehicle Facts & Figures '81* (Detroit: Motor Vehicle Manufacturers Association of the United States, Inc., 1981).

33. Norman T. Moline, *Mobility and the Small Town 1900-1930*, Research Paper no. 132 (Chicago: University of Chicago, Department of Geography, 1971).

metropolitan areas compete for the employment, trade, and patronage of the population within overlapping complementary regions.[34]

## Changes in the Characteristic Urban Spatial Models

These forces and trends have produced significant modifications in the internal spatial patterns of land uses, land values, and functions within American cities and metropolitan areas. The centrifugal and centripetal forces which were described in Charles Colby's classic paper in 1933 still work.[35] The balance between these opposing forces, however, has shifted notably in most cities, and the resultant spatial forms of the urban areas are in some ways significantly different. Since no large cities can be transformed within the span of a few decades because of the inertia and momentum of existing infrastructure, sociological affinities, and institutions, the classic forms--circumferential, wedge, and multiple nuclei--still exist in combination in most cities and metropolitan areas, but with important modifications.

Throughout the past four decades, cities have continued to expand rapidly in area by extension of the radial tentacles which were originally based upon mass transit facilities and pre-automobile roads, by development of new tentacles especially along the newer express and interstate highways, and by development of newly urbanized land in the interstitial areas between the older radii. In many instances, the interstitial development has been facilitated by circumferential arterial highways or "beltways" forming, with the radials, a spiderweb pattern.[36] Intersections of major highways, both of the modern expressway or freeway type and of conventional design, have become the loci for traffic-generating nuclei, including shopping centers, office clusters, high-density high-rise and other residential developments, and institutions such as universities. Many of these characteristically represent new forms, and in some instances functions as well, which were rare or unknown a half century ago.

## Changing Metropolitan Land Use Morphology

### Residential Areas

During the depression decade of the 1930s, the federal governments of both the United States and Canada each initiated

---

34. Mayer and Corsi, "Northeastern Ohio Urban Complex," pp. 109-177.

35. Colby, "Centrifugal and Centripetal Forces."

36. U.S. Department of Transportation Federal Highway Administration, *The Land Use and Urban Development Impacts of Beltways* (Washington: U.S. Government Printing Office, 1980); Michael Chernoff, "The Effects of Superhighways in Urban Areas," *Urban Affairs Quarterly* 16, no. 3 (March 1981): 317-336.

policies and programs relating to urban development, especially
housing, which substantially transformed urban spatial patterns
during the postwar era.  In the United States, the Federal Housing
Administration was established to administer a program of
government-guaranteed loans to financial institutions, whereby such
institutions were protected against default of the mortgages which
they issued to homeowners.  Thus, middle-income families and
individuals, who could otherwise not afford the kind of housing
which they desired, were offered loans at lower interest rates and
with longer periods of amortization.  Although the effects of this
policy were not great during the 1930s when even these loans were
commonly insufficient to produce much new housing and during the war
period when restrictions on materials and labor largely prevented
civilian home construction, the pent-up postwar demand for housing
combined with the availability of lower-cost financing to produce
millions of new homes.

The new housing was principally on and beyond the peripheries
of the cities.  The postwar baby boom demanded a rapid acceleration
of the rate of building.  Because many cities, especially in the
East and Midwest, were underbounded, few sites were available within
the "central cities" of the metropolitan areas or in some of the
contiguous older suburban communities.  Economies of scale
encouraged large-scale mass-production of housing, and in large part
because of federal actions, supplemented in some instances by the
states, financing of large-scale subdivision developments for
housing was relatively easy for large operators.  They, in turn
required large tracts of land, which generally were available only
on the fringes of the previously urbanized areas and beyond.
Although residential construction is proceeding at a slower rate in
the early 1980s, the suburban expansion continues.  Even though the
rate of population increase of many metropolitan areas is less than
before, the conversion of rural land to urban uses has not ceased.
Family sizes are smaller, and many single persons and unattached
groups seek housing units.  The resulting demand is for fewer rooms
per housing unit, but the number of units relative to the population
is increasing.[37] Thus, even in the face of a slowing up or even a
reduction of population in some metropolitan areas, the rate of
conversion of land beyond the former built-up urbanized areas

37 . Bureau of the Census, *Social Indicators III.*

continues to increase.[38] Most of these areas are developed with lower densities than those characteristic of earlier times.

The landscape of those portions of cities and metropolitan areas developed in recent decades, and especially under the various governmental programs, is quite different than that of earlier suburban developments. Although the rectangular street pattern still prevails in many places, most of the suburban and outlying areas developed since the time of World War II, and a few earlier, conform to the "neighborhood unit" principle. Indeed, neighborhood unit development patterns are virtually mandatory if federal financial assistance is involved. The neighborhood unit, as a physical concept and pattern, was popularized by Ebenezer Howard in England in the late 1890s in the context of the "Garden City." It consists of an area, the extent of which varies with the overall density of the development, all portions of which are within walking distance. Arterial roads and streets are on the edges of the neighborhood, and the streets within it are curved, looped, and have intersections and widths of such character as to discourage through traffic while providing access within the area. Centrally located are civic buildings and spaces, including a neighborhood school, sites for other civic buildings, churches, interior parks, and playgrounds. Small shopping clusters are located at or near the corners of each neighborhood. Several neighborhoods which are contiguous form community areas, serviced by larger shopping clusters, a high school, and other facilities and functions which require higher thresholds of support than those available within individual neighborhoods; thus neighborhoods nest within communities in a hierarchical relationship.[39]

The neighborhood unit concept was proposed for application in centrally-located urban areas where large-scale demolition and rebuilding was planned.[40] In post-war planning for urban areas, generally, the neighborhood unit concept was superimposed upon older and deteriorated areas in the process of urban renewal.[41] But its most widespread application was in suburban and peripheral areas, where extensive new developments were constructed to accommodate the

38 . Clawson, *Suburban Land Conversion*; A. Allan Schmid, *Converting Land from Rural to Urban Uses* (Washington, D.C.: Resources for the Future, Inc. 1968).

39 . Ebenezer Howard, *Garden Cities of Tomorrow,* reprinted (London: Faber and Faber, 1951).

40 . Clarence Arthur Perry, "The Neighborhood Unit: A Scheme of Arrangement for the Family-Life Community" in *Neighborhood and Community Planning,* vol. 7 of the Regional Survey of New York and Its Environs (New York: Regional Plan Association, 1929).

41 . Miles Colean, *Renewing Our Cities* (New York: Twentieth Century Fund, 1953).

huge post-war demand for housing.[42]

Concommitant with the building of large expanses of tract housing in many instances was the provision of shopping centers, industrial buildings, and other facilities which not only supplied the residents of the tracts and of other areas nearby, but also furnished employment both to the local residents and to commuters from other parts of the respective metropolitan areas. Reverse commuting from more centrally located areas as well as peripheral movements between home and work, supplemented, and in some instances largely supplanted the more common commuting patterns toward the urban cores.[43]

Development of massive relatively low-density suburban and peripheral tracts was regarded by many planners in the immediate post-war period as a partial solution to the problem of deteriorated areas in the "inner cities," where congestion was thought to be associated with concentrations of social, economic, and physical problems. The "new towns" as conceived by Ebenezer Howard in England at the turn of the century, and which were proliferating there after World War II, were to siphon off substantial numbers of persons from the older congested areas of the large cities and provide lower-density living conditions as well as employment opportunities. They were regarded as partially independent spatial units minimizing the need for commuting long distances between home and work, while at the same time providing access to nearby open country. Greenbelts--permanently preserved open land--were to separate each of the new towns from the others and main urban mass of the central city.

In the United States, a few small neighborhood units, such as Garden City, New York, and Radurn, New Jersey, were constructed prior to World War II, while the federal government built three "new towns" in the vicinities of Washington, Cincinnati and Milwaukee.[44] After the war, with encouragement from the federal government, largely through the mortage guarantee programs of the Federal Housing Administration and the Veterans Administration, and stimulated by the proliferation of new express highways, a number of

---

42. Edward P. Eichler and Marshall Kaplan, *The Community Builders* (Berkeley: University of California Press, 1967).

43. Edward J. Taaffe, Barry J. Garner, and Maurice H. Yeates, *The Peripheral Journey to Work: A Geographic Consideration* (Evanston, Ill.: Northwestern University Press, 1963).

44. Albert Mayer, "Greenbelt Towns Revisited," reprinted from *Journal of Housing* 24, nos. 1, 2, and 3 (January, February, and March 1967) (Washington, D.C.: Department of Housing and Urban Development, 1968); Joseph L. Arnold, *The New Deal in the Suburbs: A History of the Greenbelt Town Program 1935-1954*q (Columbus: Ohio State University Press, 1972).

"new towns" were developed by private enterprise. Some, such as the
Levittowns in the fringe areas of New York and Philadelphia, were
not substantially different from the "urban sprawl" which
characterized much of suburbia. Others, however, more nearly
resembled the new towns of postwar Britain and other countries, with
adjacent open areas, with interior shopping centers, and with
inclusion of areas for industry. One of the first was Park Forest,
Illinois, south of Chicago. It was followed by two of the best
known: Reston, Virginia, near the outer fringe of the commuting area
of Washington, D.C., and Columbia, Maryland, near Baltimore but also
within the commuting zone of Washington.[45]

More recently, the "new towns" concept has been subject to
criticism, because, far from needing reductions in population to
relieve overcrowding, many of the central cities, especially of the
older metropolitan areas, as well as some in the newer large cities
of the South and West, find that their fiscal problems are
exascerbated by out-migration, and major urban policy has shifted,
with increased emphasis upon measures to encourage re-population of
the central cities, and especially of their inner portions. In the
United States, the new towns movement has slowed to a virtual
halt.[46] The movement away from the central cities toward the outer
suburban areas and beyond, sometimes called "counterurbanization,"
however, aside from the new towns, gained considerable momentum
during the 1970s and early 1980s.

The diversities among suburban communities, to which Chauncy
Harris called attention long ago, continues to characterize
metropolitan economic, social, and spatial patterns.[47] On the other
hand, individual suburbs still tend to be relatively homogeneous
with respect to social, economic, and ethnic characteristics.[48]
Federal policy now mandates "open housing," in which discrimination
because of racial, ethnic, or other grounds is prohibited.[49]

---

45. Breckenfield, *Columbia and the New Cities.*

46. James A. Clapp, *New Towns and Urban Policy* (New York: Dunellen Company,
1971).

47. Chauncy D. Harris, "Suburbs," *American Journal of Sociology* 49, no. 1
(May 1943): 1-13.

48. Masotti and Hadden, *Urbanization of the Suburbs*; William H. Whyte Jr.,
*The Organization Man* (New York: Simon and Schuster, 1956); Herbert J. Gans, *the
Levittowners: How People Live and Politic in Suburbia* (New York: Pantheon Books,
1967).

49. Thomas A. Clark, *Blacks in Suburbs: A National Perspective* (Piscataway,
N.J.: Rutgers University Center for Urban Policy Research, 1979); Marilyn A.
Brown, "A Typology of Suburbs and Its Public Policy Implications," *Urban Geography*
2, no. 4 (October-December 1981): 288-310; Patricia Gober and Michelle Behr,
"Central Cities and Suburbs as Distinct Place Types: Myth or Fact?," *Economic
Geography* 58, no. 4 (October 1982): 371-385.

Not only have suburban areas tended toward greater
diversification than formerly, but the suburban and fringe areas
have also developed new spatial forms.[50] Four decades ago, the
typical suburban pattern consisted of radial tentacles, with
railroads having commuter service, and highways, constituting the
axes, and with clusters of commercial and high-density residential
structures along the radial routes adjacent to the train stations
and highway intersections.[51] With the ubiquity of the automobile,
much of the subsequent suburban development occurred between the
earlier axes. Thus, an exponential increase in land accessible for
urbanization occurred, and, at the same time, development took place
at generally lower densities than formerly. Combined with rising
affluence, the "American dream" of a single-family detached house on
a quarter-acre parcel was, for millions, able to be realized. The
early 1980s, however, witnessed rapid inflation, and high interest
rates, even with government-backed mortgages, deterred more and more
families from buying such homes. Two suburban residential types of
developments became widespread: higher-density clusters, including
attached single-family homes and apartment buildings, commonly under
condominium type tenure rather than the customary single ownership;
and pre-fabricated housing including "mobile homes" sited in
high-density "mobile home parks."[52]

Along with peripheral expansion of residential areas,
commercial, industrial, and institutional functions and land uses
also developed rapidly on and beyond the urban peripheries. Retail
merchandising and personal and professional service establishments
accompanied the expanding population. In many instances these
establishments selected and developed suburban sites, where they
could obtain larger land areas at lower cost, and with more
favorable constraints, than was possible at locations closer to, or
within, the central cities. Lower taxes, as well, contributed to
the suburban expansion of non-residential as well as residential
activity.

---

50. Peter O. Muller, *The Outer City: The Geographical Consequences of the
Urbanization of the Suburbs,* Resource Paper no. 75-2 (Washington, D.C.:
Association of American Geographers, 1976).

51. Robert C. Klove, *The Park Ridqge-Barrington Area: A Study of
Residential Land Patterns and Problems in Suburban Chicago* (Chicago: University of
Chicago, Department of Geography, 1942); Charles R. Hayes, "Suburban Residential
Land Values along the C.B. & Q. Railroad," *Land Economics* 33, no. 2 (May 1957):
177-181.

52. Margaret J. Drury, *Mobile Homes: The Unrecognized Revolution in
American Housing* (New York: Praeger, 1972).

## Commercial Forms

One of the most characteristic of the urban forms to emerge
after World War II is the planned shopping center. The older
retailing pattern, developed largely before the dominance of the
automobile, consisted of a hierarchy of commercial clusters, from
the neighborhood cluster, to the community-sized cluster, and the
regional shopping area, all however, subordinate to the central
business district.[53] The hierarchical arrangement of retail and
service centers within urban areas was, and is, analogous to the
central place hierarchy among trade centers within a region as
recognized by Walter Christaller in 1933. The development of retail
and service clusters within metropolitan areas, including both
central cities and suburbs during the past four decades, conforms
generally to the same pattern, but the forms of the individual
clusters depart radically from those of the past. During the era of
mass transit dominance, the clusters tended to be localized at the
intersections of major street railway routes, centering on a
transfer corner and radiating out along the intersecting streets,
declining in intensity with increasing distance. Attenuated ribbons
or strips of commercial land uses and activities tended to be
situated along the major arterial transit routes.

Later, the ribbons or strips continued to develop, but mainly
oriented to the highways, other than the limited access expressways.
Fast-food merchandisers, automobile-oriented service stations,
salesrooms, motels, and other retail and service establishments,
relatively unknown decades ago, have transformed the landscape along
the highways in and near cities. But the highest proportion--well
over half--of the retail sales in the nation occur in planned
shopping centers. These centers, like their unplanned predecessors,
range from the small local center to the massive regional center,
the concept of which spread rapidly.[54]

Large regional centers individually may contain as many as two
million square feet of selling space, five or six large department
stores, a hundred or more specialty shops, offices, restaurants,
cinemas, and interior plazas which serve as centers of socializing
and, often, as the locale of entertainment. The shopping centers
consist of an island of commercial establishments surrounded by a

53. Harold M. Mayer, "Patterns and Recent Trends of Chicago's Outlying
Business Centers," *Journal of Land & Public Utility Economics* 18, no. 1 (February
1942): 4-16; Homer Hoyt, "Classifications and Significant Characteristics of
Shopping Centers," *Appraisal Journal* 26, no. 2 (1958): 214-222.

54. Yehoshua S. Cohen, *Diffusion of an Innovation in an Urban System: The
Spread of Planned Regional Shopping Centers in the United States 1949-1968*
Research Paper no. 140 (Chicago: University of Chicago, Department of Geography,
1972).

sea of parking for as many as two thousand cars.[55] Commonly, these centers are developed in advance of residential development nearby and may serve as catalysts for such development.

Somewhat analogous to the planned regional shopping center is the free-standing, large, mass-merchandising establishment. Some are conventional department stores, but increasingly common are discount stores, which carry a broad line of merchandise. Other specialize in more limited lines. Many have 100,000 square feet of selling area or more and provide parking for hundreds, in some instances thousands, of cars. Many are outlets for regional or national chains, and in many ways they compete with the conventional department stores and the large planned shopping centers.

### New Industrial Forms

The suburban areas are increasingly the locus of manufacturing and other industrial establishments. Developments in freight transportation have facilitated the dispersion of industry out of the central urban locations along railroad lines and waterfronts, except for those industries which receive or ship large volumes of bulk commodities. Truck trailers on rail flatcars (TOFC) and containers moving in both domestic and international trade (COFC) together constitute the fastest growing portion of America's railroad traffic, providing to the railroads an amount of revenue second only to coal.[56] The transformation of the physical handling of freight--intermodalism--is both a cause and an effect of the dispersion of industry from central to peripheral urban locations and often from large cities to smaller communities.[57]

At the beginning of the twentieth century the railroads were the principal instruments for development of organized industrial districts, in which individual establishments would increase their efficiency by mutual proximity. This enabled "externalities," services which they utilized in common, to be more economically provided. Costs of transfer of goods among symbiotically related or linked establishments within the district could be carried out with minimal time and cost; and employee and executive amenities, such as financial, engineering, and protective services as well as

55. William Applebaum, *Shopping Center Strategy: A Case Study of the Planning Location, and Development of the Del Monte Center, Monterey California* (New York: International Council of Shopping Centers, 1970); George Sternlieb and James W. Hughes, *Shopping Centers U.S.A.* (Piscataway, N.J.: Rutgers University Center for Urban Policy Research, 1981).

56. *Yearbook of Railroad Facts 1982* (Washington: Association of American Railroads, 1982).

57. Robert L. Wrigley Jr., "Organized Industrial Districts with Special Reference to the Chicago Area," *Journal of Land and Public Utility Economics* 23, no. 2 (May 1947): 180-198.

utilities, could be provided jointly for the participating establishments. Among the services were, commonly, union railroad freight terminals and pickup and delivery drayage services. Later, especially after World War II, with the increased importance of truck and intermodal movements, many organized industrial districts (industrial "parks" as many of them were designated) were located at some distance from the railroads, since they could rely upon truck and intermodal movements. One result was the decline and abandonment of many formerly industrial center-city locations, which then offered opportunities for redevelopment for non-industrial uses.[58]

The organized industrial "parks" developed in recent decades differ in several respects from the earlier ones, aside from their suburban and peripheral locations. The structures are predominantly single-story, contrasting with the older multi-story manufacturing and loft buildings. The newer developments contain more open land utilized for parking, storage, attractive landscaping, and other amenities. Commonly, storage and processing of goods for metropolitan distribution represents half or more of the total activity in such districts. In some instances, proximity to an airport has been a locational factor, both for personnel travel and for the shipment and receipt of goods.[59]

### Office Environments

Although offices of large companies engaged in regional, national, and international businesses were not unknown in suburban areas and smaller communities previously, recent decades have seen a proliferation of administrative establishments of firms in locations other than the traditional central business districts. Modern communications technology has reduced, and in many instances eliminated, the need for proximity among many such establishments. Large clusters of office headquarters have developed in and near the older suburban centers, as in Evanston, Illinois and Clayton, Missouri.[60] Almost every large city has such clusters in its suburban areas. As with the deconcentration of industry within

---

58. Harold M. Mayer, "Changing Railroad Patterns in Major Gateway Cities," *Applied Geography Conferences, Papers* (Binghamton: State University of New York at Binghamton, 1979): 106-122.

59. Truman A. Hartshorn, "Industrial/Office Parks: A New Look for the City," *Journal of Geography* 72, no. 1 (January-February 1973): 33-45; Harold M. Mayer, "Centex Industrial Park: An Organized Industrial District," in *Focus on Geographic Activity,* ed. Richard S. Thoman (New York: McGaw-Hill 1964): 135-145; John R. Bale, "Toward a Geography of the Industrial Estate," *Professional Geographer* 26, no. 3 (August 1974): 291-297.

60. Earl W. Kersten, Jr., and D. Reid Ross, "Clayton: A New Metropolitan Focus in the St.Louis Area," *Annals of the Association of American Geographers* 58, no. 4 (December 1968): 637-649.

large metropolitan areas, much of the office deconcentration has been stimulated by the creation of "office parks," within which establishments, with or without functional linkages, can locate in controlled environments with compatable neighbors and with mutually required external facilities provided by the developer or the district's organization.[61]

A significant proportion of the newer office clusters is located in proximity to airports. Chicago's O'Hare and Atlanta's Hartsfield international airports, Los Angeles International and the Dallas-Forth Worth Airport, among others, have been the catalysts for nearby concentrations of corporate offices, and, associated with them, hotels, motels, numerous service businesses, and intermodal terminals. O'Hare alone employs over 30,000 people within its boundaries, and many more work in the immediate vicinity. The airports themselves constitute, in most metropolitan areas, the largest single tract of land in single ownership and control. The deregulation of airlines in the late 1970s has further stimulated deconcentration of business and industry from the older and more traditional sites, including central business districts and central city industrial areas. The airlines, old and new, have tended to concentrate at fewer but larger hub airports, thereby stimulating relatively more rapid growth of industrial and business establishments in their vicinities than in the smaller cities with less scheduled air traffic. On the other hand, the abandonment of service to smaller communities by the large air carriers has produced a demand for expansion of the network of "third level" or commuter airlines, serving as feeders to the main hubs. Although some such services are guaranteed a federal subsidy for a short time, the flexibility and uncertainty of such services is not entirely satisfactory to the many business establishments in such communities. The result is that many firms have developed alternative air transportation, including fleets of private planes. Thus, not only do the major airports with trunk-line services attract business, but the general aviation airports also serve as attractions for decentralized business establishments.

---

61 . Hartshorn, "Industrial/Office Parks;" Wolfgang Quante, *The Exodus of Corporate Headquarters from New York City* (New York: Praeger Publishers, 1976); Thomas J. Baerwald, "The Emergence of a New 'Downtown,'" *Geographical Review* 68, no. 3 (July 1978); 308-318; R. Keith Semple and Alan G. Phipps, "The Spatial Evolution of Corporate Headquarters within an Urban System," *Urban Geography* 3, no. 3 (July-September 1982f): 258-279.

## The Core of the City

The decentralization of many businesses, manufacturing establishments, and other functions, both to outlying locations within the metropolitan areas and to smaller communities elsewhere, has been concommitant with changes in the roles and spatial structures of the central portions of many cities.

In most medium-sized and larger cities of the United States and Canada, the skyscraper still dominates the profile and marks the locus of the densest concentrations of office employment and commercial activity, other than retailing.[62]

The central business districts, especially in the large cities, have evolved from their earlier status as the dominant focus of many functions to primarily the locus of business activities.[63] Night-time activity in most central business districts is much less than formerly, as the entertainment function has deconcentrated to suburban areas and to homes (television). Retailing in most cities has substantially declined; cities as large as Detroit are now without a single major department store.

There seems to be a "critical mass" of city size, above which cities--especially primate cities of extensive regions--can attract meetings and convention trade; such cities have constructed large convention halls, and massive new hotels have thrived, at the same time that older ones, including some constructed as recently as the late 1940s, have suffered from obsolescence and have either undergone substantial modernization or have closed and been demolished. In some instances, hotels were converted into residential buildings, either for the private luxury market or as subsidized housing for the poor or elderly.

Changes in the spatial patterns of internal metropolitan transportation have also had important impacts upon the central business districts and their immediate surroundings. The decline of railroad intercity passenger travel and the growth of air transportation has not only shifted much commercial activity and associated convention and hotel facilities to the vicinities of the major airports, but has at the same time been in important respects responsible for the decline of those portions of the downtown areas in proximity to the former railroad depots, many of which have been

62. Jean Gottmann, "Why the Skyscraper?," *Geographical Review* 56, no. 2 (April 1966): 190-212; Larry R. Ford, "The Urban Skyline as a City Classification System," *Journal of Geography* 75, no. 3 (March 1976): 154-164.

63. William Goodwin, "The Management Center in the United States," *Geographical Review* 60, no. 1 (January 1965): 1-16; Leland S. Burns and Wing Ning Pang, "Big Business in the Big City: Corporate Headquarters in the CBD," *Urban Affairs Quarterly* 12, no. 4 (June 1977): 533-544.

replaced by vacant land awaiting redevelopment or by new commercial, residential, or recreational uses. Similarly, technological changes in water transportation, and especially the replacement of breakbulk handling of general cargo by containerization, has caused a shifting of former port terminal locations from downtown waterfronts to more extensive sites on and beyond the edges of the cities, commonly in the direction of open water.[64] Of more widespread significance is the superimposition upon the older pattern of streets in most cities of the modern express highways or "freeways," especially after passage of the 1956 act which authorized the Interstate system, nearly completed in the early 1980s. The expressways now constitute the major arteries in most medium and large-sized cities, supplementing and in many instances supplanting the older arterial streets. The new metropolitan highway pattern is that of a spiderweb, with the radials focusing upon the central business districts, but commonly not entering them. Rather, the highways are joined to distributor loop highways surrounding the central business districts and effectively marking their boundaries.[65] In many cities, the distributor loop expressways occupy the areas designated earlier as the "zone of wholesaling and light manufacturing" or as the "core fringe." Now largely cleared of the former multi-story loft buildings which predominated in such zones, the areas are typically occupied by fringe parking facilities, both structures and non-structural open areas, no longer in demand for central business district functions.

Ridership on mass transit declined steadily after the World War II peak but bottomed out and has slowly increased after the fuel crisis of 1973. In most cities, the transit routes, both bus and fixed-guideway, focus upon the core area. Thus they serve a decreasing proportion of the workplace locations. Recreational and social travel, furthermore, is almost entirely by automobile. With the increase in automobile use, parking problems were intensified, especially in high-density areas such as central business districts, outlying shopping concentrations of the conventional type and, in some cities, high-rise apartment areas. Many cities enacted ordinances making provision of off-street parking mandatory in association with new developments. Even with the opening of the new expressway networks, traffic congestion at peak commuting times, and

---

64. Harold M. Mayer, "Some Geographic Aspects of Technological Change in Maritime Transportation," *Economic Geography* 49, no. 2 (April 1973): 145-155; and "Re-Use of Former Port Terminal Land in Central Cities on the Great Lakes," *Proceedings of Applied Geography Conference* 3 (1980): 222-239.

65. Kent A. Robertson, "The Impact of Transportation on the Central Business District," *Traffic Quarterly* 34, no. 4 (October 1980): 523-537.

the consequent delays and air pollution thereby resulting, became
intolerable. Nevertheless, except for central areas in a few of the
largest cities, planning was based upon projections of continued
dominance of the automobile for the journey-to-work.[66] Little
concern was evident for the relations between urban circulation and
land use although a few studies were made of the daily commuter
movement, especially to and from downtown areas.[67] The relations
between land uses and traffic generation, especially in central
business districts were highlighted by publication of a classic book
in 1954.[68] It was pointed out that transportation systems could not
exist or be planned without consideration of such relationships and
that land use and transportation planning studies should be
combined. Origin-destination traffic studies, which had been
applied to traffic planning in numerous cities and metropolitan
areas during the period between about 1945 and 1954, were
subsequently expanded to take into consideration the nature,
densities, and distances between land uses which generate trips.
Coincidentally, the electronic computer was then becoming available
for massive data-processing, and among its earliest civilian
applications was metropolitan transportation/land-use planning
surveys.[69] Among the first metropolitan areas to conduct such
comprehensive land-use/transportation surveys were Detroit, Chicago,
Pittsburgh, and Philadelphia.[70]

In spite of deconcentration of many of the functions which had
characterized the downtown areas of most American cities, there
continued to be many vested interests in maintaining the viability
of the urban cores. In most cities, the greatest concentration of
office activity, of historic and cultural attractions for both
residents and visitors, and of land and building values and hence of

---

66. Wilfred Owen, *The Accessible City* (Washington, D.C.: Brookings
Institution, 1972); James O. Wheeler, *The Urban Circulation Noose* (Belmont, Cal.:
Duxbury Press, 1974).

67. Gerald W. Breese, *The Daytime Population of the Central Business
District of Chicago with Particular Reference to the Factor of Transportation*
(Chicago: University of Chicago Press, 1949); Howard S. Lapin *Structuring the
Journey to Work* (Philadelphia: University of Pennsylvania Press, 1964); Robert E.
Dickinson, "The Journey to Work" in *Metropolis on the Move,* ed. Jean Gottman and
Robert A. Harper (New York: John Wiley and Sons, 1967), pp. 69-83; John Rannells,
*The Core of the City: A Pilot Study of Changing Land Uses in Central Business
Districts* (New York: Columbia University Press, 1956).

68. Robert B. Mitchell and Chester Rapkin, *Urban Traffic: A Function of
Land Use* (New York: Columbia University Press, 1954).

69. David E. Boyce, Norman D. Day, and Chris McDonald, *Metropolitan Plan
Making: An Analysis of Experience with the Preparation and Evaluation of
Alternative Land Use and Transportation Plans* (Philadelphia: Regional Science
Research Institute, 1970).

70. *Detroit Metropolitan Area Traffic Study* 1955, 2 vols.; *Chicago Area
Transportation Study,* 1960-62, 3 vols.; *Pittsburgh Area Transportation Study,*
1961-63, 2 vols.

local tax collections remained in the cores. Perceptions of the city continued to center in the downtown areas.[71] Among the important variables in relation to plans for retaining the vitality of downtowns are those associated with historic significance of buildings, their architectural significance, and the evidences of past cultural associations.[72] In many cities, clusters of prominent buildings, typically grouped around a central plaza or square, constitute the perceptual and visual center, and in recent years many such "civic centers" formed the locus of expanded public buildings and activities. In some instances, as in Chicago's Daley Plaza, large new high-rise public buildings supplemented or replaced the older and sometimes historic structures. In numerous small and medium-sized cities, especially county seats, the courthouse and other public buildings were subsequently built in other locations, but the resulting open space continues to be identified by residents of the city as the central node. In a number of cities, large buildings, or clusters of buildings within or on the edges of the downtown areas were developed as centers of entertainment and culture; typical examples are New York's Lincoln Center, Washington's Kennedy Center, the Music Center adjacent to Los Angeles's Civic Center, and Performing Arts centers in smaller cities such as Milwauee and Akron.

These developments represent attempts, some successful, to revitalize the downtown areas by providing new incentives for the public to go downtown for other than employment and at the same time to act as catalysts for other central area functions.

Many cities have succeeded in attracting large capital investments in massive clusters of buildings developed in planned multi-functional associations or, in some instances, huge single multifunctional structures. These provide attractive environments for numerous establishments, both public and private, and have to some degree arrested--and in a few instances at least partially reversed--the trend toward the suburban areas and beyond. Examples of multi-building developments are New York's World Trade Center, Chicago's Illinois Center, Pittsburgh's Gateway Center, and Detroit's Renaissance Center. Smaller cities have also developed, with combinations of public and private capital, similar unit developments, such as Constitution Plaza in Hartford and Cascade

71. Kevin Lynch, *The Image of the City* (Cambridge, Mass.: MIT Press and Harvard University Press, 1960); Anselm L. Strauss, *Images of the American City* (Glencoe, Ill.: Free Press of Glencoe, 1961), and *The American City: A Sourcebook of Urban Imagery* (Chicago: Aldine Publishing Company, 1968).

72. Pierce F. Lewis, "To Revive Urban Downtonws, Show Respect for the Spirit of the Place," *Smithsonian* 6, no. 6 (September 1975): 33-41.

Plaza in Akron. To serve the urban populations and at the same time to stimulate downtown revitalization by their presence, other planned unit developments in or adjacent to the urban cores are new campuses of universities, especially of state institutions; examples are the University of Illinois at Chicago, Georgia State University, Portland (Oregon) State University, and Cleveland State. Each of these attract many thousands of students, faculty, and staff to the downtown areas to which they are adjacent.

Attention has been devoted in many cities to the visual and perceptual environment of the downtown areas. In New York and some other cities, the zoning ordinances have been modified to provide developers with bonuses in the form of additional permitted heights and masses of buildings if they provide open plazas on their properties or public access to the lower portions of their highrise buildings.

In attempting to replicate some of the advantages of the newer planned outlying and suburban shopping centers, many cities have closed streets in their prime retail areas and developed in the beds of such streets open "malls." In some instances these malls are completely free from vehicular traffic and in other instances only transit vehicles and sometimes taxicabs are permitted during business hours. In some downtowns these malls are associated with new distributor loop highways, and commonly there are extensive off-street provisions for parking, although the supply rarely exceeds the demand.[73]

Another recent development in some downtown areas is the linking of older buildings, especially department stores, by arcades and covered spaces, somewhat analogous to the newer climate-controlled suburban shopping centers. Complementing these developments, underground passages and above-street "skywalks" connect extensive downtown blocks with each other, permitting pedestrian access to numerous establishments without exposure to the weather. Among the cities with extensive underground interconnections are Montreal, Houston, and Philadelphia, while Minneapolis, St. Paul, Milwaukee, and Spokane's downtowns have extensive networks of skywalks connecting downtown clusters of buildings.

73. Boris S. Pushkarev and Jeffrey M. Zupan, *Urban Space for Pedestrians* (Cambridge, Mass.: MIT Press, 1975); Adepoju Onikbokun, "A Comprehensive Evaluation of Pedestrian Malls in the United States," *Appraisal Journal* 43, no. 2 (April 1975): 202-218; Roberto Brambilla et al., *American Urban Malls: A Compendium* (Washington: U.S. Government Printing Office, 1977); Klaus Uhlig, *Pedestrian Areas: From Malls to Complete Networks* (New York: Architectural Book Publishing Company, 1979); Harvey M. Rubenstein, *Central City Malls* (New York: John Wiley and Sons, 1978).

Cities with waterfronts adjacent to their downtowns have, in many instances, received special attention. Extensive plans are being implemented, for example, to develop the Hudson River frontage in New York City, while on the East River the well-known South Street Seaport development combines revitalization of a deteriorated central area with preservation and reconstruction of a historic district. Similarly, the Fanuel Hall development in Boston, Penn's Landing in Philadelphia, Harbor Place in Baltimore, and Seattle's downtown waterfront have all been redeveloped as attractions for local residents and tourists, combining new commercial activity with historic preservation and reconstruction. The federal government offers various forms of aid in such developments and a program of designation of National Historic Districts has called attention to the desire to utilize the historic interest with the demand for downtown revitalization.

Thus, the central business districts of many American cities continue to be the dominant node functionally, physically, and visually, in spite of relative, and in many instances absolute, decline of retailing and other downtown functions. Surrounding the central business areas, the sites of what were formerly designated as areas of wholesaling and light manufacturing are almost everywhere declining or have been abandoned to become the axes of new loop highways and of parking facilities. But, in most cities, the peak concentrations of high-rise buildings, traffic, and consequent air pollution remain, although in many respects changed in form. A profile across the central areas of most large and medium-sized American cities no longer has a volcano shape with a negative exponential distance decay, a concave surface, as formerly. Rather, the profile is analogous to that of craters on the moon, with very sharp central peaks, then an area of very low elevation surrounded by a rim of higher elevation marking the high level of the outward expansion.

### The "Inner City" Residential Areas

The concentric zonal model of cities, developed in Chicago in the 1920s, described a zone of "transition" surrounding the urban core and, surrounding that zone in turn, a zone of low-income "workingmen's homes."[74]

---

74. Ernest W. Burgess, "The Growth of the City" in *The City,* ed. Robert E. Park, Ernest W. Burgess, and Roderick D. McKenzie (Chicago: University of Chicago Press, 1925), pp. 47-62.

Much of the attention of students of cities during the interval between the two world wars was devoted to the low-income residential areas. The correlation between low income on the one hand and the concentration of social pathology in urban areas on the other was demonstrated by many of the studies to be very high. It was, in retrospect, naively believed that improvement of housing conditions through public intervention in the real estate market would reduce many of the pathological conditions associated with the extensive low-income residential areas. Public housing programs during the 1930s provided concentrated islands of new "standard" housing with public subsidies for low-income families who met certain requirements of income within a range defined by lower as well as upper limits. A few nonprofit and limited-dividend private foundations and corporations provided clusters of housing, such as Knickerbocker Village in New York and Marshall Field Gardens and Rosenwald Homes in Chicago, for lower-middle income occupants.

But these programs, both public and private, did not go far in mitigating the physical, social, and economic problems of the millions of people and families who were resident under substandard conditions in the sprawling, generally deteriorated, and extensive low-income residential areas, which were generally described as "blighted." In 1943, a report by the Chicago Plan Commission, using the results of the Chicago Land Use Survey of the late 1930s, perhaps the most intense housing survey made up to that time of any American city, identified 23 square miles of blighted and near-blighted residential area but could recommend no solution other than virtually complete demolition and redevelopment of the entire area.[75] In many such studies, especially those of public agencies, there was little or no recognition of the human problems associated with removal of people, the breakup of their neighborhood ties, and the discrimination which they would face in seeking adequate housing elsewhere. In the low-income areas of most American cities, the preponderant population was Black, Hispanic, or of other minorities who faced the double penalty of economic inability to buy or rent satisfactory housing and discrimination because of their minority status.

World War II somewhat improved, although temporarily, the economic status of some of the low-income population, but the inability to provide adequate housing was intensified, and the unmet

---

75. Chicago Plan Commission and Works Projects Administration, *Residential Chicago: Volume One of the Report of the Chicago Land Use Survey* (Chicago: City of Chicago, 1942); Chicago Plan Commission, *Master Plan of Residential Land Use of Chicago* (Chicago: City of Chicago, 1943).

demand for housing after the war, in spite of rent controls, exacerbated the problem.

Urban redevelopment was regarded as at least a partial solution. This involved replacement of the housing inventory in many low-income areas by high-density public housing and by massive neighborhood- and community-size concentrations of housing and associated facilities through a combination of public and private capital. Some states, notably Illinois and Pennsylvania, initiated programs of public subsidies to attract private venture capital for such redevelopment. The Illinois Redevelopment Act of 1947, for example, provided a revolving fund of seventy-five million dollars of state funding, administered through the cities. These state actions constituted prototypes for the programs initiated by the federal government in the Housing Act of 1949. In addition to providing a substantial increase in federal aid for public housing, that Act, in Title I, provided for federal matching funds for urban redevelopment in "blighted areas," generally in the amount of two dollars of federal contribution for each dollar of local funds used in planning, land acquisition, relocation of businesses and residents for the site, modifying the utilities and other infrastructure, demolishing the existing buildings, and offering the site to public and private redevelopers for sale or lease, in order to create new development in accordance with a mutually agreed-upon plan, in conformance with federal standards and with a comprehensive plan for the neighborhood and the city. Thus, Title I provided for a "write down" of the land cost from current free-market values--which would inhibit private redevelopment--to "re-use value" which would be competitive with the lower price of peripheral or suburban land.

Using the provisions of Title I, many massive redevelopment projects were constructed in cities throughout the United States, between the early 1950s and the late 1960s. These were principally located in the blighted "inner city" residential areas, and they involved traumatic uprooting of many thousands of individuals and families. Most of them could not afford the rentals, nor the purchase prices, of adequate housing. Although the renewal program made provision for relocation mandatory, it proved to be far from satisfactory in most instances, and even though extensive areas, as, for example, on the Near South Side of Chicago, were cleared and redeveloped with a combination of public housing, Title I private housing, and in some instances expansion of the extent of institutions such as hospitals and universities, the direct impact often proved to be relatively minor upon the total problem of "slum clearance." The traumatic uprooting of residents, on the other hand, caused much criticism of the programs, as did the inadequate character of much of the public housing. Some of the latter was so poorly conceived, in fact, that major projects were totally abandoned within a few years, as in central Indianapolis, while in St. Louis, one of the nation's largest public housing developments was vacated and demolished a decade after its completion. In other instances, as in the Lafayette-Gratiot area of Detroit, redevelopment aborted, leaving extensive areas vacant for years following the land acquisition and clearance.

As large-scale redevelopment of inner portions of American cities continued, the process was subject to mounting criticism.[76] As an increasing number of massive renewal projects were completed, it became apparent that the negative impact of such concentrated redevelopment required modification of both the concept and the programs. Much of the criticism was directed to the fact that clearance and demolition disrupted the existing communities, a large proportion of which were based upon ethnicity and the common backgrounds of the residents. In spite of mandatory relocation provisions, a very high proportion of the dislocatees were economically, and socially, unable to locate and pay for suitable alternative housing. Small business establishments, likewise, were often forced to close because their trade was based upon their established neighborhood relationships.[77] Other criticisms were based upon the population pressures in other parts of the cities as the residents of the areas subject to redevelopment located in them. Some formerly middle-class housing, and with it the neighborhoods in which the housing was located, "filtered down" to lower-income occupancy much more rapidly than would otherwise have been the case. Also, it became evident that the amount of capital, both public and private, that would be required to redevelop sufficiently large areas of cities as to solve effectively the problems of physical blight would not generally be available. Finally, although much of the redeveloment provided adequate housing and eventually increased tax returns, the people most in need of the housing commonly could not afford Title I occupancy and many were not eligible for public housing which in many cities was insufficient to meet the demand.

---

76. Martin Anderson, *The Federal Bulldozer: A Critical Analysis* (Cambridge, Mass.: MIT Press, 1964); James Q. Wilson, ed., *Urban Renewal: The Record and the Controversy* (Cambridge, Mass.: MIT Press, 1966); Jane Jacobs, *The Death and Life of Great American Cities* (New York: Random House, 1961).

77. Brian J. L. Berry, *Commercial Structure and Commercial Blight* Research Paper no. 85 (Chicago: University of Chicago, Department of Geography, 1963).

The inhuman scale of many of the massive projects, both private and public, also drew sharp criticism. The concentrations of low-income residents in high-rise public housing was felt by many to exacerbate crime and other social problems. Other critics, however, pointed out that these problems would exist in spite of the physical pattern of housing. By the 1970s, the policy of building massive concentrations in areas subject to redevelopment was gradually modified, and few such projects were constructed thereafter.

With the general realization that, in most instances, massive land clearance and redevelopment were both impracticable and undesirable, attention gradually shifted toward other treatments of the problems of urban deterioration. Two approaches, in particular, appeared to offer advantages. One was to anticipate the physical and social deterioration which would result in the areas surrounding the inner-city blighted areas as population pressures and the uprooting of the low-income population through renewal and land clearance due to highway construction and other forces. Many residential areas were not deteriorated enough to justify large-scale renewal, but were aging and were in danger of filtering down to lower-income occupancy, overcrowding, and consequent deterioration as the peripheral movement from the areas closer to the city center took place. It became apparent that such areas needed to take steps to accommodate change in an orderly fashion. With some technical and financial aid from federal, state, and city agencies, a number of urban neighborhoods organized "grass roots" movements to arouse concern and interest in local conservation. Foremost among these was the Hyde Park-Kenwood area in the vicinity of the University of Chicago, which became a prototype of national interest in the early stages of the conservation movement in cities.[78] In many instances, universities, hospitals, and other institutions formed the nuclei of both redevelopment and conservation activities. After the Housing Act of 1949, several amendments and subsequent acts furnished incentives for institutions to participate actively in renewal and conservation of their vicinities.

With the growing realization that it was not feasible to replace extensive areas of the deteriorated portions of cities rapidly and that the traumas of displacement in some instances would outweigh the advantages of redevelopment, interest grew in conserving, insofar as practicable, the structures and

---

78. Julia Abrahamson, *A Neighborhood Finds Itself* (New York: Harper & Row, 1959, reprinted 1971 by Biblo & Tannen, New York); Peter H. Rossi, *The Politics of Urban Renewal: The Chicago Findings* (Glencoe, Ill.: Free Press of Glencoe, 1961).

infrastructures of the older portions of the cities. In some urban areas, the large-scale demolition and rebuilding approach was modified, and combined with conservation measures involving selective demolition and replacement with rehabilitation of buildings which were structurally sound. Again with federal technical and financial participation--and sometimes without it--many cities embarked upon comprehensive approaches to planning, with heavy emphasis upon the inner city and surrounding conservation areas. Section 701 of the federal planning act of 1954 provided fifty-percent of the costs of planning in cities of under 50,000 population, and in counties, to be supplied by the federal government; later the size restriction was removed and larger cities took advantage of the federal aid to expand greatly their planning activities.

Paralleling the interest in urban conservation and rehabilitation was a growing interest in the general environment and in the historical and architectural significance of urban areas and in individual buildings. A national program of preservation and reconstruction of buildings and urban districts was initiated, and in many instances this combined with the general urban conservation movement with varying degrees of effectiveness.

Conservation and rehabilitation of structures of historic and architectural interest is generally costly. The result commonly is that residents and, often, businesses which previously occupied such buildings and districts cannot afford to move back to them, and further displacement occurs. In particular, where urban areas are subjected to physical rehabilitation, they tend to be re-occupied by persons and groups of much higher economic status than that of the prior occupants. The process became known as "gentrification."[79] Among the "gentrified" districts are Georgetown in Washington, D.C., Society Hill in downtown Philadelphia, portions of the near North Side of Chicago, and many others. It is evident, however, that the process offers little if any significant help in mitigating the pathological conditions of inner-city areas and that widespread rehabilitation and conservation may actually increase the problems by uprooting persons, families, and businesses from well-established roots in the "gentrified" areas.

---

79. Martin H. Lang, *Gentrification amid Urban Decline: Strategies for America's Older Cities* (Cambridge, Mass.: Ballinger Publishing Company, 1982); David Listokin, ed., *Housing Rehabilitation: Economic, Social and Policy Perspectives* (Piscataway, N.J.: Rutgers University, Center for Urban Policy Research, 1983).

Since World War II, there has been an increasing interest among geographers in the conditions, with emphasis upon the spatial patterns, of ethnic and racial communities in cities and upon the spatial aspects of social and economic conditions associated in particular with the inner city areas.

Minorities, in particular, have received considerable attention from geographers. The rapid increase in the Black populations of many cities are evidenced in their increased influence in business, and especially in local government. Following the election of the first black mayors in Cleveland and Gary in 1968, an increasing number of American cities have had Black chief executives; these include Detroit, Atlanta, Los Angeles, and Chicago. In spite of "open housing" legislation applicable to both central cities and suburbs, the vast majority of minorities, including Blacks, tend to be concentrated in the inner portions of cities, where their potential political influence can be felt. Discrimination in the availability of housing, both because of prejudice and the lower economic status of most minorities has intensified the local concentrations in the cities. "Ghettos" have expanded, and their existence is the subject of an increasing number of geographical studies.[80]

Not all Blacks in metropolitan areas, however, are residents of the "inner city." With rising affluence, many Black families find homes in the peripheral areas of the major cities and in suburbs, which, nevertheless, mostly accept them with some reluctance.[81] Open Housing laws have somewhat mitigated the problems faced by Blacks and other minorities in seeking suburban housing. The segregation, nevertheless, remains a major problem in many cities and metropolitan areas.

Reduction of the differences in educational opportunities between minorities, especially Blacks and Hispanics in the inner cities, and others in the more affluent portions of cities and in suburban areas has been a major concern for several decades. Passage at the federal level of laws designed to improve the educational status of minorities by prohibiting discrimination in

80. Harold M. Rose, *Social Processes in the City: Race and Urban Residential Choice,* Resource Paper no. 6 (Washington, D.C.: Association of American Geographers Commission on Collge Geography, 1969), and "The Spatial Development of Black Residential Subsystems," *Economic Geography* 48, no. 1 (January 1972): 43-65; Louis Selig, "Concepts of 'Ghetto': A Geography of Minority Groups," *Professional Geographer* 23, no. 1 (January 1971): 1-4.

81. Thomas A. Clark, *Blacks in Suburbs: A National Perspective* (Piscataway, N.J.: Rutgers University, Center for Urban Policy Research, 1979), and "Race, Class and Suburban Housing Discrimination," *Urban Geography* 2, no. 4 (October-December 1981): 327-338; Robert W. Lake, *The New Suburbanites: Race and Housing in the Suburbs* (New Brunswick, N.J.: Rutgers University, 1981).

admission to schools, by provision of remedial programs, and commonly by promoting integration within the schools have met with indifferent success. Residential segregation is the heart of the problem, and in many cities and metropolitan areas federally mandated exchange of students among predominantly White schools on the one hand and schools serving predominantly minority students on the other have not been generally successful and have met with much oposition on all sides. Equal opportunities in education may or may not be related to the degree of racial and ethnic integration within the schools, but it appears obvious that integration, if desired in the schools, cannot be successful without integration of the residential neighborhoods. In the mid-1980s, school integration, a major urban problem which is largely spatial and hence of geographical concern, is far from solution.

Blacks and Hispanics in cities are not the only ethnic groups that are the subject of prolific studies by geographers and other social scientists. In recent years, there has been a large increase in the number of publications on ethnicity and ethnic spatial segregation and integration. Planners and others concerned with residential development, especially in inner city areas, are now much more aware than formerly of the existence, and the desire to preserve, the cultures of the many ethnic groups within cities.[82]

Paralleling the increasing concern for race and ethnicity in American cities is the development of an increasing literature on the geography of urban pathology, much of which occurs in the older low-income areas of central cities, although some of the negative aspects of suburbs have also received attention. Sub-fields of urban geography in the United States and Canada are attracting an increasing number of geographers. These range from poverty in general,[83] to crime,[84] and health.[85] Urban medical geography is a

82. Robert C. Weaver, "Class, Race and Urban Renewal," *Land Economics,* 36, no. 3 (August 1960): 235-251; Karl E. Taeuber, "Residential Segregation," *Scientific American* 213, no. 2 (August 1965): 12-20; Morton Grodzins, *The Metropolitan Areas as a Racial Problem* (Pittsburgh: University of Pittsburgh Press, 1958); Frederik Barth, ed., *Ethnic Groups and Boundaries* (Boston: Little Brown and Company, 1969); Nathan Glazer and Daniel Patrick Moynahan, *Beyond the Melting Pot* (Cambridge, Mass.: M.I.T. Press, 1970); Amos H. Hawley and Vincent P. Rock, eds., *Segregation in Residential Areas* (Washington, D.C.: National Academy of Sciences, 1973); Nathan Kantrowitz *Ethnic and Racial Segregation in the New York Metropolis* (New York: Praeger Publishers, 1973); Karl B. Raitz and Christopher Boerner, "Problems in Defining Ethnicity for Human Geography," *Geographical Survey* 6, no. 2 (April 1978): 15-24.

83. Richard L. Morrill and Ernest H. Wohlenberg, *The Geography of Poverty in the United States* (New York: McGraw Hill Book Co., 1971).

84. Gerald F. Pyle et al., *The Spatial Dynamics of Crime* Research Paper no. 159 (Chicago: University of Chicago, Department of Geography, 1974); Harold M. Rose, "The Geography of Despair," *Annals of the Association of American Geographers* 68, no. 4 (December 1978): 453-464; Daniel E. Georges, *The Geography of Crime and Violence, A Spatial and Ecological Perspective,* Resource Paper 78-1 (Washington, D.C.: Association of American Geographers, 1978).

major concern, and an increasing number of geographers are applying their findings in improvement of the delivery of medical services.[86]

## Open Space in Cities and Metropolitan Areas

One of the major aspects of urban and metropolitan planning and development since World War II has been that of the effective preservation of open space in the face of urban expansion. Open space takes many forms, from the "tot lot" within the city block to the extensive metropolitan park systems. Open space may, insofar as the surrounding environment permits, be preserved in essentially its natural form, or it may be made available for both passive and active recreation. With the expansion of built-up urban areas, open space is threatened if in private ownership, because the owners--whether they use the land for agriculture, golf courses, airports, or hunting preserves--cannot afford to preserve it as open space since the urban pressures generally are reflected in the taxable value of the land based on its prospective urban uses. The open space is constantly threatened, and the amenity value in an urban setting usually gives way to urbanization. The environmental movement of the 1960s and 1970s has focused attention on the values of open space preservation.

Much of the open space in the older portions of cities was secured by the public and dedicated as parks in the last half of the nineteenth century and the early twentieth century. Increased pressures to use city parks because of increased populations in their vicinities have been countered, in many instances, by increased crime in the parks and the consequent fear of many to use them. At the same time, their value is realized, and additional dedications of urban open space typically takes place on and beyond the urban peripheries. Early in the twentieth century, Ebenezer Howard pointed out the value of periperal open space, and Daniel H. Burnham and Edward H. Bennett in their *Plan of Chicago* of 1909 proposed an outer system of forest preserves for the metropolitan area, somewhat analogous to the park and boulevard system designed by Frederick Law Olmsted for what was then the periphery of Chicago in 1869.[87] This proposal was implemented a few years later in the

---

85. Jonathan D. Mayer, "Medical Geography: Some Unresolved Problems," *Professional Geographer* 34, no. 3 (August 1982); Gerald F. Pyle, *Heart Disease, Cancer and Stroke in Chicago*, Research Paper no. 134 (Chicago: University of Chicago, Department of Geography, 1971).

86. Dale D. Achabe, "The Development of a Spatial Delivery System for Emergency Medical Services," *Geographical Analysis* 10, no. 1 (January 1978): 47-64; Jonathon D. Mayer, "Response Time and Its Significance in Medical Geography," *Geographical Review* 70, no. 1 (January 1980): 79-87.

87. Norman T. Newton, *Design of the Land* (Cambridge, Mass.: Harvard University Press, 1971).

Forest Preserve District of Cook County, which acquired thousands of acres of suburban land, in large part along stream courses, thereby serving conservation and flood control purposes as well as providing for recreation. Similar systems of regional parks were established in the vicinities of many other large cities; notable examples are the systems serving the metropolitan areas of Cleveland, Akron, and Milwaukee. Denver established parks in the nearby Rocky Mountain area.

Threatened with encroachment of urban development which would endanger the rural or open nature of their environs, many organizations located in the urban peripheries were instrumental in supporting movements for preservation of metropolitan open space.[88] In some instances, as in Cleveland, Chicago, and Milwaukee, county agencies were created for acquisition, preservation, and controlled development of peripheral lands as forest preserves and county parks. In some states, state parks serve the recreational needs of nearby urban residents. The federal government conducted extensive surveys of several metropolitan areas in the 1970s,[89] and at the same time national recreational areas and parks were established in proximity to, and partially within, a number of large cities; among them is the National Seashore in metropolitan New York, the Golden Gate area in metropolitan San Francisco, the Indiana Dunes National Lakeshore near Chicago, and the Cuyahoga Valley National Recreation Area between Cleveland and Akron.

In addition to providing for the recreational needs of urban residents, these open spaces, guaranteed continuation as such under public ownership and control, not only serve various conservation needs, but also give a varied form to what otherwise would be uninterrupted urban sprawl.

On the other hand, private open space also may serve public needs if protected against incompatible developments. Scenic easements represent one form of protection, increasingly used in many urban areas. Institutional open space with public access, such as university campuses, churchyards, etc., may also have general value as open space. Cemeteries constitute open space, not only in

---

88. Rutherford H. Platt, *The Open Space Decision Process: Spatial Allocation of Costs and Benefits* Research Paper no. 142 (Chicago: University of Chicago, Department of Geography, 1972); August Heckscher, *Ocean Spaces: The Life of American Cities* (New York: Harper & Row, 1977); James S. Lemonides and April L. Young, "Provision of Public Open Space in Urban Areas," *Journal of the American Institute of Planners* 44, no. 3 (July 1978): 286-296; "The Conservation of Private Land, pp. Hidden Value in Open Space," in Peter Wolf *Land in America: Its Value Use and Control,* (New York: Pantheon Books, 1981), pp. 272-308.

89. U.S. Department of the Interior, *National Urban Recreation Study; Executive Report* (Washington, D.C.: U.S. Government Printing Office, 1978), and individual volumes covering metropolitan areas.

peripheral areas, but also in the interiors of built-up inner city areas, and their virtually inviolate nature offers assurance of open space in the future; they also serve social needs.[90]

## Energy and American Cities

Contemporary cities and metropolitan areas of the United States and Canada largely owe their present spatial forms to the ubiquity of the automobile, which is an inefficient user of energy. The oil crisis of 1973 focused attention upon the vulnerabilty of the urban areas to disruptions in the supply of fossil fuels and the virtual impossibility of replacing the motor vehicle as the basic form of personal transportation and the motor truck as the primary transporter of goods. As pointed out earlier, much of the past four decades took place in areas where fixed-route public transportation was not available. On the other hand, numerous studies in the 1970s demonstrated that the American public would not--and in most instances could not--give up their dependence on motor vehicles.[91]

It is not clear what ultimate effects upon the spatial patterns of American cities and metropolitan areas will result from the higher prices of motor fuel and the prospects of future shortages. Obviously, higher residential densities and shorter travel distances between home and work would reduce the demand for transportation and hence for fuel consumption. During much of the time since the acute shortage and rapidly rising prices of motor fuel in the early 1970s, there have been other variables to obscure the impacts; among these are price inflations in general, and especially the higher costs of housing, in turn the result of increasing construction costs and in part the result of rising interest rates. These factors seriously limited the ability of an increasing proportion of the population to purchase housing, and consequently there was a slowing up of the rate of construction.

There has been some evidence of a trend toward more clustering of housing. Group or row housing and high-rise apartments, generally owned as condominiums, became popular, both in central cities and in suburban areas, while the demand for single-unit detached houses decreased. With clustering, transportation demand is reduced, at the same time that the consumption of fuels for space

---

90 . William D. Pattison, "The Cemeteries of Chicago: A Phase of Land Utilization," *Annals of the Association of American Geographers* 45, no. 3 (September 1955): 245-257; Larry W. Price, "Some Results and Implications of a Cemetery Study," *Professional Geographer* 18, no. 5 (July 1966): 201-7; Richard V. Francaviglia, "The Cemetery as an Evolving Cultural Landscape," *Annals of the Association of American Geographers* 61, no. 3 (September 1971): 501-509.

91 . James J. Flink, *The Car Culture* (Cambridge, Mass.: MIT Press, 1975); Thomas Mr. Corsi and Milton E. Harvey, "Travel Behavior under Increases in Gasoline Prices," *Traffic Quarterly* 21, no. 3 (July 1977): 605-624.

heating is also reduced. On the whole, however, there is little evidence that energy scarcity is significantly affecting the spatial patterns of cities and metropolitan areas.[92] Although much higher densities than presently characteristic of American metropolitan areas would produce considerable reduction in per capita consumption of energy, it is paradoxical that the costs of re-structuring urban areas make drastic changes prohibitively expensive and generally impracticable.[93]

Electricity is virtually ubiquitous in the United States and in the settled parts of Canada. In few activities is the cost of electric power a major consideration, and electric utilities make their power available wherever there is prospective urban development. The sources of electric power, however, have shifted several times in relative importance during the four decades since World War II. Immediately after the war, many believed that nuclear power could eventually be provided at much lower cost than any other source. Pending the widespread adoption of nuclear power, however, many of the utilities, for environmental reasons, shifted from primary dependence upon coal to relatively more use of oil. This shift was encouraged by governmental policy. Although in some instances particulate matter in the air over cities was reduced, the escalating price of fuel oil during the 1970s encouraged a return to coal and an increased development of nuclear power.

Continued reduction in the rate of population growth and consequent slowing up of the increase in demand for electricty, combined with more efficient utilization of the power, resulted in consumption much below the earlier projections. Nuclear power became a major component of electric power supply; in 1960, it was responsible for slightly over one-tenth of one percent of the electric power generated in the United States; by 1981, nuclear power represented nearly twelve percent of the production of the electric utilities in the nation. However, the difficulties at Three Mile Island and the escalating costs of construction of nuclear plants, with cost over-runs of several hundred percent, made nuclear power much less attractive, and in the early 1980s, it was apparent that nuclear power would furnish, in the forseeable future, a much smaller proportion of the power needs of urban America than

---

92. Kenneth A. Small, "Energy Scarcity and Urban Development Patterns," *International Regional Science Review* 5, no. 2 (Winter 1980): 97-117; Robert W. Burchell and David Listokin, *Energy and Land Use* (Piscataway, N.J.: Rutgers University, Center for Urban Policy Research, 1982).

93. Jon Van Til, "Spatial Form and Structure in a Possible Future: Some Implications of Energy Shortfall for Urban Planning," *Journal of the American Planning Association* 45, no. 3 (July 1979): 318-329.

was earlier anticipated.  Nevertheless, the awareness, whether
justified or not, of possible dangers in the vicinities of nuclear
power plants was among the factors accounting for a slowing in the
utilization of nuclear energy.  A popular movement to prohibit
siting of nuclear plants near urban populations resulted in
cancellation of plans, in some instances, for further development
and, in other instances, a spreading out of construction time
pending further research.  In general, nuclear plants relocated at
some distance from major urban areas, and their effects upon such
areas' spatial structure has so far been slight.  On the other hand,
in a few instances, their construction and presence has enhanced the
tax base of the communities within which they are located.
Population increases due to the presence of nuclear plants nearby
has generally not occured to a significant degree, because they tend
to be located within commuting range of larger urban places which
not only supply a labor force but also have the infrastructure
required.[94]

### Urban Planning and Local Government

Planning of the spatial patterns of cities and metropolitan
areas in the United States is highly decentralized and not generally
effective, although during the past four decades a number of
innovations in the planning process are noteworthy.  Local
governments derive their powers from the several states, but the
federal government in furnishing technical and especially financial
aid to local governments, channeled in most instances through the
states, has set certain standards which are virtually mandated as
prerequisite for federal assistance, not only for planning but for
many physical, social, and economic programs.

The difficulties in establishing and carrying out planning in
urban areas springs largely from the multiplicity of governmental
bodies and their varying authorities in urban and metropolitan
areas.  At the national level there have been a number of changes in
the number of local governments between 1957 and 1977 (table 17.2).

Within most metropolitan areas, there are scores or hundreds
of individual local governments.  These include
municipalities--cities, towns, villages, and boroughs--and numerous
special-purpose governments, with or without taxing authority.  Each
government has a vested interest either in an area as a general
local government, or in one or more functions within a metropolitan

---

94. D. Pijawka and J. Chalmers, "Impacts of Nuclear Generating Plants on
Local Areas," *Economic Geography* 59, no. 1 (January 1983): 66-80.

TABLE 17.2

LOCAL GOVERNMENTS IN THE UNITED STATES, 1957-1977

| Year | Counties | Municipalities | Townships | Special districts | School districts |
|------|----------|----------------|-----------|-------------------|------------------|
| 1957 | 3,050 | 17,215 | 17,198 | 14,424 | 50,454 |
| 1977 | 3,042 | 18,862 | 16,822 | 25,962 | 15,174 |

SOURCE: *Statistical Abstract of the United States,* 1960 and 1982-83.

area or portion of it.[95] Special-district governments have especially proliferated (table 17.2). The only type of special district which has declined in numbers is the school district. This occurred through consolidation principally in rural areas where the consolidation was virtually dictated by the need for a minimum threshold of enrollment and tax base for staff and plant required to meet educational standards. Other special districts increased in numbers as the debt limits of general municipalities prevented them from financing the facilities and programs demanded by their populations. This was exacerbated by declining population in many cities, concommitant with increasing demand for social programs to serve the populations with lower incomes than those formerly resident in many of the city areas. Furthermore, numerous functions require, for efficient performance, larger areas than those embraced within the boundaries of individual municipalities or counties. The result in many urban and metropolitan areas is a patchwork of governmental units, the boundaries of few of which suitably coincide.[96]

During the first half of the twentieth century, numerous devices were developed, some ad hoc, in attempting to overcome the impedences to comprehensive planning and development of urban areas arising from the fragmented local governmental structure. Among them were sharing of facilities and services, informal Councils of Government, and many others. Among the noteworthy early special function governments were the Sanitary District of Chicago (now the Metropolitan Sanitary District of Greater Chicago), established in 1889, and the interstate Port Authority of New York and New Jersey,

---

95. Robert C. Wood, *1400 Governments: The Political Economy of The New York Metropolitan Region* (Cambridge, Mass.: Harvard University Press, 1961).

96. Donald F. Stetzer, *Special Districts in Cook County: Toward a Geography of Local Government,* Research Paper no. 196 (Chicago: University of Chicago, Department of Geography, 1975).

established in 1920. In many instances, annexations and consolidations of contiguous municipalities helped somewhat. But the most common device was the creation of special purpose authorities and districts.

General governments with jurisdiction over the entire extent of metropolitan areas are regarded as the ultimate solution by many people, but such governments are rare in the United States. One of the principal constraints is the dichotomy between many suburban interests and those of central cities. The former resist most forms of united action with their respective central cities, because they fear the added burdens, both financial and social, and the loss of political power to determine solutions to their local problems, if they were to be subject to governmental authority from the central city. In many instances the resistance is racially based as demonstrated by the resistance to the program of busing to facilitate school integration.

Metropolitan government was not unknown in the United States during the nineteenth century. It was ususally accomplished by merger of the governments of a central city with that of its county: Philadelphia in 1854, St. Louis and San Francisco, among others, later. In 1898, five counties (boroughs) were merged to form the present City of New York. In the first half of the twentieth century, although frequently suggested, formation of metropolitan governments in the United States did not take place.

The prototype for metropolitan government in North America in the twentieth century is Metropolitan Toronto, formed in 1950.[97] Other metropolitan governments were subsequently organized elsewhere in Canada. In the United States, several metropolitan general-purpose governments were organized after mid-century, in each instance by the merger of city and county governments: Miami-Dade County, Florida, Nashville-Davison County, Tennessee, Jacksonville-Duval County, Florida, and Indianapolis-Marion County, Indiana.

Comprehensive metropolitan planning in the United States was generally under the auspices of private organizations, with no powers except that of persuasion, until the 1930s. The most famous examples were in Chicago and New York, in 1909 and the 1920s, respectively.[98] Many of the principal physical elements of both were

---

97. Frederick G. Gardiner, "Metropolitan Toronto: A New Answer to Metropolitan Area Problems," in *Planning 1953* (Chicago: American Society of Planning Officials, 1953), pp. 38-47; Frank Smallwood, *Metro Toronto a Decade Later* (Toronto: Toronto Bureau of Municipal Research, 1963); Harold Kaplan, *Urban Political Systems: A Functional Analysis of Metro Toronto* (New York: Columbia University Press, 1967).

98. Daniel H. Burnham and Edward H. Bennett, *Plan of Chicago* (Chicago: The Commercial Club, 1909); *Regional Plan of New York and Its Environs* 2 plan vols. and 9 survey vols. (New York: Regional Plan Association, 1979).

largely carried out in subsequent decades. In the 1930s, the
federal government and many states actively attempted to institute
regional planning, including planning for metropolitan regions,
partly as a make-work effort, but the movement effectively halted
with the advent of World War II, to be revived more actively after
the end of the war.

As mentioned earlier, comprehensive transportation-land use
studies in many metropolitan areas during the 1950s and 1960s
furnished a factual base for planning decisions. Local governmental
fragmentation, however, greatly inhibited the planning process as
well as, in many instances, implementation of the plans. The
mandated studies under the Federal Highway Act of 1956, in spite of
their omissions and deficiencies, formed in a sense the framework
for metropolitan planning in the absence of more comprehensive
instruments.

Passage by the federal government in 1966 of the Demonstration
Cities and Metropolitan Development Act stimulated metropolitan
planning activity throughout the United States. Although the
"demonstration cities" aspect was far from successful--it became
known as the "model cities" program because many cities experienced
a different series of demonstrations in the late 1960s--the
metropolitan develoment program initiated by the act stimulated
considerable planning activity. As prerequisite for federal
assistance in numerous physical, social, and economic development
programs, the act mandated that comprehensive plans be prepared for
metropolitan areas. These plans were to be made, and frequently
revised, by state-designated metropolitan planning agencies. They
were to include comprehensively inter-related studies and plans for
land use, transportation, sewer and water systems, and many other
facilities and programs. Housing was also to be a prominent aspect
of the comprehensive metropolitan plans. Some of the requisite
agencies were already in existence and were expanded; others were
created to carry out the provisions of the act. Any major project
or program of metropolitan significance was to be submitted to the
metropolitan agency by the local governments or authorities for
review as to their conformance to the metropolitan plan. The scope
and method of comprehensive planning was spelled out in "Directive
A-95," which was generally followed.

Typical of the operation of metropolitan planning was that in
the Chicago region, in which the Northeastern Illinois Planning
Commission was the instrument for coordination. That agency is a
direct outgrowth of the *Plan of Chicago* of 1909, following which two
agencies were created: the Chicago Plan Commission to carry out
public education relative to the plan, and to lobby for its elements

within the City of Chicago, and the Chicago Regional Planning
Association within the metropolitan area outside of the city.  The
latter was quite successful in helping to bring about many aspects
of the Plan, including the metropolitan system of major highways and
the Forest Preserve District of Cook County.[99] It also assisted
local governments in their own planning and zoning activities.
Meanwhile in 1957, the Northeastern Illinois Planning Commission was
created as a quasi-governmental planning agency, and in 1967, was
designated as the regional agency under the Demonstration Cities and
Metropolitan Development Act.  In order to prevent duplication the
two metropolitan planning agencies were merged.  The Chicago Area
Transportation Study, which subsequently became a permanent state
agency, coordinated its transportation planning with the
comprehensive metropolitan planning of the Northeastern Illinois
Planning Commission, in spite of occasional conflicts.  As mandated,
public participation played an important role in the evolution of
the comprehensive metropolitan plan, which was adopted in 1968 and
subsequently revised.[100]

The regional plan for metropolitan Chicago is fairly typical
of the comprehensive regional plans of major metropolitan areas in
the United States.  It offered a series of alternative physical land
use and transportation patterns: satelite cities, peripheral
expansion, a "finger plan," and others.[101] After two years of
pre-presentation of the plan, and resulting modifications, by means
of lectures, exhibits, and intensive use of the mass media, a poll
was taken to ascertain public preference as among the alternative
general plans.  The preference was for the "finger plan," consisting
of a main urban mass and tentacles along the main transportation
radials with nodes at various points corresponding to the existing
suburban nuclei with a few additions.  Essentially the preferred
plan was an extension of the pattern which then existed.
Subsequently, development of many additional nuclei took place, and
the emerging system of express highways, development of the world's
busiest airport, and growth of residential, commercial, and
industrial land uses between the earlier radials greatly modified
the physical pattern of the region to a much larger extent than
visualized fifteen years ago.

In addition to the Highway Act of 1956 and the Demonstration
Cities and Metropolitan Development Act of 1966, numerous other

99 . Daniel H. Burnham, Jr., and Robert Kingery, *Planning the Region of Chicago* (Chicago: Chicago Regional Planning Association, 1956).

100 . Harold M. Mayer, "Chicago: Transportation and Metropolitan Planning," *Papers of the Regional Science Association* 7 (1961): 241-247.

101 . *The Comprehensive General Plan for the Development of the Northeastern Illinois Counties Area* (Chicago: Northeastern Illinois Planning Commission, 1968).

federal and state policies and acts have influenced the direction taken by planning in cities and metropolitan regions. Among the more important ones are the Environmental Protection Act of 1969, the Coastal Zone Management Act of 1972 and, prospectively, the various federal acts deregulating air, rail, and highway transportation, which can have major impacts upon the physical form and pattern of metropolitan areas in the future.

### The Form of American Cities and Metropolitan Areas in the Mid-1980s

In comparing the spatial patterns of American cities and metropolitan areas of the mid-1980s with the classical models--the concentric circle, the wedge or sector, and the multiple nuclei, which were set forth in the classic 1945 paper by Harris and Ullman, one is impressed by the fact that practically no significant changes at the gross scale have taken place. The typical metropolitan area, now as then, contains elements of all three patterns. The negative exponential distance decay curve is still generally applicable, in spite of growth of numerous new nuclei and expansion of the built-up areas. The density decline with distance from the metropolitan core is, in most instances, not as steep now, since the average density of new areas within the metropolitan regions tend to be less than the older ones. On the other hand, the core functions are somewhat different now, with declines in retail, wholesale, and entertainment functions in many central business districts, and their reinforcement in outlying nodes. The "wholesale and light manufacturing" belt surrounding the central business district has almost disappeared in many cities, to be replaced by extensive areas of derelict, lightly used, and vacant remnants of once-thriving business concentrations, together with parking lots and circumferential express highways surrounding the urban cores. Where they exist, downtown waterfronts are no longer the scenes of commercial port activity, but rather, the sites of newly redeveloped park, retail specialty market, and historic preservation projects; similarly, extensive areas formerly occupied by railroad freight and passenger depots and yards are either vacated or redeveloped for high-density residential or other uses.

Much of the "inner city" residential area remains the locus of low-income population, predominantly minorities, although rehabilitation has somewhat improved the physical condition of much of the housing. Here and there are phalanxes of high-rise buildings for the most part low-income public housing, with a sprinkling of Title I and other developments for middle-income residence. There are also vast areas of vacant land where proposed redevelopment has aborted. The central city areas tend to be more easily visible now, for the environmental regulations reducing pollution, have had some effect.

Farther out, some of the older outlying concentrations of business, both in the peripheries of the principal cities and in the older suburban nuclei, are prominent because of their new clusters of high-rise business buildings and apartment structures. New shopping centers constitute nuclei around which residential and business development has precipitated. A spider-web network of express highways links old and new nuclei, facilitating access to much more extensive areas than were accessible a generation ago. Major airports interrupt the continuity of the urban landscape in many instances, some occupying ten square miles or more, surrounded by virtually new cities comprised of office buildings, high-density residential areas, industrial districts, hotels, and motels and spawning attenuated ribbons of highway-oriented fast-food establishments, automobile dealerships and service facilities, a variety of merchandising establishments, and streams of automobiles, trucks, and buses with much higher traffic volumes than were prevalent forty years ago. In many instances, urbanization from nearby neighbors overlap, and intermetropolitan coalescence, with continuous ribbons of urban land uses extending for scores or even hundreds of miles, has resulted. Coincident with the expansion of urbanization is a reduction of population density, and with it considerable obsolescence of a partly redundant physical plant and infrastructure in the older portions of central cities and in some of the older suburbs.

With the widespread use of quantitative methods in urban geographic research, and the ability to utilize computers in processing large amounts of data, new models of urban structure are being tested against the actual patterns, including the use of technology and the recording of "real time" changes. Except in detail, however, it appears that the time has not yet come to reject the classic models, but, rather, to fine-tune them.

PROSPECT AND RETROSPECT:  METHODOLOGICAL AND
SYNTHETIC PERSPECTIVES

# Chapter XVIII

# URBAN SYSTEMS, REGIONAL DEVELOPMENT, AND THE EXTENT OF RESIDENTIAL SEGREGATION IN IRELAND: FURTHER INSIGHTS INTO THE "NATURE OF CITIES"

Jörg Güssefeldt and Walter Manshard

There are many explanations for the social phenomenon of residential segregation in towns. They can be grouped into at least ten distinct approaches.[1] One such approach is that of human ecology, rooted in the achievements in urban sociology of the Chicago School of the 1920s. The writings of Harris and Ullman can, in a broad sense, be considered as an additional elaboration of the human ecological concept.[2] Their multiple-nuclei urban model may be seen as a variation on the concentric or sectoral models of Burgess and Hoyt and as a widening of existing explanations, which better approximates reality.[3]

A brief survey of the more important theoretical explanations of human ecology clarifies why the Harris-Ullman model may be considered as an extension of the work of Burgess and Hoyt. If dominant use-systems or population groups of a town grow, they generally extend into those parts of urban space in which weaker institutions or social groups are located. The continued process of invasion by dominant elements leads to the displacement of weaker ones and thus to a succession of urban land-use and residential population patterns. Following the primacy of economic competition, the central business district of each town is progressively influenced in its development from the inside to the outside. Urban development, therefore, proceeds generally from the core to the periphery, with the simultaneous formation of economic and social

---

1. P. Korcelli, "Theory of Intraurban Structure: Review and Synthesis," *Geografia Polonica* 31 (1975): 99-131; Keith Bassett and John Short, *Housing and Residential Structure: Alternative Approaches* (London: Routledge and Kegan Paul, 1980); Jörg Güssefeldt: *Die gegenseitige Abhängigkeit innerurbaner Strukturmuster und Rollen der Städte im nationalen Städtesystem: Das Beispiel der sozialräumlichen Organisation innerhalb irischer Städte,* Freiburger Geographische Hefte, no. 22 (Freiburg, 1983).

2. Chauncy D. Harris and Edward L. Ullman, "The Nature of Cities," *Annals of the American Academy of Political and Social Science* 242 (1945): 7-17.

3. Ernest W. Burgess, "The Growth of the City," in *The City,* ed. R.E. Park, E.W. Burgess, and R.D. McKenzie (Chicago: University of Chicago Press, 1925), pp. 47-62; Homer Hoyt, *The Structure and Growth of Residential Neighborhoods in American Cities* (Washington, D.C.: Federal Housing Administration, 1939).

gradients and more homogenous spatial units and sub-centers.

Harris and Ullman have considered urban growth an important element of the internal urban development process as well. Because of the economic competition for optimal urban locations, a close connection is established between dominant use-systems and the economic base. This view, however, omits another aspect of their work, namely the importance of the functional[4] association of a town within the national settlement system and its internal urban structure. This link offers explanations for phenomena which are less easily explained by other theories. Berry[5] recognized this at an early stage when he postulated a theoretical link between the role of a town in its regional, national, and international socio-economic system and its internal structure.[6] The observations of Harris and Ullman, on the other hand, are based more on empirical generalizations. However, the idea for such a linkage, mentioned explicitly by Berry, doubtlessly came from Harris and Ullman, although it was Berry who developed a logical connection between both theoretical constructs. Using classical economic location theories, Berry deduced that towns have to fulfill three major roles. As *collectors of resources,* the location of towns is determined by raw materials. It is clear from polarization theories that towns produce backwash effects by absorbing labor, capital, and commodities from their hinterlands. As *producers of goods,* trying to obtain an optimal location in the communication network, they must transport goods (material as well as non-material) to national and international markets. As *distributors of goods and services* for the urban population as well as for residents in their hinterland, towns function as central places catering to local and regional markets.

Each town can, but may not, fulfill all three roles simultaneously. While the first two roles mentioned may vary considerably, almost every town possesses the role of a central place. Furthermore, because of the principle of agglomeration advantage, Berry concludes that each town must establish a central business district, which can be supplemented by other specialized services, which make other urban roles possible. Their location can occur within the central business district itself or in other

---

4. In this paper the term "role" is often used rather than "function," because in this context the former has a more precise definition.

5. Brian J.L. Berry, "Cities as Systems within Systems of Cities," *Papers of Regional Science Association* 13 (1964): 147-163; "Internal Structure of the City," in *Comparative Urban Structure: Studies in the Ecology of Cities,* ed. Kent P. Schwirian, (Lexington, Mass.: Heath, 1974), pp. 227-233.

6. Ibid.

locations in the town which provide a comparative advantage in the
fulfillment of their tasks. This generally leads to the formation
of several specialized centers in each town.

Following the hypothesis of Friedmann, towns have to fulfill,
besides the three classic roles mentioned above, two further ones.[7]
Towns act as *development centers* for the adoption of ideas which
will be extended into their regions.[8] It is particularly through
these spread effects that the economic integration of urban spheres
of influence takes place. These spread effects of economic change
also include cultural and social innovations. Towns, therefore,
experience a comprehensive development which, in the final analysis,
allows cultural, social, and economic progress. Towns also act as
*power centers* from which countries and regions are administered and
governed. In their position as power centers, these towns possess a
kind of self-regulatory counterbalance. "Accelerated urbanization
hastens the coming of a national mass politics based on bargaining
and compromise among competing interest groups."[9]

Assuming that the institutions for the fulfillment of these
roles are dominant urban use systems, it follows that they expand at
the expense of others. Therefore, the greater the number of roles a
town has, the greater is the displacement of less dominant uses and
the higher the dissimilarity and segregation of urban use systems.
If we start from a hierarchically organized urban structure with the
number of inhabitants as a valid indicator of its hierarchical
position, the following thesis can be postulated: The larger the
town, the higher tends to be the degree of social segregation, but
it is evident even in relatively small towns.[10] In addition to this
thesis, it can be suggested that the hierarchical order of an urban
system has not so much a deterministic as a probalistic quality.

This can be changed in the course of development: (1) because
of changes in the diffusion process,[11] when the inter-urban

---

7 . John Friedmann, "The Role of Cities in National Development," *American Behavioral Scientist* 22 (1969): 13-21; "The Spatial Organization of Power in the Development of Urban Systems," *Comparative Urban Research* 1 (1972): 153-190.

8 . The more comprehensive term "development center" is used here, since it includes the role of growth pole. The growth pole idea seems to be biased rather strongly towards economic growth and attaches less importance to social change. In the postindustrial era, social change may be quite important for the spatial organization of settlement systems. See James W. Simmons, "The Organization of the Urban System," in *Systems of Cities: Readings on Growth, Structure, and Policy,* ed. Larry S. Bourne and James W. Simmons (New York: Oxford University Press, 1978).

9 . Friedmann, p. 176.

10 . Brian T. Robson, *Urban Social Areas* (Oxford: Oxford University Press, 1975), p. 76.

11 . Allan R. Pred, "The Growth and Development of Systems of Cities in Advanced Economies," in *Systems of Cities and Information Flows,* ed. Allan R. Pred and G. Tornqvist (Lund: Lund Studies in Geography, ser. B, 38, 1973), pp. 9-82.

information exchange has changed, or (2) because inventors and adopters of innovations consider the risk of supply in little towns as small as in bigger ones,[12] and (3) because of political intervention which seeks to raise the economic development level. All three measures lead to a change in the urban system if they are limited to one or only a sub-set of towns. Through these influences, a change in the fulfillment of existing roles will occur. If in a town, for example, in addition to the existing industrial enterprises, a new industrial estate is established, the role of the town as a producer of goods will be strengthened. If, on the other hand, a new provincial government is established, the town may evolve a completely new role as a center of political power controlling a region.

From this theoretical framework the following thesis can be deduced regarding the extent of segregation within a town: the stronger the changes with regard to the fulfillment of roles of a town, the stronger is the social shape of its inhabitants. The two examples above may illustrate this. In the first case, the number of factory workers would increase greatly. In the case of a new administrative role, the result would be the residence of a new group of government officials which would obviously lead to increased social and professional differentiation, what has been mentioned as "increasing scale" by Shevky and Bell.[13] The stronger the social change taking place, the greater is the necessity to establish new residential areas that suit the needs of the new group. As a result, a positive correlation between the role of a town and the extent of residential segregation can be deduced. This phenomenon will be particularly obvious if changes affecting national settlement systems are strong and occur in short periods. In this case other groups and uses do not have the opportunity to invade other group-specific ("natural") areas. In short, the increased interest in the role of towns initiated by Harris and Ullman is useful in establishing a link between theoretical elements in the fields of human ecology and social area analysis. It is clear that both models of urban development need not compete with one another; rather they can be seen as complementary.

---

12. Brian J.L. Berry, *City Classification Handbook: Methods and Application* (New York: Wiley Interscience, 1972); Harry W. Richardson, *Regional and Urban Economics* (Harmondsworth: Penguin, 1978).

13. Eshref Shevky and Wendell Bell, *Social Area Analysis* (Stanford: Stanford University Press, 1955).

### An Empirical Examination Set in Ireland

Any empirical test of the theoretical construct developed above faces a number of difficulties. In addition to relevant diachronic data for a representative selection of urban systems, there is the need for corresponding information about internal urban areas, which should also be suitable for comparison from place to place. National surveys only rarely take into account the criterion of international comparability, and thus comparative studies face great problems. For these reasons, the present examination is limited to the Irish example, being fully aware of its limitations. This is a summary recasting of a much larger study, published elsewhere.[14] Ireland is a useful example because, in its recent history, it has passed through a series of development phases, which closely conform to Rostow's theory on economic development.[15]

Two dates, 1946 and 1971, have been chosen for analysis because they fall in the middle of two periods of similar length during which different economic policies were operating. The year 1946 marks a turning point in the economic development of Ireland. From 1926 onwards, new legislation on customs duty and taxation was in effect to protect the Irish economy from foreign competition and achieve a certain independence from the British economy. Payment of land rents to the United Kingdom, for example, was prohibited by the de Valera Government. This, together with protective tariffs, led the British to impose extra duties and a quota system on the importation of Irish products (e.g., beef cattle). These measures eventually escalated into the "Anglo-Irish Economic War," which culminated in the so-called "Coal-Cattle-Pact" of 1935, which actually increased the dependence of Ireland on Britain.[16] The latter gained, for instance, a monopoly for all coal products on the Irish market. These decisions in economic policy lead to a cumulative causation which has been described by R.D. Crotty:

> "Manufacturing industry was geared to the small protected home market and because of this its costs were too high to warrant any hope of a substantial export trade. Agricultural exports depended to a greater extent than ever on cattle, and against an expansion of cattle production there were formidable and well-nigh impenetrable barriers. An increase in non-cattle exports implied an increase in subsidies, which in turn implied a further reduction in living standard.[17]

---

14. Güssefeldt, *Die gegenseitige Abhängigkeit innerurbaner Strukturmuster.*

15. Walter W. Rostow, "The Take-off into Self-sustained Growth," *The Economic Journal* 66 (1956): 25-48.

16. Francis S.L. Lyons, *Ireland since the Famine* (London: Fontana, 1979), p. 612.

17. Raymond D. Crotty, *Irish Agricultural Production: Its Volume and Structure* (Cork: Cork University Press, 1966), p. 156.

The Irish economy moved into a phase similar to the situation in the nineteenth century, during which its main export products were affected by low prices. Capital became scarce and investment activity nearly ceased. Parts of the population reacted with increased emigration. In contrast to the more laissez-faire principles of the previous century, however, the Irish Government reacted quite differently. Already in the first years of independence it recognized that certain sectors of the economy are vital to the community. As a result of capital scarcity and the high risks involved, the provision and operation of these sectors should not be left to private enterprise alone. Therefore, between 1927 and 1945, beginning with the Agricultural Credit Corporation and the Electricity Supply Board, no less than 25 public corporations were established.[18] These public corporations were founded in all economic sectors for the production, as well as the distribution, of selected goods and services. As Lyons has noted, "It is not necessary to seek any profound philosophy of state socialism behind the emergence of this variegated collection of organisations. They were essentially responses to specific situations--the intentions of the government were strictly pragmatic."[19] These measures were not the result of an autarkical policy but rather of a government-sponsored "survival" policy, which must be seen in the light of the global economic depression on the one hand and Anglo-Irish economic difficulties on the other.

The most notable event of the postwar period was the foundation of the Irish Republic in 1948. With this step a new orientation of Irish economic policy began, of which the first important step was the establishment in 1949 of the Industrial Development Authority, followed by a further series of bills in the 1950s.[20] Closely following Rostow's theory of economic growth, the preparatory phase for "economic take-off" began after the Second World War, with a reduction of autarkical policies and new legislative measures for capital imports. At first, certain measures were retained in order to protect national industries and work places, because the government was not yet sure that local producers could compete with foreign imports. Only in 1958, when the First Economic Development Plan was passed, was it recognized "that if Ireland wished to keep pace materially with Europe,

---

18 . Lyons, *Ireland since the Famine,* p. 616.

19 . Ibid., p. 618.

20 . Eoin J. O'Malley, *Industrial Policy and Development: A Survey of Literature from the Early 1960's to the Present* (Dublin: National Economic and Social Council, report no. 56, 1981), p. 6.

competitive efficiency would have to be raised to levels obtaining elsewhere and that this aim could be furthered by accepting freer trade conditions."[21] After the failure of negotiations to join the European Economic Community (EEC), a free trade agreement was reached in 1965 between Ireland and Britain. Only in 1973, after joining the EEC, was trade with other member states facilitated. As protective customs barriers were gradually reduced (agreed upon with Britain in 1975 and the other EEC countries in 1978), free access to the Irish market became possible. The year 1946, therefore, represents the ending of an economic era and the beginning of a new orientation. Census data for 1971, on the other hand, indicate well how structures within the urban system of Ireland have subsequently changed.

## Towards a Typology of Irish Towns

In order to create an urban typology related to economic development, 28 social and economic variables were selected from the censuses of 1946 and 1971. The variables describe population density, housing conditions, income structure, age structure, and centrality. Data were transformed into rank values to accommodate slight changes in the definitions of some variables between 1946 and 1971. For each data set a principal components analysis was carried out using the rank values of the original data. In each analysis eight roots were extracted, reproducing roughly 85 percent of the variance of each data set. The correlation coefficient between the two loading patterns proved to be $r = 0.8168$, and so lends support to Berry's hypothesis regarding the connection between development and latent dimensions of an urban system.[22] The components may be labelled as (1) population density (the correlation between the loadings of the 1946 and 1971 analysis is 0.9045), (2) age structure or stage in life cycle (0.8144), (3) housing conditions (0.7969), (4) economic dependency or labor force (0.9102), (5) poverty (0.7330), (6) centrality or functional size (0.8677), (7) housing space (0.7393), and (8) occupational stratification or economic base (0.7067).

Neither loading patterns approximated a simple structure after varimax rotation, and even after oblique rotation, simple structure could not be obtained. In such a case there is a high probability of transferring the random pattern from the loadings to the scores,

---

21. Ibid., p. 16.

22. The aim here is not to test Berry's hypothesis concerning the emergence of latent dimensions of an urban system, which have been discussed in length elsewhere. See Güssefeldt, *Die gegenseitige Abhängigkeit innerurbaner Strukturmuster.*

so that they will barely, if at all, reflect any meaningful qualities of the cities. For the computation of scores we used an algorithm which produces linear combinations of the labelling variables.[23] This was done in accordance with interpretation of the loading patterns and "can be regarded as an empirical means of index construction."[24] These index values comprised the data base for a cluster analysis. The Ward-algorithm was used to combine individual cities into initial clusters, which were then optimized using an iterative algorithm minimizing within-group variances. The latter procedure has been described by Rubin as the "hill-climbing method."[25] The decision at what point to terminate the classification process was based on a variance criterion. It shows maximum values if the cluster centroids have a maximum distance from each other.[26]

For 1946, the towns of Ireland fell into four clusters. The first group was the *metropolitan* type with high population density, good housing conditions, and low degrees of economic dependency and poverty. The second cluster comprised *economically weak towns* with poor housing conditions. In the third cluster were *extremely underdeveloped towns,* with a large proportion of poor and old people. Finally, the fourth cluster of towns was characterized by *economic stagnation,* in which young families with children live under cramped housing and poor living conditions. General conditions within these types are described by selected centroids for each of the clusters (table 18.1). In the table, the last two columns show the figures for the *metropolitan type* excluding the metropolis and then of Dublin alone. This demonstrates that the other four towns of this group (Cork, Dun Laoghaire, Bray, and Cobh), although grouped in one cluster, nevertheless showed strong variations from Dublin itself. This suggests a staging in urban structural change during the development of these towns towards metropolitan status. In this process Dublin at all times kept ahead, which in view of its position in the urban hierachy and related hierarchical diffusion processes, is to be expected. It is interesting to note that in group 2 towns in 1946 only 16.8 percent

---

23. Jorg Gussefeldt, "Some Geographical Aspects of the Fallacy of Contemporary Factorial Ecology," *Karlsruher Manuskripte zur Mathematischen und Theoretischen Wirtschafts- und Sozialgeographie* 52 (1981).

24. Philip H. Rees, "Factorial Ecology: An Extended Definition, Survey and Critique of the Field," *Economic Geography* (suppl.) 47 (1971): 222.

25. J. Rubin, "Optimal Classification into Groups: An Approach for Solving the Taxonomy Problem," *Journal of Theoretical Biology* 15 (1967): 103-144.

26. Jürgen Bähr, "Gemeindetypisierung mit Hilfe quantitativer statistischer Verfahren," *Erdkunde* 25 (1971): 249-264.

TABLE 13.1

GROUP CENTROIDS OF SELECTED VARIABLES OF CITY TYPES, 1946

| DIMENSIONS (selected variables) | Group centroids | | | | Total mean | Group I excluding Dublin | Dublin |
|---|---|---|---|---|---|---|---|
| | I | II | III | IV | | | |
| DENSITY (Population/hectare) | 37.27 | 28.02 | 11.59 | 10.88 | 21.55 | 32.32 | 57.08 |
| HOUSING SPACE (Persons/dwelling) | 3.92 | 4.13 | 3.99 | 4.29 | 4.14 | 3.87 | 4.10 |
| HOUSING CONDITIONS (Percent dwellings with bath) | 40.93 | 16.81 | 20.94 | 20.21 | 21.45 | 39.15 | 57.08 |
| POVERTY (Percent dwellings without toilet) | 2.45 | 20.63 | 25.32 | 18.42 | 18.22 | 2.86 | 0.80 |
| OCCUP. STRATIFICATION (Percent clerical workers) | 8.83 | 5.34 | 4.07 | 4.70 | 5.41 | 8.60 | 9.76 |
| LABOR FORCE (Percent males occupied) | 57.37 | 56.41 | 45.56 | 58.45 | 55.83 | 56.85 | 59.44 |
| AGE STRUCTURE (Percent children aged 0-4) | 9.74 | 10.97 | 7.44 | 10.96 | 10.37 | 9.62 | 10.22 |

of the dwellings had a shower or bath. Furthermore, it seems a testimony to poverty as well as backwardness, that nearly one-fifth (18.2 percent) of all urban dwellings had no toilets, while in Dublin only 0.8 percent of all dwellings lacked such conveniences.

The regional distribution of city types according to the statistical analysis shows a clear pattern (figure 18.1).[27] The metropolitan type (type 1) included Dublin, Cork, and their neighboring towns of Dun Laoghaire, Bray, and Cobh. Their distribution suggests hierarchical and spatial expansion elements of a diffusing development process and indicates that only the country's two main cities were able to profit from such spread effects. The towns of type 2, characterized by poor housing conditions as a result of economic weakness, concentrated in two regions: between Arklow and Wexford on the east coast (including Waterford, Clonmel, and Limerick) and as far as Tralee in the southwest, and the towns of Drogheda, Dundalk, and Navan in the northeast. This group included many small ports, the economic development of which was hampered during the period of autarky in the 1930s and 1940s. Towns of type 4, which differed from the second type mainly in occupational structure, standard of dwellings, and population density, were distributed in a continuous region in the central lowland and the northwest. Location of towns of the more underdeveloped type (type 3) appeared in rather disjunct locations and were characterized by distinct remoteness within the urban system. In addition to Killarney, which displayed the characteristics of this type as early as 1841, Youghal in the southwest and Ballinasloe and Castlebar in the west belong to this category. Compared with those of type 2, type 3 places had higher economic dependency, lower income levels, an age structure with fewer children and more aged, and a greater degree of poverty.

If the general economic framework described above is related to the diffusion hypothesis, in which a dependency between the invention and adoption of innovations and economic development is envisaged, this offers an explanation of why the Irish urban system in 1946 comprised only four types.[28] While at the top of the system structural similarities can be observed, as a consequence of hierarchical diffusion, the great majority of the 40 towns, however, belonged to two other groups. If the dwelling standard is used as

---

27. For identification of towns, see table 18.2, which includes key numbers applicable to figure 18.2 also. The numbers of inhabitants (both for 1946 and 1971) also indicate the relatively small size of Irish cities and towns.

28. Paul O. Pedersen, "Innovation Diffusion within and between National Urban Systems," *Geographical Analysis* 2 (1970): 203-254.

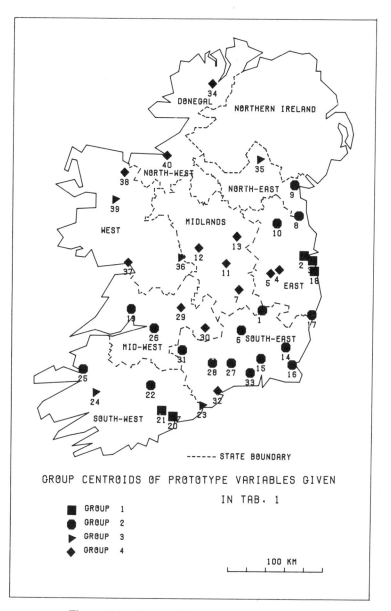

Figure 18.1. Types of Irish cities and towns in 1946

TABLE 18.2

POPULATION AND CLASSIFICATION OF IRISH URBAN PLACES,
1946 AND 1971

| Place | Urban Type* | | Population ('000)[a] | |
|-------|------|------|------|------|
| | 1946 | 1971 | 1946 | 1971 |
| Carlow | 2 | 3 | 7.5 | 10.4 |
| Dublin | 1 | 1 | 506.1 | 679.8 |
| Dun Laoghaire | 1 | 1 | 44.7 | 98.4 |
| Naas | 4 | 4 | 3.8 | 5.1 |
| Newbridge | 4 | 4 | 3.2 | 6.4 |
| Kilkenny | 2 | 2 | 10.3 | 13.3 |
| Portlaoighise | 4 | 4 | 3.2 | 6.5 |
| Drogheda | 2 | 2 | 15.7 | 20.1 |
| Dundalk | 2 | 3 | 18.6 | 23.8 |
| Navan | 2 | 3 | 4.1 | 6.7 |
| Tullamore | 4 | 3 | 5.9 | 7.5 |
| Athlone | 4 | 4 | 8.4 | 11.6 |
| Mullingar | 4 | 4 | 5.4 | 9.3 |
| Enniscorthy | 2 | 2 | 6.0 | 6.6 |
| New Ross | 2 | 3 | 4.9 | 5.2 |
| Wexford | 2 | 2 | 12.3 | 13.3 |
| Arklow | 2 | 3 | 4.9 | 7.0 |
| Bray | 1 | 1 | 11.1 | 15.8 |
| Ennis | 2 | 1 | 5.9 | 10.4 |
| Cobh | 1 | 1 | 5.6 | 7.1 |
| Cork | 1 | 1 | 89.9 | 134.4 |
| Mallow | 2 | 2 | 5.2 | 6.5 |
| Youghal | 3 | 3 | 4.8 | 5.6 |
| Killarney | 3 | 5 | 6.0 | 7.5 |
| Tralee | 2 | 2 | 9.9 | 13.3 |
| Limerick | 2 | 1 | 43.0 | 63.0 |
| Carrick on Suir | 2 | 3 | 4.9 | 5.0 |
| Clonmel | 2 | 2 | 9.9 | 12.3 |
| Nenagh | 4 | 3 | 4.5 | 5.2 |
| Thurles | 4 | 2 | 6.0 | 7.1 |
| Tipperary | 2 | 2 | 5.3 | 5.6 |
| Dungarvan | 4 | 2 | 5.3 | 5.6 |
| Waterford | 2 | 2 | 29.3 | 33.7 |
| Letterkenny | 4 | 4 | 2.9 | 5.2 |

TABLE 18.2, Cont.

| Place | Urban Type* | | Population ('000)[a] | |
|-------|------|------|------|------|
| | 1946 | 1971 | 1946 | 1971 |
| Monaghan | 3 | 5 | 4.7 | 5.3 |
| Ballinasloe | 3 | 5 | 5.4 | 6.0 |
| Galway | 4 | 4 | 20.4 | 29.4 |
| Ballina | 4 | 2 | 6.1 | 6.4 |
| Castlebar | 3 | 5 | 5.0 | 6.5 |
| Sligo | 4 | 2 | 12.9 | 14.5 |

SOURCE: Census of Population, 1946, 1971.

*For typology, see text and Figures 1 and 2.

[a]Includes suburbs and enivirons of all towns, if any.

an indicator of economic development, the actual regional distribution stands in contrast to the expected theoretical pattern. In an area between the economically well-developed cities of Dublin and Cork we should, for instance, expect the more developed towns. In fact, the opposite was the case. Given the general economic conditions of the period, it appears that in these locations little private investment had taken place and there was limited adoption of the innovations of previous development phases. A barrier to diffusion through the urban system led to a slow-down so that spread effects can be traced only in the immediate hinterlands of the two largest centers. In addition, state economic intervention led to a stronger equalization of towns in the lower ranks of the hierarchy, which in turn influenced the spatial distribution pattern.

The development typology of towns altered somewhat by 1971, and for this more recent date probably five types can be distinguished. The metropolitan type (type 1) now comprised seven towns, which show extreme centroids for population density, housing conditions, and poverty. The second group (type 2), as in 1946, possessed characteristics which were the very opposite of type 1 in housing conditions but with the highest measures of housing space. Type 3 shows extremes for age structure, poverty, and occupational stratification (about 38 percent were skilled and unskilled laborers). Type 4 was characterized by lowest housing space. Type 5, on the other hand, shows four extreme group centroids for population density, age structure, labor force, and occupational stratification and represents characteristics largely drawn from type 3 in 1946. By 1971, this type no longer reflects underdeveloped towns but rather a traditional type of *small town with special functions,* such as tourism for Killarney. The group centroids of prototype variables of city types permit a somewhat more precise description (table 18.3).

The regional distribution of urban development types in 1971 shows that at the top of the urban hierarchy there has been further diffusion downwards (figure 18.2). Limerick and its neighboring town, Ennis, now also belonged to the metropolitan group. Since this development may have been influenced by the foundation of the Shannon Free Airport Estate, it suggests the strength of the correlation between economic development and urban structure. In addition, this finding seems to support the thesis that as a consequence of economic transformation a convergence of urban structure occurs with that of the metropolis. Furthermore, it is clear that in 1971 the majority of towns in the southeast belonged to type 2, characterized by inferior dwelling conditions. This indicates a direct relation to regional per capita income. The remaining three towns of this region were members of type 3: Carlow, New Ross, and Carrick on Suir showed a slight improvement in dwelling conditions. However, as the data demonstrate, they did not have the same success in decreasing poverty. This is also true for Navan and Dundalk, which in 1946 still belonged to the second group. They were now joined by Ballina and Sligo in the west and northwest, which in 1946 belonged to a group with better dwelling conditions. In their development up to 1971, they could not keep up their lead. This, in turn, points up the deceleration effect of income diffusion in the northwest.

The separation between the different clusters has been tested in two ways. On the one hand, a multiple discriminant analysis was performed on the same index-values as used in the cluster analyses. On the other hand, the same analysis was carried out using the raw data to make sure that the indices are valid representations of the original variables.[29] It is impossible to give the results here in detail, but in every test the null hypothesis was rejected, in almost all cases at the 5 percent level. This indicates a high probability that the 40 investigated Irish towns fell into sharply discriminated clusters of multi-dimensional definition.

---

29. The SPSS program DISCRIMINANT provides four inferential tests. First it gives the results of an univariate F-test of difference between the group centroids. A second F-test shows the significance of separation between two particular group centroids in the discriminant space. Third, a modified Wilk's Lambda indicates the significance of the discriminating power of each variable included in the model, and, fourth, chi-square tests of the significance of each discriminant function are computed.

TABLE 18.3

GROUP CENTROIDS OF SELECTED VARIABLES OF CITY TYPES, 1971

| DIMENSIONS (selected variables) | Group centroids | | | | | Total mean | Group I excluding Dublin | Dublin |
|---|---|---|---|---|---|---|---|---|
| | I | II | III | IV | V | | | |
| DENSITY (Population/hectare) | 33.47 | 23.54 | 12.87 | 13.43 | 8.57 | 19.61 | 30.85 | 49.20 |
| HOUSING SPACE (Persons/dwelling) | 41.9 | 4.10 | 4.23 | 4.43 | 4.18 | 4.21 | 4.18 | 4.28 |
| HOUSING CONDITIONS (Percent dwellings with bath) | 78.87 | 61.82 | 64.76 | 72.78 | 72.32 | 68.43 | 77.51 | 87.05 |
| POVERTY (Percent dwellings without toilet) | 1.37 | 1.61 | 4.10 | 2.39 | 3.12 | 2.42 | 1.51 | 0.55 |
| OCCUP. STRATIFICATION (Percent clerical workers) | 12.99 | 10.08 | 9.05 | 10.09 | 8.69 | 10.22 | 12.24 | 17.50 |
| LABOR FIRCE (Percent males occupied) | 51.69 | 51.90 | 51.55 | 48.64 | 43.84 | 50.41 | 51.24 | 54.44 |
| AGE STRUCTURE (Percent children aged 0-4) | 11.65 | 11.45 | 12.15 | 12.05 | 9.31 | 11.53 | 11.80 | 10.74 |

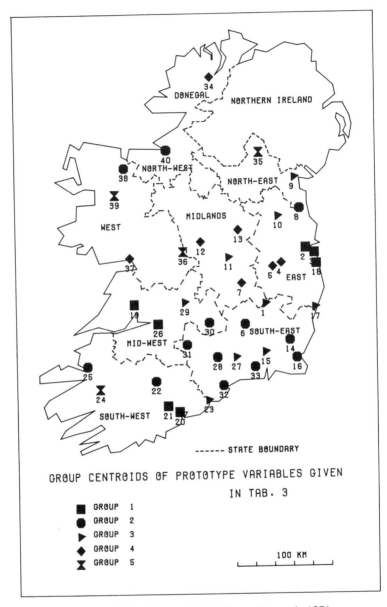

Figure 18.2.   Types of Irish cities and towns in 1971

### Diffusion and Development in the Irish Urban System

A comparison of the 1946 and 1971 typologies, without considering by which dimensions the difference between the metropolitan type and the other clusters is brought about, reveals a remarkable stability in spatial distribution patterns.[30] With a certain amount of generalization, one can suggest that the greater the relative structural deviation of a town from that of the metropolis, Dublin, the lower its rank in the urban hierarchy. The spread of economic development, which is here defined as a convergence of other towns with the structural characteristics of the metropolis, is influenced by processes that produce three separate effects. First, there is the *hierarchy effect,* which becomes apparent when towns at the top of the rank-size distribution belong to the metropolitan cluster. If the functional prerequisites for the adoption of growth-inducing innovations are lacking, towns of higher rank may be left behind in favor of lower ranking centers. Second, there is the *neighborhood effect,* which expresses itself in the fact that innovation centers form joint metropolitan areas with their smaller neighbors. Since this neighborhood effect also causes outstanding growth in these parts of the system, it may lead to the formation of agglomerations. And third, there is the *deceleration effect,* which in terms of economic development may lead to the formation of negative distance gradients, and thus to further increases in regional disparities.

All three effects can lead to very different outcomes in national and regional economic development. The hierarchical effect underlies wider spaced inter-urban relationships, by which development impulses may be transmitted to the nodes within the periphery. Their strength also influences the degree of integration of the regions. A stronger integration may again cause a higher national economic level, following the principle of comparative advantage, particularly if the regions are able to specialize.

If, however, the neighborhood effect is stronger than the hierachy effect, the former influences the growth center and leads to exponential growth at the expense of the periphery. As with the development of an agglomeration, a progressively higher input of social capital is necessary, which is then no longer available elsewhere, so that the disparities between growth center and periphery are increased. If, on the other hand, the hierarchical effect is greater than the neighborhood effect in the vicinity of

---

30. The concordance measure shows an index value of 0.7385 regarding the similarity of the two cluster solutions. See William M. Rand, "Objective Criteria for the Evaluation of Clustering Methods," *Journal of the American Statistical Association* 66 (1971): 846-850.

the growth center, the latter effect can also be achieved from the centers in the periphery and thereby speed up its development.

The deceleration effect, which can have manifold causes, may lead to a strengthening of backwash effects, which may increase regional disparities. This is a form of cumulative causation. A deceleration of growth-inducing innovations leads to regional stagnation, so that income rates and capital supplies lag behind those in growth centers. This may result in a slackening provision of better infrastructure needed for population and industrial development. Consequently, fewer industries with their regional multiplier effects would locate there, which in turn would cause further economic stagnation and underdevelopment. At the same time, a poor job and service environment would encourage the population to leave, which, in Ireland's case, has traditionally meant overseas emigration. Thus, the loss of a highly qualified laborforce provides a clear linkage to the underdevelopment of the national economy. Migration from a region generally means a decrease of population potential, by which a region may lose its functional prerequisites to adopt innovations. Thus, the vicious circle is twice circumscribed.

On the other hand, this "downward spiral" may be changed by a hierarchical diffusion process, as demonstrated by the example of Limerick. Between 1946 and 1971, Limerick joined the metropolitan cluster, an indication that its role within the urban system had changed significantly during this period. The increase of professional workers documents this shift in role. While the general population increased 1.5 times, the number of professional workers grew 3.7 times. By contrast, the corresponding figures for Dublin were 1.3 and 1.6 respectively.

### Comparative Analysis of Residential Segregation

The term *internal differentiation* means the disproportionate distribution of elements among various characteristic classes in well defined parts of a total area. However, *segregation* means the disproportionate spatial distribution of different social groups of inhabitants in an area such as a town. The measurement of segregation requires (a) a selection and analysis of certain characteristics of stratification and (b) a determination of disproportionality. While appropriate characteristics are simple to select, the definition of disproportionality is more problematic. The latter is beyond the scope of this essay. There is, however, a general agreement on ways of measuring the degree to which a social group in a particular town is or is not segregated. The index of dissimilarity (ID) measures the differences between the distribution of two social groups. The index of segregation (IS) measures the differences in distribution between a certain social group and an aggregation of all other groups. The indices are useful for a comparison of the degree of segregation between different towns.[31] Unfortunately, a direct comparison between 1946 and 1971 was not possible, since administrative boundaries have changed considerably during the period and the same data were not available for both years. Therefore, the inter-urban comparison relates only to 1971.

As a source for the description of social strata in the leading Irish towns, the socio-economic groups of the Small Area Classification file (second series) of the 1971 Irish Census have been used. The group covering "farmers and other agricultural occupations and fishermen" was omitted, since their number in towns is very small. The two groups of "higher professional workers" and "employers and managers" were amalgamated into one class (HPEM). Also the "lower professional workers" and "salaried employees" were unified into one class (LPSE). The data for the other classes, "intermediate non-manual workers" (INMW), "other non-manual workers" (ONMW), "skilled manual workers" (SKIL), "semi-skilled manual workers" (SEMI), and "unskilled manual workers" (UNWM), were adopted without change. With these modifications, the residential segregation of seven different socio-economic groups was calculated for four major towns. For the inter-urban comparison of segregation indices, a division of the Dublin/Dun Laoghaire Conurbation into 194 wards and district electoral divisions, of Cork into 74, Limerick into 37, and Waterford into 24 wards was used.

The segregation indices reveal, as expected, the U-shaped correlation between social rank and degree of segregation (table 18.4). In addition, with the exception of the semi-skilled manual workers in Cork, it is clear for major Irish towns that the more extreme the rank position of a social group is, the higher the index of segregation. This confirms "that residential segregation is greater for those occupation groups with clearly defined status than for those groups whose status is ambiguous."[32] In the middle of the social pyramid the differentiation by residential area is less clear, as is apparent from the index values for the intermediate non-manual workers (who could have been labelled clerical and kindred service workers), other non-manual workers (other service workers), and skilled manual workers (craftsmen). These findings largely replicate results obtained from towns in other countries.

31. Otis D. Duncan and Beverly Duncan, "A Methodological Analysis of Segregation Indexes," *American Sociological Review* 20 (1955): 210-217; idem, "Residential Distribution and Occupational Stratification," *American Journal of Sociology* 60 (1955): 493-503.

32. Duncan and Duncan, "Residential Distribution and Occupational Stratification," pp. 493-503.

TABLE 18.4

INDICES OF RESIDENTIAL SEGREGATION OF EACH
SOCIO-ECONOMIC GROUP IN FOUR IRISH CITIES,
1971

| City | Socio-economic groups* | | | | | | |
|------|------|------|------|------|------|------|------|
| | HPEM | LPSE | INMW | ONMW | SKIL | SEMI | UNMW |
| Waterford | .3587 | .2254 | .1802 | .0910 | .1585 | .2134 | .2360 |
| Limerick | .5351 | .4364 | .1787 | .1406 | .1630 | .3260 | .3767 |
| Cork | .4577 | .3588 | .1603 | .1441 | .1480 | .3479 | .3304 |
| Dublin/Dun Leoghaire | .4649 | .3150 | .1866 | .1577 | .1899 | .3219 | .3682 |

*Key to abbreviations:

HPEM: Higher professional workers, employers and managers

LPSE: Lower professional workers, salaried employees

INMW: Intermediate non-manual workers (clerical and kindred
service workers

ONMW: Other non-manual workers (other service workers)

SKIL: Skilled manual workers (craftsmen)

SEMI: Semi-skilled manual workers

UNMW: Unskilled manual workers

It might have been expected, on the basis of earlier studies,
that socio-economic segregation would be higher in larger towns.[33]
Present results, however, quite clearly contradict this expectation.
Limerick, for instance, a town about one-tenth of the population
size of Dublin/Dun Laoghaire, showed a similar or higher degree of
segregation for four of the seven socio-economic groups used in the
analysis. On the other hand, Waterford, the smallest town
considered, followed the expected pattern (table 18.4). In general,
the segregation measures suggest a two-level classification of Irish
towns, which corresponds with the results of the cluster analysis

33 . Robson, *Urban Social Areas.*

described above. This lends support to the supplementary hypothesis regarding the link between the roles of towns in an urban system and the extent of their social segregation.

The connection between urban role and social segregation becomes clearer when considering the more disaggregated dissimilarity indices (table 18.5). The largest indices appear at the top and bottom of the social pyramid. Again the marked differences for Limerick are striking. Here the dissimilarity between higher professions, managers, and employers, on the one hand, and unskilled manual workers, on the other, reaches a value (0.7745) that elsewhere would be regarded as typical only for ethnic segregation.

These dissimilarity indices also underline another interesting theoretical aspect. Feldman and Tilly have concluded that it is "a general tendency of workers to identify themselves with others of similar or higher rank and to differentiate themselves from others of lower rank. For high-ranking occupations, this is evidently one of excluding others, while for low-ranking occupations, it is a matter of including themselves."[34] It is precisely the dissimilarity of the skilled manual workers vis-à-vis other social groups that supports this assertion. The differences between their distribution and that of the other blue collar workers in the four Irish towns in 1971 (SEMI,UNMW) are generally higher than the distribution of the next higher group of clerical and service workers. While Feldman and Tilly's "inclusion principle" appears to operate in all cities in the same way, their "exclusion-principle" seems to apply more strongly the more rapid the social change, engendered by a rapid change in the roles of a city in the urban system.[35]

## Internal Patterns of Segregation

How these two principles operate concretely within cities remains a question. In order to deal with it, a measure of segregation in different parts of a city, at the ward level, for example, is desirable. Unfortunately, there appears to be no consensus about measuring segregation for smaller areal units, as there is for the town as a whole. The argument that segregation could only be measured if smaller units are further subdivided,

---

34. Arnold S. Feldman and Charles Tilly, "The Inter-action of Social and Physical Space," *American Sociological Review* 25 (1960): 877-884.

35. Variation of index figures can be influenced, of course, by the difference in size of administrative divisions in the towns. This influence, however, is rather small because the average number of inhabitants of the administrative units are 1,200 in Waterford, 1,400 in Limerick, 1,500 in Cork, and 3,700 in Dublin/Dun Laoghaire. In each city the "lower professionals and salaried employees" show the smallest relative frequencies: 6.2 percent in Waterford, 7.6 percent in Limerick, 9.7 percent in Cork, and 8.5 percent in Dublin/Dun Laoghaire.

TABLE 18.5

INDICES OF DISSIMILARITY IN RESIDENTIAL DISTRIBUTION
AMONG SOCIO-ECONOMIC GROUPS IN MAJOR IRISH CITIES
1971

|  | HPEM | LPSE | INMW | ONMW | SKIL | SEMI* |
|---|---|---|---|---|---|---|
| **Waterford** | | | | | | |
| LPSE | .1744 | | | | | |
| INMW | .2307 | .1890 | | | | |
| ONMW | .3837 | .2648 | .2048 | | | |
| SKIL | .3839 | .2693 | .2296 | .1459 | | |
| SEMI | .5074 | .3734 | .3259 | .1492 | .2030 | |
| UNMW | .4778 | .3668 | .3164 | .1987 | .2318 | .1295 |
| **Limerick** | | | | | | |
| LPSE | .2293 | | | | | |
| INMW | .3889 | .3212 | | | | |
| ONMW | .5554 | .4768 | .2156 | | | |
| SKIL | .5641 | .4803 | .2252 | .1083 | | |
| SEMI | .7283 | .6708 | .4174 | .2415 | .2712 | |
| UNMW | .7745 | .7117 | .4535 | .2894 | .3145 | .1273 |
| **Cork** | | | | | | |
| LPSE | .1629 | | | | | |
| INMW | .3577 | .2620 | | | | |
| ONMW | .5171 | .4356 | .2282 | | | |
| SKIL | .4892 | .3968 | .2075 | .1097 | | |
| SEMI | .6786 | .6175 | .4291 | .2485 | .2764 | |
| UNMW | .6743 | .6052 | .4163 | .2138 | .2527 | .1187 |
| **Dublin / Dun Laoghaire** | | | | | | |
| LPSE | .1802 | | | | | |
| INMW | .3662 | .2224 | | | | |
| ONMW | .5210 | .4113 | .2521 | | | |
| SKIL | .5220 | .4091 | .2448 | .1065 | | |
| SEMI | .6495 | .5647 | .4159 | .2090 | .2498 | |
| UNMW | .6754 | .6007 | .4566 | .2372 | .2922 | .1261 |

*Key to abbreviations given in Table 4.

however, overstates the procedural difficulties.[36]

Segregation within sub-areas of a town can be determined by using the differences in the spatial distributions between two social strata. By analogy, the difference between two frequency distributions as a measure of segregation in sub-units may be used. One frequency distribution is given by the observed distribution of inhabitants in different social classes, the other is the theoretical or expected distribution.[37] The usual test statistic derived from any goodness-of-fit tests between a data set and a theoretical frequency distribution can now provide a measure of the extent of segregation, and in the present case the Kolmogorov-Smirnov statistic D, which is simply the maximum absolute difference between the theoretical and the observed cumulative probability distributions, was employed.

The resulting segregation measures for the case of Limerick show clearly that the majority of most highly segregated wards in 1971 were localized in a sector between the central business district and the western boundary of the town (figure 18.3). Another sector with lower than average segregation ran in the opposite direction, while north of the center a more concentric spatial order can be recognized. With such well-defined variations in residential segregation in mind, hypotheses about their provenance and relation to other social dimensions will now be explained.

### An Attempt to Explain the Extent of Segregation

Hypotheses about the extent of segregation will be developed and expressed as structural equations, which can be tested empirically by a path-analytical causal model. To begin with, it is reasonable to suggest that the "inclusion principle" will operate more strongly the more adequate and budget-priced the dwellings are in a ward. The simplest way to minimize housing costs, under constant quality constraints, is through higher plot ratios, which lead to a higher population density. Hence, middle-rank status groups, such as skilled manual workers (later referred to as a "sub-status" social dimension) will be better represented, the better the housing conditions and the higher the population density.

---

36. Jürgen Friedrichs, *Stadtanalyse: Soziale und räumliche Organisation der Gesellschaft* (Reinbek bei Hamburg: Rororo, 1977), p. 224.

37. Assuming that the extent of segregation in each tract must equal 0 if all indexes of segregation and dissimilarity equal 0, then the latter is derived from: $E(Pij) = Pi.P.j/P$ (for $i=1,2,...,k$ tracts and $j=1,2,...,m$ social classes), where $E(Pij)$ is the expected frequency of people in tract i belonging to class j, $Pi.$ the total population in tract i, $P.j$ the city's population in class j, and p the total population in the city.

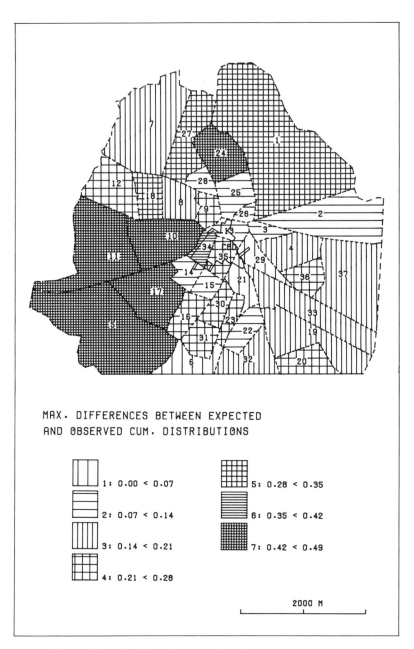

MAX. DIFFERENCES BETWEEN EXPECTED
AND OBSERVED CUM. DISTRIBUTIONS

1: 0.00 < 0.07      5: 0.28 < 0.35

2: 0.07 < 0.14      6: 0.35 < 0.42

3: 0.14 < 0.21      7: 0.42 < 0.49

4: 0.21 < 0.28

2000 M

Figure 18.3.   Residential segregation of socio-economic groups
in Limerick, Ireland

But the latter will have a negative influence on the overall social
rank of a district. We assume a positive correlation between
population density and stress on the human and natural environment.
Furthermore, if members of higher social classes try to escape from
this growing stress by movement to wards with better amenities, then
a gradually "filtering down" process comes into play. Consequently,
the social rank of a ward will be less, when more lower and middle
class people have included themselves and the population density is
higher. Supposing that good housing conditions combined with low
density (producing high housing costs) diminish the effect of the
"inclusion principle" and operate rather as the "exclusion
principle," then high social rank may be expected. Therefore, the
extent of residential segregation will be higher, the better the
housing conditions connected with low population density and the
higher the social status combined with low values of the sub-status
dimension.

In order to give empirical expression to such possible
relationships, the scores of a comparative factorial ecology of the
four cities are used to measure complex defined attributes of their
sub-areas at the ward level. The results of these analyses produced
six factors that accounted for 80 to 83 percent of the variance of
the original 75 variables for the several cities. Three expected
dimensions were clearly identified: social status, age structure,
and housing conditions. Three further axes appeared which are
interpreted as sub-dimensions of the first three factors. They may
be seen as the outcome of development processes in the cities:
population density as a sub-dimension of social status (in Waterford
it was still included in the latter). Another sub-dimension can be
interpreted to have split off from the status dimension with a high
loading, among others, on the proportion of "skilled manual
workers." It is here labelled "sub-status" and is clearly
associated with the Feldman-Tilly "inclusion principle." The sixth
factor, a sub-dimension of age structure, is of little present
interest. The signs of the loadings have been rearranged, where
necessary, to give, for example, to high positive scores on the
status dimension the meaning of high social status and vice versa.
Again the scores are linear combinations computed from the
z-standardized raw data of the leading variables in the loading
pattern, which represent correlated attributes.[38]

---

38. Güssefeldt, *Die gegenseitige Abhängigkeit innerurbaner Strukturmuster.*

The hypotheses discussed above can be formalized in terms of the following structural equations, in which the signs show the direction of the mode of operation:

1. + Sub-status = f (+ population density, + housing conditions)
2. − Social rank = f (+ sub-status, + population density)
3. + Residential segregation = f (+ housing conditions, − population density, + social rank, − sub-status)

The interdependence between the roles of cities and the extent of residential segregation can even be tested at this stage of the analysis. Assuming that the members of the metropolitan city type have to fulfill similar roles in the national city system and noting that in 1971 Limerick, Cork, and Dublin/Dun Laoghaire belonged to it, then the signs of the parameters should be constrained to be equal among the cities. Furthermore, this test may be strengthened if it is postulated that an overall causal model should produce a significant variance reduction in each city respectively, that is, the parameters are constrained to be equal between the cities.

These two constraints make it clear that the usual methods of estimating the path coefficients by multiple regression analysis cannot be applied in this case. Therefore, a mathematical model introduced by Jöreskog has been employed which, in its fourth version as a computer program entitled LISREL IV, has been widely used in the social sciences.[39] LISREL ( = LInear Structural RELations) provides for the simultaneous estimation of linear structural equation systems by maximum likelihood methods.[40] It is beyond the scope of this paper to give a description of the methods.[41]

The results are shown in figure 18.4 in the usual form, where the figures beside each arrow represent the direct causal effects. In one case the diagram seems to contradict one of the hypotheses because it indicates a positive direct causal effect of population

39. Karl G. Jöreskog, "A General Method for Estimating a Linear Structural Equation System," in *Structural Equation Models in the Social Sciences,* ed. Arthur S. Goldberger and Otis D. Duncan (New York: Seminar Press, 1973), pp. 85-112. The assistance of Klaus Opwis is acknowledged for advice in operating the program and suggestions for interpreting the output.

40. Karl G. Jöreskog and Dag Sörbom, "A General Computer Program for Estimation of Linear Structural Equation Systems by Maximum Likelihood Methods," University of Uppsala, 1978.

41. However, the equation of the model, given in the usual notation with reference to multiple regression analysis, clarifies the difference: BY = GX + E, wherein Y is the matrix of endogeneous (dependent) and X the matrix of exogeneous (independent) variables: matrices B and G describe the causal effects among the dependent variables and between the exogenous and endogenous variables respectively, that is, they hold the needed path coefficients; and E is the ususal error term. A decomposition of the correlations from these coefficients, the covariances of the variables, and the total causal effects of the exogenous on the endogenous variables can be derived.

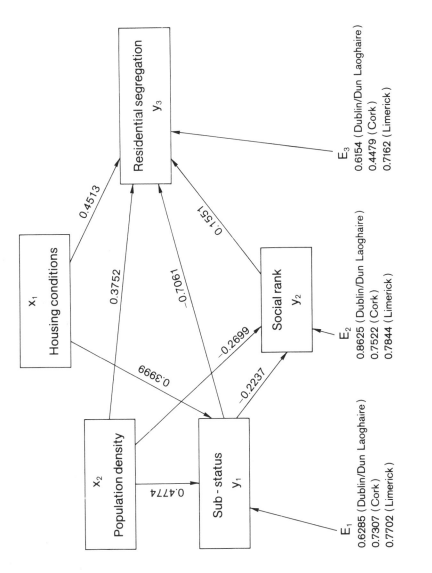

Figure 18.4. Causal model of residential segregation

density on the residential segregation, while a negative one has
been hypothesized. However, by referring to table 18.6 it can be
seen that the population density has a two-fold influence on
residential segregation. On the one hand, the direct positive
effect appears because there were more wards within the investigated
cities which show above-average density and segregation and which
also featured low class residences. This influence is incorporated
in the second equation. On the other hand, the indirect causal
effect of population density on residential segregation appears to
be negative and, thus, corresponds with the third hypothesis.

The direct and indirect causal effects of population density
on segregation nearly neutralize each other, as can be seen from the
total causal effect. This shows clearly that the model as specified
cannot be used to predict the extent of segregation. A somewhat
similar problem applies to the direct and indirect effects of
housing conditions on segregation, which again accords with the
second and third hypotheses. It is suggested that these two-fold
influences result from the two different principles hypothesized by
Feldman and Tilly.[42] They cause U-shaped relationships between the
two factorial dimensions and segregation, so that their influences
in a linear model become visible as positive, as well as negative,
causal effects.

All the path coefficients in the model, as mentioned earlier,
are constrained to be equal between the different cities. LISREL IV
provides a chi-square statistic for the goodness of fit, which is
rather unusual. The null hypothesis, then, is that the model holds,
and then the test statistic is distributed as chi-square. In the
present case the test statistic has a value of 27.6086 with 19
degrees of freedom and an error probability of 0.0913. Thus, the
null hypothesis cannot be rejected at the 5 percent level. A second
analysis without any constraints on the parameters was carried out.
One of the results gave a goodness-of-fit statistic of 6.7047 with 3
degrees of freedom and an error probability of 0.0819. The
difference between these two chi-square values is distributed as
chi-square as well, if the specified hypothesis concerning the
constraints of parameters holds. The difference yields a value of
20.9039 with 16 degrees of freedom and is less than the tabulated
chi-square of 26.3 at the 5 percent level. Therefore, the
hypothesis that the causes of residential segregation within the
metropolitan group of cities are probably the same is not rejected.

---

42. Feldman and Tilly, "The Inter-action of Social and Physical Space," pp.
877-84.

TABLE 18.6

PATH COEFFICIENTS AND DECOMPOSITION OF CORRELATION COEFFICIENTS

| Dependent variables | Independent variables | Effects | | | |
|---|---|---|---|---|---|
| | | Total causal | Direct causal | Indirect causal | Indirect correlative |
| Sub-status | Density | 0.4774 | 0.4774 (10.0429) | 0.0 | -0.0831 |
| | Housing | 0.3999 | 0.3999 (8.4119) | 0.0 | -0.0992 |
| Social rank | Density | -0.3767 | -0.2699 (4.6953) | -0.1068 | 0.0186 |
| | Sub-status | -0.2237 | -0.2237 (3.9020) | 0.0 | -0.0923 |
| Segregation | Density | -0.0204 | 0.3752 (7.1595) | -0.3956 | -0.0831 |
| | Housing | 0.1551 | 0.4513 (9.2390) | -0.2962 | 0.0042 |
| | Sub-status | -0.7408 | -0.7061 (13.0380) | -0.0347 | 0.3138 |
| | Social rank | 0.1551 | 0.1551 (3.2263) | 0.0 | 0.0885 |

NOTE: Figures given in brackets are z-values which indicate the significance. One-tailed tests are appropriate because the signs are included in the hypotheses. The critical value of a standard normal deviate at the 5 percent level is z=1.6449.

In general, then, the results support the hypotheses. However, the problems discussed above and the error terms, which are the proportions of "unexplained" variance, given in figure 18.4, show that this attempt at an explanation of the extent of segregation represents an addition to, rather than a replacement for, other approaches. Only in Cork did the model account for more than 50 percent of the variance of residential segregation.

## Conclusion

Cities are of outstanding importance as transmitters of economic and social development. In a diffusionary system they are hierarchically-organized adopters initiating appropriate changes that have intensified economic integration at the regional level. Within this development different effects can be distinguished. First, the hierarchical effect is an inter-urban link by which the process of development is transferred to the urban centers in the periphery. Thus, it promotes relocation diffusion. Second, the neighborhood effect promotes expansion diffusion which only affects cities and towns in the vicinity of innovation centers. The population agglomeration that goes with it needs progressively higher investments of social capital which are then not available to the periphery. Therefore, the neighborhood effect may cause greater disparities between core and peripheral regions.

In the realm of policy implications, it is suggested that Irish national policy must concentrate on establishing the functional prerequisites for the diffusion of innovations and encourage people to accept innovations. Thus, diffusion down the urban hierarchy will accelerate and the periphery will profit more rapidly from new economic developments, which in turn will have positive effects on the national economy. Instead of this, an actual policy of reinforcing the smaller peripheral centers in the western "Designated Areas" has been set up, which is intended to induce a development directly opposed to the otherwise effective process of hierarchical diffusion.

It may seem premature to reach conclusions regarding the interdependence between the role of a town and the extent of residential segregation when the empirical analysis is rather inconclusive. The lack of time-series data and the change of boundaries within the cities precluded a more controlled study. Nevertheless, the results indicate that the hypotheses offered here may hold. Limerick provides a good example, especially as the town's role in the Irish urban system has changed significantly

since 1946. This is just one example, however, and further research
is necessary to test these ideas further.

The path-analytical model of segregation shows that a
significant amount of residential segregation can be explained by
the suggested hypotheses. The most notable finding was that within
the metropolitan group of towns, the causes of segregation in 1971
were probably the same. In nearly all causal relations variables
were included which are directly related to decisions at various
political and administrative levels. Population density, for
example, is dependent on building plot ratios, which are required by
the local authorities. The construction of multi-family housing
structures as well as other housing conditions are related to
political decisions. Even in the status dimension, a variable such
as "local authority dwellings" has significance.

Assuming that segregation prevents social change, because
people have difficulty shaking-off the standards of a specific
social and spatial environment, with its attendant norms of
behavior, then segregation probably does not promote the necessary
willingness among the population to adopt innovations. Indeed,
political and administrative decisions have the very opposite
effect, or at least serve to maintain the status quo. Therefore,
Irish urban development policy should be altered in accordance with
the avowed political aims of accelerating economic development.

# Chapter XIX

# "THE NATURE OF CITIES" AND BEYOND

Brian J.L. Berry

Chauncy Harris and Edward Ullman wrote "The Nature of Cities" while the world was at war.[1] The urban-industrial growth that had accompanied the Third Kondratiev Wave of the industrial era had ended by the great depression. Recovery was slow, masked by the needs of a wartime economy. The dramatic transformations of the Fourth Kondratiev Wave--now, too, almost ended--were then but dimly discerned. It was a time to take stock of what had emerged and to provide a benchmark against which future change could be assessed. In so doing, Harris and Ullman helped form the views of generations of urbanists who followed.

They wrote of the rapid growth of great cities, supported by their roles as central places, strategic locations on transport networks, and concentration points for specialized economic activities such as mining, manufacturing, or recreation. Such great cities, they said, grew axially along principal transport routes, displayed concentric rings of growth and land use around their central business districts and other nuclei, and were marked by the continuing tension between the advantages of urban concentration and a local environment that was often poor for man. The forces of urban growth were, they felt, strongest in the manufacturing belt of the northeastern United States, where the interdependent nature of most industries served to reinforce the advantages of urban concentration. This contrasted with the much narrower raw material dependency of urban industry found in hinterland regions elsewhere in the country.

Yet at the very time they wrote, the economy of the United States was on the verge of a transformation that accompanied the upswing of the Fourth Kondratiev Wave in the 1950s and 1960s--the passage from a goods-producing economy dominated by manufacturing industries concerned with transformation of raw materials into

---

1. Chauncy D. Harris and Edward L. Ullman, "The Nature of Cities," *Annals of the American Academy of Political and Social Science* 242 (1945): 7-17.

finished products to a service economy dominated by knowledge-based industries concerned with transforming data into useful information.

In 1920, ten years before the end of the Third Kondratiev, the extractive and manufacturing industries accounted for 62 percent of United States employment; by 1970, ten years before the Fourth Kondratiev ended, this had shrunk to 37 percent. The service industries grew from 38 to 63 percent of the labor force in the same half century, with the greatest expansion in the growth-producing services such as finance, insurance, real estate, and corporate management.

Accompanying this transformation, the nation's great cities first grew explosively, slowed, and then in the 1970s began to decline. Today, the heartland-hinterland organization of the national economy and the core-orientation of its constituent specialized industrial cities have been succeeded by a national settlement system composed of broadly similar metropolitan regions sprawling across the national landscape, mutually interdependent parts of a completely urbanized society. The loci of growth and development have been transferred from former core regions and central cities of the northeastern manufacturing belt to the amenity-rich sunbelt and exurban environments of the former periphery. The industrial and occupational structures of these metropolitan regions have become increasingly similar, as have their income distributions and the consistency of their responses to national growth and change. Concern has switched from the economies of location to the social forces guiding urban change.[2]

### Contemporary Urban Change: A Case

Let us examine these shifts in one case, Pittsburgh, a city that typified the earlier process of industrially driven urban concentration and which was the first of the nation's metropolitan regions to register population losses as the goods-producing economy faltered.

From 1960 to 1980, metropolitan Pittsburgh's population shrank from 2,405 to 2,264 ~~million~~ thousand, but declining family sizes and increasing numbers of single-member households resulted in the number of households increasing by 118,000 in the same period. In response to these mixed signals, a speculative housing industry overbuilt, constructing 219,000 new housing units, largely in the suburbs. In turn, 85,000 excess housing units were removed from the stock, mostly in the least desirable parts of the central city and

---

2. Portions of this discussion appeared previously in my book *Comparative Urbanisation* (Basingstoke, UK: Macmillan, 1982).

the older mill towns as families moved out to climb the housing
ladder. Vacancy rates soared in older neighborhoods. Overall,
population densities became lower and much more uniform across the
metropolitan region.

Manufacturing employment shrank in the two decades by 65,000,
from 37.3 to 22.0 percent of the total labor force. Extending the
time period somewhat, from the onset of the recession beginning in
1957 through the end of yet another recession in 1983, Pittsburgh's
primary metals industries registered 98,000 lost jobs. But total
nonfarm employment grew by 172,000 between 1960 and 1980, from
776,000 to 948,000. Most of the employment growth came in
government, in nonprofit services, and in producer services--the
complex of corporate activities that include central administrative
offices, finance, insurance and real estate, legal and business
services, and the like. Collectively, these three sectors increased
their share from 27.4 to 41.2 percent of the labor force, or from
203,000 to 392,000 jobs, as Pittsburgh was transformed from a raw
materials processing center to a full participant in an information
processing society (table 19.1).

These industry shifts were accompanied by changes in the
metropolitan region's occupational distribution and, in turn, by
progressive polarization of earnings and the social structure. From
1959 to 1979, professionals and managers grew from 19 to 26 percent
of the total labor force while craft workers, operatives, and
laborers shrank from 41 to 31 percent (table 19.2).

The occupation shifts were driven both by different patterns
of employment in growing and declining industries and by changes in
the mix of occupations within industries. In 1970, 57 percent of
those employed in manufacturing, but only 5 percent of those
employed in producer services, were craft workers or operatives.
Conversely, 16 percent or less of the workers in manufacturing,
distribution, or retailing were managers, professionals, or
technicians, whereas 36 percent of those employed in producer
services and 55 percent of those employed by non-profits were in
this category (table 19.3).

Pittsburgh's heavy industrial growth had produced a well-paid,
unionized blue collar middle class with a distinctive life style and
a commensurate urban structure. Yet since 1960, the shifting
industrial and occupational mix has produced progressively greater
inequality which is radically altering the urban form. When
considering the distribution of employment by earnings groups within
industries in 1970, declining sectors such as manufacturing had the

TABLE 19.1

DISTRIBUTION OF EMPLOYMENT AMONG MAJOR INDUSTRIES

| | 1959 | | 1969 | | 1979 | |
|---|---|---|---|---|---|---|
| | Number | Pct. | Number | Pct. | Number | Pct. |
| Extraction | 11,488 | 1.5 | 8,075 | 0.9 | 12,368 | 1.3 |
| Construction | 32,158 | 4.3 | 41,200 | 4.8 | 56,211 | 5.9 |
| Manufacturing | 276,350 | 37.3 | 254,503 | 29.6 | 209,315 | 22.0 |
| Distributive services | 86,941 | 11.7 | 93,462 | 10.9 | 97,069 | 10.2 |
| Producer services | 99,895 | 13.5 | 143,061 | 16.6 | 182,148 | 19.1 |
| Retail services | 104,363 | 14.1 | 126,542 | 14.7 | 148,684 | 15.6 |
| Mainly consumer services | 27,329 | 3.7 | 30,843 | 3.6 | 36,484 | 3.8 |
| Nonprofit | 31,833 | 4.3 | 56,731 | 6.6 | 80,896 | 8.5 |
| Government | 71,200 | 9.6 | 105,800 | 12.3 | 129,400 | 13.6 |

SOURCE: U.S. Department of Commerce

TABLE 19.2

DISTRIBUTION OF EMPLOYMENT AMONG OCCUPATIONS

| | 1959 | | 1969 | | 1979 | |
|---|---|---|---|---|---|---|
| | Number | Pct. | Number | Pct. | Number | Pct. |
| Professional/ Technical | 100,535 | 12.08 | 137,318 | 15.77 | 156,996 | 16.51 |
| Managerial | 58,227 | 7.00 | 63,328 | 7.27 | 92,876 | 9.77 |
| Clerical | 128,573 | 14.34 | 157,918 | 18.13 | 166,144 | 17.48 |
| Sales | 68,215 | 8.20 | 69,202 | 7.95 | 94,519 | 9.94 |
| Craft workers | 137,141 | 16.48 | 134,848 | 15.48 | 126,644 | 13.32 |
| Operatives | 145,915 | 17.50 | 145,519 | 16.71 | 123,389 | 12.98 |
| Service workers | 86,480 | 10.39 | 111,037 | 12.75 | 132,066 | 13.89 |
| Laborers | 60,196 | 7.23 | 47,371 | 5.44 | 52,986 | 5.57 |
| Farm workers | 6,330 | 0.76 | 4,361 | 0.50 | 5,131 | 0.54 |

SOURCE: U.S. Department of Commerce

TABLE 19.3

OCCUPATIONAL DISTRIBUTION AMONG INDUSTRIES

IN THE PITTSBURGH SMSA, 1970

|  | Manufac-turing | Distri-bution | Retail | Consumer Services | Govern-ment | Producer Services | Non-Profit Services |
|---|---|---|---|---|---|---|---|
| Managers, Officers | 4.55 | 10.16 | 12.40 | 6.25 | 9.23 | 9.30 | 3.36 |
| Professional/ Technical | 11.74 | 6.56 | 2.31 | 4.67 | 10.38 | 26.95 | 51.63 |
| Craft Workers | 23.62 | 18.23 | 7.30 | 15.97 | 4.22 | 3.10 | 2.09 |
| Sales | 2.67 | 8.62 | 29.21 | 1.24 | 0.44 | 10.67 | 0.19 |
| Operatives | 33.29 | 21.87 | 10.10 | 11.05 | 2.68 | 2.07 | 1.55 |
| Clerical | 13.84 | 24.14 | 15.39 | 9.78 | 41.95 | 34.66 | 15.00 |
| Laborers | 7.60 | 7.12 | 4.64 | 4.02 | 4.20 | 1.19 | 0.53 |
| Service | 2.58 | 3.30 | 18.65 | 47.01 | 26.89 | 12.06 | 25.64 |

SOURCE:   U.S. Department of Commerce

TABLE 19.4

DISTRIBUTION OF OCCUAPTIONS AMONG

EARNINGS GROUPS

PITTSBURGH SMSA, 1970

|  | High | Medium | Low |
|---|---|---|---|
| Manufacturing | 16.29 | 59.58 | 24.02 |
| Distributive Services | 16.72 | 48.72 | 34.56 |
| Retail Services | 14.71 | 46.61 | 38.68 |
| Consumer Services | 10.92 | 28.26 | 60.81 |
| Government | 19.61 | 7.34 | 73.04 |
| Producer Services | 36.25 | 15.84 | 47.81 |
| Non-Profit Services | 54.99 | 3.83 | 41.17 |

SOURCE:   U.S. Department of Commerce

heaviest concentration of middle-income jobs;  growing sectors such as producer services had earnings distributions split between the top and the bottom earnings categories (table 19.4).

The consequence is to be seen in the distribution of workers by earnings. Changes in the earnings distribution of Pittsburgh's workers in the brief period 1971-1974 show that there was both rapid growth of better-paid workers at the top and a substantial downward shift of earnings in the middle (figure 19.1).  The pattern of progressively greater polarization was repeated nationwide.  Between 1960 and 1975, the proportion of the U.S. labor force earning between plus of minus 20 percent of the national average wage shrank from 35.9 to 27.8 percent (table 19.5).  Inequality takes many forms.  This was a period in which there were rapid increases in female employment and labor force participation (table 19.6).  But a high proportion of all female employees are concentrated in lower-paying clerical, sales, and service occupations, and as male earnings have slipped the two-worker household has become a necessity to maintain a reasonable standard of living.

Black males found their employment opportunities in the 1960s and 1970s in better-paying jobs as craft workers and operatives. But these are the very occupations that have been under the greatest pressure.  The last hired have been the first to be fired, and this doorway into the economic mainstream has been closed.  As a result, unemployment rates, particularly among Black youth unable to obtain entry-level jobs, have increased to more than 40 percent.

On the other hand, 30 percent of Pittsburgh's professional jobs are held by White women, as well as 23 percent of the technical and 11 percent of the managerial jobs.  The earnings from these positions, often combined with those of similarly employed housemates in two-partner households, are resulting in a new affluent elite with changing life styles and different demands for housing, location, and community facilities.

The effects of these shifts on urban structure are to be seen at the extremes.  There has been both gentrification of neighborhoods close to a downtown reshaped by Renaissance I and II, and intensification of the city's underclass.  Between the two, less dramatically but equally pervasively, are the forces operating on the middle classes, including a spiralling away of the outer city and the accelerating decline of the inner city.

Renaissance I and II is the way that Pittsburghers think of the public-private partnership that has transformed downtown since 1945.  in the first phase, Renaissance I, Pittsburgh's most powerful

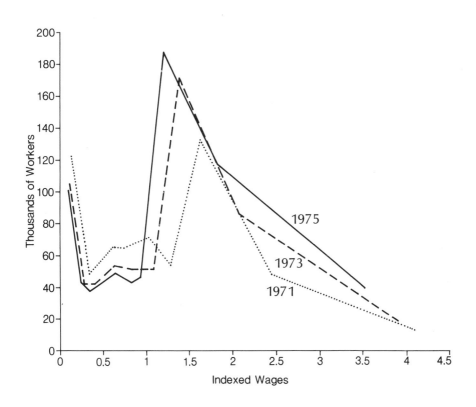

Figure 19.1.   Distribution of workers by earnings in the Pittsburgh SMSA, 1971, 1973, and 1975

TABLE 19.5

1960 AND 1975 DISTRIBUTION OF TOTAL U.S. LABOR FORCE AMONG
EARNINGS CLASSES AND DISTRIBUTION OF 1960-1975
JOB INCREASES IN THE SERVICES

| Earnings classes (US avg wage = 1.00) | Distribution of total US labor force (percentages)[a] | | 1960-1975 job increases in services[b] | |
|---|---|---|---|---|
| | 1960 | 1975 | Numbers of jobs (,000) | Percentage |
| 1.60 and above | 10.9 | 12.0 | 1,947 | 9.5 |
| | 31.6 | 34.2 | | 35.0 |
| 1.59 to 1.20 | 20.7 | 22.2 | 5,224 | 25.5 |
| 1.19 to .80 | 35.9 | 27.8 | 2,311 | 11.3 |
| .79 to .40 | 24.1 | 28.4 | 9,205 | 44.9 |
| | 32.5 | 38.0 | | 53.8 |
| .39 and below | 8.4 | 9.6 | 1,829 | 8.9 |
| TOTAL | 100.0 | 100.0 | 20,516 | 100.0 |

SOURCE: Thomas M. Stanback, Jr. and Thierriz J. Noyelle, *Cities in Transition* (Totowa, NJ: Allanheld, Osmun, 1982), p.39.
Based on U.S. Bureau of the Census, Survey of Income and Education (for 1975) and U.S. Bureau of Labor Statistics, Tomorrow's Manpower needs, National Industry-Occupational Matrix (for 1960).

[a] Excludes Agriculture, Mining, and Public Administration

[b] TCU, Wholesale, Retail, FIRE, Corporate Services, Consumer Services and Non-profit.

TABLE 19.6

SELECTED PITTSBURGH WORKFORCE CHARACTERISTICS

| | Percent of Workforce Female | Female Labor Force Participation Rate | Percent of Workforce Part-time |
|---|---|---|---|
| 1960 | 28.6 | 29.3 | 13.6 |
| 1970 | 34.2 | 34.0 | 18.5 |
| 1980 | 40.0 | 43.1 | 20.8 |

SOURCE: U.S. Department of Commerce

citizen, Richard King Mellon, was persuaded in 1945 to support
formation of a private-sector organization, the Allegheny Conference
on Community Development, that would take leadership in effecting
urban change. Through the conference, the city's corporate
leadership joined with the city and county governments, and
particularly with Mayor David L. Lawrence, to make significant
environmental improvements in smoke and flood control, to rebuild
the golden triangle, and to set in motion other economic and
physical changes throughout the Pittsburgh region. Pittsburgh
remains the nation's third largest corporate headquarters city, and
a key element in Renaissance I was persuasion of major corporations
not only to remain headquartered downtown, but to build new highrise
office buildings there.

Mutual trust between the public and private sectors dissolved
in the period 1970-8, when the city's agenda switched to social
development, and a new mayor, Peter Flaherty, was elected on a
platform of fiscal conservatism and a cutting of ties to labor, the
business community, and the democratic machine. Different agendas
led the Allegheny conferences and the Mayor's office in different
directions.

It remained for a new Mayor, Richard Caliguiri, elected in
1977, to commit the city to "another renaissance"--this time led and
effected more by the city than the Allegheny conference. In
1945-52, there had been a critical shortage of office space in
Pittsburgh that was filled by the first wave of Renaissance I
construction between 1952 and 1960. A subsequent shortage was met
by completion of major headquarters complexes, including that of
U.S. Steel, in 1971 and 1972. By 1977-78, there was an office space
shortage once again, and this helped Caliguiri marshall private
sector support for the wave of high-rise office construction that
marked Renaissance II.

Parenthetically, Pittsburgh's waves of reconstruction were
synchronous with the nations's 7-11 year short-term business cycles
(the Juglar cycles that are superimposed upon the 50-year Kondratiev
long waves). Office construction peaked in the late 1950s, early
1970s, and early 1980s, separated by periods of decreasing vacancies
and increasing rents--if, that is, one wants an alternative model to
that of the public-private partnership!

The downtown renaissance has had its effects. Young
professionals employed in the downtown's headquarters complexes and
growing producer services and nonprofit economy have begun to
rehabilitate decaying homes and to restore blighted inner-city

neighborhoods. This process of gentrification came relatively late to Pittsburgh, where a conservative corporate community has long demanded conformity to traditional family arrangements and lifestyles. But come it has, driven by the growth of professional employment outside the traditional corporations, by life style shifts in the postwar baby boom generation, and sparked by the desire of Pittsburgh's history and landmarks foundation to restore a mid-nineteenth century north side neighborhood and a south side architect's desire to anchor renewal of a decaying shopping street around an artists' colony. Subsequently, condominium conversions have increased in the city's Victorian and Edwardian neighborhoods, where elegant old homes are too large or too demanding for today's smaller professional households. In this respect, Pittsburgh is now a full participant in a process that is transforming selected neighborhoods in the central cities of those metropolitan areas in which the headquarters functions of new information economy are concentrated.

Neither is Pittsburgh an exception to another nationwide trend--rapid increase of births out of wedlock, of female-headed households, of welfare dependency, and of social pathology including violent crime in the minority community. Pittsburgh's hill district was the inspiration for television's award-winning program "Hill Street Blues." There, a Black community isolated in what had been the city's least desirable location--the hill top between steel industry smokestacks--was jerked into activism in the late 1960s and targeted for every social and physical renewal program that came along. Yet today it remains economically depressed, socially isolated, and increasingly abandoned as those with options move away and transfer housing vacancies into the area. Removal of the "lower hill" residential areas during Renaissance I planted underclass pockets elsewhere, and they too have grown and spread. And as job market changes reduce the very opportunities that Black males had sought for escape, the tangle of pathologies has intensified. William Julius Wilson advances the hypothesis that with the rapid growth in numbers of young persons who see but little opportunity, "a self-sustaining chain reaction is set off that creates an explosive increase in the amount of crime, addiction, and welfare dependency," a hypothesis particularly appropriate for the most densely settled ghetto neighborhoods. Just as the gentrifiers are creating their own new sub-culture, so a different sub-culture has emerged out of the specific circumstances, life changes, and position in the class structure of minority youth.

There are other forces working in the middle class, for whom spatial and social mobility remain connected. In the outer city--the newer suburbs, the exurbs, and the small towns beyond--the forces of dispersion continue to run their course. The leading edge of change is at the periphery. In housing, a highly fragmented and speculative building industry consistently overshoots demand for growth and replacement supply, producing excess supplies that lower the values and limit the maintenance of the older stock, some of which ends up as abandonments in older neighborhoods. Yet continuing demand for the new impels development towards amenity-rich locations, or to architectural and community designs intended to create new amenity values. In consequence, a substantial share of all new housing constructed in the past decade has been built in non-metropolitan areas.

Parallel trends are evidenced in industrial and office parks and in retail development. Formerly a response to residential growth, new large-scale retail developments have contributed to an increasingly differentiated form of dispersion. Successive new technologies have led to reevaluation of older forms and structures as shopping centers have evolved from purely retail ventures to "downtowns on the periphery" that form the space around them. Increasing differentiation appears to be the overarching trend, as new developments are keyed more closely to income, age, ethnic, and other life-style characteristics of the markets they serve (table 19.7).

Meanwhile, the inner city is afflicted by two sets of downward pressures, the first that of filtering from the outer city and the second that of the structural shifts in the job market we have discussed earlier. For the young with education, loyalty perforce gives way to the logic of exit. For the middle-aged, there is the immobility of unrealizable equity in softening housing markets, perhaps undergirded by the income security net as unionized corporations shrink or close their production facilities. A sense of hopelessness pervades--of the passing of opportunity. No longer is there an image of a ladder of success leading up and out to the suburbs and beyond, but rather of missing rungs and wider gaps. Instead of the fluidity of the traditional system of status achievement there is the greater rigidity of social class. A society in which diverse subcultures are intensifying is, simultaneously, a society in which its subcultural communities coexist but seldom interpenetrate--and if this indeed be true, future urban change will be guided by a very different social dynamic.

TABLE 19.7

METROPOLITAN AND NON-METROPOLITAN HOUSING, 1980[1]

|  | Non-Metropolitan | Metropolitan |
|---|---|---|
| Total Units | 24.1 million | 56.0 million |
| New Units | | |
|    Conventional | 6.5 million | 9.4 million |
|    Mobile Homes and Trailers | 1.8 million | 0.5 million |
| New Units[2] as a Share of<br>   Total Units | 34.4% | 17.7% |
| Owner-Occupied Housing | 79.4% | 59.6% |
|    Median Distance from Home<br>    to Work | 12.0 miles | 8.3 miles |
|    Median Travel Time to<br>    Work | 22.2 minutes | 20.6 minutes |
|    Median Value | $47,000 | $53,500 |
|    Increase in Median Value,<br>    1970-1980 | 264% | 196% |
|    Median Value of New<br>    Housing[2,3] | $61,300 | $73,000 |
|    Median Monthly Housing<br>    Costs[4] | $363 | $369 |
|    Median Monthly New Housing<br>    Costs | $426 | $497 |
| Median Rent[5] | $223 | $258 |

[1]Data are for year-round, occupied housing

[2]Constructed April 1970 or later.

[3]Conventionally built housing.

[4]For units with a mortgage. Includes taxes, insurance, utilities fuel and mortgage.

[5]For nonsubsidized rental units.

## The Social Dynamics Driving Urban Change

As yet no new theory has been developed to help guide our understanding of this social dynamic, or to explain its human consequences. At least the broad outlines can be sketched, however, if we examine the tensions between increasing societal scale and mobility and the intensity of social interactions in a truly national society on the one hand, and increasing insistence upon a mosaic of small and coherent communities with predictable life styles within a context of intensifying cultural pluralism on the other. That these factors are key is a consequence of the emergence of the new information economy and the convergence of the industrial and occupational structures of the nation's great metropolitan regions.

Scale measures the extent of a given network of relationships. Three aspects of increasing societal scale are important. First, widening of the radii of interdependence means that, whether individuals know it or not, they become mutual means to individual ends; the intensity of interdependence increases. Second, increasing scale produces an increasing range, and content of communications flows. Third, as a result there is a widening span of compliance and control within given social organizations, a preeminence of large-scale organizations, nationwide spans of control, and progressively similar division of labor and rewards. What has developed is a stratification system cutting across widely varying geographical and cultural sub-regions of the country, creating *national citizens*.

This nationwide quality, together with its accompaniment, increasing mobility, has quite different consequences as one moves down the social hierarchy. The high mobiles are those with college education and higher incomes, working for large corporate or governmental organizations, in the mid-twenty to mid-forty age span. The low mobiles are the blue collar employees and other working-class people, whose lives are built around kinship and ethnic ties within local neighborhoods. When the high mobiles move, it involves a shift from one urban region to another, but in moving they scarcely change their life style; there is a tendency to move between near-identical social environments, and indeed, their assessment of the quality of life in a community centers on the characteristics of its social environment. This attachment to a type of environment that sustains a particular life style is the key to the way in which contemporary Americans have adjusted the need to retain a locally based sense of security and stability to the emergence of a nation-wide highly mobile society.

The ability to be both national citizens and to preserve the integrity of a particular life style within a particular environment has been facilitated by a change in the nature of human interaction. Increasingly, interaction on primary and secondary levels of involvement is being supplemented by a form of interaction even more abstracted from the deeper layers of personality: *tertiary interactions* leading to tertiary relationships. If a primary relationship is one in which the individuals are known to each other in many role facets whereas a secondary relationship implies a knowledge of the other individual only in a single role facet, then a tertiary relationship is one in which only the *roles* interact. The individuals playing the role are interchangeable and, in fact, with the computerization of many interactions, are even dispensable, at least at the point of immediate contact. What are interacting are not *individuals* in one role capactiy or another but the *functional roles* themselves. Such tertiary relationships can *only* be maintained under conditions of *physical* isolation; once supplemented by physical contact, they tend to revert to the secondary. Thus, the isolation of different communities within urban regions promotes role, and life-style stereotyping via perceptions created by mass media imagery, particularly television, and many people behave to others as if these perceptions are correct.

Earlier urban theorists thought that the growth of large-scale organizations, centralization of organizational control, increasing functional division of labor, and wide-spread use of the automobile were all reducing the significance of the local community. But neither the predicted decline in heterogeneity nor increasing homogeneity through blending in the "melting pot" have occurred; rather, the coalescence of society has facilitated an elaborate internal subdivision.

First, the extent to which many of the immigrant groups have been assimilated into the larger society now appears to be quite limited. The process of assimilation involves several steps or sub-processes (table 19.8). Using this sequence, White Protestant Americans are the most assimilated; indeed it is they who constitute the mainstream or host society. Yet in primary group life, even they tend to form cliques. Much of the New England upper class has consisted, for example, of a group of self-conscious Yankee families clustered in their own exclusive social institutions.

At the other extreme, Black Americans display minimal assimilation. They are by and large acculturated, but there is

TABLE 19.8

THE PROCESS OF ASSIMILATION

| Type of Stage of Assimilation | Sub-process or Condition |
|---|---|
| 1. Cultural or behavioral assimilation | Change in cultural patterns to those of host society |
| 2. Structural assimilation | Large-scale entrance into cliques, clubs and institutions of host society or primary-group level |
| 3. Marital assimilation | Large-scale intermarriage |
| 4. Identification assimilation | Development of a sense of people-hood based exclusively on host society |
| 5. Attitude receptional assimilation | Absence of prejudice |
| 6. Behavioral receptional assimilation | Absence of discrimination |
| 7. Civic assimilation | Absence of value or power conflict |

minimal structural, marital, and identificational assimilation. They continue to experience widespread prejudice and discrimination, and conflicts are increasing rather than decreasing. Where there have been deliberate attempts to integrate, as with busing school children, racial frictions escalated, and the result has been greater polarization rather than increased tolerance.

Jewish Americans have become a thoroughly Americanized group, acculturated to the American middle-class way of life. Yet, at the same time, there is an increasing emphasis on "being Jewish," including association with Jewish culture, religion, and organizational life. Third and later generation Jews, in particular, are seeking to temper assimilation with separate group identity.

As for other groups, Japanese Americans have experienced the pluralistic development of a congruent Japanese culture within the larger American society, while for both Indian and Mexican Americans there remains a conflict between subcultural and majority values.

In the case of other ethnic groups, especially the blue-collar eastern and southern European Catholics, expressions of cultural pluralism are increasing, too. When the heterogeneity of American cities was caused primarily by the influx of successive immigrant waves, the policy of encouraging assimilation was taken for granted ideologically. Consumers might demonstrate a wide range of behaviors and preferences, but this variety was viewed as being both temporary and expendable. A White, middle-class "Americanized" standard could be imposed from the outside and justified in terms of the shared higher goal of assimilation. People behaved the way they did only because they had not yet *learned* the better way. The segregated local residential community was regarded as a passing entity which might be maintained only so long as temporary patterns of racial and socio-economic segregation persisted, but ultimately the local community would decline as people found other, preferable, non-territorial bases for association. Territorial groups were, it was felt, coercive in character and far less attractive than voluntary forms of association. The latter would shortly replace local community ties and these "interest communities" would result in a more faithful response from government and big business. The local community would decline then as racial and socio-economic segregation declined and interest communities replaced residential communities.

What is indicated in American urban regions today is, however, that a new type of heterogeneity exists and is intensifying. This heterogeneity must be understood from the different ideological position of cultural pluralism. In such a framework, the forms of community that emerge are in no way vestigial remnants of a more fragmented localized society.

As Gerald Suttles has pointed out, a useful point at which to begin to understand this different ideological position is by retrieving the cognitive maps of childhood. For the child, awareness of the city radiates outward, with the density of information diminishing rapidly with the distance from home. The area of comfortable familiarity constitutes the experience of neighborhood.

Yet cities do not consist of an infinitely large number of neighborhoods, each centering on one of millions of inhabitants only a slight spatial remove from his fellows. Rather there is a small number of social labels applied to definable geographical areas. Because population characteristics of a city are continuously variable, with no clear demarcation between one side of the street and the other, society imposes categorical labels on specific geographical realms. Neighborhood categories are not simply found in nature, but are consensually imposed definitions.

A neighborhood label, once affixed, has real consequences. For outsiders it reduces decision-making to more manageable terms. Instead of dealing with the variegated reality of numerous city streets, the residents can form a set of attitudes about a limited number of social categories and act accordingly. For those who live within it, the neighborhood defines areas relatively free of intruders, identifies where potential friends are to be found or where they are to be cultivated, minimizes the prospects of status insult, and simplifies innumerable daily decisions dealing with spatial activities. Thus the mental map of neighborhoods is not superfluous cognitive baggage, but performs important psychological and social functions.

The boundaries of neighborhoods are set by physical barriers, ethnic homogeneity, social class, and other factors that together contribute to the definition of homogeneous areas that are supportive of particular life styles. But if a neighborhood exists first as a creative social construction, it nonetheless possesses a number of important properties. First, it becomes a component of an individual's identity, a stable judgmental reference against which people are assessed. A neighborhood may derive its reputation from several sources: first, from the master identity of the area of which it is a part; second, through comparison and contrast with adjacent communities; and third, from historic claims. In this framework, the idea of a community as first and foremost a group of people bound together by common sentiments, a primordial solidarity, represents an over-romaticized view of social life. Communities do lead to social control, they do segregate people to avoid danger, insult, and status claims; but whatever sentiments are engendered by neighborhoods are strictly tied to functional realities.

There are multiple levels of community organization in which the resident participates. The smallest of these units is the *face block*. For children it is the prescribed social world carved out by parents. It is here that face-to-face relations are most likely, and the resulting institutional form is the block association. Next, is the *defended neighborhood* or *minimal named community,* which is the smallest segment of the city recognized by both residents and outsiders as possessing a particular character and which possesses many of the facilities needed to carry out the daily routine of life. Third, the urban resident also participates in the *community of limited liability,* a larger realm possessing an institutionally secure name and boundaries. The concept emphasizes the intentional, voluntary, and especially the differential involvement of residents in their local communities. Frequently an external agent, such as a community newspaper, is the most important guardian of such a community's sense of boundaries, purpose, and integrity. Finally, even larger segments of the city may also take shape in response to environmental pressures, creating an *expanded community of limited liability*. Thus an individual may find himself picketing to keep a highway not just out of his neighborhood, but out of the entire south side. In this way, varied levels of community organization are created as responses to the larger social environment. The urban community mirrors the social differentiation of the total society.

The communities in which Americans thus live vary in their racial, ethnic, and socio-economic composition and thus in their available life styles, in their physical features, which can be used to create images and boundaries, and in their historic claims to a distinct reputation or identity. Members of a mobile society select among communities in terms of the life style they are perceived to offer. What, then, are some of the principal life-style differences that are to be found within American society today, setting aside the differentiation associated with cultural intensification based on race and ethnicity?

They appear to arise from the experience by all Americans of two common developmental processes: (1) passage through stages of the life cycle, with especially sharp breaks associated with the transition from one state to another, as in marriage, family expansion, entry into the labor force, retirement, etc., and (2) occupational career trajectories that may necessitate, preclude, or otherwise pattern geographical mobility alongside social mobility. These developmental processes are cross-cut by several different value systems: *familism,* in which a high value is placed upon family living and a corresponding devotion of time and resources to family life; *careerism,* in which there is an orientation toward upward social mobility and a corresponding disposition to engage in career-related activities, at least to a partial neglect of family ties; *localism,* a parochial orientation implying interests confined to a neighborhood and reference to groups whose scope is local; and *cosmopolitanism,* an ecumenical orientation implying freedom from the binding ties to a locality and reference to groups whose scope is national rather than local, so that the cosmopolitan resides in a place but inhabits the nation.

From these bases, one can distinguish between *working-class communities, ghettos,* and *ethnic centers* where the broad pattern of interaction is one where informal meeting places, street corner gangs, church groups, and precinct politics tend to dominate the collective forms of communal life; *middle income, familistic areas,* in which informal relations seem to be heavily shaped by the management of children and formal organizations are much more extensively developed than in lower income areas; the *affluent apartment complex* and the *exclusive suburb,* which generally have a privatized mode of interaction and organization, social clubs, private schools, country clubs, and businessmen's associations; and *gentrified neighborhoods,* which characterize those central cities whose downtowns have been transformed, as in the case of Pittsburgh, by the headquarters of the new information economy.

What typifies the latter cases is *subcultural intensification*--the strengthening of the beliefs, values and cohesion both of groups emerging within expanding urban systems as new cultural values and norms are established by the changing occupational structures and rewards systems of the workplace. Two ingredients are involved: growth of "critical masses" such that subcultural institutions can develop (e.g. political power, and national churches for ethnic groups, hangouts for "bohemians," bookstores for the intellectuals, museums for artists, new communities for the elderly, and "turfs" for each group) which strengthen the subculture and attract more of its members to the city; and contrasts with other subcultures that intensify people's identification with and adherence to their own.

What has emerged in America as a result of these changes is a *mosaic culture* in which a number of parallel and distinctively different life styles coexist. While one result is divisive tendencies for the society as a whole, at another level mutual harmony is produced by mutual withdrawal into homogeneous communities isolated from groups with different life styles and values. Each of the nation's major metropolitan regions replicates the mosaic. There is a high resulting degree of expressed satisfaction by residents with their communities, and the option for those who are dissatisfied to move to an alternative that is more in keeping with their life-style requirements. Thus, even as occupational distributions and life style choices are becoming more polarized, direct social conflict is minimized.

Restructuring of the residential mosaic is occurring apace but most, locked in their own social worlds, remain ignorant of the shifts. The native of cities may indeed be a mirror of the society that maintains them, but for most the coexistence of interdependence and ignorance means that the view is "through a glass, darkly."

# Chapter XX

# TRANSATLANTIC ORBITS:  THE INTERPLAY IN THE EVOLUTION OF CITIES

## Jean Gottmann

"Orbits" has become a commonly used term since satellites, space shuttles, and other artifacts have been orbiting around the Earth.  Used in astronomy to describe the trajectory of celestial bodies that gravitate along more or less regular routes, "orbit" also designates the cavity that contains and protects the eye, within which the eyeball rotates and moves.  In the latter sense orbit defines a frame delimiting the field of an individual's vision.

Geographers nowadays are often on the move, much more than it used to be the case.  Their work and research require fieldwork, and the orbits within which they pursue it, that is, something like the field of their professional vision, have usually lengthened and diversified.  Chauncy Harris has been a geographer long orbiting various parts of the globe.  During the forty years that I have known him, we met in a great many varied places, chiefly in rather large cities like Chicago, New York, Philadelphia, Washington, Paris, Lisbon, Tokyo, Oxford, and many others.  Mostly his orbits, like mine, revolved around the North Atlantic.  It seems fitting, therefore, in a book honoring his career, to reflect on the interplay in the evolution of cities on the two sides of the North Atlantic, a cultural and economic orbit especially familiar to me as well as to Chauncy Harris.

### The Evolution of Cities

Cities evolve constantly.  The constant change going on inside a large urban community seems to be a basic characteristic of the concept of the city.  The dynamic change is what really makes the difference between a town and a city.  A dynamic town, unless it fades away, usually rises to city rank.  In a real city things are constantly brewing; change may be gradual, in some periods more accelerated than others, but it develops constantly, more substantially than local people perceive it.

Buildings change more slowly than the population and life styles they contain. However, the pace of change has greatly accelerated throughout the world since the middle of the nineteenth century, and increasingly so since 1920. These changes both in the built environment and in the socio-economic circumstances of the city are generally resented by the local leadership. I have often found that, unless it displaced them, the first instinctive reaction of the rank and file of the city people, especially of those who feel underprivileged, is to welcome changes in the built environment. New buildings, new activities at first often arouse new hopes for improvement of everybody's condition. Moreover, "modernization" is generally taken as a sign of progress and of enhancing the status of the place.

The "established" leadership stratum looks at change differently. It usually distrusts large-scale innovation that may herald or even implement modifications in the established structures, unsettle social hierarchies and political processes. Also, most people's tastes are formed early in life, and adapting to new landscapes and styles takes time and tolerance. Baudelaire, who lived through the beginnings of the renewal of Paris in the 1840s and 1850s, expressed this resistance well in a verse: "The lively city changes faster than a mortal's heart." What would he have said had he witnessed the rise of the Eiffel Tower? Still, Baudelaire, while a good analyst of it, was surely not a spokesman for the Parisian establishment. A later and more conservative poet, Theophile Gautier took long detours around Paris to avoid the sight of the Eiffel Tower. Similar attitudes could be observed among good Parisians in recent years towards the Centre Pompidou! The latter is, however, a loved attraction for large crowds of youngsters.

The twentieth century has seen forests of skyscrapers, large and high blocks of flats, and a frequent use of glass and metal structures arise in many cities in various countries. In the past, it took at least a century for a new architectural style to be accepted for a few monumental buildings. Then, it may have spread, but only within a restricted geographical compass reflecting a certain cultural zone. The speed of the diffusion of the new styles has been such both in time and in space, particularly since 1920 and even more since 1950, that the evolution of cities in the twentieth century took on a completely different allure and significance from what these may have been in past ages.

I was born in 1915, the year when Patrick Geddes published his

famous book entitled *The Evolution of Cities*,[1] a milestone in the
history of planning.  I read it when 25 yers old and found it very
interesting, its historical and analytical method stimulating, but
the basic philosophy in some way hopelessly outdated.  Twenty years
of inter-wars life in Paris and a little travelling to some other
places had created the feeling of a too rapidly moving present, of
processes in which the mortals' hearts will bleed but cities will
overcome it all.

Since then, some forty years of transhumance over the North
Atlantic has also taught me to beware of projections in time and
generalizations in space.  Surely some processes repeat themselves
through history and in different countries; certain diffusions or
evolution patterns are repeated for different innovations.  But the
city is far too complex an entity, made of too many human beings,
groups and shifting interests; it has so many diverse
characteristics, many of them unstable, and is submitted to the
influence of so many outside factors, that it could not be easily
predictable.

In the spring of 1953, while touring the large crystalline
plateau of the Ardennes, which extends from northeastern France into
Belgium and Luxembourg, I visited Rocroi, a French frontier
stronghold town designed in the sixteenth century in the shape of a
pentagonal wheel, with radio-concentric streets, probably by Italian
military engineers.  In the seventeenth century, its ramparts were
reinforced by Vauban.  A market-town in a poor rural depopulating
region, Rocroi seemed fossilized; some empty houses were badly in
need of repairs; only two notable structures stood outside the
walls--the railway station and the gas service station.  Means of
transportation had improved but seemed to have taken more life out
of Rocroi than contributed to it.  A few hours earlier, I had
visited across the border the city of Luxembourg.  The capital of
the Grand-Duchy was another strong small city, a castle town, dating
back to the Middle Ages.  Its population around 1700 must hardly
have been larger than Rocroi's.  But in 1953, although still a small
city by European standards, it looked thriving, a capital and an
international crossroads.  Some of the contrast in the evolution of
these two places may be explained by physical circumstances.
Luxembourg stood in a *Gutland* on the periphery of the Ardennes, iron
ore mines were discovered and worked, and so forth.  Still, there is
no doubt that the political function of capital city has been

---

1. Patrick Geddes, *Cities in Evolution: An Introduction to the Town
Planning Movement and to the Study of Civics,* reprint of 1915 ed. with new
introduction by Percy Johnson-Marshall (New York: H. Fertig, 1968).

essential to differentiate the evolution of Luxembourg from other nearby towns, despite the small size of the city (only 75,000 in 1983) and of the State.

The striking contrast between these two neighboring towns may serve to illustrate, first, the way in which a city reflects the economy and society of the region around it, and second, the importance of the function it has in relating that region to the outside world. The role of cities must be to serve as *hinges* between the region (or country) within their immediate orbit and the wider orbit in which each city's life revolves in the world at large. That role also used to be rather stable, only seldom changing, due to great events in the past. In this century, both kinds of orbits are being modified constantly by rapid shifts of local or worldwide portent. The evolution of the Grand-Duchy of Luxembourg, which by its size could well be assimilated nowadays to a metropolitan region, has led it in the last 150 years from the status of a feudal land reputed for its forests and wolves, to that of a center of European Community politics and of international offshore banking. Its present prosperity and functions have neither been planned nor even expected.

I went to look at the Ardennes in 1953 mainly because a few months earlier, starting my study of the State of Virginia,[2] I was impressed and puzzled by the differences I observed in the settlement and economy of the Piedmont regions in Virginia on the one hand and North Carolina or Pennsylvania on the other. A large natural region, divided into political segments which correspond to somewhat different cultural elements and traditions, produces different types of urban life and of networks of cities. This was obvious comparing Virginia to North Carolina. The differences between the cities of their Piedmonts, or their Tidewaters, appeared much greater than the differences between their land uses and types of rural settlement. Cities, that is, urban places of substantial size and diversified activities, became far more independent from their natural regional environments than rural countrysides. This is no novelty, but it takes on special significance when related to the historical past and cultural background. The determinism in a city's evolution is at least of a triple nature: there are the elements of *location* (which encompasses the natural and human regional environment), the *inner economic orgnization,* proper to the city and rather fluid nowadays, and the *external orbit* in which the

---

2. Eventually published as Jean Gottmann, *Virginia at Mid-Century* (New York: Holt, 1955).

city's life revolves, a dynamic network certainly related to location and inner structure but governed by external forces resulting from what happens in distant places.

Modern evolution has enormously increased the radius, scope, and complexity of most cities' external orbits and has made their inner structures more dependent on external forces. Geographers have been aware of this essential trend for a long time. Statements to this effect may be found repeatedly since the 1880s on in the works of Mackinder, Ratzel, and Vidal de la Blache. Still, the majority of the scholars in the generations that followed continued to emphasize the impact of the local or regional circumstances. These have certainly remained influential to this day but mainly in building up cultural variation and political differentiation, and in resisting the full impact of the momentous changes in the modern world as a whole. One could see in the vogue, in the mid-twentieth century, of quantitative models such as the rank-size rules and the hierarchies implied in central place theories derived from Christaller, devices to regionalize the external orbits and simplify the growing complexity of their dynamics. Chauncy Harris was first to apply such quantitative analysis to the Soviet Union network of cities.[3]

Two broader theoretical approaches have been applied to the study of modern urban evolution in more fecund manner: the techno-economic and the socio-cultural. The former emphasizes the economic forces shaping and modifying urban form and society, especially as determined by the advances of technology and the techniques of management. The latter focuses on the interplay between the established social system and local cultures on the one hand and the momentum of change caused by demographic, ethnic, and ideological kinetics of the time and country on the other hand. The conflicts and problems generated mainly by this socio-cultural momentum have greatly broadened the field of urban studies, attracting to it many more social scientists and creating new fields of research, such as "social geography," and "urban sociology." To compare how these various approaches and factors interacted on the two sides of the North Atlantic, it has seemed necessary to consider separately the techno-economic dynamics first and then the socio-cultural kinetics.

---

3. Chauncy D. Harris, *Cities of the Soviet Union* (Chicago: Rand, McNally and Co., for the Association of American Geographers, 1970).

## The Search for the Good Life

Aristotle said that groups of people gathered to form cities in search of security and that they remained in cities for the sake of a good life. For some time this explanation of urban settlement has been disputed. A vast literature and a long history of troubles and of legislation to quell them has claimed that, to the contrary, life in cities is hard and bad, that the good life is to be found outside, in the countryside where the patricians' villas, the old manors, and castles are. As this debate went on for millennia urbanization proceeded and cities grew, multiplied, and expanded. In the second half of the twentieth century, the condemnation of city living reached a quasi-hysterical pitch. Simultaneously urbanization generalized and accelerated. In the more advanced economies, which, even in periods of depression, enjoyed a higher level of living and a more generous welfare state, the proportion of agricultural and mining workers dropped to one-tenth or less of the total labor force, so that 90 percent of the population lived from urban pursuits, whether in dense or scattered settlements.

Cities were in crisis in many cases but they grew, either in residential population or in the extent of suburban and metropolitan territory. One could tinker with the precise definition and meaning of the terms "city" and "urban," and with the statistics of inward and outward city migration. But it remains that, on the whole, throughout the world, higher standards of health, national wealth, and greater consumption of goods and services have been related to higher levels of urbanization. Between the facts observed *in vivo,* or on the maps, and the clamor against cities, especially large cities, one could not help recognizing a clear contrast and contradiction. Critics of the cities have often answered with the argument that people were still gathering in or around cities, because they were compelled to do so by economic and technocratic forces, and the results were not a good life but an evil situation.

It is usually agreed, however, by both sides of this momentous debate, which seems to involve a great deal of mankind's future, that cities do not *have* to dissolve; they could be made much better. Furthermore, there is seldom heard a call for the sacrifice of all modern technology, a return to medieval, if not prehistoric, methods of tilling the land, of hauling loads, of using masses of controlled (or enslaved ?) human labor. On the contrary we hear that modern techniques and adequate economic planning could more than ever bring about a new golden age, the really good life. It was only a matter of reforming the laws, of adopting and implementing the right kind of planning.

My experience after almost half a century of observations on both sides of the Atlantic does not confirm such a simplistic view of the enormously complex process of modern urbanization. In the ideas, methods, and legislation concerning cities and urban planning there has been a great deal of transatlantic interplay and, indeed, of interaction in the twentieth century. I shall not go so far as to suggest that North America and Western Europe formed a sort of common market for urban technology and ideology; such a formula would not be correct as will soon be shown. But there exists one vast transatlantic orbit in which all the main planning policies, technological innovations, and methods of management are exchanged, attempted, at least debated. The outcome, however, does not provide a straight, generally appliable solution.

Let us first consider approaches to urban *design*. All those who took part in the designing--architects, planners, administrators, geographers, politicians, and businessmen--moved freely around within the transatlantic orbit. They used a *common lore* of ideas and techniques. It may take several volumes to demonstrate in detail this interplay. Certainly the North Atlantic has been and remains the large portion of space on this planet most intensely criss-crossed by ships and airplanes, telephone connections and other telecommunications, people, goods, and messages. The results in terms of evolution of cities are nevertheless strikingly at variance, not only between Anglo-America on the one hand and continental Europe on other, but even on the two sides of the Channel between England and France, or between Switzerland and Belgium.

First of all, the same ideas are not understood and accepted in the same way. In the 1960s, the Urban Design Committee of the American Institute of Architects tried to assess, and re-assess, the situation in American cities. A large project, involving many experts, was undertaken. The four articles published as a result in 1962-63 in the *Journal of the American Institute of Architects* are well worth re-reading.[4] The same names of master-designers, the same famous models repeatedly recur on these pages: the ancient monuments of Greece and Italy, the masters of the Italian Renaissance and the modern giants: Fourier, L'Enfant, Haussmann, Ebenezer Howard, Frank Lloyd Wright, Le Corbusier, Burnham, Raymond Unwin, Patrick Geddes, Abercrombie, the team of the Bauhaus, and so on. The Committee discussed the historic precedents, the roots, and modern concepts of

---

4 . *Journal of the American Institute of Architects* 38, no. 6; 39, no. 2; 39, no. 4; and 39, no. 6 (December 1962, February, April, and June 1963).

urban design, guidelines for the visual survey, basic principles in
the practice of urban design . . . It was magnificent, dedicated
soul-searching by the leaders of American town planning, all
architects, of course, at a time when American models, though
largely inspired by European thought, immediately found powerful
resonance in Europe.

The master-designers were architects, that is, both artists
and technocrats. They believed that, as Matthew A. Rockwell put it
when introducing the project,

> Throughout history man has sought to gain greater control over his
> physical environment, according to the needs and preferences of his
> times. His attention has been largely focused on the shaping of his
> cities. His successes, while sporadic, are marked by magnificent levels
> of achievement and artistry . . . As Carl Feiss has recently written:
> 'A major conversion of architectural practice is now taking place: the
> comprehensive architecture of whole communities.' This task is as
> difficult as it is necessary. Healthy cities are fundamental to healthy
> societies.5

The pages that follow in that series do not quite support the
main points of this statement. Historic precedents of fully planned
communites abound, such as the ancient Greek town of Miletus, the
medieval *bastides* of Languedoc, Rocroi, Versailles, Philadelphia,
Pa., and Washington, D.C., to mention only a few. But did the
architects actually structure the whole community? Or did they only
design the built environment amid which the community adapted,
evolved, pursued a more-or-less healthy existence? A certain
confusion may be detected in the four articles of this report
between the city's infrastrucuture (that is, buildings, streets,
open spaces) and the life of the people that formed the local
community. Certainly, both are closely related. The interaction
between the two has always been much more effective and involved
than that between container and contained. But what this
relationship actually is has never been clearly brought out.

The designers seem to believe that what they design, if
actually built, determines a great deal the sort of community that
lives there. Still, it is obvious that the form of the city is
often modified against the will of its inhabitants. And it is just
as true that, in dynamic periods of history, such as the last 500
years for the transatlantic orbit, tastes and socio-economic
structures change faster than the buildings they use. Traditionally
in Europe the built environment lags behind the people's needs.
That lag may be explained by the impulses provided by technological
innovation and the ensuing economic evolution. Thus, the industrial

---

5. Matthew A. Rockwell, "Introduction" to series on the architecture of
towns and cities, *Journal of the American Institute of Architects,* 38, no. 6
(December 1962), p. 43.

revolution attracted crowds of workers into towns before proper
housing, schools, and parks were provided for them. Recent urban
growth failed to develop adequate means of traffic and
transportation throughout urbanized areas, leading to congestion in
the buildings and on the streets, in the trains, buses, and other
channels of traffic. Altogether, modern urban change brought a
double set of contrasting worries in both Europe and North America,
on one hand, the size and congestion of the rapidly developing
cities, mainly the larger ones, and on the other the blight and
plight of the declining towns, especially of smaller size. In
France, Paris has been a classical example of the former category,
Rocroi typical of the latter.

Similar trends could be observed in the other countries within
the orbit under consideration here. In the Canadian Prairie or even
in Illinois, one could see many examples of these trends in the
twentieth century, and in the 1960s one felt sorry for many small
towns of Saskatchewan or Southern Illinois. Only a few of them
blessed with some special function or industry were holding their
own. The State of Illinois created in a half dozen smallish towns,
small university campuses which revived those places, such as
Carbondale, Edwardsville, and Charleston, but others nearby were
sad sights, despite resounding names like West Frankfurt, Venice,
and even Cairo. Shawneetown, on the mighty Ohio River, long ago an
important business center, is just a ghost town visited by tourists,
who wonder at the urban fossil.

There are many "ghost towns" in the American West, chiefly on
abandoned mining sites. But that sort of fate has befallen also
deserted towns along the rivers that used to be the essential
arteries of trade and transportation in the eastern United States,
and also along railway lines in the Canadian Prairie. Economic
activities on a local or regional scale needed local market towns,
transactional and servicing centers in past centuries. In the
twentieth century, with larger-scale operations and easy means to
overcome distance, transactions and services concentrated in a
smaller number of selected locations. These were not always the
larger metropolises, as Detroit and St. Louis have discovered, but
in places endowed with proper *hosting environments* for transactions
on a large geographical scale and with a great diversity of
ancillary services. Historians quote the episode of the Bank of
Shawneetown refusing, around 1830, credit to help develop a place
called Chicago in northern Illinois; it was too far from

Shawneetown![6] The thinning out of agricultural populations and, for a time, the concentration of manufactures may be cited as an illustration of the power of technological and economic forces. Europe did not quite have ghost towns but concentration factors worked efficiently to empty the countryside.

Concentration led to congestion and social conflict in the larger and more successful metropolitan areas. The European cities lost much of their quality of life in the nineteenth century as a result of the growth of manufactures and of wealth, due to economic and imperial expansion. Decentralization, or at least deconcentration, became the essential worry of London and Paris then and, even more, during the twentieth century. North America came to the same concerns after 1920 and more acutely after 1950. Urban designers of different origins offered a recipe for the good life in an urbanized and industrialized country, to cure the ills of over-concentration and congestion, which has been very popular for a century: surplus growth was to be resettled in well-planned new towns. The *new towns* were to be small, rather self-contained, preferably *Garden Cities*. While the creation of new urban places, many of which became cities, has been a normal occurrence in the process of land settlement for ages, few of these were originally and systematically planned, except perhaps by colonial powers (for example, Spain in the Americas). Each of these towns established a center amid unstructured territory. The new towns, advocated in the nineteenth century and often implemented in the twentieth, proceeded from a special philosophy of decentralization of congested large cities not only to relieve the pressures within them but even more to provide an urban environment conducive to a good life. The French dreamers Ledoux and Fourier started the concept (especially the "phalanstere"). Ebenezer Howard really formulated both the theory and plan of modern new towns in his *Garden Cities of To-morrow* first published in 1898.[7] All the nineteenth century new-town proposals were offered as expressions of social reforms, to achieve, with the good life, a better society. Howard offered the most reasonable design, and he was considered the real father of the new town theory.

---

6. *The WPA Guide to Illinois: The Federal Writer's Project Guide to 1930s Illinois,* with a new intro. by Neil Harris and Michael Conzen (New York: Pantheon, 1983), p. 436.

7. See Ebenezer Howard, *Garden Cities of To-morrow,* with an intro. by Lewis Mumford (Cambridge, Mass.: Massachusetts Institute of Technology Press, 1965).

What developed under the "new towns" label varied greatly from one country to another and evolved fast. Books have been written repeatedly on this theme and I shall not attempt to summarize the ideas, the implementation, and the debates that arose. It is, however, relevant to make two points at this juncture. First, while the same ideas and technical means were available and well-known throughout the whole transatlantic orbit, the implementation or lack of it varied with national and regional cultures and politics. Second, planners used the new town ideas more to decentralize large cities than to achieve social reform. In France, after 1960, new towns, particularly around Paris, were aimed at a better structure of sweeping suburban sprawl. Once again, a type of built environment became the aim, the purpose and the ingredients for a good urban life. It was expected to determine human mood and behavior. When one considers the diversity of towns and experiments that ensued in a dozen countries, one realizes that the population in fact determined the outcome locally, especially the use of what was built.

New towns helped to decentralize. In a few cases they did not alleviate the pressures in the neighboring central city. In other cases they sucked out so much of the growth from the central city, when the latter was not booming, that only more decline and greater problems ensued for the central old nucleus, modifying the sort of crisis that developed but also deepening or accelerating it. Liverpool and Newcastle-on-Tyne may be cases in point. The basic facts that I have observed in my own urban transhumance indicate that the evolution of society and regional cultural diversity have been essential factors in determining both the forms and the conflicts in the evolution of cities. In brief, the people have used cities and suburbs for their purposes and ideas; they have not obeyed or even respected what the planners and architects have tried to impose on the city attempting to control the population and the quality of life.

### The City Is the People

Under that title, the American architect Henry Churchill published in 1940 a thoughtful and stimulating book.[8] He thought the population, with its tastes, moods, and diverse trends, should be given more attention by architects and city planners, because that was the most determinant factor in urban evolution. I remember vividly a long conversation once with Henry Churchill in Rittenhouse

---

8. Henry Stern Churchill, *The City Is the People,* 2nd ed. (New York: W.W. Norton, 1962).

Square in Philadelphia, while I was working on my book on Megalopolis.[9] He had been traveling recently in France. He spoke of the gradual change he observed, visiting churches in the south of France, in the expression of the Madonnnas, from the soft and benevolent expression of the ones of Provence to the severe and rigorous of those near the Spanish Pyrenees. He also referred to the symbolism of monuments in Paris, that the Arc de Triomphe signaled the end of a long period opened by Greco-Roman architects, while the Eiffel Tower heralded the new era of history opening up in our century with skyscraping, liberation from old molds, and new engineering taking over the design of the environment. Gifted artists just express the trends and traditions in the local people's spirit.

In 1966, the Council of the World Society for Ekistics, founded a year earlier at meetings in London, met in Paris to elaborate the statutes of the association. We sat in the gold and purple splendour of one of the most decorated rooms of the Palais-Royal. Constantinos Doxiadis spoke on the definition of *Ekistics,* a new "science of human settlements." Listening to him Buckminster Fuller registered disapproval by saying, "I do not think we should emphasize 'settlements.' I see much of the young all around the world; they are not interested in settlement." Asked by the chairman, Lord Llewellyn-Davies, what the youth was then interested in, Bucky answered: "Unsettlement." Since 1967, he was many times proven right on both sides of the Atlantic. That our time is one of unsettlement in all the meanings of the word is not the result of urbanization, and the consequent problems could not be solved just by urban policy and design. Rather, modern cities and urban change are a product of the unsettlement. They should be managed taking into account these kinetics decided upon by the people.

Concluding its report, the A.I.A. Urban Design Committee had taken into consideration human scale and human vision, popular needs and traditions. It still emphasized form as a determinant:

> *Form* is the idea; *design,* its fulfilment. As the scale of design increases in a city, as the participations multiply, we have what David Crane calls the city of a thousand designers. They are the many people who act on the basis of the form concept which is furnished in an urban design plan. The thousand designers fulfil the promise of the initial form.[10]

---

9. Jean Gottman, *Megalopolis: The Urbanized Northeastern Seaboard of the United States* (New York: Twentieth Century Fund, 1961).

10. *Journal of the American Institute of Architects,* 39, no. 6 (June 1963), p. 74.

Architects are not alone in being preoccupied with form. So are
also the geographers, as form delineates sections of space and
provides some geometrical frame and appearance of stability. In our
time, however, these approaches seem outdated. Moreover the purely
morphological approach is constricting for the understanding of the
dynamic phenomena developing in modern urban space.

Let us return to what has happened since Ebenezer Howard to
the new towns concept. The Garden City Howard offered for to-morrow
by 1900 would have been excellent for the nineteenth century.
Welwyn Garden City has been a success, but this was because it
evolved very fast after the 1930s into a satellite in the regional
orbit of London, taking on a character which would have greatly
surprised Howard, if he could have looked at it in 1985. It
influenced the thinking of Rexford Tugwell, director of the U.S.
Resettlement Administration in 1935-36, when he proposed a Greenbelt
Town Program. The program was defeated, for it seemed too
disturbing to those already established in the areas concerned, and
too "socialist" to the consensus of powerful private interests
working on urbanization. Some new towns were nevertheless
established in the United States after careful planning: first, to
answer wartime urgent needs, such as Levittown, New York, and Oak
Ridge, Tennessee; later, in congested interurban locations and by
private rather than government initiative, such as Levittown,
Pennsylvania; Reston, Virginia; and Columbia, Maryland.

In France new towns succeeded on the contrary as governmental
foundations on public land. The decisive step there was the first
master plan for the Region of Paris, prepared and applied by Paul
Belouvrier. He visualized a half-dozen new towns with populations
of 2-400,000 each to deconcentrate and structure the growth of
central Paris from 1967 on. Some of these foundations have taken on
substantial size and are achieving success. But they are, in 1985,
just better planned suburbs of a large, still expanding metropolis
with a good deal of green space within and around them.

Paris is still extending tentacles beyond what is officially
recognized as its region. In Rouen, the old capital of Normandy,
new residential neighborhoods have recently arisen next to the
railroad station to house families, one member of which works in the
heart of Paris. A good electrified rail service makes the
arrangement attractive and benefits the "inner cities" of both Paris
and Rouen. A comparable relationship shapes up between Paris and
Orleans to the south.

Indeed, the attitudes towards the central city and the suburban periphery differ greatly on the continents of Europe and North America. In the United States the middle class has always preferred to live *uptown* while working *downtown*. Not so in Europe. As a gradual gentrification of society occurs, due to the shift of the majority of the labor force to qualified services (better paid, more specialized, and requiring higher education), large masses acquire, therefore, new lifestyles, generally of higher standing and status, despite the aberrant vogue of blue jeans. This effect of techno-economic progress has met with different reactions on the two sides of the ocean.

In France the people with status prefer to stay close to the business center, whether they work there or not. The uptown is a belt immediately surrounding the downtown. The former may expand farther away from the original kernel but only following an expansion of the downtown and in the same direction. Thus the best sections of Paris are in the Ville de Paris or along the main axes of historical royal moves to suburban castles: St. Germain-en-Laye, Versailles, and, to some extent, Fontainebleau. The best suburbs like Neuilly or Rueil-Malmaison line the road (and the new R.E.R. line) to St. Germain. When Haussmann rebuilt Paris between 1850 and 1868, he "cleaned up" the central district and pushed the poorer working masses out to the suburbs. This has not been forgotten. The French move to the suburban periphery only if and to the extent that they cannot do otherwise.

In American cities the tradition was opposite: status came with uptown residence. With the gentrification of society, an immense suburban and metropolitan sprawl developed, taking urbanization out of bounds. The emptying central districts of cities were taken over partly by the expansion of offices and other institutional uses of the land, and partly by the poor migrants flowing into the cities in the hope of a better life, that is, better jobs, better schools for their children, and more welfare from richer communities. The result has been often an active and expanding central business district surrounded by a belt of "refugee camps" housing the newcomers who hope to fit themselves first into the lower occupations abandoned by established groups and later to benefit by the process of general gentrification.

Social conflicts between the wealthy and the poor have always been a standing feature of city life and growth. My contemporaries complain bitterly nowadays about the insecurity, criminality, and hostility they feel in modern cities. I am not sure at all that this moaning is not basically caused by short memories. To-day, even wealthy people dare to go about their business in cities without being guarded by armed escort which was a necessity, generally accepted, in the cities and towns of days of yore. Let us turn to the medieval history of Florence, or the normal atmosphere of seventeenth century Paris or Amsterdam--all very civilized places--to realize that there was *less* security there then than what we now enjoy. Statistics of criminality are now better made, urban populations and the middle classes amidst them are much more numerous, and the carrying and use of arms is not as readily accepted.

## Orbits and Diversity

Such historical comparisons do not mean, of course, that the unsettlement of our time is not disturbing and troublesome. Cities have immense problems. Adapting to the speed and complexity of modern change is not easy. It is undoubtedly a good thing that we have now realized to what extent the city is the people and how necessary it is to study and improve the condition of the people in those gigantic artifacts that are the urbanized areas of the late twentieth century.

Each country, each region must be allowed to search for its own solutions, its own style of life. No stereotyped recipe will do for a diversity of communities. Perhaps those who concern themselves with the interplay of forces, factors, and places within urban orbits of large and small scale should ponder an idea offered by various modern scholars in different fields. As evolution of living beings proceeds, the major change is not only size but much more the functional alteration or *mutation,* which restructures the organization in some of their organs. The brain does not produce higher quality of thought by growing bigger, but it may achieve such progress by changes within its organization, the way it functions. The same can be said of society. In 1776, Adam Smith observed that the division of labor in a community increases with the size of the market, and he gave large cities as examples. But the size of a market may increase or decrease independently of the number of the potential consumers, as we have experienced in recent years of depression. It is a function of the organization of the market.

Anthropology and history have shown evolution that accompanied the march of civilization has led to increasing human diversity. British, Italian, or French settlements scattered around the planet have produced a constantly growing variety of communities, of groups

at variance from the original kernel.  The concentration of
population in large metropolitan agglomerations may very well
increase this diversifying process around the world.  The
"melting-pot" idea is far too simple for human behavior.  Human
diversity is just beginning to be studied.  It holds enormous
promise for the students and cultural leaders of cities, and of the
orbits each of the cities construct for themselves, to achieve in an
interdependent world the role which they think fits them best.

# THE CONTRIBUTORS

**DAVID H. K. AMIRAN** is Professor Emeritus of Human Geography at the Hebrew University of Jerusalem and Director of the Institute for Jerusalem Studies. He has served as President of the Israel Geographical Society. He is the dean of Israeli geography, and spent a year as a visiting Professor of Geography at the University of Chicago. He has co-edited *The Atlas of Israel* (Hebrew ed. 1956-64, English ed. 1970), *Coastal Deserts: Their Natural and Human Environments* (1973), and played a crucial developmental role in the publication of the 2-volume *Atlas of Jerusalem* (1973). He has also co-authored *Development Towns in Israel* (1969) and *Lakhish: Realization of a Plan* (1978).

**JACQUELINE BEAUJEU-GARNIER** is Professor of Geography at the Sorbonne, Paris. She has served as President of the Société de Géographie, Paris, and is Co-Director of the major French geographical periodical *Annales de Géographie* and has been since 1940 the General Secretary of the periodical *Information Géographique*. She has published many books and monographs, among which those translated into English are *Urban Geography* (1967), *France* (1975), and *Geography of Population* (1967, rev. 1978). Other major works include *La population française* (1977), *La géographie de commerce* (1977), *Atlas et géographie de Paris et la region d'Ile-de-France* (1977), and the multi-volume *La France des villes* (1978-1980) prepared under her direction.

**BRIAN J. L. BERRY** is Dean of the School of Urban and Public Affairs and University Professor of Urban Studies and Public Policy at Carnegie-Mellon University, Pittsburgh. Previously he taught at Harvard University, following a long period on the faculty of the University of Chicago (1958-76). He is a member of the National Academy of Sciences and was President of the Association of American Geographers in 1978-79. Among his most influential writings and edited works are *Geography of Market Centers and Retail Distribution* (1968), *Geographic Perspectives on Urban Systems* (1970), *Urbanization and Counterurbanization* (1976), *The Human Consequences of Urbanization* (1977, rev. 1981), *Contemporary Urban Ecology* (1977), and *The Open Housing Question* (1979).

**MICHAEL P. CONZEN** is Associate Professor of Geography at the University of Chicago, and member of the Center for Urban Research and Policy Studies at the University, having previously taught at Boston University from 1971-76. He is the author of *Frontier Farming in an Urban Shadow* (1971), co-author of *Boston: A Geographical Portrait* (1976), and editor of *Chicago Mapmakers: Essays on the Growth of the City's Map Trade* (1984).

**KAZIMIERZ DZIEWOŃSKI** is Professor of Geography at the Institute of Geography and Spatial Organization, Polish Academy of Sciences, Warsaw. He is both a geographer and a planner. He has served as Chairman of the Commission on National Settlement Systems of the International Geographical Union (1976-1984). His co-authored works include *Rozwój i Rozmieszczenie Ludnosci Polski w XX Wieku* (1967), *Przksztalcenia Przestrzenno-Gospodarczej Struktury Kraju* (1978), and he co-edited *Urbanization and Settlement System: International Perspectives* (1984).

**SPERIDIÃO FAISSOL** is Professor of Geography in the Departamento de Geografia of the Instituto Brasileiro de Geografia e Estatistica in Rio de Janeiro. He was a Vice-President of the International Geographical Union (1976-1984). His books include *Problemas Geograficos Brasileiros: Analises Quantitativas* (1972), and *Tendencias Atnais na Geografia Urbano/Regional: Teorizacao e Quantificacao* (1978).

**NORTON S. GINSBURG** is Professor of Geography at the University of Chicago and Executive Secretary of the Norman Wait Harris Memorial Foundation in International Relations there. He has served as President of the Association of American Geographers (1970-71). He has edited and co-authored numerous works, including *The Pattern of Asia* (1958), *Essays on Geography and Economic Development* (1960), the *Atlas of Economic Development* (1961), *Pacem in Maribus III: The Mediterranean Marine Environment and Development of the Region* (1974), *China: Urbanization and National Development* (1980), and *China: The 80s Era* (1984). He has been General Editor of the Prentice-Hall series *Foundations in Economic Geography* and is Co-Editor of *The Ocean Yearbook*.

**JEAN GOTTMANN** is Professor Emeritus of Geography in the University of Oxford where he was Head of the School of Geography from 1968 to 1984. He was awarded an honorary LL.D. by the University of Wisconsin in 1968, a D.Sc. by Southern Illinois University in 1969, and a D.Let. at the Université de Paris in 1970. His many books include *Virginia at Mid-Century* (1955, rev. 1969), *Megalopolis: The Urbanized Northeastern Seaboard of the United States* (1961), *The Significance of Territory* (1973), *The Coming of the Transactional City* (1983), and *La Città Invincibile: Una Confutazione dell' Urbanistica Negativa* (1983), and he has also edited *Metropolis on the Move: Geographers Look at Urban Sprawl* (1966), and *Centre and Periphery: Spatial Variation in Politics* (1980).

**JÖRG GÜSSEFELDT** is Privat-Dozent in the Institut für Kulturgeographie der Albert-Ludwigs-Universität, Freiburg, West Germany. He has recently published *Die gegenseitige Abhängigkeit innerurbaner Strukturmuster und Rollen der Städte im Nationalen Städtesystem: Das Beispiel der sozialräumlichen Organisation innerhalb irischer Städte* (1983).

**MARIA TERESA GUTIÉRREZ de MacGREGOR** is Professor of Population and Urban Geography in the Instituto de Geografía, Universidad Nacional Autónoma de México, and was Director of the Institute from 1971 to 1977. She holds doctorates from the Universidad Nacional Autónoma de México (1965) and the Université de Paris (1969). Her major publications include *Desarrollo y Distribución de la Populación Urbana en México* (1965) and *Geodemografía del Estado de Jalisco* (1968).

**GEORGE W. HOFFMAN** is Professor Emeritus of Geography at the University of Texas at Austin and Acting Secretary of the East European Program at the Woodrow Wilson International Center for Scholars, Smithsonian Institution, Washington, D.C. His major books include *The Balkans in Transition* (1963), *Regional Development Strategy in Southeast Europe* (1972), *The European Energy Challenge: East and West* (1985), and such edited works as *A Geography of Europe* (1953, 5th ed. 1983), *Eastern Europe: Essays in Geographical Problems* (1971), *Federalism and Regional Development: Case Studies on the Experience in the United States and the Federal Republic of Germany* (1981).

**HOU REN-ZHI** is Professor of Geography and Chairman of the Department of Geography at Beijing University, Peoples Republic of China, a position he has held since 1978. Previously he was Professor and Chairman of the Department of Geological Geography there from 1952 to 1962, and Vice Director of Studies at the University 1962-66. He holds a Ph.D. from the University of Liverpool. He is currently a member of the Beijing City Planning Commission and Chairman of the Beijing Cultural Relics Preservation Committee. His books include *The Origins of Tianjin Village* (1945), *Historical Beijing City* (1962, 3rd ed. 1983), *The Theory and Practice of Historical Geography* (1979), and *Talks on the History of Beijing* (1982).

**SHINZO KIUCHI** is Professor Emeritus of Geography at Seijo University. Previously he had a long career at the University of Tokyo, where he was Professor from 1956 to 1970. He was a Vice-President of the International Geographical Union (1972-80). He is the author of many publications on urban geography in Japanese. He is well-known internationally for his editing of two publications in English, *Japanese Cities: A Geographical Approach* (1970), and *Geography in Japan* (1976), both publications of the Association of Japanese Geographers.

**AKIN L. MABOGUNJE** is Professor of Geography at the University of Ibadan, Nigeria (since 1965). He was President of the International Geographical Union from 1980 to 1984. His major books include *Yoruba Towns* (1962), *The Urbanization of Nigeria* (1968), *Growth Poles and Growth Centres in the Regional Development of Nigeria* (1971), *Regional Mobility and Resource Development in West Africa* (1972), *The Development Process: A Spatial Perspective* (1981), and an edited work *Regional Planning and National Development in Tropical Africa* (1977).

**WALTER MANSHARD** is Professor of Geography and Director, Institut für Kulturgeographie der Albert-Ludwigs-Universität, Freiburg, West Germany. He has also served as Director of the Division of Environmental Sciences and Natural Resources Research of UNESCO (1969-73) and as Vice-Rector for Natural Resources of the United Nations University, Tokyo (1977-80). He was Secretary General-Treasurer of the International Geographical Union, 1976-1982. His major books include *Tropical Agriculture: A Geographical Introduction and Appraisal* (1968, Engl. transl. 1974), *Afrika südlich der Sahara* (1970), *Die Städte des Tropischen Afrika* (1977), and *Renewable Resources and the Environment: Pressing Problems in the Developing World* (1981).

**HAROLD M. MAYER** is Professor of Geography at the University of Wisconsin-Milwaukee, following a long career at the University of Chicago (1950-68), and Kent State University (University Professor 1968-74). He currently serves as a Commissioner of the Port Authority of Milwaukee. Following *The Port of Chicago and the St. Lawrence Seaway* (1957), he co-edited the influential *Readings in Urban Geography* (1959), and his major publications since include *Chicago: Growth of a Metropolis* (1969), *The Spatial Expression of Urban Growth* (1969), *The Great Lakes Transportation System* (1976), and *Land Uses in American Cities* (1983).

**PETER SCHÖLLER** is Professor of Geography and Director of the Geographisches Institut der Ruhr-Universität, Bochum, West Germany (since 1964). He is author of *Die Deutschen Städte* (1967) and editor and co-author of many volumes, including *Allgemeine Stadtgeographie* (1969), *Zentralitätsforschung* (1972), *Trends in Urban Geography: Reports on Research in Major Language Areas* (1973), and *Bibliographie zur Stadtgeographie: Deutschsprachige Literatur 1952-1970* (1973), *Ostasien* (1978), and *Federal Republic of Germany: Spatial Development and Problems* (1980). More recently he has contributed a series of research articles on many aspects of the cities of Japan. His latest work is *Hong Kong: Finanz- und Wirtschafts-Metropole; Entwicklungspol für Chinas Wandel* (1985).

**THEODORE SHABAD** is Editor of *Soviet Geography*, member of the editorial staff of the *New York Times*, and Adjunct Lecturer in Geography at Columbia University. He is the recipient of an honorary degree of Doctor of Humane Letters from the University of Wisconsin-Milwaukee (1985). His major works include *Geography of the U.S.S.R.: A Regional Survey* (1951), *China's Changing Map: National and Regional Development, 1949-71* (1956, rev.1972), *Basic Industries of the U.S.S.R.* (1969), *Gateway to Siberian Resources* (1977), *The Soviet Energy System: Resource Use and Policies* (1979), and a co-edited volume *Soviet Natural Resources in the World Economy* (1983).

**AVIE S. SHACHAR** is Associate Professor of Geography at the Hebrew University of Jerusalem, Chairman of the Israeli National Commission of the International Geographical Union, and Editor of *City and Region*. He has co-authored *Development Towns in Israel* (1969), and served as Co-Editor of the 2-volume *Atlas of Jerusalem* (1973).

**RAM LOCHAN SINGH** is Professor Emeritus of Geography and Co-Director of the International Centre for Rural Habitat Studies at the Banares Hindu University in Varanasi, India. He has also served as Vice-Chancellor of Meerut University. He is author of *Bangalore: An Urban Survey* (1964). He edited *India: A Regional Geography* (1971), *Rural Settlements in Monsoon Asia* (1972), and *Urban Geography in Developing Countries* (1973), and co-edited with Rana P.B. Singh such volumes as *Place of Small Towns in India* (1979), *Rural Habitat Transformation in World Frontiers* (1980), and *Environmental Appraisal and Rural Habitat Transformation* (1984). He is Chief Editor of the periodical *National Geographical Journal of India*.

**RANA P. B. SINGH** is a faculty member of the Department of Geography, Banares Hindu University, Varanasi, India, and co-Director of the International Centre for Rural Habitat Studies at the University. He has published *Clan Settlements in the Saran Plain: A Study in Cultural Geography* (1977), co-authored *Changing Japanese Rural Habitat: Perspective and Prospect of Agricultural Dimension* (1981), and co-edited *Man, Culture, and Settlement: A Festschrift presented to Professor R. L. Singh* (1977), as well as various volumes of the Centre.

**HERBERT WILHELMY** is Professor Emeritus of Geography in the Geographisches Institut der Eberhard-Karls-Universität, Tübingen, West Germany. As a sequel to his acclaimed *Südamerika im Spiegel seiner Städte* (1952) he recently published *Die Städte Südamerikas* in two volumes (1984-85). Other books include *Die La Plata-Länder* (1963), *Deutsche geographische Forschung in der Welt von Heute: Festschrift für Erwin Gentz* (1970), *Geographische Forschungen in Südamerika* (1980), and *Welt und Umwelt der Maya: Aufstieg und Untergang einer Hochkultur* (1981). He is an editor of *Stuttgarter Geographische Studien, Tübinger Geographische Studien*, and co-editor of *Zeitschrift der Gesellschaft für Erdkunde zu Berlin* and Westermann's *Das Geographische Seminar*.

**MICHAEL J. WISE** is Professor Emeritus of Geography in the London School of Economics and Political Science. He has also served as Pro-Director of the School. He has been President of the International Geographical Union (1976-80), of the Royal Geographical Society (1980-82), of the Institute of British Geographers (1974), and of Section E of the British Association for the Advancement of Science (1965), and a member of many important commissions. His alma mater, the University of Birmingham, has awarded him an honorary D.Sc. He has authored *The West Midlands* (1958) and *Industrial Location: A Geographical Approach* (1960), has edited *Birmingham and Its Regional Setting* (1950), and contributed numerous articles in economic and urban geography.

# THE UNIVERSITY OF CHICAGO
## DEPARTMENT OF GEOGRAPHY
### RESEARCH PAPERS (Lithographed, 6×9 inches)

#### LIST OF TITLES IN PRINT

133. SCHWIND, PAUL J. *Migration and Regional Development in the United States.* 1971. 170 p.

134. PYLE, GERALD F. *Heart Disease, Cancer and Stroke in Chicago: A Geographical Analysis with Facilities, Plans for 1980.* 1971. 292 p.

135. JOHNSON, JAMES F. *Renovated Waste Water: An Alternative Source of Municipal Water Supply in the United States.* 1971. 155 p.

136. BUTZER, KARL W. *Recent History of an Ethiopian Delta: The Omo River and the Level of Lake Rudolf.* 1971. 184 p.

139. MCMANIS, DOUGLAS R. *European Impressions of the New England Coast, 1497–1620.* 1972. 147 p.

140. COHEN, YEHOSHUA S. *Diffusion of an Innovation in an Urban System: The Spread of Planned Regional Shopping Centers in the United States, 1949–1968,* 1972. 136 p.

141. MITCHELL, NORA. *The Indian Hill-Station: Kodaikanal.* 1972. 199 p.

142. PLATT, RUTHERFORD H. *The Open Space Decision Process: Spatial Allocation of Costs and Benefits.* 1972. 189 p.

143. GOLANT, STEPHEN M. *The Residential Location and Spatial Behavior of the Elderly: A Canadian Example.* 1972. 226 p.

144. PANNELL, CLIFTON W. *T'ai-chung, T'ai-wan: Structure and Function.* 1973. 200 p.

145. LANKFORD, PHILIP M. *Regional Incomes in the United States, 1929–1967: Level, Distribution, Stability, and Growth.* 1972. 137 p.

146. FREEMAN, DONALD B. *International Trade, Migration, and Capital Flows: A Quantitative Analysis of Spatial Economic Interaction.* 1973. 201 p.

147. MYERS, SARAH K. *Language Shift Among Migrants to Lima, Peru.* 1973. 203 p.

148. JOHNSON, DOUGLAS L. *Jabal al-Akhdar, Cyrenaica: An Historical Geography of Settlement and Livelihood.* 1973. 240 p.

149. YEUNG, YUE-MAN. *National Development Policy and Urban Transformation in Singapore: A Study of Public Housing and the Marketing System.* 1973. 204 p.

150. HALL, FRED L. *Location Criteria for High Schools: Student Transportation and Racial Integration.* 1973. 156 p.

151. ROSENBERG, TERRY J. *Residence, Employment, and Mobility of Puerto Ricans in New York City.* 1974. 230 p.

152. MIKESELL, MARVIN W., editor. *Geographers Abroad: Essays on the Problems and Prospects of Research in Foreign Areas.* 1973. 296 p.

153. OSBORN, JAMES F. *Area, Development Policy, and the Middle City in Malaysia.* 1974. 291 p.

154. WACHT, WALTER F. *The Domestic Air Transportation Network of the United States.* 1974. 98 p.

155. BERRY, BRIAN J. L., *et al. Land Use, Urban Form and Environmental Quality.* 1974. 440 p.

156. MITCHELL, JAMES K. *Community Response to Coastal Erosion: Individual and Collective Adjustments to Hazard on the Atlantic Shore.* 1974. 209 p.

157. COOK, GILLIAN P. *Spatial Dynamics of Business Growth in the Witwatersrand.* 1975. 144 p.

159. PYLE, GERALD F. *et al. The Spatial Dynamics of Crime.* 1974. 221 p.

160. MEYER, JUDITH W. *Diffusion of an American Montessori Education.* 1975. 97 p.

161. SCHMID, JAMES A. *Urban Vegetation: A Review and Chicago Case Study.* 1975. 266 p.

162. LAMB, RICHARD F. *Metropolitan Impacts on Rural America.* 1975. 196 p.

163. FEDOR, THOMAS STANLEY. *Patterns of Urban Growth in the Russian Empire during the Nineteenth Century.* 1975. 245 p.

164. HARRIS, CHAUNCY D. *Guide to Geographical Bibliographies and Reference Works in Russian or on the Soviet Union.* 1975. 478 p.

165. JONES, DONALD W. *Migration and Urban Unemployment in Dualistic Economic Development.* 1975. 174 p.

166. BEDNARZ, ROBERT S. *The Effect of Air Pollution on Property Value in Chicago.* 1975. 111 p.

167. HANNEMANN, MANFRED. *The Diffusion of the Reformation in Southwestern Germany, 1518–1534.* 1975. 248 p.

168. SUBLETT, MICHAEL D. *Farmers on the Road. Interfarm Migration and the Farming of Noncontiguous Lands in Three Midwestern Townships. 1939–1969.* 1975. 228 pp.

169. STETZER, DONALD FOSTER. *Special Districts in Cook County: Toward a Geography of Local Government.* 1975. 189 pp.

170. EARLE, CARVILLE V. *The Evolution of a Tidewater Settlement System: All Hallow's Parish, Maryland, 1650–1783.* 1975. 249 pp.

171. SPODEK, HOWARD. *Urban-Rural Integration in Regional Development: A Case Study of Saurashtra, India—1800–1960.* 1976. 156 pp.

172. COHEN, YEHOSHUA S. and BERRY, BRIAN J. L. *Spatial Components of Manufacturing Change.* 1975. 272 pp.